ISBN 978-1-330-38142-7
PIBN 10046105

1 MONTH OF FREE READING

at

www.ForgottenBooks.com

By purchasing this book you are eligible for one month membership to ForgottenBooks.com, giving you unlimited access to our entire collection of over 700,000 titles via our web site and mobile apps.

To claim your free month visit:

www.forgottenbooks.com/free46105

English
Français
Deutsche
Italiano
Español
Português

www.forgottenbooks.com

Mythology Photography **Fiction**
Fishing Christianity **Art** Cooking
Essays Buddhism Freemasonry
Medicine **Biology** Music **Ancient**
Egypt Evolution Carpentry Physics
Dance Geology **Mathematics** Fitness
Shakespeare **Folklore** Yoga Marketing
Confidence Immortality Biographies
Poetry **Psychology** Witchcraft
Electronics Chemistry History **Law**
Accounting **Philosophy** Anthropology
Alchemy Drama Quantum Mechanics
Atheism Sexual Health **Ancient History**
Entrepreneurship Languages Sport
Paleontology Needlework Islam
Metaphysics Investment Archaeology
Parenting Statistics Criminology
Motivational

THE EMPIRE

AND

THE PAPACY

918-1273

BY

T. F. TOUT, M.A.

PROFESSOR OF MEDIÆVAL AND MODERN HISTORY
AT THE OWENS COLLEGE, VICTORIA UNIVERSITY

PERIOD II

RIVINGTONS

34 *KING STREET, COVENT GARDEN*

LONDON

1·903

[Fourth Edition]

PREFACE

THE absence of any existing text-book, narrating with any approach to fulness the history of the period with which this work is concerned, induced the writer to think that the most useful course that he could pursue would be to cover as much of the whole ground as his space allowed. Finding that there was not room to treat all the aspects of European history with the same fulness, the author resolved to limit himself to the central struggle between the Papacy and the Empire, and to the events directly connected with it. He has therefore only busied himself with the affairs of Scandinavia, the Baltic lands, and the Slavonic kingdoms of the East so far as they stand in direct relation to the main currents of European history. The history of the Mohammedan Powers has been treated in the same way, and even Christian Spain has only been allowed a very small number of pages. This necessary limitation has afforded more room for the main purpose of the writer, which has been to narrate, with some amount of detail, the political and ecclesiastical history of the chief states of Southern and Western Europe, and in particular of Germany, Italy, France, and the Eastern Empire. The expansion of the Latin and

626831

Catholic world at the expense of both the Orthodox Greeks and the Mohammedans, stands so much in the forefront of the history of the period that it could not be neglected, though the writer has avoided treating the Crusades in much detail. Some account of the general movements of thought and of the development of the ecclesiastical system and of the religious orders seemed to him necessary for the understanding even of the political history of a time when everything was subordinated to the authority of the Church. He has, however, endeavoured to bring this into some sort of connection with the political history of the period, and has not felt it in his power to enlarge upon the general history of civilisation in the way adopted by the very valuable *Histoire Générale de l'Europe*, edited by MM. Lavisse and Rambaud. He has, however, frequently availed himself of the help of that book in his selection and arrangement of his facts, and would like to refer his readers to it for such parts of the history as do not fall within his scheme. He has indicated in notes at the beginning of the various chapters some useful authorities in which readers will find a more detailed account of various aspects of the time.

In conclusion, the writer must express his thanks to his wife, who has helped him materially in nearly every part of the book, and has taken the chief share in preparing the maps, tables, and index.

MANCHESTER, *May* 1898.

CONTENTS

MAPS

GENEALOGICAL TABLES

APPENDIX

BIBLIOGRAPHICAL NOTE

To the general modern authorities for French history for this period must now be added the valuable new *Histoire de France* edited by M. Ernest Lavisse (Hachette), of which the three half-volumes covering this period are now published. They are · *Les Premiers Capétiens* (987-1137), by Achille Luchaire, II. ii. ; *Louis VII., Philippe Auguste, Louis VIII.*, by Achille Luchaire, III. i. ; and *Saint Louis, Philippe le Bel, les derniers Capétiens directs*, by Ch..V. Langlois, III. ii.

CHAPTER I

INTRODUCTION

General Characteristics of the Period—The End of the Dark Ages—The Triumph of Feudalism—The Revival of the Roman Empire and Papacy —The Struggles of Papacy and Empire—The Spread of Religion and Civilisation—The Crusades and the Latin East—The Growth of National Monarchies.

IT is a trite thing to say that all long periods of European history are ages of transition. The old order is ever passing gradually away, and a new society is ever springing up from amidst the ruins of the dying system that has done its work. But the period with which this book is concerned is transitional in no merely conventional sense. We take up the story in the early years of the tenth century, when the Dark Ages had not yet run their course. We end it in the closing years of the thirteenth century, when the choicest flowers of mediæval civilisation were already in full bloom. Starting at the end of a period of deep depression and degradation, we have to note how feudalism got rid of the barbarian invaders, and restored the military efficiency of Europe at the expense of its order and civilisation. We learn how the revival of the Roman Empire again set up an effective and orderly political power, and led to the revival of the Church and religion, and the subsequent renewal of intellectual life. But the Empire was never more than a half-realised theory; and while the world had theoretically one master, it was in reality ruled by a multitude of petty feudal chieftains. Thus was brought about

The general characteristics of the period.

PERIOD II.
A

the universal monarchy of the Papacy, the Crusades, the monastic revivals, the strong but limited intellectual renascence of the twelfth century, and the marvellous development of art, letters, and material civilisation that flowed from it. The conflict of Papacy and Empire impaired the efficiency of both, and made possible the growth of the great national states of the thirteenth century, from which the ultimate salvation of Europe was to come. Turbulent as was the period during which these great revolutions were worked out, it was one of many-sided activity, and of general, but by no means unbroken, progress. It was the time of the development and perfection of all the most essential features of that type of civilisation which is called mediæval. It was the age of feudalism, of the Papacy and Empire, of the Crusades, of chivalry, of scholasticism and the early universities, of monasticism in its noblest types, of mediæval art in its highest aspects, and of national monarchy in its earliest form. Before our period ends, the best characteristics of the Middle Ages had already manifested themselves. Fertile as were the fourteenth and fifteenth centuries in their promise of later developments, they bore witness only to the decline of what was most characteristic of the period that we now have to consider.

Let us dwell for a moment on some of the leading features of this period in a little more detail.

We begin in a time of gloom and sorrow. The Carolingian Empire, which had united the vigour of the barbarians with **The Dark Ages.** the civilisation of the Roman world, had broken up. The sacred name of Emperor had been assumed so constantly by weaklings that it had ceased to have much hold upon the minds of men. The great kingdoms, into which the Carolingian Empire had resolved itself, seemed destined to undergo the process that had destroyed the parent state. The East Frankish realm—the later Germany—was breaking up into its four national duchies of Saxony, Franconia, Bavaria, and Swabia. The West Frankish realm was the prey of the rivalry of the Carolings and the Robertians. The Middle Kingdom was in still worse plight. Italy had fallen away under a line of nominal Italian or Lombard kings, but the south was Greek or Saracen, and the north was in hopeless confusion. The northern parts of the Middle Kingdom, to which alone the name Lotharingia clung, were tending towards their ultimate destiny of becoming a fifth national duchy of the German realm, though their loyalty for the Carolingian house brought them more than once back to the West Frankish kingdom. The lands between this restricted Lotharingia and the Mediterranean had become the kingdom of Arles or Burgundy by the union, in 932, of the two Burgundian states that had grown up in the days of chaos. But of the six kingdoms which now represented the ancient Empire, not one was effectively governed. The administrative system of the Carolingians had altogether disappeared. The kings were powerless, the Chureh was corrupt, the people miserable and oppressed, the nobles self-seeking and brutal. The barbarian invader had profited by the weakness of civilisation. The restored Rome of Charlemagne, like the old Rome of Constantine and Theodosius, was threatened with annihilation by pagan hordes. The Norsemen threatened the coasts of the west; the Saracens dominated the Mediterranean, captured the islands, and established outposts in southern Gaul and Italy. The Slavs overran Germany. The Magyars threatened alike Germany and Italy. Everywhere civilisation and Christianity were on the wane.

Yet the darkest hour was already past when the tenth century had begun. The feudal system had saved Europe from its external enemies. The feudal cavalry and the feudal castle had proved too strong for the barbarians. The Norse plunderers had gone home beaten, or had settled with Rolf in Neustria, or with Guthrum in eastern England. The Saracens had been driven from Italy, and were soon to be chased out of Provence. The Wends and the Magyars were soon to feel the might of

The end of the Dark Ages.

Henry the Fowler.   The Saxon dukes were restoring the East Frankish realm.   The Robertians were getting the upper hand in France.   Even the consolidation of the two Burgundies made for unity. ⸤In the east the Macedonian dynasty was ruling over the Greek Empire in uneventful peace, and extending its sway to the farthest limits of Asia Minor. In Spain the Christians had definitely got the better of the Moors. ⸤The break-up of the Caliphate robbed Islam both of its political and religious unity, and destroyed for the time its capacity for aggression.⸥   The

Feudalism. first gleams of a religious revival began with the foundation of Cluny.   But despite all these glimpses of hope, the state of western Europe was still deplorable.   The feudal nobles were the masters of the situation. Their benefices were rapidly becoming hereditary, their authority more recognised and systematic.   But no salvation was to be expected from a system that was the very abnegation of all central and national authority.   It was but little more than organised anarchy when the west had to depend upon a polity that made every great landholder a petty tyrant over his neighbours.   The military strength of feudalism had given it authority.   Its political weakness was revealed when the feudal baron had to govern as well as fight.

Feudalism was not long in undisputed possession of the field. ⸤From the revival of the German kingdom by the

The Holy Roman Empire. Saxon kings sprang the Holy Roman Empire of the German nation, beginning with the coronation of Otto the Great in 962.   Less universal, less ecclesiastical, less truly Roman than the Carolingian Empire, the Empire of the Saxons and Franks was based essentially upon the German kingship, yet was ever trying to outgrow its limitations, and to claim in its completeness the Carolingian heritage.   Within a century of the coronation of Otto, the revived Empire included in its sphere the German, Italian, Burgundian, and Lotharingian realms—in short, all the Empire of Charles the Great, save the West Frankish states, ruled since

987 by Hugh Capet and his descendants. Moreover, the Empire had pushed forward the limits of Christianity and civilisation in the barbarous north and east. It had extended its direct rule over a wide stretch of marchlands. The Scandinavians, Wends, Poles, Bohemians, and Hungarians all received the Christian faith from missionaries profoundly impressed with the imperial idea, and their conversion involved at least temporary dependence upon the power that again aspired to be lord of the world. At home the Emperors checked and restrained, though recognising and utilising, the feudal principle. In their fear of the lay aristocracy, no less than in their zeal for religion and order, they associated themselves closely with the work of reforming the Church. But the restoration of religion soon involved the restoration of Papacy and hierarchy, and thus they raised up the power before which Emperors were finally to succumb. Yet the Empire did not fall until it had kept central Europe together for nearly three centuries, at a time when no other power could possibly have accomplished the task. From the coronation of the Saxon to the fall of the Hohenstaufen, the Holy Roman Empire had no small claim to the lordship of the world.

The darkest hour of the State was the darkest hour of the Church. The last faint traces of the Carolingian revival of religion disappeared amid the horrors of Danish, Saracen, and Hungarian invasions. The feudalism that saved Europe from the barbarians now began to infect what remained of Christian life with its own ferocity, greed, and lust. The spiritual offices of the Church were becoming heritable property, dissociated from all effective spiritual duties. But amidst the turmoil of feudal times, a few nobler spirits sought salvation from the wickedness that lay thick around them in the solitude of the cloister. Before the end of the tenth century, the Cluniac revival presented to Europe an ideal of life very different from feudal militarism. In alliance with the Empire, the Cluniacs restored religion in central Europe, and missionaries, working in their spirit, spread the Gospel beyond the bounds of the Empire among the barbarians of the north and east. But from Cluny also came new theories of the province of the Church, which soon brought religion into sharp conflict with the temporal authority. When the power of the State lay almost in abeyance, it was natural that the Church should encroach upon the sphere it left vacant. From Cluny came the Hildebrandine Reformation, and from the theories of Hildebrand sprang two centuries of

The struggles of Papacy and Empire.

conflict between Papacy and Empire. The great struggle of Popes and Emperors (the highest expression of the universal struggle of the spiritual and temporal swords), was the central event of the Middle Ages. It first took the form of the Investiture Contest, but when the Investiture Contest had been ended by the substantial victory of the Church, the eternal strife was soon renewed under other pretexts. It inspired the contest of Alexander III. with Frederick Barbarossa, of Thomas of Canterbury with Henry of Anjou, of Innocent III. with half the princes of Europe, and the final great conflict between the successors of Innocent and Frederick II. At last the Empire succumbed before the superior strength of the Papacy. But the Hohenstaufen were soon revenged; and, within two generations of the death of Frederick II., the victorious Papacy was degraded from its pride of place by its ancient ally.

From the triumphs of Hildebrand and his successors sprang the religious revivals that enriched the Middle Ages

Religious and monastic revivals.

with all that was fairest and most poetical in the life of those times. The Cistercians and the Carthusians revived the ideals of St. Benedict, with special precautions against the dangers before which the old Benedictine houses had succumbed. The orders of Canons Regular sought to unite the life of the monk with the work of the clerk. They paved the way for the more complete realisation of their ideal in the thirteenth

century, when the mendicant orders of Friars arose under
Francis and Dominic. From the monastic movement sprang
a revival of spiritual religion and a renewed interest in
the world of thought and art. The artistic
impulses of the time found their highest expression in the vast and stern Romanesque minsters of the
older orders, and in the epic literature of the *chansons de
geste.* The transition during the twelfth century from
Romanesque to Gothic architecture, and the parallel change
in vernacular literature from the epic to the romance, mark
a new development in the European spirit. Side by side
with them went the great intellectual renascence of the same
momentous century. While an Anselm sought to enlist philosophy in the service of the Church, an Abelard began to
question the very sources of authority. In Abelard the intellectual movement outgrew its monastic parentage, and in his
conflict with Bernard the dictator of Christen- Revival of
dom, the old and the new spirit came into the speculative
sharpest antagonism. The systematic schoolmen activity.
of later ages had neither the independence of Abelard nor the
limitation of Bernard. Learning passed from monastic to
secular hands, but the scholastic philosophy was already
enlisted on the side of the Church, and active as was its
intelligence, it henceforth worked within self-appointed limits.
Side by side with the revival of philosophy, came the work
of Irnerius and Gratian, the revival of the sys- Law.
tematic study of Civil Law, and the building up
of the great structure of ecclesiastical jurisprudence. From
the multiplication of students and studies sprang the organisation of teachers and learners into the universities. The
From the ignorance and barbarism of the tenth Universities.
century, there is a record of continuous progress until the end
of our period. Yet the thirteenth century does not only illustrate the crowning glories of the Middle Ages: it suggests new
modes of thought that indicate that the Middle Ages themselves are passing away. The triumph of the Church bore

with it the seeds of its own ruin, in the world of thought as well as in the world of action.

From the Hildebrandine revival sprang also the Crusades, and the combination of the military and religious ideals of the Latin world in the pursuit of a holy war for the recovery of Christ's Sepulchre. The Turkish advance was checked ; the Eastern Empire was saved from imminent destruction ; and a series of Latin states in Syria and Greece extended the scope of western influence at the expense of Orthodox and Mohammedan alike. But the diversion of the Fourth Crusade to overthrow the Empire of Constantinople indicates the high-water mark of the Latin Christian power in the East ; and the change in the current of western ideas made the Crusades of the thirteenth century but vain attempts to restore a vanished dream. Before the end of our period, the Christian domination in the East had shrunk to the lordship of a few Greek islands. The Palæologi brought back Byzantine rule to the Byzantine capital ; and the strongest kings of the West could not save the remnants of the Latin states in Syria. The Mongol invasions threatened Christian and Saracen alike. While the western prospects were so fair, in the East barbarism was on the highway to ascendency.

The Crusades and the Latin rule in the East.

The failure of the Empire to rule the world led to a feudal reaction, that was not least felt in the lands directly governed by the Emperors. Our period witnesses both the triumph and the decay of feudalism. It is the time when feudal ideas prevailed all over the western world, following the Crusaders into the burning deserts of Syria, and the lands of the Eastern Emperors. The Normans took feudalism to southern Italy and Sicily, and developed the feudalism that they already found in England. Even Scandinavia evolved a feudalism of its own, and the sons and grandsons of the followers of William the Conqueror planted feudal states side by side with the Celtic tribalism of

The Feudal Age.

Wales and Ireland. For nearly four centuries the mail-clad feudal horseman was invincible in battle, and the stone-built feudal castle, ever becoming mor complex and elaborate in structure, was impregnable except to famine. The better side of feudal social ideals—chivalry, knighthood, honour, and courtesy—did something to temper the brutality and pride of the average baron, and found powerful expression in the vernacular literatures, written to amuse nobles and gentry. But before our period ends, the days of feudal ascendency were over. Hopeful of triumph in Germany, where the German state suffered by its kings' pursuit of the imperial vision, feudalism found in Italy a powerful rival in strong municipalities closely allied with the Church. In western Europe it was beginning to give ground. The greater feudatories crushed their lesser neighbours, and built up states that were powerful enough to stand by themselves. The Church, though fitting itself into the feudal organisation of society, could never repose simply on brute force. The towns, whose separate organisation was, in some *The Towns.* parts of Europe at least, as much the result of military, as of economic necessities, became the centres of expanding trade and increasing wealth. Within their strong walls they were able to hold their own, and claim for themselves a part in the social system as well as baron or bishop. But feudalism had at last met its master. With its decline before the national spirit, we are on the threshold of modern times.

The division of the Empire into local kingdoms, begun at the treaty of Verdun, paved the way for the modern idea of a national state. The Empire stifled the early *The growth* possibilities of a German nation, and Empire and *of national* Papacy combined to make impossible an Italian *monarchies.* nation. But in France other prospects arose. Through its virtual exclusion from the Empire, France had been delivered from some very real dangers. The early Capetians were shadows round which a mighty system revolved; but they had

a lofty theory and a noble tradition at their back, and the time
at last came when they could convert their theory into practice.
Philip Augustus made France a great state and nation.
Power passes from Germany to France. Under St. Louis the leadership of Europe passed
definitely from the Germans to the French—from
the people ruled by the visionary world-Empire
to the people ruled by a popular and effective
national monarchy. The alliance between France and the
Church, the preponderance of French effort in the Crusades,
the spread of the French tongue and literature as the common
expression of European chivalry, had made the French nation
famous, long before a large proportion of the French nation
had been organised into a French state. The Spanish peoples
acquired strong local attachments; the English became
conscious of their national life. Alfonso the Wise of Castile
and Edward I. of England rank with St. Louis and Philip the
Fair. Even Frederick II. owed his strength to his national
position in Germany and Naples, rather than to his imperial
aspirations. Before our period ends, the national principle
had clearly asserted itself. Trade, art, literature, religion
began to desert cosmopolitan for national channels, and
the beginnings of the system of estates and representative
institutions show that the great organised classes of mediæval
society aspired to share with their kings the direction of the
national destinies. The Empire had fallen; the Papacy was
soon to be overthrown; feudalism was decayed; the cosmopolitan culture of the universities had seen its best days. It
is in the juxtaposition of what was best in the old, and what
was most fertile in the new, that gives its unique charm to
the thirteenth century. The transition from the Dark Ages
to the Middle Ages had been worked out. There were
signs that the transition was beginning that culminates in the
Renascence and the Reformation.

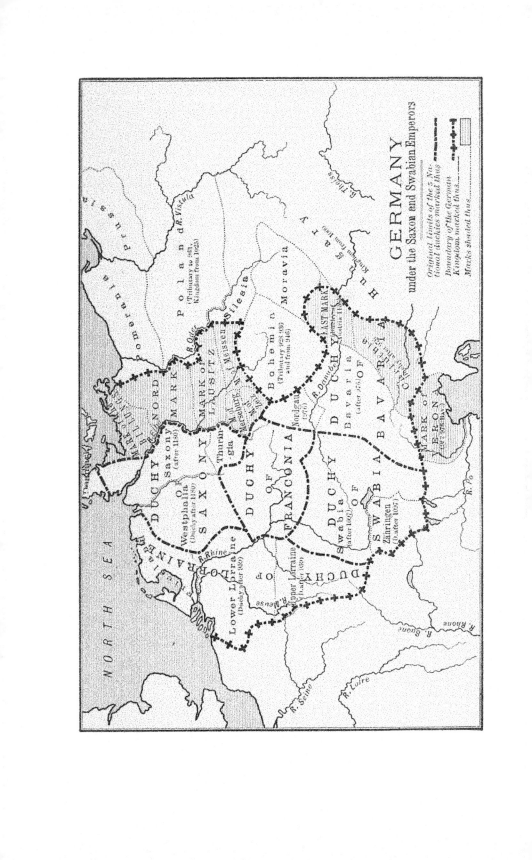

CHAPTER II

THE SAXON KINGS OF THE GERMANS,
AND REVIVAL OF THE ROMAN EMPIRE BY OTTO I. (919-973) [1]

The Transference of the German Kingship from the Franks to the Saxons—
The Reign of Henry the Fowler—The Defence of the Frontiers and the
Beginnings of the Marks—Otto I.'s Rule as German King—The Feudal
Opposition and its Failure—The First and Second Civil Wars—The
Reorganisation of the Duchies—The Marks established—Battle on the
Lechfeld—Otto's Ecclesiastical Policy—His Intervention in Italy and its
Causes—Italy in the Tenth Century—Degradation of the Papacy—
Theodora and Marozia—Alberic and John XII.—Otto's Second Inter-
vention in Italy—His Coronation as Emperor—His later Italian Policy
His Imperial Position and Death.

THE death of Conrad I., in December 918 (see Period I.
pp. 475-7), ended the Franconian dynasty. In April 919 the
Election of   Franconian and Saxon magnates met at Fritzlar
Henry the   to elect a new king. On the proposal of Eber-
Fowler, 919.   hard, Duke of Franconia, and brother of the dead
king Conrad, Henry, Duke of the Saxons, called Henry the

[1] Giesebrecht's *Geschichte der deutschen Kaiserzeit* gives a full account
of German and Italian history from 919 to the latter part of the reign of
Frederick I. Richter and Kohl's *Annalen des deutschen Reichs im
Zeitalter der Ottonen und der Salier*, include an excellent series of
extracts from the original sources. Prutz's *Staatengeschichte des Abend-
lands im Mittelalter* (vol. i. Oncken's Series) is a popular working-up of
the whole period. A French account is in Zeller's *Histoire de l'Alle-
magne*; while Lavisse and Rambaud's *Histoire générale du ive Siècle à
nos jours*, vols. i. and ii., is certainly the best presentation of the general
history of the early Middle Ages. Bryce's remarkable essay on *The Holy
Roman Empire*, and Fisher's detailed *Medieval Empire* are the best books
in English. The facts are related in Henderson's *History of Germany
during the Middle Ages*, and in Milman's *History of Latin Christianity*.
Gregorovius' *Geschichte der Stadt Rom im Mittelalter* is now translated.

12

Fowler, was elevated to the vacant throne. Henry had been already marked out for this dignity, both by the great position of his house and nation, and by the wish of the last king. Yet the voluntary abdication of the Franconian and the transference of the monarchy to the Saxon forms one of the great turning-points in the history of the German nation. The existence of a separate German state had been already secured by the work of Louis the German and Arnulf of Carinthia. Yet so long as the sceptre remained in the Carolingian hands, the traditions of a mighty past overpowered the necessities of the present. Down to the death of Conrad, the Franks were still the ruling nation, and the German realm was East Frankish rather than German. The accession of the Saxon gave the best chance for a more general development on national lines. For of all the five nations of Germany, the Saxons were the least affected by the Carolingian tradition. Christianity was still less than a century old with them, and formal heathenism still lingered on in the wilder moors and marshes of the north. Roman civilisation was still but a sickly exotic; and, free from its enervating influences, the Saxons still retained the fierce barbaric prowess of the old Teutonic stock, while the primitive Teutonic institutions, which were fast disappearing in the south before the march of feudalism, still retained a strong hold amidst the rude inhabitants of northern Germany. In the south the mass of the peasantry were settling down as spiritless and peaceful farmers, leaving the fighting to be done by a limited number of half-professional soldiers. But among the Saxons every freeman was still a warrior, and the constant incursions of heathen Danes and Wends gave constant opportunities for the practice of martial habits. The old blood nobility still took the leadership of the race. Not only were the Saxons the strongest, the most energetic, and most martial of the Germans, but the mighty deeds of their Ludolfing dukes showed that their princes were worthy of them. It was only the strong arm of a mighty warrior that could save Germany from the manifold evils that beset it from within and without. The Ludolfings had already proved on many a hard-fought field that they were the natural leaders of the German people. The dying Conrad simply recognised accomplished facts, when he urged that the Saxon duke should be his successor. The exhausted Franconians merely accepted the inevitable, when they voluntarily passed over the hegemony of Germany to their northern neighbours.

There were, however, insuperable limitations to the power of the first Saxon king of the Germans. Henry the Fowler

Henry's German policy.

was little more influential as king than as duke. There was no idea whatever of German unity or nationality. The five nations were realities, but beyond them the only ties that could bind German to German were the theoretical unities of Rome—the unity of the Empire and the unity of the Church. From the circumstances of his election and antecedents, Henry could draw no assistance from the great ideals of the past, by which he was probably but little influenced. He feared rather than courted the support of the churchmen. When the Church offered to consecrate the choice of the magnates by crowning and anointing the new king, Henry protested his unworthiness to receive such sacred symbols.

Thus Germany became a federation of great duchies, the duke of the strongest nation taking precedence over the others with the title of king. Even this result was obtained only through Henry's strenuous exertions. His power rested almost entirely on the temporary union of the Saxons and Franconians. The southern and western nations of Germany were almost outside the sphere of his influence. Lotharingia fell away altogether, still cleaving to the Carolings, and recognising the West Frankish king, Charles the Simple, rather than the Saxon intruder. Henry was conscious of the weakness of his position, and discreetly accepted the withdrawal of Lotharingia from his obedience, receiving in return an acknowledgment of his own royal position from Charles the

Simple. Swabia and Bavaria were almost as hard to deal with as Lotharingia. They had taken no practical share in Henry's election, and were by no means disposed to acknowledge the nominee of the Saxons and Franconians. It was not until 921 that Henry obtained the formal recognition of the Bavarians, and this step was only procured by his renouncing in favour of Duke Arnulf every regalian right, including the much-cherished power of nominating the bishops. Henry was no more a real king of all the Germans than Egbert or Alfred were real kings over all England. His mission was to convert a nominal overlordship into an actual sovereignty. But he saw that he could only obtain the formal recognition necessary for this process by accepting aecomplished facts, and giving full autonomy to the nations. His ideal seems, in fact, to have been that of the great West Saxon lords of Britain. He strove to do for Germany what Edward the Elder and Athelstan were doing for England. It is, from this point of view, of some political significance that Henry married his eldest son Otto, afterwards the famous Emperor, to Edith, daughter of Edward, and sister of Athelstan. Yet, like England, Germany could hope for national unity only when foreign invasion had been successfully warded off. The first condition of internal unity was the cessation of the desolating barbarian invasions which, since the breakup of the Carolingian Empire, had threatened to blot out all remnants of civilisation. Saxony had already suffered terribly from the Danes and Wends. To these was added in 924 a great invasion of the Magyars or Hungarians, the Mongolian stock newly settled in the Danube plains, and still heathen and incredibly fierce and barbarous. The Magyars now found that the Bavarians had learnt how to resist them successfully, so that they turned their arms northwards, hoping to find an easier foe in the Saxons. Henry, with his Franks and Saxons, Invasion of barbarians checked. had to bear the full brunt of the invasion, and no help came either from Swabia or Bavaria. Henry had the good luck to take prisoner one of the Hungarian leaders, and by restoring his captive and promising a considerable tribute, he was able to procure a nine years' truce for Saxony. Two years later the Magyars again swarmed up the Danube into Bavaria, but Henry made no effort to assist the nation which had refused to aid him in his necessity.

Thus freed from the Magyars, Henry turned his arms against the Danes and the Wends. In 934 he established a strong mark against the Danes, and forced the mighty Danish king, Gorm the Old, to pay him tribute. He was even more successful against the Slavs. In 928 Brennabor (the modern Branden-

The defence
of the
frontiers and
the begin-
nings of the
Marks.

burg), the chief stronghold of the Havellers, fell into his hands, and with it the broad lands between the Havel and the Spree, the nucleus of the later East Mark. But more important than Henry's victories were his plans for the defence of the frontiers. He planted German colonists in the lands won from the barbarian. He built a series of new towns, that were to serve as central strongholds, in the marchland districts. The Saxon monk Widukind tells us how Henry ordered that, of every nine of his soldier-farmers, one should live within the walls of the new town, and there build houses in which his eight comrades might take shelter in times of invasion, and in which a third part of all their crops was to be preserved for their support, should necessity compel them to take refuge within the walls. In return, the dwellers in the country were to till the fields and harvest the crops of their brother in the town. Moreover, Henry ordered that all markets, meetings, and feasts should be held within the walled towns, so as to make them, as far as pos-sible, the centres of the local life. Some of the most ancient towns of eastern Saxony, including Quedlinburg, Meissen, and Merseburg, owe their origin to this policy. Henry also improved the quality of the Saxon cavalry levies, teaching his rude warriors to rely on combined evolutions rather than the prowess of the individual horseman. So anxious was he to utilise all the available forces against the enemy, that he settled a legion of able-bodied robbers at Merseburg, giving them pardon and means of subsistence, on the condition of their waging war against the Wends.

The effect of these wise measures was soon felt. Henry had laid the foundation of the great ring of marks, whose organisation was completed by his son. He had also inspired his subjects with a new courage to resist the barbarian, and a new faith in their king. When the nine years' truce with the Hungarians was over, the Saxons resolved to fight rather than continue to pay them a humiliating tribute. A long series of victories crowned the end of Henry's martial career. He was no longer forced to strictly limit himself to the defence of his own duchy of Saxony, and the southern nations of Germany *Henry's triumph and death, 936.* could honour and obey the defender of the German race from the heathen foe, though they paid but scanty reverence to the duke of the Saxons. Lotharingia reverted to her allegiance after the sceptre of the western kingdom had passed, on the death of Charles the Simple, from her beloved Carolings. Yet Henry never sought to depart from his earlier policy, and still gave the fullest autonomy to Saxon, Bavarian, and Lotharingian. He still lived simply after the old Saxon way, wandering from palace to palace among his domain-lands on the slopes of the Harz, and seldom troubling the rest of the country with his presence. Yet visions of a coming glory flitted before the mind of the old sovereign. He dreamed of a journey to Rome to wrest the imperial crown from the nerveless hands of the pretenders, whose faction fights were reducing Italy to anarchy. But his end was approaching, and the more immediate task of providing for the succession occupied his thoughts. His eldest son, Thankmar, was the offspring of a marriage unsanctioned by the Church, and was, therefore, passed over as illegitimate. By his pious wife Matilda, the pattern of German housewives, he had several children. Of these

Otto was the eldest, but the next son, Henry, as the first
born after his father had become a king, was looked upon
by many as possessing an equally strong title to election.
The king, however, urged on his nobles to choose Otto as
his successor. He died soon after, on 2nd July 936, and was
buried in his own town of Quedlinburg, where the pious care
of his widow and son erected over his remains a great church
and abbey for nuns, which became one of the most famous
monastic foundations of northern Germany. ' He was,' says
the historian of his house, ' the greatest of the kings of Europe,
and inferior to none of them in power of mind and body '
But Henry's best claim to fame is that he laid the solid
foundations on which his son built the strongest of early
mediæval states.

Otto I. was a little over twenty years of age when he
ascended the throne. While his father had shunned the
Comnation of
Otto I., 936. consecration of the Church, his first care was
to procure a pompous coronation at Aachen. As
strong a statesman and as bold a warrior as his father,
the new king was so fully penetrated with the sense of
his divine mission, and so filled with high ideals of king-
craft, that it was impossible for him to endure the limitations to his sway, in which Henry had quietly acquiesced.
Duke Eberhard of Franconia was the first to resent the
pretensions of the young king. He felt that he was the
author of the sway of the Saxon house, and resolved to
exercise over his nation the same authority that he had
wielded without question in the days of King Henry. Mean-
The attack
on the duke-
doms, and the
First Civil
War, 938-941. while, the death of Duke Arnulf of Bavaria gave
Otto an opportunity of manifesting his power to
the south. He roughly deposed Arnulf's eldest
son, Eberhard, who had refused to perform
him homage, and made his younger brother Berthold duke,
but only on condition that the right of nominating to the
Bavarian bishoprics, which had been wrung from the weakness
of Henry, should now be restored to the crown. Moreover,

he set up another brother, Arnulf, as Count Palatine, to act as a sort of overseer over the new duke. But while Franconia and Bavaria were thus deeply offended, Otto's own Saxons were filled with discontent at his policy. They resented Otto's desire to reign as king over all Germany, as likely to impair the dominant claims of the ruling Saxon race. They complained that he had favoured the Franks more than the Saxons, and the sluggish nobles of the interior parts of Saxony were disgusted that Otto had overlooked their claims on his attention in favour of Hermann Billung and Gero, to whom he had intrusted the care of his old duchy along with the government of the Wendish marches. Thankmar, the bastard elder brother, Henry, the younger brother who boasted that he was the son of a reigning king, were both angry at being passed over, and put themselves at the head of the Saxon malcontents. In 938, a revolt broke out in the north. The faithfulness of Hermann Billung limited its extent, and the death of Thankmar seemed likely to put an end to the trouble. But Henry now allied himself with Duke Eberhard of Franconia; and Duke Giselbert of Lotharingia, Otto's brother-in-law, joined the combination. A bloody civil war was now fought in Westphalia and the Lower Rhineland. The army of Otto was taken at a disadvantage at Birthen, near Xanten; but the pious king threw himself on his knees, and begged God to protect his followers, and a victory little short of miraculous followed his prayer. However, the rebels soon won back a strong position, and the bishops, headed by Archbishop Frederick of Mainz, intrigued with them in the belief that Otto's term of power was at an end. But the king won a second unexpected triumph at Andernach, and the Dukes of Franconia and Lotharingia perished in the pursuit. Henry fled to Louis, king of the West Franks, whose only concern, however, was to win back Lotharingia from the eastern kingdom. At last Henry returned and made his submission to his brother; but before long he joined with the Archbishop

of Mainz in a plot to murder the king. This nefarious
design was equally unsuccessful, and Henry, under the
influence of his pious mother, sought for the forgiveness of
his injured brother. At the Christmas feast of 941 a reconciliation was effected. The troubles for the season were
over.

Otto now sought to establish his power over the nations
by setting up members of his own family in the vacant
duchies. Franconia he kept henceforth in his

The reorgani-
sation of the
duchies.

own hands, wearing the Frankish dress and
ostentatiously following the Frankish fashions.
Over Lotharingia he finally set a great Frankish noble,
Conrad the Red, whom he married to his own daughter,
Liutgarde. The reconciled Henry was made Duke of
Bavaria, and married to Judith, the daughter of the old
Duke Arnulf. Swabia was intrusted to Otto's eldest son,
Ludolf, who in the same way was secured a local position
by a match with the daughter of the last duke. But the
new dukes had not the power of their predecessors. Otto
carefully retained the highest prerogatives in his own hands,
and, by the systematic appointment of Counts Palatine to
watch over the interests of the crown, revived under another
name that central control of the local administration which
had, at an earlier period, been secured by the Carolingian
missi dominici.

The new dukes soon fell into the ways of their predecessors. They rapidly identified themselves with the local
traditions of their respective nations, and quickly

Its failure.
The Second
Civil War,
953.

forgot the ties of blood and duty that bound
them to King Otto. Henry of Bavaria and
Ludolf of Swabia soon took up diametrically
different Italian policies, and their intervention on different
sides in the struggle between the phantom Emperors, that
claimed to rule south of the Alps, practically forced upon
Otto a policy of active interference in Italy. Ludolf was
intensely disgusted that his father backed up the Italian

policy of Henry, and began to intrigue with Frederick of Mainz, Otto's old enemy. Conrad of Lotharingia joined the combination. Even in Saxony, the enemies of Hermann Billung welcomed the attack on Otto. At last in 953 a new civil war broke out which, like the troubles of 938, was in essence an attempt of the 'nations' to resist the growing preponderance of the central power. But the rebels were divided among each other, and partisans of local separatism found it doubly hard to bring about an effective combination. The restless and turbulent Frederick of Mainz died during the struggle. Conrad and Ludolf made their submission. A terrible Hungarian inroad forced even the most reluctant to make common cause with Otto against the barbarians. But the falling away of the dukes of the royal house had taught Otto that some further means were necessary, if he desired to continue his policy of restraining the 'nations' in the interest of monarchy and nation as a whole. That fresh support Otto found in the Church, the only living unity outside and beyond the local unities of the five nations.

Even King Henry had found it necessary, before the end of his reign, to rely upon ecclesiastical support, especially in his efforts to civilise the marks. There the fortified churches and monasteries became, like the new walled towns, centres of defence, besides being the only homes of civilisation and culture in those wild regions. But King Henry had not removed the danger of Wendish invasion, and the civil wars of Otto's early years gave a new opportunity for the heathen to ravage the German frontiers. In the midst of Otto's worst distress, Hermann Billung kept the Wends at bay, and taught the Abotrites and Wagrians, of the lands between the lower Elbe and the Baltic, to feel the might of the German arms. His efforts were ably seconded by the doughty margrave, Gero, of the southern Wendish mark. By their strenuous exertions the Slavs were for the time driven away from German territory, and German rule was extended as far as the Oder, so that a whole ring

The organisation of the Marks.

of organised marchlands protected the northern and eastern frontiers. These marks became vigorous military states, possessing more energy and martial prowess than the purely Teutonic lands west of the Elbe, and destined on that account to play a part of extreme prominence in the future history of Germany. Owing their existence to the good-will and protection of the king, and having at their command a large force of experienced warriors, the new margraves or counts of the marches, who ruled these regions, gradually became almost as powerful as the old dukes, and, for the time at least, their influence was thrown on the side of the king and kingdom. Under their guidance, the Slav peasantry were gradually Christianised, Germanised, and civilised, though it took many centuries to complete the process. Even to this day the place-names in marks like Brandenburg and Meissen show their Slavonic origin, and a Wendish-speaking district still remains in the midst of the wholly Germanised mark of Lausitz. To these regions Otto applied King Henry's former methods on a larger scale. Walled towns became centres of trade, and refuges in times of invasion. Monasteries arose, such as Quedlinburg, and that of St. Maurice, Otto's favourite saint, at Magdeburg. A whole series of new bishoprics—Brandenburg and Havelberg, in the Wendish mark; Aarhus, Ripen, and Schleswig, in the Danish mark — became the starting-points of the great missionary enterprise that in time won over the whole frontier districts to Christianity. Hamburg became the centre of the first missions to Scandinavia. Never since the days of Charles the Great had the north seen so great an extension of religion and culture. There was many a reaction towards heathenism and barbarism before the twelfth century finally witnessed the completion of this side of Otto's work.

The Hungarians were still untamed, and, profiting by the civil war of 953, they now poured in overwhelming numbers into south Germany. But the common danger was met by common action. On 10th August 955, Otto won

a decisive victory on the Lechfeld, near Augsburg, at the
head of an army drawn equally from all parts of Germany,
and including among its leaders Conrad the Red, The battle
the former Duke of Lorraine, who died in the on the
fight. This crushing defeat damped the waning Lechfeld, 955
energies of the Magyars, and the carrying out of the same
policy against them that had been so successful against their
northern neighbours resulted in the setting up of an east
mark (the later Austria), which carried German civilisation
far down the Danube, and effectually bridled the Magyars.
In these regions Henry of Bavaria did the work that Hermann
Billung and Gero were doing in the north. The final defeat
of the barbarian marauders, and the wide extension of German
territory through the marks, are among Otto's greatest titles
to fame. Moreover, Otto forced the rulers of more distant
lands to acknowledge his sovereignty. In 950 he invaded
Bohemia, and forced its duke, Boleslav, to do him homage.
Nor did he neglect the affairs of the more settled regions
of the west. Already in 946 he had marched through north
France as far as the frontiers of Normandy, striking vigorous
blows in favour of the Carolingian Louis IV.—who had
married his daughter Gerberga, Duke Giselbert's widow—
against his other son-in-law, Hugh the Great, the head of the
rival Robertian house [see page 69]. He also took under his
protection Conrad the Pacific, the young king of the Arelate.

In civilising the marks Otto had striven hard to use
the Church to secure the extension of the royal power.
But the lay nobles were not slow to see that Otto's
trust in bishops and abbots meant a lessening Otto's
of their influence, and resented any material ecclesiasti-
extension of ecclesiastical power. The Saxon cal policy.
chieftains — half-heathens themselves at heart — did their
very best to prevent the Christianisation of the Wends,
knowing that it would infallibly result in a close alliance
between the crown and the new Christians against their
old oppressors. Even the churchmen of central Germany

watched Otto's policy with a suspicious eye. Typical of
this class is Archbishop Frederick of Mainz, the centre of
every conspiracy, and the would-be assassin of his sovereign.
If his policy had prevailed, the Church would have
become a disruptive force of still greater potency than

ECCLESIASTICAL DIVISIONS OF GERMANY
showing the growth of the provinces Magdeburg and Hamburg-Bremen.

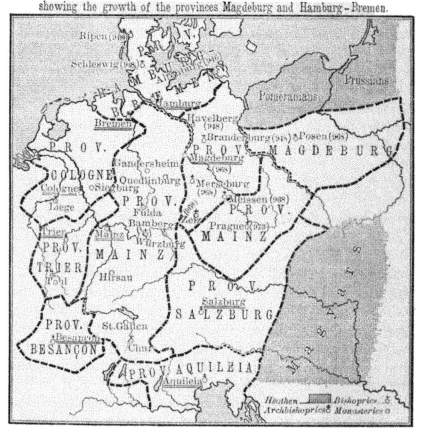

the dukedoms. But a new school of churchmen was
growing up willing to co-operate with Otto. His youngest
brother, Bruno, presided over his chancery, and made
the royal palace as in Carolingian times the centre of the
intellectual life of Germany. Bruno 'restored,' as we are

told, 'the long-ruined fabric of the seven liberal arts,' and, like our Alfred, was at the same time the scholar and the statesman. From his efforts sprang that beginning of the general improvement of the German clergy that made possible the imperial reformation of the Papacy. Moreover, Bruno carried out a reform of discipline and of monastic life that soon made Germany a field ripe to receive the doctrines that were now beginning to radiate from Cluny to the remotest parts of the Christian world. Side by side with the religious revival came the intellectual revival that Bruno had fostered. Widukind of Corvey wrote the annals of the Saxons; the abbess Hrotswitha of Gandersheim sang Otto's praises in Latin verse, and wrote Latin comedies, in which she strove to adopt the methods of Terence to subjects chosen in order to enhance the glories of religious virginity. The literary spirit touched Otto himself so far that he learnt to read Latin, though he never succeeded in talking it. Under Bruno's care grew up a race of clerical statesmen, far better fitted to act as Otto's ministers than the lay aristocracy with its insatiable greed, ruthless cruelty, and insufferable arrogance. It now became Otto's policy, since he had failed to wrest the national duchies to subserve his policy, to fill up the great sees with ministerial ecclesiastics of the new school. The highest posts were reserved to his own family. His faithful brother, Bruno, became Archbishop of Cologne, and was furthermore intrusted with the administration of Lotharingia. Otto's bastard son, William, succeeded the perfidious Frederick as Archbishop of Mainz. Otto now stood forth as the protector of the clergy against the lay nobles, who, out of pure greed, were in many cases aiming at a piecemeal secularisation of ecclesiastical property. The incapacity of a spiritual lord to take part in trials affecting life and limbs had already led to each bishop and abbot, who possessed feudal jurisdiction, being represented by a lay 'Vogt' (*advocatus*) in those matters with which he was himself incompetent to deal. The lay nobles sought to make their 'advocacy' the pretext of a gradual extension of their power until the bishop or abbot became their mere dependant. But this course was not to the interest of the crown. If the domains of the crown were to be administered by the local magnates or to be alienated outright, if the jurisdiction of the crown was to be cut into by grants of immunities to feudal chieftains, it was much better that these should be put into spiritual rather than into secular hands. Otto therefore posed as the protector and patron of the Church. Vast grants of lands and immunities were made to the bishops and abbots, and the appointment to these high posts, or at least the investiture of the prelates with the symbols of their office, was carefully kept for the king. The clergy, who in the days of Henry had feared lest the king should lay hands on their estates, joyfully welcomed Otto's change of front. It was not clear to them as it was to Otto, that the royal favour to the Church was conditional on the Church acting as the chief servant of the State. Otto would brook no assertion of ecclesiastical independence, such as had of old so often set bounds to the empire of the Carolings. He desired to attach the Church to the State by chains of steel; but he carefully gilded the chains, and the German clergy, who were neither strong theologians nor sticklers for ecclesiastical propriety, entered as a body into that dependence on the throne which was to last for the best part of a century, and which was in fact the indispensable condition of the power of the Saxon kings in Germany. The unity of the Church became as in England the pattern of the unity of the State, and in a land which had no sense of civil unity, Saxon and Frank, Lorrainer and Bavarian were made to feel that they had common ties as citizens of the Christian commonwealth.

The first efforts of Otto towards the conciliation and subjection of the clergy were surprisingly successful. He next formed a scheme of withdrawing eastern Saxony and the Wendish march from obedience to the Archbishop of Mainz, and setting up a new Archbishop of Magdeburg as metropolitan of these regions. It

Resistance of William of Mainz.

was a well-designed device to give further unity to those
warlike and loyal regions upon which Otto's power was
ultimately based. But his own son, Archbishop William,
violently opposed a scheme which deprived the see of Mainz
of the obedience of many of its suffragans. William's repre-
sentations to Rome induced the Pope to take no steps to
carry out Otto's plan. The king was deeply incensed, but
the check taught him a lesson. He learnt that after all, the
German Church was not self-contained or self-sufficing. Over
the German Church ruled the Roman Pope. He could only
ensure the obedience of the German Church by securing the
submission or the co-operation of the head of the Christian
world. So long as the Pope was outside his power, Otto's
dream of dominating Germany through churchmen seemed
likely to end in a rude awakening. To complete this aspect
of his policy required vigorous intervention in Italy.

The condition of Italy had long been one of deplorable
anarchy. After the death of the Emperor Berengar in 924
had put an end to the best chance of setting up a national
Italian kingdom, things went from bad to worse. The
Saracens, having plundered its coasts, settled down in its
southern regions side by side with the scanty remnants of the
Byzantine power. Thus all southern Italy was withdrawn
altogether from the sphere of western influence. But in
the centre and north things were far worse. The inroads of
the barbarians were but recently over, and had left their
mark behind in poverty, famine, pestilence and disorder.
Great monasteries like Subiaco and Farfa were in ruins.
The Hungarians had penetrated to the heart of central Italy.
The Saracens from their stronghold of Freinet, amidst the
'mountains of the Moors' of the western Riviera, had
devastated Provence, and had held possession of the passes
of the Alps. If the growth of feudalism, with State of
its permanent military system and its strong Italy,
castles, had already repelled the barbarians, the 924-950.
price paid for deliverance was the cutting up of sovereignty

among a multitude of petty territorial lords. The rising tide
of feudal anarchy had almost overwhelmed the city civilisation
which had been, since Roman times, the special feature of
Italian life.   A swarm of greedy feudal counts and marquises
struggled against each other for power, and a series of phantom
Emperors reduced to an absurdity the once all-powerful name
of Cæsar.   There was still a nominal Italian or Lombard
king, who claimed the suzerainty over all northern and central
Italy.   But in their zeal for local freedom, the Italians had encouraged quarrels for the supreme power.   'The Italians,' said
Liutprand of Cremona, 'always wish to have two masters, in
order to keep the one in check by the other.'   After the death
of the Emperor Berengar, in 924 [see Period I. pp. 463-7],
Rudolf of Burgundy reigned for nearly three years.   On his
fall in 926, Hugh of Provence was chosen his successor, and
held the name at least of king till his death in 946.   There
then arose two claimants to the Italian crown—Lothair, son
of Hugh of Provence, and Berengar, Marquis of Ivrea, the
grandson of the Emperor Berengar.   Neither was strong
enough to defeat the other, and both looked for help from
the warlike Germans.   It is however significant that they
sought support, not from the distant Saxon king, but
from the neighbouring dukes of Swabia and Bavaria, whose
dominions extended to the crest of the Alps.   Lothair begged
the help of Ludolf of Swabia, while Berengar called in Henry
of Bavaria.   The latter gave the most efficient assistance, and
Lothair in despair was negotiating for help from Constantinople
when he was cut off by death (950), leaving his young and
beautiful widow, Adelaide of Burgundy, to make what resistance she might to Berengar of Ivrea.   But there was no
chance of a woman holding her own in these stormy times,
and Adelaide was soon a prisoner in the hands of the victorious
marquis.   She naturally looked over the Alps to her German
friends and kinsfolk, and both Ludolf and Henry, already on
the verge of war on account of their former differences as to
Italian policies, were equally willing to come to her assistance.

Henry now raised pretensions to the great city of Aquileia and the north-eastern corner of. the Italian peninsula. He now aspired, as the protector of Adelaide, his former foe, to unite the Bavarian duchy with the Italian kingdom. Ludolf, more active than his uncle, appeared in the valley of the Po intent on a similar mission. Otto, ever on the watch to prevent the extension of the ducal powers, saw with dismay the prospect of his brother's or son's aggrandisement. He resolved by prompt personal intervention to secure the prize for himself.

In 951, Otto successfully carried out his first expedition to Italy. He met with no serious resistance, and on 23rd September entered in triumph in to Pavia, the old capital of the Lombard kings. Adelaide was released from her captivity, and appeared in Pavia. Otto, who was now a widower, forthwith married her, assumed the crown of Italy, and fruitlessly negotiated with the Pope to bring about his coronation as Emperor. But Otto soon crossed the Alps, leaving Conrad of Lorraine to carry on war against Berengar. Next year, however, a peace was patched up. Berengar was recognised as vassal king of Italy, with Otto as his overlord, and the lands between the Adige and Istria—the mark of Verona and Aquileia—were confirmed to Duke Henry, who thus drew substantial advantage from his brother's intervention. The revolt of Ludolf and Conrad in 953 was largely due to their disgust at Otto's vigorous and successful defeat of their schemes.

Otto, King of Italy, 951.

Nine years elapsed before Otto again appeared in Italy. Though he needed the help of the Papacy more than ever, its condition was not one that could inspire much hope. It was the period of the worst degradation into which the Roman See ever fell. For more than a generation the Popes had almost ceased to exercise any spiritual influence. The elections to the Papacy had been controlled by a ring of greedy and corrupt Roman nobles, conspicuous among whom was the fair but dissolute Theodora and her daughters Marozia, wife of the Marquis

Position of the Papacy, 914-960.

Alberic I. of Camerino, and the less important Theodora the younger. Imperialist partisans like Liutprand of Cremona have drawn the character of these ladies in the darkest and most lurid colours ; but, allowing for monastic exaggeration, it is hard to see how the main outlines of the picture can be untrue. With all their vices, they did not lack energy. Pope John X. (914-928), an old lover and partisan of Theodora, was not destitute of statecraft, and did much to incite the Italians to drive away the Saracens of the south ; but, quarrelling with Marozia, he had to succumb to her second husband, Guido, Marquis of Tuscany. After John's death in prison in 928, Marozia became mistress of Rome, and made and unmade Popes at her pleasure. She married as her third husband, Hugh of Provence, the nominal king of the Italians, and procured the election of her second son, a youth of twenty, to the Papacy, under the name of John XI. About 932 her elder son, Alberic II., a strong, unscrupulous but efficient tyrant, whose character found many parallels in later Italian history, drove his father-in-law out of Rome, and reduced the city to some sort of order under his own rule. His policy seems to have been to turn the patrimony of St. Peter into an aristocratic republic, controlled by his house, and leaving to the Pope no functions that were not purely spiritual. He took the title of 'Prince and Senator of all the Romans.' He kept his brother, Pope John XI. (931-936), and the subsequent Popes, in strict leading-strings, and retained his power until his death in 954. His dreams of hereditary power seemed established when his young son Octavian succeeded him as a ruler of Rome, and in 955 also ascended the papal throne as John XII.

John XII., But the new Pope, who thus united the ecclesi-
955-964. astical with the temporal lordship of Rome, looked upon things purely with the eye of a skilful but unscrupulous statesman. His great ambition was to make his house supreme throughout middle Italy, and he soon found that King Berengar, whose claims grew greater now

that Otto was back beyond the Alps, was the chief obstacle in the way of carrying out his designs. He therefore appealed to Otto for aid against Berengar. In 957 Ludolf of Swabia was sent by his father to wage war against Berengar, but, after capturing Pavia, Ludolf was carried off by fever, and Berengar then resumed his successes. In 960 John sent an urgent appeal to Otto to come to his assistance.

Otto had, as we have seen, long felt the need of the support of the Papacy in carrying out his schemes over the German Church. The wished-for opportunity of effecting a close alliance with the head of the Church was now offered by the Pope himself, and the monastic reformers, disciples of Bruno, or of the new congregation of Cluny, urged him to restore peace and order to the distracted Italian Church. In 961 Otto procured the election and coronation of Otto, his young son by Adelaide, as king of the Germans. In August he marched over the Brenner at the head of a stately host. On 31st January 962 he entered Rome. On 2nd February he was crowned Emperor by John XII. Otto crowned Emperor, 962.

The coronation of Otto had hardly among contemporaries the extreme importance which has been ascribed to it by later writers. Since the fall of the Carolingians there had been so many nominal emperors that the title in itself could not much affect Otto's position. Neither was the assumption of the imperial title the starting-point so much as the result of Otto's intervention in Italy. But the name of Roman Emperor, when assumed by a strong prince, gave unity and legitimacy to Otto's power both over Germany and Italy. And in Germany no less than in Italy there was no unity outside that which adhered to the Roman tradition. Yet the imperial title made very little difference in the character and policy of Otto. He never sought, like Charles the Great, to build up an imperial administrative system or an imperial jurisprudence. Even in Germany there was still no law but the local laws of the five Consequences of the revival of the Roman Empire.

nations. And there was no effort whatever made to extend
into Italy the rude system on which Otto based his power in
Germany.   Still the combination of the legitimacy of the
imperial position with the strength of the Teutonic kingship
did gradually bring about a very great change, both in Germany
and Italy, though it was rather under Otto's successors than
under Otto himself that the full consequences of this were
felt.   Yet Otto was the founder of the mediæval ' Holy Roman
Empire of the German Nation,' and the originator of that
close connection of Germany with Italy on which both the
strength and the weakness of that Empire reposed.   Modern
Germans have reproached him for neglecting the true
development of his German realm in the pursuit of the
shadow of an unattainable Empire.   The criticism is hardly
just to Otto, who was irresistibly led into his Italian policy
by the necessities of his German position, and who could
hardly be expected to look, beyond the immediate work
before him, to far-off ideals of national unity and national
monarchy that were utterly strange to him and to his age.
Otto came into Italy to win over the Pope to his side.   He
looked upon his Roman coronation as mainly important,
because it enabled him to complete his subjection of the
German Church with the help of his new ally Pope John.

The first result of the alliance of Pope and Emperor was
the completion of the reorganisation of the German Church
for which Otto had been striving so long.   The Pope held
a synod at St. Peter's, in which Otto's new archbishopric of
Magdeburg was at last sanctioned.   But Otto, who looked
upon the Pope as the chief ecclesiastic of his Empire, was as
Otto's   anxious to limit Roman pretensions as he had been
motives.   to curb the power of the see of Mainz.   He issued
a charter which, while confirming the ancient claims of the
Papacy to the whole region in middle Italy that had been
termed so long the patrimony of St. Peter, reserved strictly
the imperial supremacy over it.   He provided that no Pope
should be consecrated until he had taken an oath of fealty

to the Emperor. The Pope was thus reduced, like the German bishops, to a condition of subjection to the state.

Otto now left Rome to carry on his campaign against Berengar, who had fled for refuge to his Alpine castles. John XII. now took the alarm, and quickly allied *Otto's later* himself with his old foe against his new friend. *Italian policy* Otto marched back to Rome, and in 963 held a *962-973.* synod, mostly of Italian bishops, in which John was deposed for murder, sacrilege, perjury, and other gross offences, and a new Pope set up, who took the name of Leo VIII., and who was frankly a dependant of the Emperor. John escaped to his strongholds, 'hiding himself like a wild beast in the woods and hills,' and refusing to recognise the sentence passed upon him. The need of fighting Berengar again forced Otto to withdraw from Rome. During his absence the fickle citizens repudiated his authority, and called back John. But hardly was the youthful Pope restored to authority than he suddenly died in May 964. His partisans chose at once as his successor Benedict V.

Otto now hurried back to Rome, and attended a synod, held by Leo VIII., which condemned Benedict and reaffirmed the claims of Leo. There was no use in opposing the mighty Emperor, and Benedict made an abject submission. Sinking on his knees before Otto, he cried, ' If I have in anywise sinned, have mercy upon me.' He was banished beyond the Alps, and died soon afterwards. His fall made patent the dependence of the Papacy on Otto. A last revolt of the Romans was now sternly suppressed. When Otto, flushed with triumph, marched northwards against Berengar, Leo's successor, John XIII., humbly followed in his train. The young king Otto now crossed the Alps, and accompanied his father on a fresh visit to Rome, where, on Christmas day 967, John XIII. crowned him as Emperor. Henceforth father and son were joint rulers. Otto had done his best to make both German kingdom and Roman Empire hereditary.

PERIOD II.   C

The last years of Otto's reign were full of triumph.　Secure in the obedience of the Church, he ruled both Germany and Italy with an ever-increasing authority.　The Magdeburg archbishopric received new suffragans in the sees of Zeiz, Meissen, and Merseburg.　A new era of peace and prosperity dawned.　The German dukes were afraid to resist so mighty a power.　The division of Lotharingia into the two duchies of Upper and Lower Lorraine which now took place was the first step in the gradual process that soon began to undermine the unity of the traditional 'nations' of the German people.　Beyond his Teutonic kingdom the kings of the barbarous north and east paid Otto an increasing obedience.　The marauding heathens of an earlier generation were now becoming settled cultivators of the soil, Christian and civilised.　Their dukes looked up to Otto as an exemplar of the policy which they themselves aspired to realise.　The dukes of Poland and Bohemia performed homage to Otto as Emperor. Ambassadors from distant lands, France, Denmark, Hungary, Russia, and Bulgaria, flocked around his throne.　He intervened with powerful effect in the West Frankish kingdom.　He aspired to the domination of southern Italy, and, having won over to his side the powerful Pandulf, prince of Capua and Benevento, he enlarged that prince's dominions and erected them into a mark to withstand the assaults of the Arabs and Greeks of southern Italy.　But while waging war against the Mohammedans, Otto was anxious to be on good terms with the Romans of the East. The accession of John Zimisces to the Eastern Empire [see pages 161-162] gave Otto his opportunity.　The new lord of Constantinople offered the hand of Theophano, daughter of his predecessor Romanus II., as the bride of the young Otto II., with Greek Italy as her marriage portion.　The Emperor welcomed the opportunity to win peacefully what he had sought in vain to acquire by war.　Early in 972 Theophano was

Marginal note: Otto's imperial position, 962-97[3].

Marginal note: Marriage of the young Otto and Theophano, 972.

crowned by John XIII. at Rome, and immediately afterwards married to the young Emperor. The gorgeous festivities that attended this union of East and West brought clearly before the world the reality of Otto's power.

Otto was now growing old, and had outlived most of his fellow-workers. His brother Henry had died soon after the battle on the Lechfeld. His bastard son William had already sunk into a premature grave. Now came the news of the death of the faithful Hermann Billung. In the spring of 973 Otto went on progress for the last time through his ancestral domains on the slopes of the Harz. Death came upon him suddenly as he was celebrating the Whitsuntide feast in his palace at Memleben. *Death of Otto I., 973.*

He was buried beside his first wife, the English Edith, in his favourite sanctuary of St. Maurice of Magdeburg, raised by his care to metropolitan dignity. His long and busy life had not only restored some sort of peace and prosperity to two distracted nations, but his policy had begun a new development of western history that was to last nearly three centuries, and was to determine its general direction up to the Reformation. He had built up a mighty state in an age of anarchy. He had made Germany strong and peaceful, and the leading power of Europe. He had subjected the Church and pacified Italy. Under him the Roman Empire had again acquired in some real sense the lordship of the civilised world.

THE CRESCENTII.

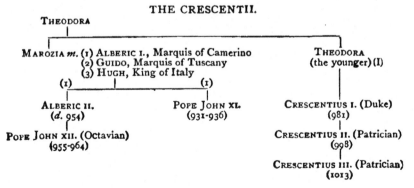

CHAPTER III

THE GERMAN EMPIRE AT THE HEIGHT OF ITS POWER;
THE LATER SAXON AND EARLY SALIAN EMPERORS
(973-1056)[1]

The reign of Otto II.—Break-up of Bavaria—Projects of Crusade—War and Alliance with Greek Empire—The Reign of Otto III.—Regency of Theophano and Bavarian Revolt—Otto and the Bishops—Gerbert of Aurillac—Visionary Schemes of Otto—His failure—Reign of Henry II.— The two Conrads—Reign of Conrad II.—His Italian and Slavonic Policy —Union of Arelate and Empire—Fiefs declared Hereditary—Aribert— Reign of Henry III.—His Policy in the East, France, Germany, and Italy —Synod of Sutri—Death of Henry III.

OTTO II. was eighteen years of age when the death of his father made him sole ruler. His education and surround-
Otto II.,   ings gave his policy a very different direction from
973-983.   that of Otto I. The elder prince was purely
German, and even in winning the imperial crown sought to subserve a Teutonic object. His son, born and reared in the purple, Burgundian or Italian on his mother's side, and married to a Byzantine Emperor's daughter, took wider views. To Otto II. Italy was as important as Germany, and his ambition was to weld the two realms together in a solid imperial unity, while constantly keeping his eyes even beyond these two kingdoms. To him the Emperor's lordship of the world was a reality, and he strove with all the force of an ardent, impetuous, and impulsive nature to give effect to his ideal. But while Otto II.'s short reign witnessed the Empire assuming a more universal character, it also saw the first signs of that essential incompatibility between the position of German

[1] For authorities see note to chapter ii.

king and Roman Emperor which, in after ages, was to bear such bitter fruit.

Despite the quietness of Otto I.'s last years, the difficulties against which the old Emperor had struggled still remained. The separatist spirit of the national dukedoms still lived on in Bavaria, and had only been temporarily glossed over by the good understanding between Otto I. and Duke Henry. Judith, the widow of Duke Henry, now ruled Bavaria in the name of her son Henry II., surnamed the Quarrelsome, while she controlled Swabia through her influence on her daughter Hedwig, and Hedwig's aged husband, the Swabian Duke Burkhard. Otto II. saw the danger of a close union between the two southern duchies, and, on Burkhard's death, invested his nephew Otto, Duke Ludolf's son, with Swabia. Judith and her partisans were instantly aroused. A new civil war was threatened, in which the Bavarians did not scruple to call in the help of the Bohemians and Poles. But the young Emperor's vigorous measures proved fatal to the attempted rebellion, and Otto took the opportunity of his triumph to lessen the influence of the Bavarian dukes by intrusting, to separate margraves, the east mark, on the Danube (the later Austria), and the north mark between the Danube and the Bohemian Forest. The great highland marchland of Carinthia and Carniola, with which still went the Italian March of Verona, or Friuli, was constituted a seventh duchy. The rest of the Bavarian duchy was consigned to the care of the faithful Otto of Swabia. Judith was shut up in a convent. Henry the Quarrelsome fled to Bohemia, whence he made subsequent unsuccessful attempts to recover his position. Thus the Emperor triumphed, but he had simply to do over again the work of his father. It was a thankless business, and showed how insecure were the very foundations of the German kingdom. But for the rest of his short reign Germany gave Otto but little trouble. The extension of Christianity among Wends, Poles, and Bohemians gave Magdeburg and Mainz new suffragans in the Bishops

[marginal note:] Break-up of the Bavarian Duchy, 976-8.

of Gnesen and Prague, though renewed attacks on the
marches soon taught Otto that the Christianised Slavs were
scarcely less formidable enemies than their heathen fathers
had been.

In 978 Otto marched with a great army almost to the walls
of Paris to avenge on the Carolingian king, Lothair, his
War with   attempt to withdraw Lorraine from the imperial
France, 978. obedience [see page 70]. Few of his acts bring
out more clearly his imperial position than this long progress
through hostile territory. But Italy was the scene of Otto II.'s
most famous actions, and best illustrates his high conception
of the imperial dignity. Rome was, as usual, a constant
source of trouble. A series of insignificant Pontiffs succeeded
John XIII.; but above them towered the noble Roman,
Crescentius   Crescentius, Duke of the Romans, perhaps the
at Rome, 980. son of the younger Theodora, Marozia's sister, who
aspired to renew the great part played by Alberic II. In
980 Otto crossed the Alps for Italy, and on his approach the
opposition was shattered. In 981 he restored the Pope to
Rome, whence he had fled from fear of Crescentius, and
forced Crescentius himself to withdraw into the seclusion of
a monastery, where a few years later he died. The need of
protection still kept the Papacy faithful to the imperial
alliance.

Otto now assumed new responsibilities directly flowing
from his position as Emperor. The Mohammedan lords of
Sicily had re-established themselves in southern Italy, and
threatened the march of Benevento. Otto marched to the
Campaigns   help of the Lombard Duke of Benevento. At the
against   same time he sought to make a reality of the
Greeks and
Saracens,   cession of Greek Italy, the promised portion of
981-982.   Theophano, but which, owing to the unwillingness of the Byzantines, had never actually come into his
hands. In 981 and 982 Otto carried on successful war in
southern Italy. A whole series of Greek towns—Salerno,
Bari, Taranto—fell into his hands. In the summer of 982

Otto traversed the old road of Pyrrhus, along the Gulf of Taranto, and defeated the Arabs at Cotrone (the ancient Croton), slaying Abul Cassim, the Ameer of Sicily, in the fight. A few days later Otto fell into a Saracen ambush as he pursued his route along the narrow road between the Calabrian mountains and the sea. His army was almost destroyed, though he himself, after a series of remarkable adventures, succeeded in eluding his enemies.

Germans and Italians vied with each other in their efforts to restore the Emperor's preponderance. In 983 a remarkable Diet assembled at Verona, in which the magnates of Germany and Italy sat side by side to show that the two realms constituted but one Empire. The spirit that a century later inspired the Crusades first appeared in this remarkable assembly. It was resolved to follow the Emperor on a holy war against the Mussulmans. That the succession might be peacefully secured during his absence the magnates chose as their future ruler the little Otto, his three-years-old son by Theophano. Preparations were then made for the war against Islam. But the rising commercial city of Venice, jealous of the imperial policy, and already enriching itself by trade with the enemies of the Christian faith, refused to supply the necessary ships for an expedition against Sicily, the centre of the infidel power. Otto sought to block up the land approaches to the recalcitrant town, but, secure in her impregnable lagoons, Venice was able to defy the Emperor. The news of a Wendish invasion now came from Germany; and the disturbed condition of Rome again demanded Otto's personal presence. There he laboured with feverish earnestness to prepare for his mighty task; but there he was smitten with a sudden and deadly disease, that carried him off on 7th December 983. He was only twenty-eight years old. His body was buried, as became a Roman Emperor, in the Church of St. Peter's. The difficulties which had proved almost too much

Diet of Verona and projected Crusade, 983.

Death of Otto II., 983.

for the strong and capable grown man, were now to be faced, as best they might be, by his young widow Theophano, the regent of the new lord of the world, a child scarcely four years of age.

The German Empire rested almost entirely on the warlike character of its head, and any failure of the central military power involved the gravest evils. A wave of heathen re-action burst from the Wendish and Danish lands into the very heart of the Saxon Empire. In the south, Islam, excited by the threatened Crusade, menaced the centre of the Christian world. It seemed as if the Empire of the Ottos was on the verge of dissolution, when Henry the Quarrelsome, the deposed

Revolt of Henry of Bavaria, 984. Duke of Bavaria, came back, and, by claiming the regency from Theophano, added the terrors of internal discord to those of barbarian invasion. At first Henry made good progress, and, advancing in his claims, began to covet the crown itself. The Dukes of Poland and Bohemia paid him homage, and Lothair of France eagerly supported him. It was more important that Henry had won over many of the bishops, who, as the natural result of Otto I.'s policy, had the balance of power in their hands. He also secured the person of the young Otto III. But, as the Archbishop of Magdeburg favoured Henry, the lay nobles of the Wendish mark, who hated their clerical supplanters, and Archbishop Willegis of Mainz, who still looked with detestation on the mushroom primacy on the Elbe, declared for Theophano. The adhesion of the mass of the Saxon nation at last secured the victory of the Greek. Henry was forced to submit, and was pacified by being restored to his duchy of Bavaria.

Otto III. owed his throne to the clergy. The influence of the bishops kept Germany quiet during the regency of Theophano. The fall of the last of the West

Regency of Theophano, 983-991. Frankish Carolingians, and the accession of Hugh Capet in 987, prevented any further danger from the French side, while on the east, the Margrave

Eckhard of Meissen hurled back the Slavonic invaders, and cleverly set the Bohemians and the Poles by the ears. Adelaide, Otto's grandmother, ruled Italy from the old Lombard capital of Pavia. She was less fortunate than her daughter-in-law, with whom, moreover, her relations were not cordial. Rome fell away almost altogether, so that a French synod at Reims (995) was able, with good reason, to denounce the scandals that degraded the Papacy, and to threaten that France, like the east, might be provoked into breaking off all connections with the See of Peter. John Crescentius, son of the man driven by Otto II. into a cloister, renewed the policy of his father, and, taking the name of Patrician, ruled over Rome with little opposition.

Theophano died in 991. No new regent was appointed, but a council of regency set up, prominent among its members being the Empress Adelaide, Willegis of Mainz, Eckhard of Meissen, and Henry, Duke of Bavaria, son and successor of Henry the Quarrelsome. The composition of this body was a *Rule of the bishops and education of Otto, 991-996.* further proof of the extension of ecclesiastical influence. But an even more significant indication of this was the fact that the young king was brought up almost entirely under the direction of highly-placed churchmen. Willegis of Mainz, and Bernward, Bishop of Hildesheim, the future saint, were the two prelates most directly responsible for his education. The result was that, though the young king spent his early years amidst his fierce and half-barbarous Saxon subjects, he became still less of a German than Otto II., and was possessed by ideals that stand in the strongest contrast with those of his predecessors. Bernward caused him to be schooled in the best culture of his time, and gave him an abiding love of letters and learned men. He also strongly inspired the quick-witted and sympathetic youth with the ascetic views and the sacerdotal sympathies of the Cluniacs. Thus Otto became enthusiastically religious, and ever remained a devout pilgrim to holy places and seeker out of inspired anchorites

and saints.   Moreover, Otto inherited from Theophano all
the high Byzantine notions of the sacredness of the Empire,
and, seeking to combine the two aspects of his education, his
mind was soon filled with glowing visions of a kingdom of
God on earth, in which Pope and Emperor ruled in harmony over a world that enjoyed perfect peace and idyllic
happiness.   Otto's ideals were generous, noble, and unselfish ;
but in the iron age in which he lived they were hopelessly
unpractical.   The young king lived to become the 'wonder
of the world' and the 'renewer of the Empire.'   But his early
death came none too soon to hide the vanity of his ambitions.
At best, he was the first of that long line of brilliant and
attractive failures which it was the special mission of the
mediæval Empire to produce.

In 996 Otto attained his legal majority, and crossed the
Alps to seek his coronation at Rome as Emperor.   The king
Otto's
coronation
at Rome, 996. and his army marched as though bound on a
pilgrimage, or like the crusading hosts of a cen-
tury later.   As they entered the Lombard plain,
the news came that the Papacy was vacant, and a deputation
of Romans, tired of the tyranny of Crescentius, begged Otto
to nominate a new Pope.   The young king at once appointed
his cousin, Bruno, grandson of Conrad the Red and Lint-
Gregory V.,
996-999. garde, daughter of Otto I., a youth of four-and-
twenty, and a zealous champion of the Cluniacs,
who took the name of Gregory v.   On 25th May 996, Otto
was crowned by Gregory at Rome.

Pope and Emperor strove at once to embody their theories
in acts.   The proceedings of the anti-papal synod of Reims
were annulled ; its nominee to the see of Reims, Gerbert of
Aurillac, was forced to yield up his post to the worldly
Arnulf that the synod strove in vain to depose.   The whole
French episcopate bowed in submission before the new Pope,
and Gerbert soon repudiated his earlier teachings.   The
French king, Robert, was visited with the severest censures
of the Church for contracting a marriage within the prohibited

degrees. The holy Adalbert, the apostle of Bohemia, but driven from his see of Prague by a pagan reaction, was sternly ordered to return to his bishopric, or, if that were impossible, to engage in a new mission to the heathen. Adalbert chose the latter alternative, and his early death at the hands of the heathen Prussians made him the proto-martyr of the new order that Otto and Gregory were striving to introduce. But while the two enthusiasts were busy in the regeneration of the universe, they were unable to maintain themselves in the very centre of their power. A new Roman rebellion brought back Crescentius. Only through the help of the iron soldiery of the Saxon borders, headed by the valiant Eckhard of Meissen, could Otto win back the Eternal City to his obedience. In 998 Rome surrendered, and Crescentius atoned for his rebellion on the scaffold.

Fall of Crescentius, 998.

An early death now cut off Gregory v., and Otto raised Gerbert of Aurillac[1] to the papal throne. Gerbert was quite the most remarkable man of his age. A poor Frenchman of obscure birth from the uplands of the centre, he received his first schooling in a cloister at his native Aurillac, where he took the monastic vows. Borrel, a pious Count of Barcelona, made his acquaintance while visiting Aurillac on a pilgrimage, and took him back with him to the Spanish march. There Gerbert abode some years, and there he acquired that profound knowledge of mathematics which had perhaps filtered into the march from the Mussulman schools of Cordova, and which gave him in the unlearned north a reputation for extraordinary learning, if not for magical skill. Ever eager for knowledge, he aecom-panied his patron to Italy, and attracted the notice of Otto i. Finally he settled down at Reims, attracted by the fame of

Gerbert of Aurillac.

[1] Havet's *Lettres de Gerbert* (Picard's 'Collection de Textes'), with the editor's introduction, are a chief authority for Gerbert's history and policy. See also an article on Gerbert by Mr. R. Allen, in the *English Historical Review*, vol. vii. pp. 625-668.

a certain archdeacon who taught in the cathedral school.
The good Archbishop Adalbero made Gerbert 'scholasticus'
of the school at Reims.   Accompanying the archbishop
to Italy, Gerbert received from Otto II. the headship of
Columban's old abbey of Bobbio, and speedily reformed its
lax discipline.   On Otto II.'s death, the angry monks drove
him away, and he went back to Reims and resumed his
teaching as 'scholasticus.'   He dominated the policy of the
archbishop in the critical years that saw the accession of
Hugh Capet to the French throne [see pages 70-71], but on
Adalbero's death was ungratefully passed over by Hugh,
whose interests procured the election of Arnulf, an unlearned
but high-born Carolingian, to the great see.   A few years
later, Arnulf was deposed by the synod of 995, and Gerbert
put in his place.   But Arnulf still claimed to be archbishop,
and Gerbert went to Italy to plead his cause with Gregory v.
Finding his chances hopeless, he closely attached himself to
Otto III., with whom he had strong affinities in character.
Gerbert loved pomp and splendour, was attracted by Otto's
high ideals, and was of a pliant, complaisant, and courtier-like
disposition.   He was made Archbishop of Ravenna to com-
pensate him for the loss of Reims.   When elevated to the
Papacy, he chose to call himself Sylvester II.   As Sylvester I.
had stood to the first Christian Emperor, so would Sylvester II.
stand to the new Constantine.   Under him the close alliance
of Pope and Emperor was continued as fervently as during
the lifetime of Gregory v.

Otto's plans grew more mystical and visionary.   Rome,
and Rome alone, could be the seat of the renewed Empire,

Visionary   and Otto began the building of an imperial palace
schemes of   on the Aventine on the site of the abode of the
Otto and
Sylvester II., early Cæsars.   He abandoned the simple life of a
999-1003.   Saxon etheling, which had been good enough for
his father and grandfather, and secluded his sacred person
from a prying world by all the devices of Byzantine court-
etiquette and Oriental exclusiveness.   His court officials

dropped their old-fashioned Teutonic titles, and were renamed after the manner of Constantinople. The chamberlain became the *Protovestiarius*, the counsellor the *logothetes*, the generals were *comites imperialis militiæ*, and their subordinates *protospatharii*. The close union of the Pope and Emperor in a theocratic polity was still better illustrated by the institution of the *judices palatii ordinarii*. They were of the mystic number of seven, ecclesiastics by profession, and were to act as supreme judges in ordinary times, but ·.ere also to ordain the Emperor (a new ceremony to be substituted for coronation) and to elect the Pope. But apart from its fantastic character, the whole policy of Otto depended upon a personal harmony between Pope and Emperor. Even under Otto himself this result could only be secured by the Emperor's utter subordination of his real interests to the pursuit of his brilliant but illusive fancies.

Otto's cosmopolitan imperialism soon brought him in collision with Germany, and especially with the German Church. He set up a new archbishopric at Gnesen in Poland, where reposed the relics of the martyred Adalbert, and surrounded it with the mystical number of seven suffragans. In the same way, Sylvester, in recognising Stephen, the first Christian Duke of Hungary, as a king, established a Hungarian archbishopric at Gran. These acts involved a recognition of the national independence of Poland and Hungary. Wise as they were, they were resented in Germany as being directly counter to the traditional Saxon policy of extending German influence eastwards, by making the bishops subject to the German metropolitans at Magdeburg and Salzburg. The practical German bishops saw with disgust the Emperor giving up the very corner-stone of the policy of Henry and Otto I. The deep differences of sentiment came to a head in a petty dispute as to whether a new church for the nuns of Gandersheim should be consecrated by Bernward of Hildesheim, the diocesan, who favoured Otto's fancies, or by the metropolitan

[marginal note: Opposition to Otto III. in Germany.]

Willegis of Mainz, who bitterly lamented the outlandish ideas
of his old pupil.   Sylvester upheld Bernward, but the German
bishops declared for Willegis, and paid no heed to the papal
censures that followed quickly on their contumacy.   They
refused even to be present at the Councils in which Sylvester
professed to condemn the Archbishop of Mainz.   The German
clergy were thus in open revolt from Rome, and they were,
as we have seen, the leaders of the German nation.

While the outlook was thus gloomy in Germany, the march
of events in Italy gave but little encouragement to Pope and

Breakdown
of Otto's
system in
Italy.

Emperor, and demanded the personal presence of
Otto, who had been forced to return to Germany
in the vain hope of appeasing the general opposition to his policy.   Before he crossed the Alps
for the last time, Otto went to Aachen, and, if we can believe
one of his followers' statement, visited the vaults beneath
the venerable palace-chapel to gaze upon the corpse of
Charles the Great, sitting as in life upon a throne, with
crown on head and sceptre in hand.   When he reached the
south, he found to his dismay that lower Italy had fallen
altogether from his obedience, and that even Tivoli, in the
immediate neighbourhood of Rome, had rebelled against
him.   Otto made feverish efforts to restore his authority.
He clamoured for Byzantine help, and begged for a Byzantine
wife.   He paid a flying visit to the Venetian lagoons, seeking
for a fleet from the great Doge Peter Orseolo.   But worse
news now reached him.   Rome itself now rose in revolt, and
Otto, postponing in despair his warlike operations, could only
find consolation in visits to the holy Romuald in his inaccessible island hermitage amidst the swamps of Ravenna, and
in the practice of penances, mortifications, and scourgings.
Recovering his energy, he now sought to obtain an army from
Germany to procure, as in the old days, the subjection of
Italy; but it was the very moment of the crisis of the
Gandersheim struggle, and no German help was forthcoming.
A sharp fever now attacked Otto at the very moment of

the collapse of all his plans. He died on 23rd January 1002, at Paterno, near Rome, when only twenty-two years old. With him perished his lofty ambitions. Death of He had made himself the wonder of the world; Otto III., but all that he had accomplished was to play the 1002. game of the high ecclesiastical party. The tendency of his policy, like the latter Carolings, was to subordinate the visionary Empire to the practical Papacy, thus exactly reversing the ideas of the great Saxons, and bringing out in its most glaring contrast the incompatibility of the union of the German kingship with the imperial claims to universal domination. Within a year Sylvester II. followed him to the tomb.

For eighty years the Saxon kings and emperors had succeeded from father to son, and even a minority had not broken down the tendency towards heredity which Henry II., seemed rapidly divesting the German kingdom of 1002-1024. the elective character which it had shared with the Empire itself. Otto III.'s death without direct heirs now reminded the German magnates that they still could choose their king, and, in the absence of any strong claimant, there was a whole swarm of aspirants after the vacant dignity. The friends of the Saxon traditions, which Otto III. had so violently set at naught, hoped for the election of the brave and experienced Eckhard of Meissen; but as Eckhard was travelling to the south to pursue his candidature, he was murdered to satisfy a private revenge. His removal secured the appointment of Henry, Duke of Bavaria, the son of Henry the Quarrelsome, and the nearest kinsman of competent age and position to the dead ruler. Thus the throne was retained in the hands of the Saxon house, though it now was held by a branch that had long attached itself to the traditions of its southern duchy. Bavarians, Lorrainers, and Franks accepted Henry at once; the Saxons and Swabians only after a short hesitation.

It was a great thing that the succession had been peaceably settled. Yet the new king had neither the power nor the energy of the Ottos. Raised to the throne by the great magnates, Henry II. never aspired to carry on the despotic traditions of the earlier Saxon kings, but thought to rule with the help of frequent Diets and Councils. He had more authority over the Church, and his personal piety and zeal for good works, in which he was well supported by his wife Cunigunde, procured for him in after times the name and reputation of a saint, and in his own day kept him on good terms with the clergy, though he was never their slave. He used his bishops and abbots as instruments of his temporal rule, and systematically developed Otto III.'s system of making the bishops and abbots the local representatives of the imperial power by granting them the position of Count over the neighbouring Gau. On one great matter he gave much offence to the German bishops. He set up a new bishop-

Henry II. and the Church.

ric at Bamberg in Franconia, laying in 1004 the foundations of its new cathedral, and conferring on it such extensive privileges that every bishop in Germany was annoyed at the new prelate holding a position next after the archbishops, while the Archbishop of Mainz resented the merely nominal ties of obedience that bound the Bishop of Bamberg to him as his metropolitan. Henry was a friend of the Cluniac monks, and it was through his efforts that these zealous Church reformers first got a strong position in Germany.

Henry had no trouble with the Hungarians, whose great king, St. Stephen, the founder of the settled Magyar state,

Henry II. and the Slavs.

was his brother-in-law and friend. But it was among his chief cares to uphold the old Saxon supremacy over the Slavs, which Otto III. had generously or fantastically neglected. Poland was now a formidable state, and its Duke Boleslav, who had become a terror to the marks before the death of Otto, aspired to build up a strong Slavonic power, and drive back the Germans over the Elbe. It was no longer the frontier warfare of the days after Otto the Great's victories. It was rather a stern fight between two vigorous nations, in which Henry only won the

upper hand after long and costly efforts. Even at the last
he was forced to hand over the mark of Lausitz to the Poles,
to be held as a fief of the German kingdom. Henry's laborious
policy, his shrinking from great efforts, and his fixed resolve
to concentrate himself on little objects within his reach, stand
in the strongest contrast to the vast ambitions of his predecessor. Yet, in his slow and determined way, Henry brought
back the German kingdom to a more national policy, and
did much to restore the havoc wrought by Otto's vain
pursuits of impossible ideals. As a German king, he was in
no wise a failure, though he raised the monarchy to no new
heights of power.

Henry's success in Germany was closely connected with
his failure in Italy. Under his cautious rule the plans of
Otto III. were quickly lost sight of. On the death of Sylvester II., the Papacy fell back into its old dependence on
the local nobles. At first a third Crescentius, son of Otto III.'s
victim, assumed his father's title of Patrician, ruled Rome at
his pleasure, and nominated two puppet Popes in succession.
But a stronger power arose, that of the Counts of Tusculum.
Before long a series of Tusculan Popes, set up by the goodwill of these powerful lords, again degraded the Papacy, and
threatened to deprive it of the obedience and respect of
Europe. It was the same in the secular as Henry II.
in the spiritual sphere. Before the German suc- and Italy.
cession had been settled, Ardoin, Marquis of Ivrea, had
got himself elected King of Italy, and held his own
for many years against the partisans of Henry reinforced
by German armies. In 1004 Henry went over the Alps,
and submitted to be elected and crowned king at Pavia,
though the Ottos had borne the Italian crown without con-
descending to go through such formalities. Despite this
Ardoin long maintained himself. At last, in 1013, Henry
went down to Italy again, and on 14th February 1014 received the imperial diadem from Pope Benedict VIII. But no
striking result followed this renewal of the Empire. Benedict,

who was a zealous partisan of the Count of Tusculum, now sought, by advocacy of the Cluniac ideas, to maintain himself against an Antipope of the faction of Crescentius. In 1020 Benedict visited Germany to consecrate the cathedral of Bamberg, and signalised his visit by taking Henry's foundation under his immediate care. It seemed as if the old alliance of Papacy and Empire were renewed. Next year Henry crossed the Brenner at the head of a strong German army, which traversed all Italy, in three divisions, commanded respectively by Henry himself, the Patriarch of Aquileia, and the Archbishop of Cologne. But by the time the Lombard dukes of Capua and Salerno had made their submission, and Henry was marching through Apulia, a deadly sickness raged in his host and compelled its immediate retreat. Next year Henry was back in Germany. It is significant that the office of Count Palatine of Italy ceased to exist during his reign. The Emperor was no longer an effective ruler of the peninsula.

In the latter years of his life Henry attached himself still more strongly to the Cluniac party, and, as with Otto III., his friendship for foreign priests brought him into renewed conflict with the German bishops. Aribo, Archbishop of Mainz, led the opposition to Henry and Benedict. But just as the conflict was coming to a head, Benedict VIII. died (1024). He was quickly followed to the grave by Henry himself. With him perished the last king of the male stock of the Ludolfing dukes of Saxony. His dull and featureless reign was but a tame conclusion to the brilliant period of the Ottos

The ecclesiastical differences that had troubled Germany during Henry II.'s lifetime lay at the root of the party struggles

The two Conrads, 1024.

that now raged round the appointment of his successor. As in Henry's case, there was no specific candidate marked out by birth and special fitness for the choice of the German nation. The bishops, led by Aribo of Mainz and Burkhard of Worms,

resolved to take full advantage of this freedom of election
to prevent the accession of any prince inclined, like the
late Emperor, to favour the spread of Cluniac ideas. They
therefore urged the claims of Conrad of Swabia. Conrad
was the great-grandson of Conrad the Red and his wife Liutgarde, Otto the Great's daughter, and consequently nephew
of Pope Gregory v., and descended from the Ludolfings on
the female side. Though only the possessor of part of his
rich family estates in the Rhineland, Conrad had made a
lucky marriage with the widowed Gisela, Duchess of Swabia,
the granddaughter of Conrad, king of Arles, and a descendant of the Carolingians. This gave him the guardianship
of the young Duke Ernest of Swabia, Gisela's son by her
former husband, and secured for him a leading position
among the German magnates. Conrad was a valiant and
experienced warrior, and an intelligent statesman, possessing a clear head and a strong will, resolutely bent on
securing practical objects immediately within reach. He
had persistently held aloof from the ecclesiastical policy of
his predecessor, with whom he had been more than once
in open feud. He was still more hostile to his cousin, Conrad,
Duke of Carinthia, the son of another Conrad, a younger
brother of his father Henry, who, through the caprice of their
grandfather, had inherited the mass of the Rhenish estates
of Conrad the Red, usurping the position of the elder line.
This second Conrad was now the candidate of the Cluniac
party against Conrad of Swabia. But the great prelates
were still all-powerful; despite the opposition of the
Lorrainers, among whom Cluniac ideas had gained a firm
hold, Conrad of Swabia was elected king. His path to the
throne was made smooth by the generosity of his rival,
who, at the last moment, abandoned his candidature,
and voted for his cousin. Aribo of Mainz Conrad II.
crowned Conrad in his own cathedral, regard- 1024-1039.
less of the claims of the rival Archbishop of Cologne, the
diocesan of Aachen, the proper place for the coronation.

But Aribo refused to confer the crown on Gisela, since the Church regarded her marriage with Conrad as irregular by reason of their affinity.   Pilgrim of Cologne now saw his opportunity for making terms with the victor.   He gave Gisela the crown which Aribo had denied her.   Thus Conrad entered upon his reign with the support of all the leaders of the German nation.   The younger Conrad remained faithful to his old rival; while his younger brother Bruno, who became Bishop of Toul, soon became one of the greatest supports of the new dynasty.

When Conrad II. became king, he found everything in confusion: but within two years of his accession he had in-
Italian policy.   fused a new spirit and energy into every part of his dominions.   His first difficulty was with Lorraine, whose two dukes had opposed his election, and now refused to acknowledge its validity.   They sought the help of King Robert of France, whose weak support availed them but little.   Conrad soon put down their rebellion, and with almost equal ease quelled the revolt of his ambitious and unruly step-son, Ernest of Swabia.   Germany was thus appeased, but Italy, where the imperial power had become very feeble in the later part of the reign of Henry II., was still practically outside Conrad's influence.   His authority was only saved from complete ruin by the policy of the Lombard bishops, who saw in the Emperor their best protection against the proud and powerful lay aristocracy, and especially against the warlike margraves, who now aspired to renew the part played by Ardoin of Ivrea.   But conscious that they did not possess sufficient strength to continue successfully a policy in which even Ardoin had failed, the leaders of the north Italian nobility looked elsewhere abroad for help to counterbalance the German soldiery of the Emperor.   When King Robert of France rejected their advances, they found what they sought in William V., the Duke of Aquitaine and Count of Poitou, an aged and experienced warrior, and a strong friend of the Cluniacs, who

hoped to find in Italy a suitable endowment for his young son William. This was the first occasion in which the policy of calling in the French to drive out the Germans was adopted by the Italians. But the times were not yet ripe for the intervention of a French prince in Italy. William crossed the Alps, but found that he could make but little progress against the vigorous opposition of the Lombard bishops, headed by Aribert of Milan, and tried to make up for his weakness in Italy by uniting himself with the Lorraine rebels, and by stirring up an anti-German party in the kingdom of Arles. But nothing came of his elaborate schemes, and in 1025 he went home in disgust.

Early in 1026 Conrad crossed the Brenner, and in March received the Lombard crown from Aribert in the cathedral of Milan. Pavia, the old Lombard capital, shut its gates on the Emperor, who was thus unable to be hallowed in the usual place. For a whole year Conrad remained in northern Italy, and gradually forced his enemies to make their submission. In the spring of 1027 the way to Rome at last lay open, and on Easter Sunday Conrad was crowned Emperor by Pope John xix. The function was one of the most striking and memorable ceremonies in the whole history of the mediæval Empire. It was witnessed by two kings—Rudolf iii., the last of the kings of Arles, and Canute of Denmark, the conqueror of England and Norway, then at Rome on a pilgrimage. But the clear head of Conrad was not in the least turned by the mystic rite. Content that his twofold coronation gave him a firm hold over Italy, he quickly recrossed the Alps and resumed his proper work as a German king, taking good care that there should be no clashing between his German and Italian interests. Before his return he visited southern Italy, and ensured the obedience of the Lombard dukes, who still guarded the frontier against the Greeks of Calabria.

On his return to Germany, Conrad felt that his power was sufficiently secure to take steps towards retaining the Empire

Conrad's imperial coronation, 1027.

in his own family. In 1028, he persuaded the magnates to elect, and Pilgrim of Cologne to crown, as his successor his Fall of Ernest eldest son, Henry, who was but ten years of of Swabia, age. This act roused the jealousy of the greater 1030. nobles, who found in Conrad's son-in-law, Ernest of Swabia, an eager champion of their views. Ernest again plunged into revolt; and when pardoned, at the instance of his mother the Empress, still kept up his close friendship with the open rebel, Werner of Kyburg, Count of the Thurgau, a district including the north-eastern parts of the modern Switzerland. In 1030 Conrad ordered Ernest to break off from all dealings with his friend, and, as a sign of his repentance, to carry out in person the sentence of outlawry and deprivation pronounced against him. Ernest refused to give up Werner, whereupon Conrad deprived him of his duchy. Bitterly incensed with his father-in-law, the young duke left the palace, and wandered from court to court, seeking help to excite a new rebellion. But Conrad was so strong that neither foreign prince nor discontented German noble would make common cause with Ernest. In despair he took to a wild robber life of adventure, lurking with a few faithful vassals amidst the ravines and woods of the Black Forest. Before the summer was out Ernest was overpowered and slain. His commonplace treason and brigandage were in after ages glorified in popular tales, that make his friend Werner a model of romantic fidelity, and he himself a gallant and chivalrous warrior. After his fall, Conrad reigned in peace over Germany.

The inroads of the Hungarians and Poles now forced fresh wars on Conrad. In 1030 he waged a doubtful contest against Hungary Stephen of Hungary. In the succeeding years he and Poland, obtained great successes against the Poles, winning 1030-1032. back in 1031 Lausitz and the other mark districts that Henry II. had been forced to surrender to their king Boleslav, and compelling his successor Miecislav, in 1032, to do homage to him for the whole of his kingdom. But great as were Conrad's successes in the east, they were surpassed by his brilliant acquisition of a new kingdom in the west, where in 1032 he obtained the possession of the kingdom of Arles.

The kingdom of Arles or Burgundy had fallen into evil days. During the long reigns of Conrad the Pacific (937-993) and Rudolf III. (993-1032) all power had fallen into the hands of the territorial magnates, and now the threatened extinction of the royal house seemed likely to plunge the Arelate into worse confusion. Rudolf III. was old and childless, and had long sought to make arrangements to prevent the dissolution of his kingdom with his death. In 1007 he had concluded with Henry II., his nephew, an agreement by which Burgundy was to fall on his death to the German monarch, but the Burgundian nobles had more than once forced him to renounce his treaty. An increasing sense of his powerlessness drew Rudolf, who was Gisela's uncle, more closely to Conrad II. He hurried to Rome to be present at his coronation, and he trusted entirely to him for protection against his turbulent nobility. The contract of succession was renewed, and on Rudolf's death, in 1032, Conrad entered into possession of the Arelate. Count Odo of Champagne set himself up as a rival and national king, but the German portions of the Arelate favoured Conrad from the beginning. In 1033 he was chosen king, and crowned at Ueberlingen, near Constance; and in 1034 Odo was forced into submission, while Conrad triumphantly wore his crown at Geneva and received the homage of the lords of Burgundy. Henceforward the kingdom of Arles was indissolubly united with the Empire. Despite the small amount of power which even the strongest Emperors could exercise in the Arelate, the acquisition was one of no small importance. The Arelate was for the most part a Romance land, and its union with the Empire made the Empire less German, and, for some generations at least, prevented the natural tendency to union between France and the Burgundian lands from being carried out. Moreover, the

Union of the Arelate with the Empire, 1032.

acquisition of the Arelate, by virtue of a contract of succession, increased the already strong tendency towards hereditary monarchy in Germany and Italy.   Again, Burgundy was the chief home of the Cluniacs, and one very important consequence of its absorption by Conrad was a gradual increase of Cluniac influence all over the Empire.   And most of all, the new-won kingdom was useful to the Emperors as acting as a sort of buffer-state to protect Italy from French interference. The attempt of William of Poitou had taught Conrad the necessity of thus guarding the Italian frontier.   For the next few generations the acquisition of the Arelate made such projects more difficult.   Supplementing the final adhesion of Lotharingia to the Eastern Kingdom, the lapse of the Arelate completed the absorption of the 'Middle Kingdom' in the German Empire.   Of the threefold partition of Europe by the Treaty of Verdun in 843, only the ancient dominions of Charles the Bald—France, in the narrower sense—were outside the powers of the Emperor.   Henceforth Conrad ruled not only all the lands that had gone in 843 to Louis the German, but also over the districts that had then fallen to the share of the Emperor Lothair.   Two-thirds of the Carolingian Empire were thus concentrated under Conrad.

Ten years of Conrad's rule had now brought the Holy Empire to a point of solid prosperity that was seldom surpassed.   But Conrad saw that there were still great dangers inherent in his position, and foremost among these was the smallness of the number of the feudal dignitaries with whom he had direct legal dealings.   There were no longer indeed the five national dukedoms in their old united strength and dignity. There were no longer dukes of Franconia; Lorraine was already divided into two distinct duchies, of Upper and Lower Lorraine.   Swabia was showing signs of a similar tendency to bifurcation ; Bavaria, after the rearrangement of 976, was in a much less imposing position than under the Saxon Emperors, and even in Saxony the margraves

Feudal benefices declared hereditary.

were a strong counterpoise to the more imposing but
not more powerful dukes. In the last generations the
more vigorous of the counts and margraves had shaken
off their dependence on the dukes, and aspired to stand
in immediate relations with the Emperor. Yet the whole
drift of the time was towards feudalism, and towards
making a limited number of tenants-in-chief, whether dukes,
margraves or counts, the sole persons with whom the Emperor
had any direct relations. Secure in their own hereditary
tenure of their fiefs and allodial properties, the great lords of
Germany claimed an absolute control over all their vassals.
The old tie of national allegiance that bound every subject to
his sovereign had fallen into neglect as compared with the
new link of feudal dependence of vassal on lord. The leading
tenants-in-chief considered that their powers over their vassals
were so absolute that it was the bounden duty of a tenant to
follow his lord to the field, even against his overlord. With
the same object of strengthening their own position, the
great lords strove to prevent the fiefs of their vassals from
assuming that hereditary character which they had already
acquired in practice, if not in theory, for their own vast
estates.

Conrad showed a shrewd sense of self-interest in posing as
the friend of the lesser tenants against the great vassals of
the crown. Whether he also secured the best interests of
Germany is not quite so clear. The great vassals were strong
enough to maintain order; the lesser feudalists had neither
their resources nor their traditions of statecraft. It was too
late to revive with any real effect the national tie of allegiance,
and the scanty means of an early mediæval king had always
made somewhat illusory great schemes of national unity.
Conrad did his best for the protection of the under-tenants by
establishing for them also that hereditary possession of their
benefices which gave them some sort of permanent position
over against their overlords. This was secured in Germany
by a mere recognition of the growing custom of heredity,

though in Italy a formal law was necessary to attain the same end. Another advantage won by Conrad by this action was that in securing the recognition of the principle of heredity in every fief, he made a long step towards securing the heredity of the crown. For Conrad, much more distinctly than his Saxon predecessors, sought definitely to make both the royal and imperial crown hereditary in his house. As a further step towards breaking down the greater nobility, he strove to get rid of the national duchies altogether. He persuaded the Bavarians to elect the young King Henry as their duke, and, on the death of his last stepson, gave Swabia also to his destined successor. On the death of his old rival, Conrad of Carinthia, the great Carinthian mark was also handed over to Henry. At the end of Conrad's reign, Saxony and Lorraine were the only duchies still held by independent princes. Like his predecessors, Conrad used the bishops as the means of carrying on the government and checking the growth of the lay aristocracy. Following the example of the chief ecclesiastics, he encouraged the development of a new class of hereditary *ministeriales*, who devoted their lives to the service of the crown, and soon built up a new official body that enabled his successors to largely dispense with the interested help of the episcopate in carrying on the daily task of the administration of the kingdom.

Conrad was so successful with this policy in Germany and Burgundy that he desired to extend it to Italy. But the spirit of independence was already deeply rooted south of the Alps, and the very prelates who had called Conrad to help them against their lay rivals, now looked with suspicion on a policy that deprived churchman and lay noble alike of their cherished immunities. Aribert of Milan had long aspired to a position of almost complete independence. His dream was to make the see of St. Ambrose a sort of North Italian patriarchate, and at the same time he wished to combine with ecclesiastical aseen-dency an organised temporal power. His twofold ambition

Conrad's strife with Aribert, 1036-1039.

was exactly that of the Papacy at a later period, and for the moment Milan seemed stronger than Rome. The citizens of Milan, more obedient to their bishops than the turbulent Romans, were zealous partisans of Aribert; but the smaller nobles, who saw in the fulfilment of his plans the destruction of their own independence, rose as one man against him. Civil war broke out in Lombardy between the friends and foes of Aribert. So dangerous was the outlook that in 1036 Conrad again crossed the Alps in the hope of restoring peace in North Italy.

Aribert was summoned to a Diet at Pavia; but he loftily declared that he would surrender no single right of the church of St. Ambrose, and was soon in open war against the Emperor. Conrad saw his only chance of overcoming the archbishop in winning over the smaller nobility to his side. In 1037 he issued the famous edict which made fiefs hereditary in Italy, thus doing for the south by a single stroke what gradual custom and policy had slowly procured for the north. He also promised to exact from his vassals no greater burdens than those already usually paid to him. But these measures, though increasing the party of Conrad in Italy, were not enough at once to overcome Aribert, who, secure in the hearty support of the Milanese citizens, defied not only the threats of Conrad but also the condemnation of Rome, which the Count of Tusculum, who then occupied the papal throne, willingly put at the service of the Emperor. In 1038 Conrad was forced by urgent business to recross the Alps, leaving Aribert unsubdued. Next year he died suddenly at Utrecht. 'No man,' says a Saxon annalist, 'regretted his death.' Yet if Conrad was unpopular, he was singularly successful. Though he had failed to get the better of Aribert, he had obtained his object in everything else that he undertook. He left the royal authority established on such a solid basis that his son, King Henry, already crowned King of Germany and Burgundy, and already Duke of Bavaria and Swabia, now stepped into the complete possession of his

father's power, as if he were already the heir of an hereditary
state.   Henry III. was the first German king to succeed
without opposition or rebellion.

Henry III. was now two-and-twenty years of age, and had
been carefully educated for his great position.   Gisela had
Henry III., procured for him the best of literary teachers,
1039-1056. while Conrad himself had taken care that he
should excel in all knightly exercises, and go through a
sound drilling in war, law, and statecraft.   He had already
won martial glory against the Poles and Hungarians, while
he had acquired political experience as virtual, if not
formal, co-regent with his father.   He was now able to take
up his father's work, and while carrying it on essentially in
the old lines, to infuse it with a new spirit.   For the gifted
young king, though inheriting to the full the practical wisdom
of his father, soared far above the cold self-seeking and
hard selfishness of the least attractive of the great German
Emperors.   Under his strong and genial rule, the Holy
Empire again became a great ideal, though it was now an
ideal that had little that was visionary or fantastic about it.
The seventeen years of his reign witnessed the culminating
point of the power of the mediæval Empire.   Under him
Germany effectively ruled the destinies of the world.   The
early troubles that had attended the building up of the
kingdom were over.   The later troubles that sprang from the
struggle of the ecclesiastical and temporal power had not yet
begun.

A series of signal triumphs in the east first proclaimed to
the world the greatness of the new king.   Poland, Bohemia,
and Hungary were all alike matters of concern to Henry.
Poland,   But Poland, so mighty a few years before, was
Bohemia, and distracted by civil strife, and attacked by the
Hungary
made fiefs of rising power of Bohemia, now the strongest
the Empire. Slavonic state.   It was a light matter for Henry to
retain Poland as a feudatory of the Empire.   But it involved
a long struggle before Bohemia, under its warlike Duke

Bretislav, could be forced to accept the same position. It was Bretislav's ambition to make himself a king, and to secure for the Bohemian bishopric at Prague the position of an archbishopric, so that a great Slavonic kingdom, independent both in Church and State, might centre round the Bohemian table-land. But Henry forced his way through the mountains of the border and threatened Prague itself. In despair Bretislav did homage to him for Bohemia and Moravia, and even for the outlying district of Silesia, which he had conquered from the weak Polish monarchy and made an integral part of the Bohemian kingdom. Even greater difficulties beset Henry in Hungary, where a heathen reaction had set Aba, a member of the hero race of Arpad, on the throne. In 1042 Henry invaded Hungary and dethroned Aba, but the Hungarian king was soon restored, and it was not until a third expedition in 1044 that Henry finally succeeded in destroying his power. Aba's defeat secured the complete triumph of the German king. Peter, the new king of Hungary, performed homage to Henry, thus making Hungary, like Poland and Bohemia, a fief of the Empire. In 1045 Henry visited Hungary, and received the submission of the Magyar magnates. In pious gratitude for his victory Henry sent the gilded lance, which Peter had given to him as an emblem of his dependence, as a votive offering to the Papacy. A few years later another Arpad, Andrew, dethroned the weak Peter, and gave a more national direction to the fierce Magyar nation, though he was too conscious of Henry's power to break openly with him. With a row of vassal kingdoms extending to the extremest eastward limits of Roman civilisation, the Holy Empire was fast becoming in a very real sense the mistress of the world.

With all his power, Henry could not hope to obtain from the princes of the west the same formal acknowledgment of his supremacy that he had wrested from the lords   Henry III. of the east. The France of Henry I. was indeed and France. feeble and helpless, but the early Capetian monarchy was still the centre of a great system, and its feudatories, though constantly at war with their king and with each other, would be likely to make common cause against a German pretender to universal rule.   Henry III. was content to keep on friendly terms with his neighbours beyond the Rhine, and, as a good means of securing French friendship, he chose a wife from among the greater vassals of the Capetian throne.   In 1043 he married Agnes of Poitou, the youngest daughter of that Count William of Poitou who, in his youth, had competed with Conrad the Salic for the crown of Italy.   Agnes exercised henceforth strong influence over her husband, and in particular upon his ecclesiastical policy.

With the eastern kings paying him tribute and the monarch of the west seeking his friendship, Henry had now leisure to improve the internal condition of his dominions.   Despite all that his predecessors had done, Germany and Italy were still in the utmost disorder.   Conrad II.'s policy of encouraging **Henry III.** the smaller nobility had tended to increase the **and Germany.** private wars and local feuds that made existence so difficult and dreary for the simple freeman, and so dangerous even to the great lord.   Henry now made strenuous efforts to restore peace to Germany.   At a diet at Constance Henry solemnly forgave all his enemies, and craved their forgiveness in turn, calling upon the magnates to follow his example and lay aside their feuds with each other.   Some degree of success followed this appeal, especially as Henry had partly abandoned his father's policy of concentrating the national duchies in his own hands.   Germany was so vast that it could hardly be effectively ruled from a single centre, and Henry hoped that henceforth the dukes whom he set up would be faithful ministers, and not champions of local independence.

Italy demanded Henry's utmost care, and the critical position of the Papacy closely connected his policy with his attitude towards the Church.   Since his marriage with Agnes, Henry had become more attentive to the

teachings of Cluny, and was keenly alive to the scandals
which still disgraced the Roman Church. No ecclesiastical
reformation could be complete which did not begin with
the head of the Church, and it was only by a great
manifestation of his power that Henry could purify   Henry III.
the Papacy. The Counts of Tusculum still kept   and Italy.
their tight hold over the Roman Church, which had almost
become their hereditary possession. After two brothers—the
reforming Benedict VIII. (1012-1024) and the reactionary
John XIX. (1024-1033)—had held in turn St. Peter's chair,
a third member of the Tusculan house, their nephew, Benedict IX., succeeded, despite his extreme youth, to the papal
throne (1033). His excesses soon gave occasion to universal
scandal, and in 1044 the Romans set up an Antipope in
Sylvester III. Family influence still upheld Benedict, but next
year new troubles arising, he sold the Papacy in a panic to
a new pretender, who called himself Gregory VI., and who,
despite his simoniacal election, soon attracted the reformers
around him by his zeal in putting an end to abuses. But
Benedict soon repented of his bargain, and sought to regain
his position as Pope. The result was that three rival claimants
to the Papacy distracted Rome with their brawls, and none
of them had sufficient power to get rid of the others.

A synod assembled at Rome, and called on Henry III.
to put an end to the crisis. In 1046 he crossed the Alps,
and held a Church Council at Pavia, in which he issued an
edict condemning simony. In December 1046 he held
another synod at Sutri, near Rome, where two   Synod of
of the three claimants to the Papacy were de-   Sutri, 1046.
posed. The third claimant was deposed in a third synod
held in Rome itself. Suidgar, Bishop of Bamberg, was chosen
Pope through Henry's influence, and enthroned on Christmas
Day as Clement II., conferring on the same day the imperial
crown on Henry and Agnes. Accompanied by Clement,
the Emperor made a progress through southern Italy,
which he reduced to submission. Grave troubles on the

Lower Rhine now brought Henry back to Germany; yet even in his absence his influence remained supreme in Italy. Clement II. died in 1048; but a whole succession of German Popes, the nominees of the Emperor, were now accepted by the Romans with hardly a murmur. The first of these— Damasus II., formerly Poppo, Bishop of Brixen, died after a few weeks' reign. His successor, the Emperor's kinsman, Bruno of Toul, took the name of Leo IX. (1048-1054). Short as was his pontificate, the result of his work was epoch-making in several directions. During the reign of his successor, Victor II. (1054-1057), Henry III. paid his second and last visit to Italy, the results of which we will speak of later. No sooner was he over the Alps than a rebellion broke out in Bavaria that necessitated his immediate return. The presence of the Emperor soon extinguished the revolt, but the rising taught Henry the insecurity of his position, and he now sought to conciliate his foes.

In the summer of 1056 Henry held his court at Goslar, where he was visited by Victor II.; but in September he fell

Death of Henry III., 1056. sick, and had only time to take further measures to secure his son's succession, when death overtook him, on 5th October, in the thirty-ninth year of his age. Under him the mediæval Empire attained its apogee. Germany was now almost a nation; Italy a submissive dependency; the Papacy had been reformed, and the Church purified. A child of six years old was now called to the throne, whose burden had been almost too heavy for his father. With the accession of Henry IV. the decline of the Empire begins.

GENEALOGY OF THE SAXON AND SALIAN EMPERORS

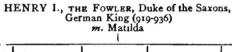

HENRY I., THE FOWLER, Duke of the Saxons,
German King (919-936)
m. Matilda

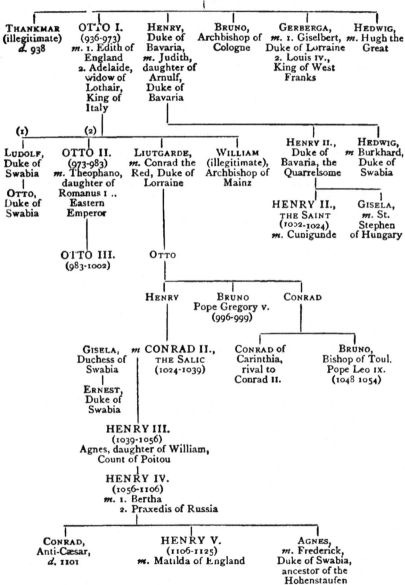

THANKMAR (illegitimate) *d.* 938

OTTO I. (936-973) *m.* 1. Edith of England 2. Adelaide, widow of Lothair, King of Italy

HENRY, Duke of Bavaria, *m.* Judith, daughter of Arnulf, Duke of Bavaria

BRUNO, Archbishop of Cologne

GERBERGA, *m.* 1. Giselbert, Duke of Lorraine 2. Louis IV., King of West Franks

HEDWIG, *m.* Hugh the Great

(1) LUDOLF, Duke of Swabia
|
OTTO, Duke of Swabia

(2) OTTO II. (973-983) *m.* Theophano, daughter of Romanus I .. Eastern Emperor

LIUTGARDE, *m.* Conrad the Red, Duke of Lorraine

WILLIAM (illegitimate), Archbishop of Mainz

HENRY II., Duke of Bavaria, the Quarrelsome
|
HENRY II., THE SAINT (1002-1024) *m.* Cunigunde

HEDWIG, *m.* Burkhard, Duke of Swabia

GISELA, *m.* St. Stephen of Hungary

OTTO III. (983-1002)

OTTO

HENRY

BRUNO Pope Gregory V. (996-999)

CONRAD
|
CONRAD of Carinthia, rival to Conrad II.

BRUNO, Bishop of Toul. Pope Leo IX. (1048 1054)

GISELA, Duchess of Swabia
|
ERNEST, Duke of Swabia

m CONRAD II., THE SALIC (1024-1039)

HENRY III. (1039-1056) Agnes, daughter of William, Count of Poitou

HENRY IV. (1056-1106) *m.* 1. Bertha 2. Praxedis of Russia

CONRAD, Anti-Cæsar, *d.* 1101

HENRY V. (1106-1125) *m.* Matilda of England

AGNES, *m.* Frederick, Duke of Swabia, ancestor of the Hohenstaufen

CHAPTER IV

FRANCE AND ITS VASSAL STATES
UNDER THE LAST CAROLINGIANS
AND THE EARLY CAPETIANS, 929-1108 [1]

The last Carolingians—Hugh the Great—Election of Hugh Capet, and its results—The first four Capetians, Hugh, Robert II., Henry I., Philip I. The great Fiefs under the early Capetians—Normandy—Brittany—Flanders — Vermandois — Champagne and Blois — Anjou — Burgundy Aquitaine and Poitou — Toulouse — Beginnings of French influence.

WHILE the first great Saxon kings were reviving the power of their eastern kingdom, the expiring Carolingian house

The last Carolingian Kings of the West Franks.

still carried on an unavailing struggle for the possession of the old realm of the West Franks. Charles the Simple was the last Carolingian to exercise any real authority in France. He had obtained a powerful ally by his concession of Normandy to Rolf and his vikings. He had witnessed the revolt of the Lotharingians from Germany to France, and had

Charles the Simple, 896-929.

attained many successes through their support. Yet the concluding years of his reign were troubled in the extreme, until he succumbed before the formidable coalition of Robert, Count of Paris, the brother of the dead King Odo, and the chief representative

---

[1] Luchaire's *Institutions Monarchiques de la France sous les Premiers Capétiens* (987-1180) includes, besides its detailed studies of institutions, an admirable summary of the political history. Special works include Lot's *Les Derniers Carolingiens*, Monod's *Études sur l'Histoire de Hugues Capet*, and Pfister's *Étude sur le Règne de Robert le Pieux*.

of the new order, with his two mighty sons-in-law, Herbert, Count of Vermandois, and Rudolf, Duke of Burgundy. Robert got himself crowned king in 922, but was Robert, slain in battle in 923, leaving his famous son, 922-923. Hugh the Great, too young to succeed to his disputed kingdom. This left Rudolf of Burgundy as king of the Franks, or, rather, of those who still resisted Charles the Rudolf, Simple [see Period I., pp. 503-5]. When Charles 923-936. died in prison in 929, Rudolf had no longer a nominal rival. He reigned until his death in 936. But his power was miserably weak, and real authority still resided with the great feudatories, whose possessions had now become hereditary for so long a time that they were now associated by close ties to the districts which they ruled.

Hugh the Great was a man of very different calibre from his fierce ancestors. Robert the Strong, the founder of the house, had been a warrior pure and simple. His sons, Odo and Robert, the two dukes who had in turn grasped the sceptre, had faithfully followed in his footsteps. Wanting in policy and statecraft, they had been less powerful as kings than as dukes. Hugh the Great, the first statesman of the Robertian house, was a shrewd tactician, Policy of who saw that his fortunes could best be estab- Hugh the lished by playing a waiting game. He heaped Great. up treasure, and accumulated fresh fiefs, but on the death of his Burgundian brother-in-law he declined the royal dignity, preferring to exercise an unseen influence over a king of his own choice to exposing himself to the certainty of exciting the jealousy of every great lord in France, by raising himself above them as their king.

There was only one sacred family which every lord admitted to be above himself. Even in its humiliation the Carolingian name was still one to conjure with. As Hugh Louis IV., would not be king himself, he wisely fell back on 936-954. the legitimate stock of the West Frankish royal house. He turned his eyes over the Channel, where Louis, son of Charles the Simple, and his West Saxon queen, Eadgifu, daughter of Edward the Elder, was living quietly at the court of his uncle Athelstan. Louis was only fifteen years old, and was likely to be grateful to his powerful protector. He was elected king by the Frankish lords, and duly crowned at Reims. In memory of his exile he was called 'Louis from beyond sea' (*Ultramarinus, Outremer*). In the list of French kings he is reckoned as Louis IV.

Hugh the Great was rewarded by the renewal in his favour of the title 'Duke of the French,' which had already been borne by his father Robert in the days of Charles the Simple. This title suggested a power, half military and half national, The Duke of analogous to that held by the dukes of the nations the French. in Germany. But if this were the case, Hugh's power as duke would have probably been restricted to 'Francia,' a region which, in common speech, was now limited to the Gaulish regions north of the Seine. It is not clear, however, that the power of the Duke of the French had any territorial limitation other than that of the limits of the West Frankish kingdom as prescribed by the treaty of Verdun. Wherever Louis ruled as 'king,' Hugh wielded authority as 'duke.' He was a permanent prime minister, a mayor of the palace, a justiciar of the Anglo-Norman type, rather than a territorial duke. Indeed, Hugh's chief domains were not in 'Francia' at all. Despite his possession of Paris, his chief fiefs were still in the cradle of his house, the district between the Seine and Loire, to which the term Neustria was now commonly applied. Here his authority stretched as far westwards as the county of Maine, which he had obtained in his youth from the weakness of Rudolf of Burgundy. Moreover, in the lack of all central royal authority, half the chief vassals of the north had thought it prudent to commend themselves to the mighty lord of Neustria, and, with the Duke of Normandy at their head, had become his feudal dependants. Hugh was no longer simply a great feudatory. Even in name, he was the second man in Gaul. In fact, he was a long way the first.

The last Carolingians were in no wise puppets and do-nothings like the last Merovingians. Louis IV. proved a strenuous warrior, with a full sense of his royal dignity. He ruled directly over little more than the hill-town of Laon and its neighbourhood, but he did wonders with his scanty resources. He married a sister of Otto the Great, and with German help was able to press severely his former patron. But Otto soon withdrew beyond the Rhine, and Louis, deprived of his help, and ever planning schemes too vast for his resources, was soon altogether at Hugh's mercy. In 946 he was driven out of Laon: 'the only town,' as he complained, 'where I could shut myself up with my wife and children, the town that I prefer to my life.' In his despair he laid his wrongs before King Otto and a council of bishops at Ingelheim. Hugh prudently yielded before the threatened thunders of the Church. He renewed his homage to King Louis, and restored Laon to him. 'Henceforth,' says the chronicler, 'their friendship was as firm as their struggles had formerly been violent.' When Louis died suddenly in 954, his thirteen-year-old son, Lothair, was chosen king through Hugh's influence. Two years later the great duke died.

Hugh the Great's son and successor was also named Hugh. He is famous in history by the surname of 'Capet,' which he obtained from bearing the cope of the abbot of St. Martin's at Tours, but which, like most famous surnames, has no contemporary authority. Brought up in his father's school, he was clear-headed, cunning, resourceful, and cold-blooded. He soon extended the power of his house, establishing one of his brothers in Burgundy, and marrying Adelaide, the heiress of Poitou, so as to be able to push forward claims in the lands beyond the Loire. Both in policy and resources he overmatched the young king Lothair, who tried as he grew up to play his father's part; but his means were too small, and he embarked on contradictory policies which destroyed

Hugh Capet and King Lothair, 954-986.

each other. His father had relied upon the support of Otto I., but Lothair, tempted by the long tradition of loyalty which bound Lotharingia to the Carolingian house, sought to find a substitute for his dwindling patrimony in northern France by winning domains for himself in that region. The strong Saxon kings would not tolerate the falling away of Lorraine from their Empire. Otto II. invaded France [see page 38] and vigorously punished the presumptuous Carolingian. Henceforth Lothair had no support against the subtle policy of the new Duke of the French. He even alienated Adalbero, the famous Archbishop of Reims, and the last prominent ecclesiastical upholder of the tottering dynasty, so that he repudiated the traditional policy of his see, and allied himself with the duke and the Emperor. Gerbert, the 'scholasticus' of Adalbero's cathedral school, and the author of his policy, established an alliance between Hugh Capet and Otto III., and was soon able to boast that Lothair was but king in name, and that the real king was Duke Hugh. After losing the support of the Germans and of the Church, the Carolingians had absolutely nothing left but their own paltry resources. Yet Lothair gallantly struggled on till his death,

Louis V., in 986, after a nominal reign of thirty-two years.
986-987. His son, Louis V., who had reigned jointly with him since 979, succeeded to his phantom kingship, and contrived to win over Duke Hugh, at whose instigation he led an expedition into Poitou. But Louis also quarrelled with Archbishop Adalbero, and alienated the Church. Adalbero intrigued against him, and the prelate's triumph was hastened by Louis' premature death in the hunting-field (987). He was the last of the Carolingian kings.

For a century the Robertian house had struggled with the house of Charles the Great. Its premature triumph

Election of under Odo and Robert had put off the final day
Hugh Capet, of success. But the patient and shrewd policy
987. of Hugh the Great and Hugh Capet was at last rewarded with victory. Louis V. left no son. His uncle

Charles, Duke of Lower Lorraine, was his nearest heir, but was in no position to push forward his pretensions. The pear was at last ripe, and Hugh Capet had no longer any motive for avoiding the semblance of the power, of which he had long enjoyed the reality. Adalbero and Gerbert now showed great activity. Adalbero harangued the barons and bishops on the duty that lay before them. 'We know,' he said, 'that Charles of Lorraine has his partisans who pretend that the throne belongs to him by hereditary right. But we believe that kingship is not acquired by hereditary right, but that we ought only to raise to that dignity the man who is marked out, not only by nobleness of birth, but by wisdom, loyalty, and magnanimity.' The magnates took the cue, and elected Hugh king of the French. The Church ratified the choice of the nobles by the solemn coronation of the new king at Noyon. The Duke of the Normans and the Count of Anjou lent him the support of their arms. The Emperor recognised Hugh, on condition that he waived all claims over Lotharingia.

The revolution of 987 was easily accomplished, because the old order was so nearly dead. It involved no striking change in form. The Capetian kings posed as the lawful successors of the Carolingians : they had the same conceptions of sovereignty, and followed the same principles of Its government. Yet those are not far wrong who results. regard the accession of Hugh as the starting-point of all later French history. It is easy to exaggerate the nature of the change. It is unsafe to make the change of dynasty a triumph of one race over another. It has been the fashion to say that, with the last of the Carolingians, disappear the last of the Teutonic conquerors of Gaul, and that their power had passed on to the Romanised Celts whom they had ruled so long. But there is no scrap of evidence to prove that the later Carolings were different in tongue, ideas, or policy from the Robertian house. There was no real national feeling in the tenth century, and, if there were, no proof that the one

house was more national than the other.   Nevertheless, the
passing away of the line of Charles the Great does complete
the process which the Treaty of Verdun had begun.   The
Capetian king had a limited localised power, a power that in
due course could become national; and if he looked back, like
the Carolings, to the traditions of imperial monarchy and
order, he had no temptation to look back, as the Carolings
were bound to look back, to the imperial ideas of universal dominion.   He had no claim to rule beyond the
limits ascribed to the West Frankish kingdom in the Treaty
of Verdun.   He was king of the French, the new Romance
people that had grown up as the result of the amalgamation
of conquering Frank and conquered Roman.   He spoke the
infant French tongue ; his ambitions were limited to French
soil ; he represented the new nationality that soon began to
take a foremost place amidst all the nations of Europe.   But
the triumph of the Capetian was not even in anticipation a
simple national triumph.   It was only in after ages, when France
had become great, that she could look back and see in his
accession the beginnings of her separate national monarchy.
Personally, Hugh Capet was doubtless, like Harold of England some two generations later, an embodiment of the
new national character and energy.   But, less fortunate than
Harold, he had time enough to live to show how powerless was a national hero, amidst an order of society in which
the national ideal could have no place.   He was rather the
mighty feudatory, raised by his own order to a position of
pre-eminence to represent the predominance of feudal ideas.
The Carolings had fallen, not because of their own weakness,
and still less by reason of any want of sympathy between
them and the French nation.   They were pushed out of power
because France had become so fully feudalised that there was
no room for an authority that had no solid basis of feudal
support.   France had become divided among a series of great
fiefs.   None of these fiefs fell to the ruling family, which
was thus, as the result of the preponderance of the feudal

principle, deprived of revenue, army, lands, and reputation. Hugh Capet inherited all that had kept the Carolingian power alive so long; but in addition to that he could supplement the theoretical claims of monarchy by right divine, by the practical arguments drawn from the possession of one of the strongest fiefs. Thus the new dynasty saved the monarchy by strengthening it with a great fief. No doubt the feudatories acted unwisely in having a king at all. But a nominal monarchy was part of the feudal system, and the barons could console themselves by believing that in becoming king of the French, Hugh still remained one of themselves. He was not surrounded with the mystic reverence due to the descendants of Charlemagne. As Harold, in becoming king of the English, did not cease to be earl of the West Saxons, so Hugh, in ascending the French throne, was still in all essentials the count of Paris. Harold and Hugh alike found but a questioning obedience in the great earls and counts, who looked upon the upstart kings as their equals. The Norman Conquest destroyed Harold before it could be early demonstrated what a long step in the direction of feudalism was made by his accession. Hugh Capet and his successors had time to bear the full brunt of the feudal shock. The most powerful of dukes proved the weakest of kings. It was only gradually that the ceremonial centre, round which the cumbrous fabric of French feudalism revolved, became the real heart of French national life. Yet, even in the feeble reigns of the first four Capetian kings, it is plain that France had begun a new existence. The history of the Carolingians is a history of decline. The history of the Capetians is a story of progress. While beyond the Rhine and Alps the continuance of the imperial theory choked the growth of German and Italian national life, the disappearance of these remnants of the past proved a blessing to Gaul. The history of modern Europe is the history of the development of nationalities. That history may be said in a sense to begin with the establishment of the first of an unbroken dynasty of national kings over what was destined to become one of the greatest of modern nations.

It is only with these limitations that the election of Hugh can be regarded as a triumph either of feudalism or of nationality. But it is entirely true that Hugh's accession was the triumph of the Church. Adalbero, and Gerbert working through Adalbero, really gave Hugh the throne. Gerbert could truly boast that the Church had revived the royal name after it had long been almost dead among the French. Amidst the horrors of feudal anarchy, the sounder part of the Church still upheld in monarchy the Roman tradition of orderly rule, and taught that the king governed by God's grace, because without a strong king the thousand petty tyrants of feudalism would have no restraint upon their lust and greed. But even this was an ideal far beyond the vision of the tenth century; though in later generations it was to bear fruit. The immediate results of Hugh Capet's election were far different from its ultimate results. The conditions upon which his brother magnates had elected him king meant in practice that they should enjoy in their territories the same power that he enjoyed on his own domain. Save his theoretical pre-eminence, Hugh got very little from his royal title. The only resources on which he could depend implicitly were those which he derived from his own lands and vassals. There was no national organisation, no royal revenue, and practically no royal army, as the term of feudal service was too short to carry on a real campaign, even if the king could have trusted his vassals' levies. The royal title involved responsibilities, but brought with it little corresponding power.

Struck by the contrast between their weakness and the commanding position of later French kings, historians have dwelt with almost exaggerated emphasis on the powerlessness of Hugh Capet and his first three successors. Yet the early Capetians were not so feeble as they are sometimes described.

The French king was still the centre round which the feudal system revolved. He had a store of legal claims and traditions of authority, which at any favourable moment he could put into force. He was the only ruler whose authority extended even in name all over France. He inherited the traditions of the Carolingians and Merovingians, and, rightly or wrongly, was regarded as their successor. Moreover, the lay fiefs were, luckily for the monarchy, cut up by the great ecclesiastical territories, over which the king stood in a better position. Though feudal in a certain sense, the great Church dignitary was never a mere feudalist. His power was not hereditary. On his death the custody of the temporalities of his see passed into the royal hands, and it was the settled royal policy to keep churches vacant as long as possible. Only in a few favoured fiefs, like Normandy, Brittany, and Aquitaine, did the *regale* slip altogether into the hands of the local dukes. Moreover, the disputes and the weakness of the chapters gave the king the preponderating voice in elections. Even stronger was the royal position in relation to the monasteries. The greatest abbeys throughout France were 'royal abbeys,' over which the king possessed the same right as over bishoprics. Weaker than the bishops, the abbots looked up even more than the secular prelates to the royal support against the grasping and simoniacal lay-lords. The king favoured the Cluniac reformers, knowing that the more earnest the Churchmen, the more they would be opposed to feudal influence. Thus it was that every great Church fief was a centre of royal influence. Over the Church lands of central France—the provinces of Sens, Reims, Tours, and Bourges—the early Capetian was a real king. Even from the point of view of material resources, the king was in every whit as favourable a position as any one of his chief vassals. His own domains were large, rich, and centrally situated. Though lavish grants to the chief monasteries, and the need of paying for each step of their upward progress by conciliating the feudal magnates, had eaten away much of the old Robertian domain ; though the great Counts of Anjou and Blois had established themselves in virtual independence within the limits of the domain of Hugh the Great, Hugh Capet still held the country between the Seine and the Loire, including the county of Paris, Orléans and its district, Senlis, Etampes, and Melun, with scattered possessions in more distant places, Picardy, Champagne, Berri, Touraine, and Auvergne.   Paris was not as yet so important a place as it afterwards became, and it is an exaggeration to make it the centre of his power.   Hugh could only conciliate his chief adviser and supporter, Bouchard the Venerable, the greatest lord of the royal domain, and count already of Vendôme, Corbeil, and Melun, by granting him his own county of Paris. The title of 'royal count' of Paris suggested that Bouchard was a royal officer rather than a simple feudatory, and after Bouchard had retired into a monastery, the county of Paris was henceforth kept strictly in the king's hands. The second Capetian acquired with Montreuil-sur-Mer a seaport near the English Channel.   For a time the Capetians held the duchy of Burgundy.   Moreover, they were men of energy and vigour who made the best of their limited resources.   But their lot was a hard one.   Even in their own domains, between the Seine and Loire, the leading mesne lords, lay and secular, exercised such extensive jurisdiction that there was little room left for the authority of the suzerain.   Besides the task—as yet hopeless-- of reducing the great vassals of the crown to order, the Capetian kings had the preliminary task of establishing their authority within their own domains.   Even this smaller work was not accomplished for more than a century.   But, luckily for the kings, each one of the great feudatories was similarly occupied.   The barons of Normandy and Aquitaine gave more trouble to their respective dukes than the barons of the Isle of France gave to the lord of Paris. Power was in reality distributed among hundreds of feudal chieftains. It was so divided that no one was strong enough to really rule at all. France suffered all the miseries of feudal anarchy, when every petty lord of a castle ruled like a little king over his own domain. Yet it was something that her contests were now between Frenchmen and Frenchmen. Something was gained in the passing away of the barbarian invasions of the tenth century.

The details of the political history of the first four Capetian reigns are insignificant, and need not be told at length. Hugh Capet reigned from 987 to 996. He had little difficulty in obtaining general recognition, even from the lords of the distant south. But he had some trouble in upholding his claims against the Carolingian claimant, Charles, Duke of Lower Lorraine, who received the powerful support of the church of Reims, after Adalbero's death, and continued for some time to maintain himself in the old Carolingian fortress of Laon. Hugh continued with wise policy to maintain his hold over the church of Reims, and so to destroy the last possible stronghold of the Carolingians. He did not even scruple to sacrifice the trusty Gerbert to serve his dynastic ambitions. Within modest limits, the reign of the founder of the new dynasty was a successful one.

The first four Capetians. Hugh, 987-996.

In the very year of his accession, Hugh provided for the hereditary transmission of his power by associating his son Robert in the kingship. On Hugh's death Robert, already with nine years' experience as a crowned king, became sole monarch. He had been a pupil of Gerbert's, and was sufficiently learned to be able to compose hymns and argue on points of theology with bishops. His character was amiable, his charity abundant; he was of soft and ready speech, and amiable manners. He showed such fervent devotion that he was surnamed Robert the Pious, and contributed more than any other Capetian king to identify the Church and the dynasty. He was not the weak uxorious prince that his enemies describe him, but a

Robert II., the Pious, 996-1031.

mighty hunter, a vigorous warrior, and an active statesman. He made constant efforts, both to enlarge his domain and establish his authority over the great vassals. He kept up friendly relations with Normandy. He married Bertha, widow of Odo I., Count of Chartres, Tours, and Blois, his father's worst enemy, in the hope of regaining the three rich counties that had slipped away from the heritage of Hugh the Great. But Bertha was within the prohibited degrees; and the Pope insisting upon the unlawfulness of the union, Robert was excommunicated, and after a long struggle gave her up. But in 1019, the establishment of Odo II. of Blois, the son of Bertha by her former marriage, in the county of Troyes, did something to avenge the lady's memory. Robert's third marriage with Constance of Arles, the daughter of a Provençal lord, led to several royal visits to his wife's native regions which was a step towards establishing Capetian influence in the south. But the men of Robert's own territories disliked the hard, greedy queen, and the clergy in particular resented her introduction, into the court of Paris, of the refined but lax southern manners. Robert's most important exploit was the conquest of Burgundy. His uncle, Duke Henry, had died without an heir, and after a struggle of fourteen years' duration, Robert got possession of the great fief; but he soon granted it to his eldest surviving son Henry, whom, faithful to his father's policy, he had crowned king in 1027. He twice went on pilgrimage to Rome, and was offered the throne of Italy by the Lombard lords, who were opposed to Conrad the Salic; yet he found much difficulty in chastising any petty lord of the Orléanais or the Beauce, who chose to defy him.

During the declining years of Robert II., Queen Constance exercised an increasing influence. She wished to set aside the young king, Henry of Burgundy, the natural heir, in favour of his younger brother Robert. But the old king insisted on the rights of the first-born, and civil war broke out between the brothers, though before long

Henry I.,
1031-1060.

they united their arms against their father. When King Robert died, the contest was renewed ; but finally Henry secured the throne for himself, and pacified his younger brother by the grant of Burgundy, which thus went permanently back to a separate line ' of rulers. Henry I.'s inauspicious beginning lost some ground to the monarchy, which under him perhaps attained its lowest point of power. But Henry, if not very wise, was brave and active. Though his resources prevented any great expeditions, he strove by a series of petty fights and sieges to protect his frontiers against two of the strongest and most disloyal of his vassals—the Count of Blois, and the Duke of Normandy. In neither case was he successful. Odo II., after a long struggle, was able to establish his power on a firm basis, both in Champagne and Blois. But after Odo's death in 1037, Henry managed to absorb some of his fiefs in the royal domain, and scored a considerable triumph by transferring Touraine from the overpowerful house of Blois to Geoffrey Martel, Count of Anjou. The young duke, William of Normandy, who owed his throne to the support of Henry, which had secured the defeat of the rebel barons at Val-ès-Dunes, soon grew so powerful as to excite the apprehensions of his overlord. In an unlucky hour, Henry broke the tradition of friendship that had so long united Rouen and Paris. He twice invaded Normandy, but on both occasions the future conqueror of England proved more than a match for him. In 1054 Henry was defeated at Mortemer, and again, in 1058, at Varaville. Another difficulty in the way of the monarchy was the fact that Henry married late, and his health was already breaking up when the eldest son, borne to him by his wife Anne of Russia, was still a child. Nevertheless, in 1059, Henry procured the coronation of his seven-year-old son Philip at Reims, and the great gathering of magnates from all parts of France that attended the ceremony showed that the succession to the throne was still an event of national interest. Yet with all his weakness, Henry I. held firm to the ancient traditions of the

Frankish monarchy. When the reforming Pope Leo IX. held his synod of Reims to denounce simony, Henry was so jealous of the Pope that he prevented the French prelates from attending it. He watched with alarm the results of the absorption of Lorraine and the kingdom of Arles in the Empire, and boldly wrote to Henry III., claiming by hereditary right the palace at Aachen, possessed by his ancestors, and all the Lotharingian kingdom kept from its rightful owners by the tyranny of the German king. It is significant that the weakest of the early Capetians should thus pose against the strongest of the Emperors as the inheritor of the Carolingian tradition.

In 1060 Henry died, and the little Philip I. was acknowledged as his successor without a murmur. During his
Philip I., 1060-1108.
minority, Count Baldwin v. of Flanders held the regency, paying perhaps more regard to his interests as a great feudatory, than to his duty to his ward. It was possibly owing to this attitude that Baldwin allowed his son-in-law, William the Bastard, to fit out the famous expedition which led to the conquest of England, and thus gave one of the chief vassals of France a stronger position than his overlord. The year after the battle of Hastings Baldwin of Flanders died, and henceforward Philip ruled in his own name. As he grew up, he gained a bad reputation for greed, debauchery, idleness, and sloth. Before he attained old age he had become extraordinarily fat and unwieldy, while ill-health still further diminished his activity. Yet Philip was a shrewd man, of sharp and biting speech, and clear political vision. His quarrel with the Church was the result of his private vices rather than his public policy. As early as 1073 he was bitterly denounced by Gregory VII. as the most simoniac, adulterous, and sacrilegious of kings. But he gave most offence to the Church when, in 1092, he repudiated his wife, Bertha of Holland (with whom he had lived for more than twenty years), in favour of Bertrada of Montfort, the wife of Fulk Réchin, Count of Anjou, whom he married after a complaisant

bishop had declared her former union null. This bold step brought on Philip's head not only the arms of the injured Fulk, and of Bertha's kinsfolk, but a sentence of excommunication from Urban II. (1094). Though a way to reconciliation was soon opened up by the death of Bertha, the Pope nevertheless persisted in requiring Philip to repudiate his adulterous consort. Philip never gave up Bertrada, and never received the full absolution of the Church. Nevertheless, the war which he carried on against the Papacy did not cost him the allegiance of his subjects, though to it was added a long conflict with Gregory VII.'s ally, William the Conqueror. So weak was he that he dared not prevent the holding of councils on French soil at which he was excommunicated, and the great crusading movement proclaimed. But Philip was more active and more shrewd than his ecclesiastical enemies thought. He turned his attention with single-minded energy towards the increase of the royal domain, preferring the inglorious gain of a castle or a petty lordship to indulging in those vague and futile claims by which his three predecessors had sought in vain to hide their powerlessness. He took possession of the lapsed fief of Vermandois, and, not being strong enough to hold the district in his own hands, established there his brother Hugh the Great, the famous crusading hero and the father of a long line of Capetian counts of Vermandois, who were all through the next century among the surest supports of the Capetian throne. Philip also absorbed the Vexin and the Valois, thus securing important outworks to protect his city of Paris from Normandy and Champagne. By his politic purchase of Bourges, Philip for the first time established the royal power on a solid basis south of the Loire. But the weak point of Philip's acquisitions was that he had not force sufficient to hold them firmly against opposition. Hampered by the constant unfriendliness of the Church, broken in health and troubled in conscience, he ended his life miserably enough. Formally reconciled to the Pope before the end of his days, he died in the habit

of a monk, declaring that his sins made him unworthy to
be laid beside his ancestors and St. Denis, and humbly
consigning himself to the protection of St. Benedict.   When
the vault at Fleury closed over his remains, French history
began a new starting-point.   Philip I. was the last of the early
Capetians who were content to go on reigning without governing,
after the fashion of the later Carolingians.   It was reserved
for his successors to convert formal claims into actual possessions.   Nevertheless, the work of Philip set them on the right
track.   In his shrewd limitation of policy to matters of practical
moment, and his keen insight into the drift of affairs, the gross,
profligate, mocking Philip prepared the way for the truer
expansion of France under his son and grandson.   His reign
is the bridge between the period of the early Capetians and
the more fruitful and progressive period that begins with
Louis VI.

The history of the struggles of the Capetians and Carolingians, and of the first faint efforts of the former house to
realise some of the high pretensions of the old
The great fiefs under the early Capetians. Frankish monarchy, is only one side of the history
of France during the tenth and eleventh centuries.
Divided as was all the western world, there was
no part of it more utterly divided in feeling and interest than
the kingdom of the West Franks.   When the early Capetians
were carrying on their petty warfare in the regions between
Seine and Loire, or making their vain progresses and emphasising their barren claims over more distant regions, half a
score of feudal potentates as able, as wealthy, and as vigorous
as themselves were building up a series of local states with
foundations as strong, and patriotism as intense, as those of
the lords of Paris.   The tenth and eleventh centuries saw
the consolidation of the provincial nationalities of France, the
growing up of those strong local states which play so conspicuous a part in later mediæval French history, and which,
centuries after their absorption into the royal domain, continued to be centres of keen local feeling, and are not

crushed out of existence even by modern patriotism and the
levelling-up of the Revolution. Equally important with their
political influence was their influence on arts, language, and
literature. Into the details of this history it is impossible to
go; but without a general survey of the process, we should
lose the key to the subsequent history of France.

The first among the great fiefs of France to acquire a
distinct character of its own was Normandy, which since the
treaty of Clair-on-Epte in 911 had been handed Normandy.
over by Charles the Simple to Rolf the Ganger
and his Viking followers. The pirates gave up their wandering
life of plunder, became Christians, and tillers of the soil.
Rollo divided the lands of his duchy among his kinsfolk and
followers. In one or two generations, the descendants of the
pirate chieftains became the turbulent feudal aristocracy that
held even their fierce dukes in check, and found the little
duchy too small a field for their ambition and enterprise.
For a time they retained their Norse character. In some
districts, especially in the Bessin and the Côtentin, the great
mass of the population had become Scandinavian in tongue
and manners. Constant relations with Norwegian and
Danish kings kept alive the memory of their old home.
Harold Blue Tooth protected Duke Richard against
Louis IV. Swegen sought the help of the lord of Rouen
in avenging the massacre of St. Brice on the English. But
the ready wit and quick adaptability of the Scandinavian
races could not long withstand the French influences surrounding them. The constant friendly relations between the
Norman dukes and both the Carolingian and Capetian kings
precipitated the change. The dukes and barons of Normandy
became French in tongue and manners. But they became
French with a difference. The French of Caen and Rouen
were more restless, more enterprising, more ambitious, and
more daring than the French of Paris and Orleans. The contemporary chroniclers saw the importance of the distinction.
'O France,' says Dudo of Saint-Quentin, 'thou wert crushed

to the earth.   Behold, there comes to thee a new race from Denmark.   Peace is made between her and thee.   That race will raise thy name and thy power to the heavens.'   Nor was this prophecy a false one.   Despite its constant turbulence, Normandy became filled with a vigorous local life that soon flowed over its own borders.   What the Normans could not teach themselves, they learnt from wandering Italians or Burgundians.   The Normans stood in the forefront of all the great movements of the time.   They upheld the Capetians against the Carolingians.   They became the disciples of Cluny, and from the Norman abbey of Le Bec soon flowed a stream of culture and civilisation that bade fair to rival Cluny itself. They covered their land with great minsters, and wrote stirring *chansons de geste* in their Norman dialect of the French tongue.   Yet they kept themselves so free of their suzerain's influence, that not even through the Church could the Capetian kings exercise any authority in Normandy.   Throughout the whole province of Rouen, the Church depended either upon the local seigneur or upon the Norman duke.   They were the champions of the Hildebrandine Papacy.   They were foremost in the Crusades.   Their duke, William the Bastard, conquered England, and in the next generation his Norman followers swarmed over Scotland, Wales, and Ireland.   Private Norman adventurers attempted to found a kingdom in Spain, and set up a monarchy in southern Italy strong enough to wrest Sicily from Islam [see pages 104-118].   Throughout the length and breadth of Europe, Norman warriors, priests, and poets made the French name famous.   With the activity of the Normans first begins the preponderance of French ideas, customs, and language throughout the western world.

The old Celtic tribal state of Brittany had been almost overwhelmed by the Norman invasions, and had lost all its former prosperity.   The most sacred shrines of **Brittany.** the vast crowd of the Breton saints were pillaged and destroyed.   At the best, the holy relics were transferred to Paris, to Orleans, or some other safe spot, far away from the marauding pagan. When Rolf got from Charles the Simple the duchy of Normandy, it is said that he asked for fresh land to plunder, while his followers learnt the arts of peace in their new home. In some vague way Charles granted him rights of suzerainty over Brittany. The Normans harried the land for another generation, and, as later in Wales and Ireland, many Norman chieftains settled down in the more fertile eastern districts of Upper Brittany. But a Celtic reaction followed. Led by Alan of the Twisted Beard (*barbe torte*), the native Bretons rose against their oppressors and made common cause with the Gallo-Roman peasantry against them. Alan became the founder of the county (afterwards duchy) of Brittany, a state half French and half Celtic, including besides 'la Bretagne bretonnante' of the western peninsula of Lower Brittany, the French-speaking lands of the Lower Loire and the Vilaine, with the purely French town of Rennes for its capital, and the equally French Nantes for its chief seaport. But despite the differences of tongue and custom, there was an essential unity of feeling in the new duchy, based on the disappearance both of the Celtic tribal system and the Gallo-Roman provincial system in favour of a feudalism that was common to Celt and Frenchman alike. Brittany, despite its composite origin, retained and still retains a marked type of local nationality, less active and energetic than the Norman, but more dogged, persevering, and enduring. When Alan Barbe-torte died in 952, Brittany had become an organised feudal state.

The county of Flanders grew up in the flat country between the Scheldt and the sea. Like Brittany, it had suffered terribly from Norman invasions. Like Brittany, it was not homogeneous in language and custom. In all the northern and eastern districts the Low Dutch tongue prevailed, but in the south-east, round Lille and Douai, French was spoken. Baldwin of the Iron Arm, a Carolingian official who became the son-in-law of Charles the Bald, distinguished himself by leading the Flemings to

Flanders.

victory against the Normans, and obtained from his father-in-law an hereditary supremacy over the whole district bounded by the Scheldt, the North Sea, and the Canche, and therefore including the modern Artois with the homage of great barons like the counts of Boulogne and Saint-Pol. Four other Counts Baldwin continued their ancestor's exploits. Of these the most famous was Baldwin v., the uncle and guardian of Philip i., and the father-in-law of William the Conqueror. It was under Baldwin v. that the Flemish towns, whose strong walls had served to shelter previous generations from the Viking marauders, first enter upon their long career of political liberty and industrial prosperity. When Baldwin v. died in 1067, the year after his son-in-law's establishment in England, mediæval Flanders had well begun its glorious but tumultuous and blood-stained career. To the south of

Vermandois. Flanders lay the Vermandois, round its chief town of Saint Quentin, and including the northern parts of the restricted 'Francia' of the tenth century. We have seen the importance of its counts in the days of the struggle of Carolingians and Capetians, and the establishment of a Capetian line of counts of Vermandois in the person of Hugh the Great, the brother of Philip i.

Champagne became the chief fief of north-eastern France. A special feature in this district was the power of the bishops, Champagne and in consequence the influence of the crown.
and Blois. The metropolitans of Reims played a great local as well as a great national part. The bishops of Châlons became counts of their cathedral city; the bishops of Troyes, the local capital, only just failed in attaining the same end. 'Everywhere,' we are told, 'the mighty oppressed the feeble, and men, like fishes, swallowed each other up.' In the course of the tenth century a strong lay power arose in this district under the counts of Troyes. During the tenth century the country was held by a branch of the house of Vermandois. In 1019 it passed, as we have seen, to the house of Blois. However, the power of the family was soon

endangered by the separation of Champagne and Blois under the two elder sons of Odo II., after his death in 1037.

The county of Blois, itself the original seat of the Capetians but carved out of their dwindling domain in favour of a hostile house, had already been united with that of Chartres. The establishment of the same house in Troyes created a state which pressed upon Paris both from the west, south, and east, and was frequently hostile to it. Before long, this powerful line began to absorb the lesser feudatories of the eastern marchland, and to make its influence felt even over the great ecclesiastical dignitaries. After the county of Vitry was transferred from the obedience of the Archbishop of Reims to the authority of the counts of Troyes, the lords of the amalgamated fiefs assumed the wider title of counts of Champagne, and became one of the greatest powers in France. Against these gains the loss of Touraine was but a small one. Odo's grandson, Stephen, Count of Blois and Chartres (1089-1102), was one of the heroes of the First Crusade, and the father, by his wife Adela, daughter of William the Conqueror, of a numerous family in whose time the house of Blois attained its highest prosperity. His second son, Theobald (II. of Champagne and IV. of Blois, called Theobald the Great, died 1152) reigned over both Blois and Champagne. His third son, Stephen, acquired not only the counties of Mortain and Boulogne but the throne of England. His fourth son, Henry, was the famous Bishop of Winchester. Though Blois and Champagne again separated under different lines of the house of Blois after Theobald's death, their policy remained united, and their influence was still formidable.

Like Blois, Anjou grew up out of the original domains of Robert the Strong. Fulk the Red, who died in 941, and was rewarded with Anjou for his prowess in Anjou. resisting the Normans, was the first hereditary Count of Anjou of whom history has any knowledge, though legends tell of earlier mythical heroes and a witch ancestress, whose taint twisted into evil the strong passions and high courage of the later representatives of the race. Though their exploits are told in a somewhat romantic form, there remains enough to enable us to form more individual impressions of the fierce, wayward Angevin lords than of most of the shadowy heroes of early feudalism. With Geoffrey Martel, great-grandson of Fulk the Red, who died in 1060, the first line of the Counts of Anjou became extinct; but his sister's son Geoffrey the Bearded got possession of the county, and became the ancestor of the famous line that later ages than their own celebrated as the house of Plantagenet. His descendants grew in dominions and influence. Touraine they had possessed since Henry I. had transferred that county from the house of Blois to Geoffrey Martel. They now turned their eyes on Maine, the border district that separated them from the Normans. This brought about a long struggle between the Norman dukes and the Angevin counts, which was not finally ended until Henry I. of Normandy and England married his daughter, the widowed Empress Matilda, to Geoffrey the Fair, from which marriage sprang the greatest of the Angevins, Henry II. of England, Normandy and Anjou.

The duchy of Burgundy was the last remaining great fief of the Capetians in northern and central France. While various kingdoms, duchies, and counties of Burgundy grew up, as we have seen, in the imperial lands beyond the Saône and the Rhone, one Richard the Justiciar, famous like all the founders of fiefs as a successful foe of the Nor man marauders, became, in 877, the first duke or marquis of that Burgundy which became a French vassal state. His brother was Boso, founder of the kingdom of Provence, his brother-in-law was Rudolf, king of Transjurane Burgundy, and his son was Rudolf, king of the French. His sons succeeded him in his rule, though for more than a century each successive duke received a fresh formal appointment; and it was not until a junior branch of the Capetian house began with Robert the Old (1032-1073), the younger brother of

Burgundy.

King Henry I., that the hereditary duchy of Burgundy can be said to have been definitively established.

South of the Loire the development of feudal states took even a more decided form than in the north. In these regions feudal separation had the freest field to run riot. There was still a nominal duke of Aquitaine, who Aquitaine. might be regarded as having some sort of vague authority over the old Aquitania that was substantially synonymous with south-western France; but neither in Gascony, nor Auvergne, nor in La Marche, nor in the Limousin was any recognition paid to this shadowy potentate. The duchy of Aquitaine seemed on the verge of sharing the fate of the kingdom of France and disappearing altogether because it stood outside the newly grown feudal system, when, like the kingdom of France, it procured a new lease of life by being granted to a house that, like the Robertians of Paris, possessed with great fiefs a firm position in the new system. In 928 Ebles, Count of Poitou, received a grant Poitou. of the duchy of Aquitaine, and in 951 William Tow-head, his son by a daughter of Edward the Elder of Wessex, was confirmed in his father's possession by Louis d'Outremer. The county that took its name from Poitiers was a substantial inheritance. It was the marchland that divided north and south, but its main characteristics were those of the north. Its uplands seldom permit the cultivation of the vine, and its manners, like its climate and tongue, were northern. As the dialects of Romance became differentiated, Poitou spoke, as it still speaks, a dialect of the north French tongue, the *langue d'oïl.* Aquitaine proper spoke the southern *langue d'oc,* and differed in a thousand ways from the colder, fiercer, ruder, more martial lands of the north. But the infusion of fresh blood from Poitou saved the Aquitaine duchy from extinction. Eight dukes of Aquitaine and counts of Poitou reigned in succession to William Tow-head, seven of whom were named William. Under this line county after county was gradually added to the original fief of Poitou. At last all the

Limousin, Auvergne, and parts of Berri owned them as at least nominal lords. Gascony, in the lands beyond the Garonne, had since 872 been ruled by a hereditary line of **Gascony.** dukes, whose favourite name was Sancho. On the extinction of this family, Gascony, with its dependencies, passed in 1062 to William VIII. of Poitiers, whose grandson William X., the last of the male stock of the house of the Guilhems, died in 1137, leaving the nominal over-lordship over the swarm of seigneurs that ruled the district between the Loire, the Pyrenees, and the Cevennes to his daughter Eleanor, whose vast inheritance made Louis VII. of France and Henry II. of England in succession successful suitors for her hand. Under the fostering care of the Williams, Aquitaine had prospered in civilisation and the arts; and their court at Poitiers, whose magnificent series of Romanesque basilicas still attests the splendour of their capital, became the centre of the earliest literary efforts of the troubadours, the poets and minstrels of the *langue d'oc*, though the southern tongue of the court was not the Poitevins' native speech.

To the east of Aquitaine the county of Toulouse became the nucleus of a sort of monarchical centralisation that, by the **Toulouse.** beginning of the twelfth century, had brought the French lands beyond the Aquitanian border, the imperial lands between the Alps and the Rhone, and the old Spanish march between the Pyrenees and the Ebro, to look to Toulouse as the source of its intellectual and almost of its political life. The lands dependent on the counts of Toulouse became emphatically the Languedoc, the region where the Romance vernacular of southern Gaul was spoken with the greatest purity and force. While the subjects of the dukes of Aquitaine had the purity of their Gascon contaminated by the Basque of the Pyrenean valleys, and the northern idiom of the lands beyond the Gironde and Dordogne, the followers of the counts of Toulouse spoke the same tongue as the Burgundian vassals of the count of Provence. or the fierce marchers ruled by the counts of Barcelona. The tongue of Oc has as much claim to be regarded as a language distinct from northern French, as northern French has to be considered separate from Italian or Spanish. It was the first Romance tongue that boasted of a strong vernacular literature, and those who spoke it were the first Romance people to attain either the luxuries or corruptions of an advanced civilisation. Its spread over southern Gaul drew a deep dividing line between northern and southern France that has not yet been blotted out. It gave the subjects of the southern feudalists, like the counts of Toulouse and the dukes of Aquitaine, a solidarity that made them almost separate nations, like the Flemings or the Bretons. Its vast expansion between the Alps and the Ebro bade fair to overleap the boundaries set by the Treaty of Verdun, and set up in those regions a well-defined nationality strong and compact enough to be a make-weight against the growing concentration of the northern French under the Capetian kings. But the civilisation of Languedoc flowered too early to produce mature fruit. We shall see how in the thirteenth century it succumbed to the ruder spirit of the north. Raymond I., the first hereditary count of Toulouse, died in 864. His successors, with whom Raymond was ever the favourite name, continued to grow in power until they had united all Languedoc early in the twelfth century. Their hereditary hostility to the dukes of Aquitaine, no less than the centrifugal tendencies of southern feudalism, which they could at best but partially counteract, prevented their authority from attaining wider limits.

Such was the France of the tenth and eleventh centuries—divided, chaotic, anarchic, and turbulent, yet full of vigorous life and many-sided activity. Its growth was slower, its exploits less dazzling than those of contemporary Germany, though perhaps it was developing on more solid and permanent lines. Even when Germany was still the chief political centre of the west, the fame of the French warrior had extended over all Europe. The alliance with the Church did much, the prevalence of the Cluniac idea did more to bring this about. The wanderings of the Normans first spread abroad the terror of the Frankish name. The Crusades became an essentially Frankish movement, and made the Frankish knight the type of the feudal warrior. But the concentration of France into a great state followed very slowly on the growth of the reputation of the individual Frenchman.

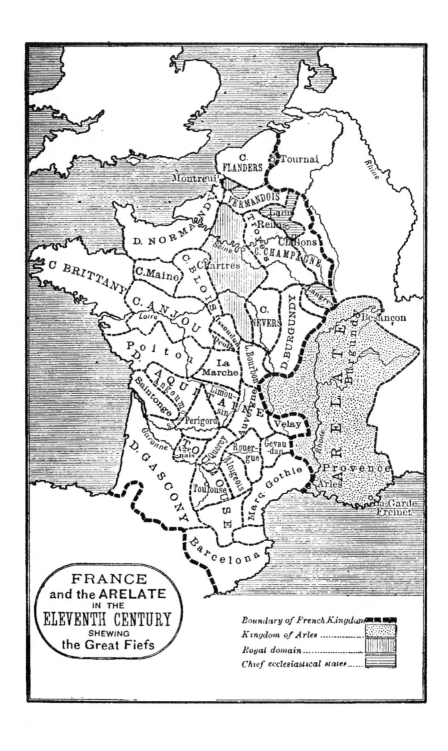

FRANCE
and the ARELATE
IN THE
ELEVENTH CENTURY
SHEWING
the Great Fiefs

Boundary of French Kingdom ......
Kingdom of Arles ....
Royal domain ....
Chief ecclesiastical states ......

GENEALOGY

WILLIAM OF BLOIS.

ROBERT THE STRONG, Duke of the French.

ODO,
King of the West Franks
(888-899).

ROBERT,
King of the West Franks
(922-923).

HUGH THE GREAT, Duke of the French (d. 956),
m. Hedwig, daughter of Henry the Fowler.

HUGH CAPET (987-996), m. Adela.

ROBERT II. (The Pious—996-1031),
m. (1) Rosala.
   (2) Bertha, daughter of Conrad, King of Arles,
       and widow of Odo I. of Blois.
   (3) Constance of Arles.

HENRY I. (1031-1060),
m. Ann   daughter of Jaroslav, Duke of Russia.

PHILIP I. (1060-1108),
m. (1) Bertha, daughter of Florence,
       Count of Holland.
   (2) Bertrada of Montfort, divorced wife of
       Fulk le Réchin, Count of Anjou.

ROBERT, Duke of Burgundy,
Ancestor of the Capetian Dukes of Burgundy.

HUGH THE GREAT,
Count of Vermandois.

RALPH, Count
of Vermandois.

ISABELLA of Vermandois,
m. Philip of Alsace, Count of Flanders.

PHILIP.

FLEURY.

LOUIS VI. (The Fat—1108-1137),
m. Adelaide, daughter of Humbert I
   Count of Maurienne.

LOUIS VII. (The Young—1137-1180),
m. (1) Eleanor of Aquitaine.
   (2) Constance of Castile.
   (3) Adela of Champagne.

HENRY,
Archbishop of Reims.

ROBERT
of Dreux.

PETER
of Courtenay.

CONSTANCE,
m. (1) Eustace, Count of Boulogne.
   (2) Raymond v. of Toulouse.

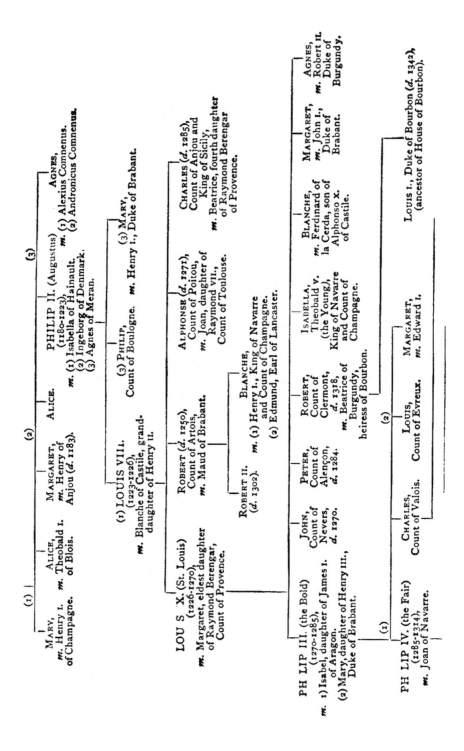

(1)

MARY,
m. Henry I.
of Champagne.

ALICE,
m. Theobald I.
of Blois.

(2)

MARGARET,
m. Henry of
Anjou (d. 1183).

ALICE.

(3)

PHILIP II. (Augustus)
(1180-1223),
m. (1) Isabella of Hainault.
(2) Ingeborg of Denmark.
(3) Agnes of Meran.

AGNES,
m. (1) Alexius Comnenus.
(2) Andronicus Comnenus.

(1) LOUIS VIII.
(1223-1226),
m. Blanche of Castile, grand-
daughter of Henry II.

(3) PHILIP,
Count of Boulogne.

(3) MARY,
m. Henry I., Duke of Brabant.

LOUIS IX. (St. Louis)
(1226-1270),
m. Margaret, eldest daughter
of Raymond Berengar,
Count of Provence.

ROBERT (d. 1250),
Count of Artois,
m. Maud of Brabant.

ALPHONSE (d. 1271),
Count of Poitou,
m. Joan, daughter of
Raymond VII.,
Count of Toulouse.

CHARLES (d. 1285),
Count of Anjou and
King of Sicily,
m. Beatrice, fourth daughter
of Raymond Berengar
of Provence.

ROBERT II.
(d. 1302).

BLANCHE,
m. (1) Henry I., King of Navarre
and Count of Champagne.
(2) Edmund, Earl of Lancaster.

PHILIP III. (the Bold)
(1270-1285),
m. 1) Isabel, daughter of James I.
of Aragon.
(2) Mary, daughter of Henry III.,
Duke of Brabant.

JOHN,
Count of
Nevers,
d. 1270.

PETER,
Count of
Alençon,
d. 1284.

ROBERT,
Count of
Clermont,
d. 1318,
m. Beatrice of
Burgundy,
heiress of Bourbon.

ISABELLA,
Theobald v.
(the Young),
King of Navarre
and Count of
Champagne.

BLANCHE,
m. Ferdinand of
la Cerda, son of
Alphonso x.
of Castile.

MARGARET,
m. John I.,
Duke of
Brabant.

AGNES,
m. Robert II.
Duke of
Burgundy.

(1)

PHILIP IV. (the Fair)
(1285-1314),
m. Joan of Navarre.

CHARLES,
Count of Valois.

(2)

LOUIS,
Count of Evreux.

MARGARET,
m. Edward I.

LOUIS I., Duke of Bourbon (d. 1342),
(ancestor of House of Bourbon).

CHAPTER V

THE CLUNIAC REFORMATION (910-1073)
AND ITALY IN THE ELEVENTH CENTURY [1]

End of the Dark Ages—Beginnings of the Cluniac Reformation—The Con-
gregation of Cluny — Cluniac ideals — Camaldoli and Vallombrosa —
Henry III. joins the Reformers—The German reforming Popes—Leo IX.—
South Italy and Sicily in the Eleventh Century—The first coming of the
Normans—Aversa—The sons of Tancred and the Conquest of Apulia—
Robert Guiscard—Leo IX. and the Normans—Battle of Civitate—Early
Career of Hildebrand—Nicholas II.—The Reform of Papal Elections—
The Normans become Papal Vassals—Milan submits to Rome—Roger's
Conquest of Sicily—Feudalism in Southern Italy.

THE Dark Ages were well over by the middle of the eleventh
century, and after a century of anarchy, even feudalism had
End of the become a comparatively tolerable form of govern-
Dark Ages. ment. The stronger military states had absorbed
their weaker neighbours, and, beyond the Alps at least, the
disintegrating tendency of feudal doctrine had received a
decided check, not only in the strong monarchy of the
Germans, but even in the growth of vigorous feudal potentates such as the margraves of the eastern frontier of the
Empire, the dukes of the Normans, and the counts of
Flanders or of Toulouse. There were again forces making

[1] Moeller's *Church History* (translated from the German), gives a bald
but full and learned summary of the ecclesiastical history of the whole
period. Gieseler's *Church History* (also translated), is valuable for its
numerous citations of original texts. Besides Gibbon's famous fifty-sixth
chapter on the Normans in Italy, Delarc's *Les Normands en Italie*
(*1016-1073*) gives an elaborate and careful account of the Norman history
in Italy up to the accession of Gregory VII.

towards order, law, and peace. The state had been saved from absolute annihilation.

The Church was not yet in so sound a position. She had outlived the worst brutalities of the tenth century, but the fierce, lawless, grasping baron, who feared neither God nor man, was still an element to be reckoned with. The revived lay-power tended of itself to correct the worst abuses. The Empire had, as we have seen, reformed the Papacy. But if the Church was to live, it could not owe its life to the patronage or goodwill of outside reformers. The Church must reform itself.

Signs of such a purification of the Church from within had long been manifest, but the little band of innovators found it no easy task to preach to a world that knew no law but the law of the stronger. As ever in the Middle Ages, a new monastic movement heralded in the work of reformation. As the Carolingian reformation is associated with Benedict of Aniane, so is the reformation of the eleventh century associated with the monks of Cluny.

In 910 Duke William the Pious of Aquitaine founded a new monastery at Cluny, in French Burgundy, a few miles from the bishop's town of Macon. He appointed The early Berno, a noble Burgundian, as its head, and pro- history of cured for it absolute immunity from all external Cluny. ecclesiastical jurisdiction save that of the Roman See. Berno strove to establish a complete and loyal observance of the rule of St. Benedict, and the piety and earnestness of his monks soon attracted attention, wealth, followers. Corrupt old communities or new foundations sought the guidance or the protection of the abbots of Cluny. But the Benedictine system was limited to a single house, and afforded no room for the crowd of disciples who wished to attach themselves to the model monastery. Odo, the second abbot (927-941), started the memorable monastic reformation which, in a few years, was embodied in the 'Consuetudines Cluniacenses,' and the 'Congregation of Cluny.' By it a plan was found for combining formal adherence to the strict rule of St. Benedict with the practical necessity of maintaining the rule of Cluny over its dependent communities. If under the old system a new house were formed under the direction of a famous monastery, the new establishment, when it had received its constitution, parted company from its parent stock, and, like a Greek colony, became independent and self-governing. The Cluniacs prevented this by regarding the daughter communities as parts of themselves. In whatsoever part of Christendom a monastery on Cluniac lines

The Congregation of Cluny.

was established, it was still in law a part of the great Burgundian convent. Its head was the arch-abbot, the abbot of Cluny. What local self-government was necessary was delegated to a prior, who was appointed by the abbot of Cluny, to whom he was responsible. From time to time the dependent communities sent representatives to the periodical chapters that met at Cluny, under the presidency of the abbot. By this means a unity of organisation, a military discipline, a control over weak brethren, and a security was procured, which was impossible under the Benedictine rule. When each monastery was as independent for all practical purposes as a modern Congregational chapel, it was impossible, in an age when public opinion hardly existed, to reform a lax community, and it was difficult for an isolated flock of unwarlike men to protect themselves from feudal violence or the equally fierce hostility of the secular clergy. Besides unity of organisation, the control exercised over the whole order of Cluny gave the brethren unity of purpose, doctrine, and policy.

Brought under the immediate jurisdiction of Rome, at a time when monastic immunities from episcopal authority had not become common, the Cluniacs taught from the beginning a high doctrine as to the power of the apostolic see. They saw that the great danger to religion was in the feudalisation of the Church. Bishops were in danger of becoming barons in mitres. Kings looked upon

prelates as officials bound to do them service, and patrons sold benefices to the highest bidder. Monasteries were often in danger of absolute secularisation. So corrupt and lax were even the better sort of regulars that the Saxon monk Widukind, the historian of his people, naïvely complains of the 'grave persecution' which beset the poor religious of his time, and laments the erroneous doctrines of some bishops who maintained that it was better that there should be a few ascetic regulars than houses filled with negligent monks, forgetting, as he innocently adds, that the tares and the wheat were ordered to grow up together until the harvest time. The chief dangers of the Church were simony and the marriage of clerks. To keep the Church apart from the world seemed to the Cluniac leaders the only possible way of securing a better state of things. Their ideal was the separation of the Church from the State, and the reorganisation of the Church under discipline such as could only be exercised by the Pope, who was to stand to the whole Church as the abbot of Cluny stood to each scattered Cluniac priory—the one ultimate source of jurisdiction, the universal bishop, appointing and degrading the diocesan bishops as the abbot made and unmade the Cluniac priors. The bishop, the secular priest, even the monk, had no rights of his own that were not ultimately derivative from the unique source of ecclesiastical authority, the chair of St. Peter. The Forged Decretals supplied convenient arguments for such a system. *Hierarchical and Papal ideals of Cluny.*
The necessities of the times supplied a sort of justification for it. Feudal anarchy made it natural for good men to identify the secular power with the works of darkness, and regard the ecclesiastical power as alone emanating from God. After-ages were to show that the remedy was almost as bad as the disease, and that there was as much danger of secular motives, greed for domination, for wealth and influence in the uncontrolled exercise of ecclesiastical authority, as in the lay power that they dreaded. But the

early Cluniacs had faith in their principles, and sought in realising them to promote the kingdom of God on earth. They lived holy and self-denying lives in an age of brutal violence and lust. A moral and an intellectual reformation preceded and prepared the way for the ecclesiastical reformation that was preached from Cluny with the fervour of a new gospel.

Under the influence of the reformed clergy, study and learning again became possible to a large class. The monastic and cathedral schools beyond the Alps became the centres of ardent study of philosophy, theology, and science. In Italy grammarians expounded the classics, and civilians commented upon the Roman law. The career of Gerbert is but typical of that of a large number of others. The Lombard Lanfranc, and the Burgundian Anselm, took the new culture over the Alps to the Norman monastery of Le Bec, and prepared the way for the new birth of learning in the twelfth century. Nor did the monastic reformation stop with **New orders** the Congregation of Cluny. In Italy in particular, **In Italy.** where a swarm of new orders arose, extreme asceticism and utter self-renunciation stood in strange contrast to the violence, greed, and profligacy that marked Italian life as a whole. Romuald of Ravenna, the spiritual director of Otto III., lived the life of a hermit, and gathered round himself great bands of solitaries from whom sprang the **Camaldoli.** order of Camaldoli, so called from an inaccessible spot in the Apennines, near Arezzo, where one of Romuald's troops of followers had settled. A monk of this order, Peter Damiani, soon took a very foremost part in the religious reformation of Italy, and first made the enthusiastic anchorites minister to the spread of the new hierarchical ideal. Not far from the hermits of Camaldoli, John Gualbert, a Tuscan **Vallombrosa.** lord, established the strict cœnobitic order of Vallombrosa. The same influence spread all over Europe, and penetrated into even the most conservative cloisters of the followers of St. Benedict. The faith, zeal, and enthusiasm of the champions of the new order carried every-thing before it. Under Henry III. the reformers had won over the Emperor himself to their cause. The strong arm of the king had purified the Papacy and handed over its direction to men of the new school. But though willing to use the help of the secular arm to carry out their forward policy, the Cluniac reformers never swerved from their conviction that lay interference with the spiritual power lay at the very root of the worst disorders of the time. Even when accepting the favours of the great Emperor, they never lost sight of the need of emphasising the independence of the spirituality. However needful was the imperial sword to free the Papacy from the Tusculan tradition, and to put down the lazy monk and the feudalist bishop, they saw clearly that it stood in the way of the full realisation of their dreams.

Henry III. won over by the reforming party.

After the synod of Sutri, a whole series of German Popes was nominated by the Emperor, and received by the Church with hardly a murmur, though the young deacon Hildebrand, soon to become the soul of the new movement, attached himself to the deposed Gregory VI. and accompanied him on his exile. But to most of the reformers the rude justice of Sutri seemed a just if irregular solution of an intolerable situation. The puritan zeal of the German Popes seemed the best result of the alliance of the Emperor and the reforming party. The first two reigned too short a time to be able to effect much, leaving it to Leo IX., the third German Pope, to permanently identify the papal throne with the spirit of Cluny.

The German reforming Popes.

On the death of Damasus, the Romans called upon Henry III., who was then at Worms, to give them another Pope The Emperor chose for this post his cousin Bruno, the brother of Conrad of Carinthia, the sometime rival of Conrad the Salic, and the son of the elder Conrad, uncle of the first of the Salian emperors. Despite his high birth, Bruno had long turned from politics to the

Leo IX., 1048-1054.

service of the Church, and had become the ardent disciple
of the school of Cluny.   As bishop of Toul, he had governed
his diocese with admirable care and prudence, and his great
influence had enabled him to confer many weighty services,
both on Henry and his father in Lorraine.   When offered the
Papacy by his kinsman, Bruno accepted the post only on the
condition that he should be canonically elected by the clergy
and people of Rome.   Early in 1049 he travelled over the
Alps in the humble guise of a pilgrim.   He visited Cluny on
his way to receive spiritual encouragement from his old
teachers for the great task that lay before him.   He there
added to his scanty following the young monk Hildebrand,
whose return to the city in the new Pope's train proclaimed
that strict hierarchical ideas would now have the ascendency
at the Curia.   Joyfully accepted by the Romans, Bruno
assumed the title of Leo IX.   For the short five years of
his pontificate, he threw himself with all his heart into a
policy of reformation.   In an Easter Synod in Rome (1049),
stern decrees were fulminated against simony and clerical
marriage.   But the times were not yet ripe for radical cure,
and Leo was compelled to depart somewhat from his original
severity.   He soon saw that the cause he had at heart would
not be best furthered by his remaining at Rome, and the special
characteristic of his pontificate was his constant journeying
through all Italy, France, and Germany.   During these
travels Leo was indefatigable in holding synods, attending
ecclesiastical ceremonies, the consecration of churches, the
translation of the relics of martyrs.   His ubiquitous energy
made the chief countries in Europe realise that the Papacy
was no mere abstraction, and largely furthered the centralisation of the whole Church system under the direction of the
Pope.   Wherever he went, decrees against simony and the
marriage of priests were drawn up.   In Germany, Henry III.
gave him active support.   In France he excited the jealousy
of King Henry I.   Invited to Reims by the archbishop for
the consecration of a church, he summoned a French

synod to that city. Alarmed at this exercise of jurisdiction within French dominions, Henry I. strove to prevent his bishops' attendance by summoning them to follow him to the field. Only a few bishops ventured to disobey their king, but a swarm of abbots, penetrated by the ideals of Cluny, gave number and dignity to the Synod of Reims, and did not hesitate to join the Pope in excommunicating the absent bishops. The restless Leo sought to revive the feeble remnants of North African Christianity, and began the renewed troubles with the Eastern Church, which soon led to the final breach with the Patriarch Cærularius [see page 167]. The all-embracing activity of Leo led to his active interference in southern Italy, where the advent of a swarm of Norman adventurers had already changed the whole complexion of affairs.

Early in the eleventh century, southern Italy and Sicily were still cut off from the rest of Europe, and, as in the days of Charlemagne, were still outposts both of the Orthodox and Mohammedan East. Sicily had been entirely Saracen since the capture of Syracuse in 877 [see Period I. pp. 460-461]. Though the predatory hordes, which landed from time to time on the mainland of Italy, had failed to establish permanent settlements, the various attempts of the Eastern Emperors to win back their former island possession had proved disastrous failures. In southern Italy the Catapan or governor of the Greek Emperors still ruled over the 'theme of Lombardy' from his capital of Bari, but in the tenth century, the Lombard Dukes of Benevento, Salerno, and Capua won back much of the ground that had been lost by their ancestors. The transient successes of Otto II. (981-2), had done something to discourage Greeks and Saracens alike, despite the ignominious failure that ultimately led to his flight [see pages 38-39]. In the early years of the eleventh century, southern Italy was still divided between Greeks and Lombards, and the growing spirit of Catholic enthusiasm made the Orthodox yoke harder to bear by those subjects of the theme of Lombardy, who were Italian rather than Greek in their sympathy. Between 1011 and 1013 Meles, a citizen of Bari, a Catholic of Lombard origin, took advantage of a Saracen inroad to revolt against the Eastern Emperor. Driven into exile by the failure of his attempt, he sought all over southern Italy

for allies to recommence the struggle. The fame of the Normans as soldiers was already known in the south of Italy, and chance now threw Meles in the way of some Norman warrior-pilgrims, whom devotion to the Archangel had taken to the sanctuary of St. Michael, in Monte Gargano, in imitation of which a Neustrian bishop had some generations before set up the famous monastery of St. Michael in Peril of the Sea.

The first coming of the Normans, 1017.

Meles proposed to the pilgrim leader, Ralph de Toeny, that he should join with him against the Greeks. Pope Benedict VIII. encouraged the enterprise, and the adventurous Normans greedily welcomed the opportunity. In 1017, Meles and his northern allies won a victory over the Greeks at Civitate in the Capitanata. 'This victory,' sang the Norman rhyming chronicler, William of Apulia, 'mightily increased the courage of the Normans. They saw that the Greeks were cowards, and that, instead of meeting the enemy face to face, they only knew how to take refuge in flight.' Other Normans flocked from their distant home on the report of rich booty and fair lands to be won on easy terms in Apulia. Meles and Ralph of Toeny. But they despised their enemy too much, and in 1019 a battle fought on the historic field of Cannæ annihilated the little Norman band. Meles and Ralph hastened over the Alps, in the hopes of interesting Henry II. in their cause. Even the death of Meles was not fatal to the fortune of his allies. Some survivors from Cannæ took service with the princes of Capua and Salerno, and the abbot of Monte Casino. They were mere mercenaries, and willingly sold their swords to the highest bidder. When Henry II. made his transient appearance in southern Italy in 1022 [see page 50], he found his chief obstacle in the new Greek fortress of Troja, obstinately defended by some valiant Normans in the pay of their old foe the Catapan.

Other Normans now flocked to the land of promise. Among these was a chieftain named Ranulf, who joined Sergius, Prince of Naples, a vassal of the Greeks, in his war against the Lombard prince Pandulf of Capua. In reward for his services Ranulf received one of the richest districts of the Terra di Lavoro, where he built in 1030 a town named Aversa, the first Norman settlement in Italy. This foundation makes a new departure in Norman policy. The Normans no longer came to Foundation of Aversa, 1030. Italy as isolated adventurers willing to sell their swords to the highest bidder. By much the same arts as those by which their brethren later got hold of the fairest parts of Wales and Ireland, the adventurers strove to carve feudal states for themselves out of the chaos of southern Italy. Whilst cleverly utilising the feuds that raged around them, they pursued their interests with such dexterity, courage, and clear-headed selfishness, that brilliant success soon crowned their efforts. Conrad II. sojourned at Capua in 1038, deposed Pandulf and confirmed Ranulf in the possession of Aversa, which he erected into a county owing homage to the Western Emperor. Three of the twelve sons of the Norman lord, Tancred of Hauteville, now left their scanty patrimony in the Côtentin and joined the Normans in Italy. Their names

The sons of were William of the Iron Arm, Drogo, and Hum-
Tancred of phrey. In 1038 they joined the Greeks under
Hauteville. George Maniaces in an attempt to expel the Mohammedans from Sicily. Messina and Syracuse were captured, but an affront to their companion-in-arms Ardouin drove the Normans back to the mainland in the moment of victory, and led them to wreak their vengeance on the Greeks by a strange compound of violence and treachery. Ardouin their friend took the Greek pay and became governor of Melfi, the key of Apulia. He proposed to the Normans that he should deliver Melfi to them, and make that a starting-point for the conquest of Apulia, which he proposed to divide between them and himself. The northerners accepted

Conquest of his proposals. In 1041 Melfi was delivered into
Apulia, 1041-2. their hands, and a long war broke out between them and their former allies. By shrewdly putting Adenulfus, the Lombard Duke of Benevento at the head of their armies, the Normans got allies that were probably necessary in the early years of the struggle. But they were soon strong enough to repudiate their associate. The divisions of the Greeks further facilitated their task. In 1042 William of the Iron Arm was proclaimed lord of the Normans of Apulia, with Melfi as the centre of his power.

In 1046 William of Apulia died, and Drogo, his brother, succeeded him. Henry III., then in Italy, recognised Drogo as Count of Apulia, while renewing the grant of Aversa to another Ranulf. He also urged the Normans to drive out of Benevento the Lombards, who after the spread of the Norman power were making common cause with the Greeks. About this time a fourth son of Tancred of Haute- Robert ville came to Italy, where he soon made himself the Guiscard. hero of the Norman conquerors. Anna Comnena, the literary daughter of the Emperor Alexius, describes Robert Guiscard as he appeared to his enemies. 'His high stature excelled that of the most mighty warriors. His complexion was ruddy, his hair fair, his shoulders broad, his eyes flashed fire. It is said that his voice was like the voice of a whole multitude, and could put to flight an army of sixty thousand men.' A poor gentleman's son, Robert was consumed by ambition to do great deeds, and joined to great bravery and strength an extraordinary subtlety of spirit. His surname of Guiscard is thought to testify to his ability and craft. Badly received by his brothers in Apulia, he was reduced to taking service with the Prince of Capua against his rival of Salerno. Events soon gave him an opportunity of striking a blow for himself.

Meanwhile, a formidable combination was forming against the Normans. Argyrus, son of Meles, had deserted his father's policy and came from Constantinople, as Patrician and Cata-pan (Governor), with special commissions from the Leo IX. turns Emperor. Unable to persuade the Normans to against the take service with the Emperor against the Persians, Normans. he soon waged war openly against them, and procured the murder of Count Drogo in 1051, but was soon driven to take refuge in Bari. Meanwhile Leo IX. had become Pope, and his all-absorbing curiosity had led him to two journeys into southern Italy, where he persuaded the inhabitants of Bene-vento to accept the protection of the Holy See against the dreaded Northmen. It looked as if the Eastern and Western Empires were likely to combine with the Papacy and the

Lombards to get rid of the restless adventurers. In 1052
Henry III. granted the duchy of Benevento to the Roman
Church, and Leo hurried from Hungary to southern Italy to
enforce his claims on his new possession.

In May 1053 Leo IX. reached Monte Casino.   There soon
flocked round him a motley army, drawn together from every

Battle of   district of central and southern Italy and eager
Civitate,   to uphold the Holy Father against the Norman
1053.   usurpers ; but the few hundred Germans, who had
followed the Pope over the Alps, were probably more service-
able in the field than the mixed multitude of Italians.   The
Normans, abandoned by their allies, united all their scanty
forces for a decisive struggle.   The armies met on 18th
June near Civitate (Civitella) on the banks of the Fortore,
the place of the first Norman victory in Italy.   The long-
haired and gigantic Germans affected to despise their
diminutive Norman foes, and the fiercest fight was fought
between the Pope's fellow - countrymen and Humphrey
of Hauteville, the new Count of Apulia, who commanded
the Norman right.   There the Norman horse long sought
in vain to break up the serried phalanx of the German
infantry.   But the left and centre of the Normans, led respectively by Richard, the new Count of Aversa, and Robert
Guiscard, easily scattered the enemies before them, and,
returning in good time from the pursuit, enabled Humphrey
to win a final victory over the Germans.   Leo IX. barely
escaped with his liberty from the fatal field.   Peter Damiani
and the zealots denounced him for his unseemly participation
in acts of violence, and the object which had induced him to
depart from his sacred calling had been altogether unfulfilled.

Peace   He retired to Benevento, where he soon came to an
between the   understanding with the Normans, giving them his
Normans
and the   apostolic blessing and absolving them from their
Pope.   blood-guiltiness.   Even in the moment of victory
the Normans had shown every respect to the head of the
Church, and self-interest now combined with enthusiasm to

make them his friends. But Leo entered into no formal treaty with them. He remained at Benevento, carefully watching their movements and corresponding with Constantine Monomachus in the hope of renewing the league against them. But his dealings with the Greek Empire soon broke down owing to the theological differences which the acute hostility of Leo and Michael Cærularius now brought to a head. Leo gave up all hope of western help when he fulminated the excommunication against Cærularius, which led at once to the final split of Catholic and Orthodox. In the spring of 1054 he returned to Rome and died. His exploits and holy life had given him a great reputation for holiness, and he was canonised as a saint. Even the disaster of Civitate and the eastern schism did little to diminish his glory.

Leo IX.'s successor as Pope was another German, Gebhard, bishop of Eichstâdt, who took the name of Victor II. (1054-1057). He continued to work on the lines of Pope Leo, though more in the spirit of a politician. During Victor's pontificate, Henry III. made his second and last visit to Italy (1055). His presence was highly necessary. His strongest Italian enemy, the powerful Marquis Boniface of Tuscany, was dead, leaving an only daughter Matilda heiress of his great inheritance. Boniface's widow Beatrice soon found a second husband in Godfrey the Bearded, Duke of Lower Lorraine, the chief enemy of Henry in Germany. In this union there was a danger of the German and Italian opposition to the Empire being combined. But the formidable league dissolved at once on Henry's appearance. Godfrey fled from Italy, and Beatrice and her daughter were led into honourable captivity in Germany. Godfrey's brother Frederick, hitherto a scheming ecclesiastic, renounced the world, and became one of the most zealous of the monks of Monte Casino. But the death of the Emperor and the long minority that followed, soon restored the power of the heiress of Boniface.

The Countess Matilda, powerful alike in Tuscany and north of the Apennines, became the most zealous of the allies of the

Position of the Countess Matilda.
Papacy. Her support gave that material assistance without which the purely spiritual aims of the Papacy could hardly prevail. At the moment when the Papacy had permanently absorbed the teachings of Cluny, it was a matter of no small moment that the greatest temporal power of middle Italy was on its side. It was a solid compensation for Leo's failure against the Normans.

We have now come to one of the real crises of history. The new spirit had gained ascendency at Rome, and the

Hildebrand's early career and character.
great man had arisen who was to present the papal ideal with all the authority of genius. Hildebrand of Soana[1] was the son of a well-to-do Tuscan peasant; he had been brought up by his uncle, abbot of the strict convent of St. Mary's on the Aventine, which was the centre of the Cluniac ideas in Rome, and where he made his profession as monk. He became the chaplain of Gregory VI. who, though he bought the Papacy with gold, had striven his best to carry out the work of reformation. When deprived of his office at Sutri, Gregory VI. had been compelled to retire to Germany with the Emperor. Hildebrand, now about twenty-five years old, accompanied his master in his exile. In 1048 the deposed Pope died, and his chaplain betook himself to Cluny, where he remained for a full year, and where, he tells us, he would have gladly spent the rest of his life. But in 1049 Leo IX. passed through Cluny on his way to Rome, and Hildebrand was commanded to accompany him. With his return to Rome his active career began. As papal sub-deacon he reorganised the crippled finances of the Holy See, and

[1] Stephen's *Hildebrand and his Times* ('Epochs of Church History'), gives a useful summary of the life and work of the future Gregory VII.; see also Stephen's essay on Hildebrand in his *Essays on Ecclesiastical Biography*. Bowden's *Life and Pontificate of Gregory VII.*, and Villemain's *Histoire de Gregoire VII.* give fuller accounts.

strengthened the hold of the Pope over the unruly citizens. As papal legate he was sent to France in 1054 to put down

MIDDLE ITALY
IN THE
ELEVENTH CENTURY.

Former papal lands usurped by secular powers ____
Former papal lands held by the Countess Matilda
Lands of the Countess Matilda
Papal territory ____

the heresy of Berengar of Tours. But the death of Leo recalled him to Italy, whence he went to the Emperor at the

head of the deputation that successfully requested the appointment of Victor II.   With this Pope he was as powerful
as with Leo.   But Victor II. died in 1057, and Frederick of
Lorraine left his newly-won abbot's chair at Monte Casino to
Stephen IX., ascend the throne of St. Peter as Stephen IX.
1057-1058.   Though a zealot for the ideas of Cluny, Stephen,
as the head of the house of Lorraine, was the natural leader
of the political opposition to the imperial house both in
Germany and Italy.   He made Peter Damiani a cardinal,
and zealously pushed forward the warfare against simony in
Germany.   Stephen's early death in 1058, when Hildebrand
was away in Germany, brought about a new crisis.   The
Counts of Tusculum thought the moment opportune to make
a desperate effort to win back their old influence.   They
terrorised Rome with their troops, and brought about the
irregular election of one of the Crescentii, who called himself
Benedict X.   The prompt action of Hildebrand preserved
the Papacy for the reforming party.   He hurried back to
Florence, and formed a close alliance with Duke Godfrey of
Lorraine, Stephen's brother, against the nominee of Tusculum.
The stricter cardinals met at Siena ând chose Gerhard, Bishop
of Florence, a Burgundian by birth, as orthodox Pope.   Gerhard
Nicholas II., held another synod at Sutri, where the Antipope
1058-1061   was formally deposed.   Early in 1059 he entered
Rome in triumph.   By assuming the name of Nicholas II.,
he proclaimed himself the successor of the most successful
and aggressive of Popes.   As Archdeacon of Rome, Hildebrand
acted as chief minister to the Pope whom he had made.
Henceforth till his death he dominated the papal policy.
While previous reformers had sought salvation by calling
the Emperor over the Alps, Hildebrand had found in Duke
Godfrey and his wife champions as effective for his purpose
on Italian soil.   With the establishment of Pope Nicholas,
through the arms of Godfrey and Matilda, the imperial alliance
ceases to become a physical necessity to the reforming party
in Italy.   Hildebrand had won for the Church her freedom.
Before long he began to aim at domination.

Nicholas II. ruled as Pope from 1058 to 1061. Within those few years, three events were brought about which enormously strengthened the position of the Papacy, already possessed of a great moral force by its permanent identification with the reforming party, and the final abasement of the unworthy local factions, that had so long aspired to wield its resources. These events were the settlement of the method of papal elections, the establishment of a close alliance between the Papacy and the Normans of southern Italy, and the subjection of Lombardy to the papal authority.

In 1059 Nicholas held a synod in the Lateran which drew up the famous decree that set aside the vague ancient rights of the Roman clergy and people to choose their bishop, in favour of the close corporation of the College of Cardinals. The decree was drawn up in studiously vague language, but put the prerogative voice into the very limited circle of the seven cardinal bishops of the suburbicarian dioceses. These were to add to themselves the cardinal priests and deacons, whose assent was regarded as including that of clergy and people at large. A Roman clerk was to be preferred if worthy, and Rome was to be the ordinary place of election; but, if difficulties intervened, any person could be chosen, and any place made the seat of election. The due rights of King Henry and his successors to confirm their choice were reserved, but in terms that suggested a special personal favour granted of his own goodwill by the Pope to a crowned Emperor, rather than the recognition of an immemorial legal right. The decree did not, as was hoped, save the Church from schisms like those of Benedict X. Neither was the pre-eminence of the suburbicarian bishops permanently maintained. But henceforth the legal right of the cardinals to be the electors of future Popes became substantially uncontested. It is not likely that this involved any real change of practice. But in embodying custom in a formal shape it gave subsequent efforts to set up Antipopes the condemnation

(marginal note: Lateran Synod and reform in Papal elections, 1059.*)*

of illegality, and so stood the Papacy in good stead in the troubles that were soon to ensue.   The council also witnessed the abject degradation of the Antipope and the recantation of the heretic Berengar of Tours.

In the years that followed the battle of Civitate, the Normans had steadily extended their power over Apulia and
The Normans
become the
vassals of
the Pope,
1059.
Calabria.   But the south of Italy is so rugged and mountainous that even the bravest of warriors could only win their way slowly.   In 1057 the valiant Count Humphrey died, leaving his sons so young that he had been constrained to beg his brother Robert to act as their protector.   But the barons of Apulia insisted that Robert should be their count in full succession to Humphrey.   Soon after Roger of Hauteville, the youngest of the twelve sons of Tancred, left the paternal roof to share the fortune of his brothers.   'He was,' says Geoffrey of Malaterra, 'a fine young man, of lofty stature and elegant proportions.   Very eloquent in speech, wise in counsel, and gifted with extraordinary foresight, he was gay and affable to all, and so strong and valiant that he soon gained the good
Roger of
Hauteville.
graces of every one.'   Robert Guiscard received Roger in a more brotherly spirit than had been shown on his own first arrival by Drogo and Humphrey. He gave him a sufficient following of troops and sent him to Calabria, where he soon established himself as lord of half the district, though under his brother's overlordship. Meanwhile, Richard of Aversa had driven out the Lombards from Capua and added it to his dominions.   The Normans were still, however, not free from danger from the Popes. Victor II. had disapproved of Leo IX.'s policy, yet before his death he had become their enemy.   Stephen IX. formed various projects against them.   But Hildebrand now turned Nicholas II. to wiser counsels.   In 1059 Hildebrand went in person to Capua and concluded a treaty with Count Richard, who, as the ally of the monks of Monte Casino, was the most friendly of the Norman chieftains to the Church.

Almost immediately the archdeacon returned to Rome with a strong Norman escort, and soon after a Norman army spread terror among the partisans of the Antipope. In the summer of 1059 Nicholas himself held a synod in Melfi, Synod the Apulian capital, where he passed canons con- of Melfi. demning married priests. After the formal session was over, the Pope made Robert Guiscard Duke of Apulia and Calabria, and 'future Duke' of Sicily, if he should ever have Robert, Duke the good luck to drive out the infidels. In return of Apulia; Robert, 'Duke by the grace of God and of St. and Richard, Duke of Peter,' agreed to hold his lands as the Pope's Capua. vassal, paying an annual rent of twelve pence for each plough-land. Richard of Capua, either then or earlier, took the same oath. Thus the famous alliance between the Normans and the Papacy was consummated, which by uniting the strongest military power in Italy to the papal policy, enabled the Holy See to wield the temporal with almost as much effect as the spiritual sword. Thus the Papacy assumed a feudal suzerainty over southern Italy which outlasted the Middle Ages. Within seven years of the Synod of Melfi, the estab-lishment of the Norman duke William the Bastard in England, as the ally of the Pope, still further bound the most restless, active, and enterprising race in Europe to the apostolic see.

The Pope now intervened decisively in the long struggle between the traditional and the strict parties in Lombardy, where the ancient independence of the arch- The Patarini bishops of Milan had long been assailed by the in Lombardy. Patarini or rag-pickers, as the reformers were contemptuously called. Lovers of old ways in the north, with the Archbishop Guido of Milan at their head, had long upheld clerical marriage as the ancient custom of the Church of St. Ambrose. Peter Damiani was now sent as papal legate to Milan to uphold the 'rag-bags' in their struggle. At a synod held in Milan, the zealous monk made short work of the married clerks and of the immemorial rights of the archbishop. Guido proffered an abject submission and received a contemptuous restitution of his archbishopric. The continuance of the friendship of God-

Milan submits to Rome. frey and Matilda secured middle Italy, as the alliance with Normans and Patarini had secured the south and the north. The strongest princes of Gaul and Burgundy were on the zealots' side. The imperialist prelates of Germany, headed by Anno of Cologne, made a faint effort to stem the tide, but the decrees fulminated by German synods against Nicholas and his work were unknown or disregarded in Italy.

The untimely death of Nicholas in no wise altered the course of events. The next Pope, Alexander II., was

Alexander II. 1061-1073. Anselm, Bishop of Lucca, who had shared with Peter Damiani in the victory over the simoniacs and married clerks in Lombardy. His appointment by the cardinals without the least reference to King Henry IV. gave the greatest offence in Germany, and brought to a head the growing tension between Empire and Papacy. A synod at Basel declared Pope Alexander's election invalid, and set up an Antipope, Cadalus, Bishop of Parma, who had been the real soul of the opposition to the Patarini in Lombardy. Honorius II. (this was the name he assumed) hurried over the Alps, and in 1062 was strong enough, with the help of the Counts of Tusculum, to fight an even battle with Alexander's partisans, and for a time to get possession of St. Peter's. But the factions that controlled the government of the young Henry IV. could not unite even in upholding an Antipope, while the religious enthusiasm, which the reforming movement had evoked, was ardently on the side of Alexander. Condemned by Anno of Cologne and his party in Germany, Honorius was rejected in 1064 by a council at Mantua. Nevertheless, he managed to live unmolested and with some supporters until his own death in 1072. His successful rival Alexander only outlived him a year. It was then time for the archdeacon himself to assume the responsible leadership of the movement which he had so long controlled. In 1073 Hildebrand became Pope Gregory VII.

The reconciliation with the Papacy stood the Normans in good stead. Henceforth they posed as the champions of Western Catholicism against Eastern Orthodoxy and Islam. Though the Norman chieftains still wrangled hotly with each other, the tide - in south Italy had definitely turned in their favour. Later triumphs of Robert Guiscard, 1068-1085. In 1071 the capture of Bari, after a three years' siege, finally expelled the Greeks from Italy. The Lombard principality of Salerno was also absorbed, and the greater part of the territories of the dukes of Benevento, save the city and its neighbourhood, which Robert Guiscard, much to his own disgust, was forced to yield to his papal suzerain. We shall see in other chapters how Robert crossed the Straits of Otranto and aspired to conquer the Greek Empire, how he came to the help of Gregory vii. in his greatest need, and how his son Bohemund took part in the first Crusade and founded the principality of Antioch. When Robert died in 1085, all southern Italy acknowledged him as its lord, save the rival Norman principality of Capua, the half-Greek republics of Amalfi and Naples, and the papal possession of Benevento.

While Robert Guiscard was thus consolidating his power in the peninsula, an even harder task was being accomplished by his younger brother Roger, sometimes in alliance, and sometimes in fierce hostility with the Duke of Apulia. The grant of Nicholas ii. had contemplated the extension of the Norman rule to Sicily. The divisions of the Mohammedan world had cut off the island from the Caliphate of the Fatimites, and its independent Ameers were hardly equal to the task of ruling the island and keeping in order a timid but refractory population of Christian serfs. The increasing power of Robert was fatal to the independence of Roger in Calabria, and he gladly accepted the invitation of the discontented Christians of Messina to deliver them from the bondage of the infidel. In 1060 Roger led his first expedition to Sicily, which was unsuccessful. But early next year he came again, and Roger's conquest of Sicily, 1060-1101.

this time the dissensions of the Mohammedans in Sicily enabled him to have friends among Saracens as well as Christians.   In the summer of 1061 Robert came to his help. Messina was easily captured, and proved invaluable as the starting-point of later expeditions.   The infidels were badly beaten at the battle of Castrogiovanni, and before the end of the year the standards of Roger had waved as far west as Girgenti.   The first successes were not quite followed up.   In 1064 the Normans were forced to raise the siege of Palermo. The compact Mussulman population of Western Sicily opposed a very different sort of resistance to the invaders from that which they had experienced in the Christian East. But the process of conquest was resumed after the capture of Bari had given Robert leisure to come to his brother's help. In 1072 Palermo was taken by the two brothers jointly. Robert claimed the lion's share of the spoil.   Roger, forced to yield him the suzerainty of the whole island, and a great domain under his direct rule, including Palermo and Messina, threw himself with untiring zeal into the conquest of the parts of the island that still adhered to Islam.   Thirty years after his first expedition, the last Saracens were expelled

The feudali-sation of Naples and Sicily.

from the rocky fastnesses of the western coasts, and the inaccessible uplands of the interior.   The Normans took with them to Italy their language, their manners, their art, and above all, their polity. On the ruins of the Greek, Lombard and Saracen power, the Normans feudalised southern Italy so thoroughly that the feudalism of Naples and Sicily long outlasted the more in-digenous feudalism of Tuscany or Romagna.   Freed from his grasping brother's tutelage after 1085, Roger ruled over Sicily as count till his death in 1101.   We shall see how his son united Sicily with Apulia in a single sovereignty, which has in various shapes endured as the kingdom of Naples or Sicily, until the establishment of a united Italy in our own days.

GENEALOGY OF THE HOUSE OF TANCRED OF HAUTEVILLE.

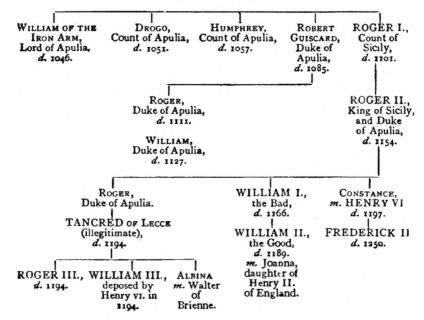

TANCRED OF HAUTEVILLE.

WILLIAM OF THE IRON ARM, Lord of Apulia, *d.* 1046.

DROGO, Count of Apulia, *d.* 1051.

HUMPHREY, Count of Apulia, *d.* 1057.

ROBERT GUISCARD, Duke of Apulia, *d.* 1085.

ROGER I., Count of Sicily, *d.* 1101.

ROGER, Duke of Apulia, *d.* 1111.

WILLIAM, Duke of Apulia, *d.* 1127.

ROGER II., King of Sicily, and Duke of Apulia, *d.* 1154.

ROGER, Duke of Apulia.

TANCRED OF LECCE (illegitimate), *d.* 1194.

WILLIAM I., the Bad, *d.* 1166.

WILLIAM II., the Good, *d.* 1189. *m.* Joanna, daughter of Henry II. of England.

CONSTANCE, *m.* HENRY VI *d.* 1197.

FREDERICK II *d.* 1250.

ROGER III., *d.* 1194.

WILLIAM III., deposed by Henry VI. in 1194.

ALBINA *m.* Walter of Brienne.

CHAPTER VI

THE INVESTITURE CONTEST (1056-1125)

Minority of Henry IV.—Regency of Agnes—Rivalry of Adalbert and Anno—
The Saxon Revolt—Election of Gregory VII.—Beginnings of the Investi-
ture Contest—Canossa and its results—Rudolf of Swabia and Guibert of
Ravenna—The Normans and Gregory VII.—Victor III. and Urban II.—
Last years of Henry IV.—Henry V. and Pascal II.—Calixtus II. and the
Concordat of Worms—Death of Henry V.

WHILE the Cluniac movement had at last attained ascendency over the best minds of Europe, and a swarm of monastic
reformers had prepared the way for the great revival of
spiritual religion and hierarchical pretensions; while in Italy
strong papalist powers, like the Countess Matilda and the
Normans of the south, had arisen to menace the imperial
authority, the long minority of Henry IV. sapped
the personal influence of Cæsar over Italy and
brought about a lengthened period of faction and
weak rule in Germany. On Henry III.'s death, his son,
Henry IV., was a boy of six. The great Emperor's power
secured the child's undisputed succession, but was too
personal, too military in its character to prove any safe-
guard against the dangers of a long minority. Nor did
the choice of ruler during Henry IV.'s nonage improve the
state of affairs. Henry III.'s widow, Agnes of Poitou, a
pious well-meaning lady, acted as regent for her son, but
her weakness of will and inconsistency of conduct
gave full scope to discontented nobles ready to
take advantage of a woman's sway. The lay
nobles availed themselves of her helplessness to
plunder and despoil the prelates, while they complained that
Agnes neglected their counsels for those of low-born courtiers

120

and personal favourites. After six years of confusion the Empress was driven from power. Anno, Archbishop of Cologne, a vigorous, experienced, and zealous prelate, full of ambition and violence, joined himself with Otto of Nordheim, the newly appointed Duke of Bavaria, Count Egbert of Brunswick, and some of the bishops, in a well-contrived plot to get possession of the young king. In May 1062 the three chief con- Abduction of Henry by Anno of Cologne, 1062. spirators visited the king at his palace of Saint Suitbert's, situated on an island in the Rhine, some miles below Düsseldorf, now called Kaisers- werth. One day after dinner Anno persuaded the boy king to inspect an elaborately-fitted-up barge. As soon as Henry had entered the boat, the oarsmen put off and rowed away. Henry was soon frightened and plunged into the water, but Count Egbert leapt in and rescued him. The king was pacified by flattery and taken to Cologne. The crowd cried shame on the treachery of the bishop, but Henry remained in his custody, and Agnes made no serious attempt to regain her authority, but reconciled herself with Anno and retired into a monastery. Anno proposed to the magnates that the regency should be exercised by the bishop of the diocese in which the king happened to be staying. By carefully selecting the king's places of abode, he ‑ thus secured the reality of power without its odium. By throwing over the Antipope he procured the support of the Hildebrandine party, and was likened by Peter Damiani to another Jehoiada. But his pride and arrogance soon raised him up enemies ; and young Henry, who never forgave his abduction, bitterly resented his tutelage.

Adalbert, Archbishop of Bremen, took the lead among Anuo's enemies. He was a man of high birth, Rivalry of Adalbert of Bremen and Anno of Cologne, 1065-1070. great experience, and unbounded ambition, an old confidant of Henry III., and filled with a great scheme for making his archbishopric a permanent patriarchate over the infant churches of Scandi- navia. He made himself personally attractive to the king, who contrasted his kindness and indulgence with the austerity of Anno. By Adalbert's influence Henry was declared of age to govern on attaining his fifteenth year in 1065. Henceforth Adalbert disposed of all the high offices in Church and State, and growing more greedy as he became more successful, excited much ill-will among the religious by plundering the monasteries right and left. He appropriated to himself the two great abbeys of Lorsch and Corvey, and sought in vain to propitiate his enemies by allowing other magnates, including even his rival Anno, to similarly despoil other monasteries. The king was made so poor that he hardly had enough to live on. But Adalbert at least sought to continue the great traditions of statecraft of Henry III., and showed more policy and skill than the crowd of bishops who had previously shared power with Anno. At last, in 1066, the nobles combined against Adalbert at a Diet at Tribur, and Henry was roundly told that he must either dismiss Adalbert or resign his throne. Adalbert retired to his diocese, and Anno and Otto of Nordheim again had the chief control of affairs. But neither party could rule with energy or spirit, and Henry, now nearly grown up, showed no decided capacity to make things better. The young king was tall, dignified, and handsome. He was affable and kindly to men of low rank, with whom he was ever popular, though he could be stern and haughty to the magnates, whose power he feared. He had plenty of spirit and fair ability. But he had been brought up so laxly by Archbishop Adalbert that he was headstrong, irresolute, profligate, and utterly deficient in self-control. He never formulated a policy, and if he championed great causes, he did so blindly and in ignorance. Married to Bertha, daughter of the Marquis Odo of Turin, in 1065, he gave offence both to her powerful kinsfolk and to the strict churchmen by refusing to live with her, and talking of a divorce. He had now to put down open rebellions. In 1069 the Margrave Dedi strove to rouse the Thuringians to revolt, and in 1070 Otto of

Bavaria, the most important of the dukes surviving, after the death of Duke Godfrey of Lorraine in the previous year, was driven into rebellion. So divided were the German nobles, so helpless the German king, that instead of ruling the Italians, there seemed every prospect of the Italians ruling them. In 1069 Peter Damiani went to Germany as legate, and compelled Henry to reconcile himself with Bertha. Peter was horrified at the unblushing simony of the German bishops, and, on his report, Anno of Cologne and several other of the greatest prelates of Germany were summoned to Rome and thoroughly humiliated. Anno atoned for his laxity by his edifying discharge of the meanest monastic duties in his own great foundation at Siegburg, but his influence was gone and his political career was at an end His fall brought Adalbert back to some of his ancient influence. The death of the Archbishop of Bremen in 1072 unloosed the last link that connected the new reign with the old traditions.

Henry IV.'s reign now really began. A thorough Swabian, his favourite ministers were Swabians of no high degree, and he had no faith in the goodwill or loyalty of the men of the north. He had kept vacant the Saxon dukedom. On every hill-top of Saxony and Thuringia he built strong castles, whose lawless garrisons plundered and outraged the peasantry. There was ever fierce ill-will between northern and southern Germany during the Middle Ages. The policy of the southern Emperor soon filled the north with anger, and the Saxon nobles prepared for armed resistance. In 1073 Henry fitted out an expedition, whose professed destination was against the Poles. It was believed in Saxony that his real object was to subdue the Saxons and hand them over to the Swabians. Accordingly in the summer of 1073 a general Saxon revolt broke out, headed by the natural leaders of Saxony both in Church and State, including the Archbishop of Magdeburg, the deposed Duke Otto of Bavaria, and the fierce Margrave Dedi, already an unsuccessful rebel. The insurgents demanded the instant

The Saxon Revolt, 1073-1075.

demolition of the castles, the dismissal of Henry's evil coun-
sellors, and the restitution of their lands that he had violently
seized. On receiving no answer they shut up Henry in the
strong castle of Harzburg, whence he escaped with the utmost
difficulty to the friendly cloister of Hersfeld. In the course of
the summer the rebels destroyed many of the new castles.
The levies summoned for the Polish campaign refused to
turn their arms against the Saxons, and Henry saw himself
powerless amidst the general falling away. A meeting at
Gerstungen, where Henry's friends strove to mediate with
the rebels, led to a suggestion that the king should be
deposed. Only at Worms and in the Swabian cities did
Henry receive any real support. He gathered together a
small army and strove to fight a winter campaign against
the Saxons, but failed so completely that he was forced to
accept their terms. However, hostilities were renewed in
1075, when Henry won a considerable victory at Hohenburg
on the Unstrut, and forced the Saxons to make an unconditional submission. Otto of Nordheim, the Archbishop of
Magdeburg, and the other leaders were imprisoned. On
the ruins of Saxon liberty Henry now aspired to build up a
despotism.

Hildebrand was now Pope. During the funeral service of
Alexander II. at St. John's in the Lateran, a great shout arose
from the multitude in the church that Hildebrand
should be their bishop. The cardinal, Hugh
the White, addressed the assembly. 'You know,
brethren,' he said, 'how, since the time of Leo IX., Hildebrand has exalted the Roman Church, and freed our city.
We cannot find a better Pope than he. Indeed, we cannot
find his equal. Let us then elect him, who, having been
ordained in **our** church, is known to us all, and thoroughly
approved by us.' There was the great shout in answer:
'Saint Peter has chosen Hildebrand to be Pope!' Despite
his resistance, Hildebrand was dragged to the church of
St. Peter ad Vincula, and immediately enthroned. The

Election of Gregory VII., 1073.

cardinals had no mind to upset this irregular election, strangely contrary though it was to the provisions of Nicholas II. The German bishops, alarmed at Hildebrand's reputation for severity, urged the king to quash the appointment, but Henry contented himself with sending to Rome to inquire into the circumstances of the election. Hildebrand showed great moderation, and actually postponed his consecration until Henry's consent had been obtained. This Henry had no wish to withhold. On 29th June 1073 Hildebrand was hallowed bishop. By assuming the name of Gregory VII., he proclaimed to the world the invalidity of the deposition of his old master at the Synod of Sutri.

The wonderful self-control which the new Pope had shown so long did not desert him in his new position. Physically, there was little to denote the mighty mind within his puny body. He was of low stature, short-legged and corpulent. He spoke with a stammer, *His character and policy.* and his dull complexion was only lighted up by his glittering eyes. He was not a man of much learning or originality, and contributed little towards the theory of the papal or sacerdotal power. But he was one of the greatest practical men of the Middle Ages; and his single-minded wish to do what was right betokened a dignity of moral nature that was rare indeed in the eleventh century. His power over men's minds was enormous, even to their own despite. The fierce and fanatical Peter Damiani called him his 'holy Satan.' 'Thy will,' said he, 'has ever been a command to me—evil but lawful. Would that I had always served God and St. Peter as faithfully as I have served thee.' Even as archdeacon he assumed so great a state, and lived in such constant intercourse with the world, that monastic zealots like Damiani were scandalised, and some moderns have questioned (though groundlessly) whether he was ever a professed monk at all. Profoundly convinced of the truth of the Cluniac doctrines, he showed a fierce and almost unscrupulous statecraft in realising them that filled even Cluny with alarm./His ideal was to reform the world by establishing a sort of universal monarchy for the Papacy. He saw all round him that kings and princes were powerless for good, but mighty for evil. He saw churchmen living greedy and corrupt lives for want of higher direction and control. Looking at a world distraught by feudal anarchy, his ambition was to restore the 'peace of God,' civilisation, and order, by submitting the Church to the Papacy, and the world to the Church. 'Human pride,' he wrote, 'has created the power of kings; God's mercy has created the power of bishops. The Pope is the master of Emperors. He is rendered holy by the merits of his predecessor, St. Peter. The Roman Church has never erred, and Holy Scripture proves that it never can err. To resist it is to resist God.' For the next twelve years he strove with all his might to make his power felt throughout Christendom. Sometimes his enthusiasm caused him to advance claims that even his best friends would not admit, as when William the Conqueror was constrained to repudiate the Holy See's claims of feudal sovereignty over England, which, after similar pretensions had been recognised by the Normans in Sicily, Gregory and his successors were prone to assert whenever opportunity offered. The remotest parts of Europe felt the weight of his influence. But the intense conviction of the righteousness of his aims, that made compromise seem to him treason to the truth, did something to detract from the success of his statecraft. He was too absolute, too rigid, too obstinate, too extreme to play his part with entire advantage to himself and his cause. Yet with all his defects there is no grander figure in history.

Gregory realised the magnitude of his task, but he never shrank from it. 'I would that you knew,' wrote he to the Abbot of Cluny, 'the anguish that assails my soul. The Church of the East has gone astray from the Catholic faith. If I look to the west, the north, or the south, I find but few bishops whose appointments and whose lives are in accordance with the laws of the Church, or who govern God's people through love and not through worldly ambition. Among princes I know not one who sets the honour of God before his own, or justice before gain. If I did not hope that I could be of use to the Church, I would not remain at Rome a day.' From the very first he was beset on every side with difficulties. Even the alliance with the Normans was uncertain. Robert Guiscard, with his brother Roger, waged war against Gregory's faithful vassal, Richard of Capua; and Robert, who threatened the papal possession of Benevento, went so far that he incurred excommunication. Philip of France, 'the worst of the tyrants who enslaved the Church,' had to be threatened with interdict. A project to unite the Eastern with the Western Church broke down lamentably. A contest with Henry IV. soon became inevitable. But Gregory abated nothing of his high claims. In February 1075 he held a synod at Rome, at which severe decrees against simony and the marriage of clerks were issued. The practice of lay investiture, by which secular princes were wont to grant bishoprics and abbeys by the conferring of spiritual symbols such as the ring and staff, had long been regarded by the Cluniacs as the most glaring of temporal aggressions against the spiritual power. This prac tice was now sternly forbidden. 'If any one,' declared the synod, 'henceforth receive from the hand of any lay person a bishopric or abbey, let him not be considered as abbot or bishop, and let the favour of St. Peter and the gate of the Church be forbidden to him. If an emperor, a king, a duke, a count, or any other lay person presume to give investiture of any ecclesiastical dignity, let him be excommunicated.' This decree gave the signal for the great Investiture Contest, and for the greater struggle of Papacy and Empire that convulsed Europe, save during occasional breaks, for the next two centuries.

Up to the issue of the decree as to investitures, the relation between Gregory and Henry IV. had not been unfriendly. Henry had admitted that he had not always respected the rights of the Church, but had promised amendment for the future. But to give up investitures would have been to change the whole imperial system of government. He was now freed, by his victory at Hohenburg, from the Saxon revolt. The German bishops, afraid of the Pope's strictness, encouraged his resistance, and even in Italy he had many partisans. The Patarini were driven out of Milan, and Henry scrupled not to invest a new archbishop with the see of St. Ambrose. Even at Rome, Gregory barely escaped assassination while celebrating mass. In January 1076 Henry summoned a German council to Worms. Strange and incredible crimes were freely attributed to the Pope, and the majority of the German bishops pronounced him deposed. Henry himself wrote in strange terms to the Pope : ' Henry, king not by usurpation but by God's grace, to Hildebrand, henceforth no pope but false monk,—Christ has called us to our kingdom, while He has never called thee to the priesthood. Thou hast attacked me, a consecrated king, who cannot be judged but by God Himself. Condemned by our bishops and by ourselves, come down from the place that thou hast usurped. Let the see of St. Peter be held by another, who will not seek to cover violence under the cloak of religion, and who will teach the wholesome doctrine of St. Peter. I, Henry, king by the grace of God, with all of my bishops, say unto thee—"Come down, come down."'

In February 1076 Gregory held a great synod in the Vatican, at which the Empress Agnes was present, with a great multitude of Italian and French bishops. A clerk from Parma named Roland delivered the king's letter to the Pope before the council. There was a great tumult, and Roland would have atoned for his boldness with his life but for the Pope's personal intervention. Henry was now formally excommunicated and

Marginal notes:

The beginnings of the Investiture Contest, 1075.

Council at Worms, 1076.

Vatican Synod, 1076.

deposed. 'Blessed Peter,' declared Gregory, 'thou and the Mother of God and all the saints are witness that the Roman Church has called upon me to govern it in my own despite. As thy representative I have received from God the power to bind and to loose in Heaven and on earth. For the honour and security of thy Church, in the Name of God Almighty, I prohibit Henry the king, son of Henry the Emperor, who has risen with unheard-of pride against thy Church, from ruling Germany and Italy. I release all Christians from the oaths of fealty they may have taken to him, and I order that no one shall obey him.'

War was thus declared between Pope and king. Though the position of both parties was sufficiently precarious, Henry was at the moment in the worst position for carrying on an internecine combat. He could count very little on the support of his German subjects. Those who most feared the Pope were the self-seekers and the simoniacs, whose energy was small and whose loyalty less. The saints and the zealots were all against him. The Saxons profited by his embarrassments to renew their revolt, and soon chased his garrisons out of their land. The secular nobles, who saw in his policy the beginnings of an attempt at despotism, held aloof from his court. It was to no purpose that Henry answered the anathemas of Gregory with denunciations equally un-measured, and complained that Gregory had striven to unite in his hands both the spiritual and the temporal swords, that God had kept asunder. Hermann, Bishop of Metz, the Pope's legate in Germany, ably united the forces against him. At last, the nobles and bishops of Germany gathered together on 16th October 1076 at Tribur, where the papal legates were treated with marked deference, though Henry took up his quarters at Oppenheim, on the other bank of the Rhine, afraid to trust himself amidst his dis-affected subjects. Henry soon saw that he had no alternative but submission. The magnates were so suspicious of him that

Weakness of Henry's position in Germany.

Diet of Tribur, 1076.

it needed the personal intercession of Hugh, Abbot of Cluny, to prevail upon them to make terms with him at all.   Finally

Humiliation of Henry. a provisional agreement was patched up, upon conditions excessively humiliating to Henry.   The barons refused to obey him until he had obtained absolution from the Pope, who, moreover, had promised to go to Germany in person and hold a council in the succeeding February. Pending this, Henry was to remain at Speyer without kingly revenue, power, or dignity, and still shut off by his excommunication from the offices of the Church.   If Henry could not satisfy the Pope in February, he was to be regarded as deposed.

Abandoned by Germany, Henry abode some two months at Speyer, gloomily anticipating the certain ruin to his cause that would follow the Pope's appearance in a German council. He realised that he could do nothing unless he reconciled himself to Gregory ; and, hearing good news of his prospects in northern Italy, thought that his best course was to betake himself over the Alps, where the Pope might well prove less rigorous, if he found him at the head of a formidable band of Italian partisans.   It was a winter of extraordinary severity, but any risks were better than inglorious inaction at Speyer.

Henry's winter journey through Burgundy and Lombardy, 1076-77. Accordingly Henry broke his compact with his nobles, and towards the end of December secretly set out on his journey southward.   He was accompanied by Bertha and his little son, but only one German noble was included among his scanty following.   He traversed Burgundy, and kept his miserable Christmas feast at Besançon.   Thence crossing the Mont Cenis at the risk of his life, he appeared early in the new year amidst his Lombard partisans at Pavia.   But though urged to take up arms, Henry feared the risks of a new and doubtful struggle.   Germany could only be won back by submission.   He resolved to seek out the Pope and throw himself on his mercy.

Gregory was then some fifteen miles south of Reggio, at an

impregnable mountain stronghold belonging to the Countess
Matilda, called Canossa, which crowned one of the northern
spurs of the Apennines, and overlooked the Canossa,
great plain.   He had sought the protection of Jan. 1077.
its walls as a safe refuge against the threatened Lombard
attack which Henry, it was believed, had come over the Alps
to arrange.   The Countess Matilda and Hugh of Cluny,
Henry's godfather, were with the Pope, and many of the
simoniac bishops of Germany had already gone to Canossa
and won absolution by submission.   On 21st January 1077
Henry left his wife and followers at Reggio, and climbed
the steep snow-clad road that led to the mountain fastness.
Gregory refused to receive him, but he had interviews with
Matilda and his godfather in a chapel at the foot of the
castle-rock, and induced them to intercede with the Pope
on his behalf.   Gregory would hear of nothing but complete
and unconditional submission.   'If he be truly penitent, let
him surrender his crown and insignia of royalty into our
hands, and confess himself unworthy of the name and honour
of king.'   But the pressure of the countess and abbot at
last prevailed upon him to be content with abject contrition
without actual abandonment of his royal state.   For three days
Henry waited in the snow outside the inner gate of the castle-
yard, barefoot, fasting, and in the garb of a penitent.   On
the fourth day the Pope consented to admit him into his
presence.   With the cry 'Holy father, spare me !' the king
threw himself at the Pope's feet.   Gregory raised him up,
absolved him, entertained him at his table, and sent him
away with much good advice and his blessing.   But the
terms of Henry's reconciliation were sufficiently hard.   He
was to promise to submit himself to the judgment of the
German magnates, presided over by the Pope, with respect
to the long catalogue of charges brought against him.   Until
that was done he was to abstain from the royal insignia and
the royal functions.   He was to be prepared to accept or
retain his crown according to the judgment of the Pope as

to his guilt or innocence.   He was, if proved innocent, to obey the Pope in all things pertaining to the Church.   If he broke any of these conditions, another king was to be forthwith elected.

The humiliation of Henry at Canossa is so dramatic and so famous an event that it is hard to realise that it was but an

Results of Canossa. incident in the midst of a long struggle.   It settled nothing, and profited neither Henry nor Gregory. Gregory found that his harshness had to some extent alienated that public opinion on which the Papacy depended almost entirely for its influence.   Henry found that his submission had not won over his German enemies, but had thoroughly disgusted the anti-papal party in northern Italy, upon which alone he could count for armed support.   The Lombards now talked of deposing the cowardly monarch in favour of his little son.   But the future course of events rested after all upon the action of the German nobles, who held their Diet at Forchheim in March 1077.   To this

Diet of Forchheim, March 1077. assembly Henry was not even invited; and for the present he preferred remaining in Italy.   The Pope also did not appear in person, but was represented by two legates.   The old charges against Henry were brought up once more, and the legates expressed their wonder that the patient Germans had submitted so long to be ruled by such a monster.   Without giving Henry the least opportunity of refuting the accusations, it was determined to proceed at once to the choice of a new king.   The suffrages of the magnates fell on Duke Rudolf of Swabia.   Before his

Rudolf of Swabia, Anti-Cæsar. appointment, Rudolf was compelled to renounce all hereditary claim to the throne on behalf of his heirs, and to allow freedom of election to all bishoprics.   He was then crowned at Mainz by Archbishop Siegfried.

The news of Rudolf's election at once brought Henry back over the Alps.   He soon found that he now had devoted partisans in the land that had rejected him when he was under the ban of the Pope. He was warmly welcomed in Bavaria, in Burgundy, and especially in the great towns of the Rhineland, always faithful to the imperial cause. Civil war Rudolf's own duchy of Swabia rejected its duke between in favour of the prince who had ever loved the Henry, Swabians. Rebel Saxony was alone strongly 1077-1080. on Rudolf's side. Even the Pope could not make up his mind to ratify the action of his legates and accept Rudolf as king. For more than two years civil war raged between Rudolf and Henry. It was substantially a continuation of the Saxon revolt. At last, in January 1080, a decisive battle was fought at Flarchheim on the banks of the Battle of Unstrut, in which Henry was utterly defeated. Flarchheim, During all this time Gregory had contented 1080. himself with offers of arbitration. Though Henry practised lay investiture as freely as ever, it was not until after his defeat that the Pope once more declared himself against him. Yielding to the indignant remonstrances of Rudolf and the Saxons, he convoked a synod at Rome in March 1080, where he renewed Henry's excommunication, and again Renewed deprived him of his kingdoms of Germany and excommuni- Italy. 'Act so,' said Gregory to the assembled cation and prelates, 'that the world shall know that ye who of Henry, have power to bind and to loose in heaven, can March 1080. grant or withhold kingdoms, principalities, and other possessions according to each man's merits. And if you are fit to judge in things spiritual, ought ye not to be deemed competent to judge in things temporal?' Rudolf was now recognised as king, and another universal prohibition of lay investitures was issued.

Gregory boasted that, before the next feast of SS. Peter and Paul, Henry would have lost his throne and his life. But each fresh aggression of the Pope increased his rival's power. Henry now showed an energy and vigour that contrasted strangely with his spiritless action three years before. Both in Germany and Italy he found himself supported

by partisans as enthusiastic as those of the Pope. The
bishops of Germany declared for him, and the old foes

Guibert of
Ravenna
elected
Antipope,
June 1080.

of the Pope in Italy took courage to continue
the contest. In June Henry met at Brixen the
German and Italian bishops who adhered to his
side. This assembly declared Gregory deposed
and excommunicate, and elected Guibert, Archbishop of
Ravenna as his successor.

The new Antipope had in his youth served Henry III.,
and, as chancellor of Italy, had striven to uphold the
imperial authority during Henry IV.'s minority. He had
once been on friendly terms with Gregory, but had quarrelled
with him, and had for some time been the soul of the
imperialist party in north Italy. He was of high birth, unblemished character, great abilities, and long experience. He
assumed the title of Clement III., and at once returned to
Ravenna to push matters to extremities against Gregory.
The rash violence of the Pope had been answered with
equal violence by his enemies. There were two Popes
and two Emperors. The sword alone could decide between
them.

Fortune favoured Henry and Clement both in Germany
and Italy. On 15th October 1080 a great battle was fought

Battle on the
Elster, and
death of
Rudolf,
15th October
1080.

on the banks of the Elster, not far from the
later battlefields of Lützen. The fierce assault of
Otto of Nordheim changed what threatened
to be a Saxon defeat into a brilliant victory for
the northern army. But Rudolf of Swabia was
slain, and the victorious Saxons wasted their opportunity
while they quarrelled as to his successor. It was nearly a

Hermann of
Luxemburg,
Anti-Cæsar,

year before they could agree upon Hermann of
Luxemburg as their new king. Before this the
back of the revolt had been broken, and Henry,
secure of Germany, had once more gone to Italy.
Crossing the Brenner in March 1081, he went on progress
through the Lombard cities, and abode with Pope Clement at

Ravenna. Thence he set out for Rome, meeting little resistance on his way save from the Countess Matilda. Henry's visit to Italy, 1081.
The Normans of Naples, on whose help Gregory
had counted, made no effort to protect their
suzerain. In May Henry celebrated the Whitsun feast
outside the walls of Rome.

Gregory did not lose his courage even with the enemy
at his gate. The Romans were faithful to him, and Henry,
who saw no chance of besieging the great city successfully,
was forced to retreat northwards by the feverish heat of
summer. He retired to Lombardy, where his War between Henry and Gregory, 1081-1084.
position was unassailable. Next year he was back
again before the walls of Rome, but the occupation of Tivoli was his greatest success. In 1083
a third attack gave him possession of the Leonine city, but
even in this extremity Gregory would listen to no talk of
conciliation. 'Let the king lay down his crown and make
atonement to the Church,' was his answer to those who
besought him to come to terms. In the early months of
1084 Henry invaded Apulia and kept in check the Normans,
who at last were making a show of helping the Pope. In
March he appeared for the fourth time before Rome. This
time the Romans opened their gates, and Gregory Coronation of Henry by Guibert, 1084
was closely besieged in the castle of St. Angelo.
A synod was hastily summoned, which renewed
his deposition and excommunication. On Palm
Sunday, 1084, Guibert was enthroned, and on Easter Day
he crowned Henry Emperor at St. Peter's.

Gregory sent from the castle of St. Angelo an urgent
appeal for help to Robert Guiscard. During the troubles
of the last few years, Robert's obligations to his The Normans come to Gregory's help, 1084.
suzerain had weighed very lightly upon him, but
Henry's invasion of Apulia and the certain ruin
of the Normans in Naples if the Pope succumbed,
at last brought him to decided action. Hastily abandoning
his Greek campaign, Robert crossed over to Italy, and in May

advanced to the walls of Rome with a large and motley army, in which the Saracens of Sicily were a prominent element. Henry, who had no force sufficient to resist, quitted Rome, and soon crossed the Alps.   The Romans tried in vain to defend their city from the Normans.   After a four days' siege treason

Sack of Rome. opened the gates. Rome was ruthlessly sacked, whole quarters were burned down, hideous massacres and outrages were perpetrated, and thousands of Romans were sold as slaves.   The Normans then marched home.   Gregory could not remain in the desolate city, and followed them to Salerno.   The Antipope kept his Christmas amid the ruins of Rome, but soon abandoned the city for his old home at Ravenna.   Gregory now fell sick at Salerno.   The few faithful cardinals strove to console him by dwelling on the

Death of Gregory in exile, 1085. great work which he had accomplished. 'I set no store by what I have done,' was his answer. 'One thing only fills me with hope. I have always loved the law of God and hated iniquity.   Therefore I die in exile.' He passed away on 25th May 1085.   Less than two months afterwards, Robert Guiscard died at Corfu.

For a year after Gregory's death, the Papacy remained vacant.   At last, in May 1086, the cardinals, profiting by the Antipope's return to Ravenna, met at Rome and forced the Papacy on the unwilling Desiderius, Abbot of Monte Casino. The new Pope (who assumed the name of Victor III.), was a

Victor III., 1086-1087. close friend of Gregory's and strongly attached to his ideals. But he was too old and too weak to take up Hildebrand's task, and three days after his election he strove to avoid the troublesome dignity by flight to Monte Casino.   Next year he was with difficulty prevailed upon to return to Rome to receive the tiara.   But the partisans of the Emperor and of the Countess Matilda fought fiercely for the possession of Rome, and Victor again retreated to his monastery, where death ended his troubles three days after his return (16th September 1087).   Next time the cardinals fixed upon a Pope of sterner stuff.   Driven from Rome by the Antipope, they made their election at Terracina on 12th March 1088. Their choice fell upon the son of a baron of Champagne named Odo, who had lived long at Cluny as monk and sub-prior, and then served the Roman Court as cardinal-bishop of Ostia. Urban II. (this was the title he took) was a man of ability and force Urban II., 1088-1099. of character, as ardent as Hildebrand for the Cluniac ideals, but more careful of his means of enforcing them than the uncompromising Gregory. He made closer his alliance with the Normans, and, thanks to the help of Duke Roger, Robert Guiscard's son and successor, was able to return to Rome and remain there for some months. But the troops of the Antipope still held the castle of St. Angelo, and Urban soon found it prudent to retire. He mainly spent the first years of his pontificate in southern Italy under Roger's protection.

Meanwhile, papalists and imperialists fought hard in northern Italy. Germany was now tolerably quiet, and Henry could now devote his chief energies to Italy, which he revisited in 1090. But Urban Henry re-visits Italy, 1090. united the German with the Italian opposition to the Emperor by bringing about a politic marriage between the Countess Matilda and the young son of Welf or Guelf, Duke of Bavaria, the Emperor's most powerful adversary in Germany. Despite this combination, Henry's Italian campaigns between 1090 and 1092 were extraordinarily successful. Matilda's dominions in the plain country were overrun, and her towns and castles captured. But she held her own in her strongholds in the Apennines, rejected all compromise, and prepared to fight to the last. Henry met his first check when he was driven back in disgrace from an attempted siege of Canossa.

The papalists were much encouraged by Henry's defeat. Soon after they persuaded his son Conrad, a weak and headstrong youth, to rise in revolt against his father. Half Lombardy fell away from father to son. Before the year was out, Conrad re- Conrad of Franconia, Anti-Cæsar, 1093. ceived the Iron Crown at Milan, and Urban ventured back to

Rome. Worse was to follow. Henry's second wife, Praxedis of Russia (Bertha had died in 1087), escaped from the prison to which her husband had consigned her, and taking refuge with the Countess Matilda, gave to the world a story of wrongs and outrages that destroyed the last shreds of the Emperor's reputation. In high glee at the progress of his cause, Urban set out on a lengthened progress that reminds us of the memorable tours of Leo IX. After a long stay in Tuscany, he crossed the Apennines early in 1095, and held a great synod at Piacenza, at which the laws against simony and married clerks were renewed, while the Empress publicly declared her charges against Henry, and ambassadors from the Eastern Emperor pleaded for help, against the growing power of the Seljukian Turks. In the summer Urban crossed the Alps, and remained for more than a year in France and Burgundy, being everywhere received with extraordinary reverence. In November 1095 he held a largely attended synod at Clermont in Auvergne. Not content with his quarrel with the Emperor, he here fulminated excommunication against Philip I. of France, on account of his adultery with Bertrada, Countess of Anjou. But the famous work of the Council of Clermont was the proclamation of the First Crusade. Nothing shows more clearly the strength and nature of the papal power than that this greatest result of the universal monarchy of the Church should have been brought about at a time when all the chief kings of Europe were open enemies of the Papacy. Henry IV. was an old foe, Philip of France had been deliberately attacked, and William Rufus of England was indifferent or hostile. But in the eleventh century the power of even the strongest kings counted for very little. What made the success of Urban's endeavour was the appeal to the swarm of small feudal chieftains, who really governed Europe, and to the fierce and undisciplined enthusiasm of the common people, with whom the ultimate strength of the Church really lay.

Marginal notes:

Urban's Councils at Piacenza and Clermont, 1095.

The proclamation of the First Crusade, 1095.

Flushed with his success at Clermont, Urban recrossed the Alps in September 1096. Bands of Crusaders, hastening to the East, mingled with the papal train as he Urban's again traversed northern Italy. Rome itself now return to opened its gates to the homeless lord of the Italy, 1096. Church. In 1097 Henry IV. abandoned Italy in despair. He restored the elder Welf to the Bavarian duchy, Henry and easily persuaded the younger Welf to quit abandons his elderly bride, and resume his allegiance to Italy, 1097. the Emperor. Conrad was deprived of the succession, and his younger brother Henry crowned king at Aachen on taking an oath that he would not presume to exercise royal power while his father was alive.

Urban was now triumphant, save that his Norman allies were once more giving him trouble, and the castle of St. Angelo was still held for the Antipope. He accordingly Urban II. in again visited southern Italy, and won over Count southern Roger of Sicily, by conceding the famous privi- Italy, 1098. lege to Roger and his heirs that no papal legate should be sent into their lands without their consent, but that the lords of Sicily should themselves act as legates within their dominions. In October 1098 the Pope held a synod at Bari, Synod at restored to Catholicism by the Norman conquest Bari. in 1071. There, with a view to facilitating the Crusade, the great point of difference between the Eastern and Western Churches—the Procession of the Holy Ghost—was debated at length. Among the prelates attending the council was Anselm of Canterbury, exiled for upholding against William Rufus the principles which Urban had asserted against the Emperor and the King of France. Urban, who had been politic enough not to raise up a third great king against him by supporting Anselm, atoned for past neglect by the deference he now showed to the 'Pope of the second world.' As the council broke up, the good news came that the castle of St. Angelo had at last been captured. Urban returned to Rome and devoted himself to the work

of the Crusade.   On 29th July 1099 he died suddenly.
It was his glory that the struggle of Pope and Emperor,
which had absorbed all the energies of Gregory VII.,
sank during his pontificate into a second place.

Death of Urban II., 1099.

Though he abandoned no claim that Gregory
had made, he had the good fortune to be able to put himself
at the head of crusading Europe, while his opponent shrank
into powerless contempt.   Next year the Antipope followed
Urban to the grave.   With Clement, the schism as a real force
died.   Three short-lived Antipopes pretended to carry on his
succession until the death of the Emperor, but no one
took them seriously.   With the flight of the last pretender in
1106, formal ecclesiastical unity was again restored.

Driven out of Italy by his rebel son, Henry IV. found
Germany equally indisposed to obey him.   Both north and
south of the Alps, the real gainers in the long struggle had
been the feudal chieftains, and Germany, like Italy, was
ceasing to be a single state at all.   In 1101 the
rebellious Conrad died at Florence, bitterly re-
gretting his treason.   Henry's main object now was to restore
peace to Germany, and to effect a reconciliation with the
Church.   But the new Pope, Paschal II. (Rainerius
of Bieda, near Viterbo, elected August 1099),
renewed his excommunication, and was as unbending as his
predecessors.   Before long Paschal was able to extend his
intrigues into Germany, and in 1104 the young
King Henry raised the Saxons in revolt against
his father, and was recognised as king by the
Pope.   But the Emperor had no spirit left for a fresh contest.
At Coblenz he threw himself at his son's feet. begging only
that his own child should not be the instrument of God's
vengeance on his sins.   The young king asked for forgiveness,
and promised to give up his claims when his father was
reconciled with the Church.   The Emperor trustfully disbanded his soldiers, and was promptly shut up in prison by
his twice-perjured son.   On 31st December 1105 he formally

Death of Conrad, 1101.

Paschal II., 1099-1118.

Revolt of the young King Henry, 1104.

abdicated at Ingelheim, and abjectly confessed his offences against the Church. He was told that absolution could only come from the Pope in person, and that it was a boon that he was allowed his personal freedom. He fled from Ingelheim to Cologne, where the goodwill of the citizens showed him that he still had friends. From Cologne he went to Aachen, and from thence to Liége, whose bishop, Otbert, supported him. The Duke of Lorraine declared himself for him, and help was expected from Philip of France and Robert of Flanders. Henry now declared that his abdication was forced on him, but offered any terms, compatible with the possession of the throne, to get absolution from the Pope. But on 7th August 1106 he died at Liége, before the real struggle between him and his son was renewed. The enmity of the Church grudged rest even to his dead body. The Bishop of Speyer refused to allow the corpse of the excommunicate to repose beside his ancestors in the stately church which he himself had built, and for five years it lay in an unconsecrated chapel. *Death of Henry IV., 1106.*

On 5th January 1106 Henry v. was crowned for the second time at Mainz. The first months of his reign were disturbed by his father's attempt to regain power. When he was at last undisputed King of Germany, he found that his cold-blooded treachery had profited him very little. The Investiture Contest was still unsettled. Between 1103 and 1107 Anselm of Canterbury, restored to his see by William Rufus' death, had been carrying on a counterpart of the contest with Henry I. of England. But the personal animosities which had embittered the continental struggle were absent, and the dispute did not, as abroad, involve the larger questions of the whole relations of Church and State. It was easy, therefore, to settle it by a satisfactory compromise. Yet at the very moment when Henry had agreed to lay aside investiture with ring and staff, the envoys of Henry v. were informing Paschal that their master proposed to insist upon his traditional rights in the matter. *Henry V., 1106-1125.*

The result was that the continental strife was renewed with all its old bitterness.

For two years Henry was engaged in wars against Hungary and Bohemia. In 1110 he resolved to visit Italy to receive the imperial crown, and to re-establish the old rights of the Empire. Besides a numerous army, he took with him 'men of letters able to give reasons to all comers' for his acts, among whom was an Irish or Welsh monk named David, who wrote, at his command, a popular account of how the king had gone to Rome to extract a blessing from the Pope, as Jacob had extorted the angel's blessing.[1] He found Italy too divided to offer effectual resistance. The Countess Matilda was old, and Paschal was no great statesman

Henry's
Roman
journey.
Paschal re-
nounces the
Temporali-
ties of the
Church,
1111.
like Gregory or Urban. Early in 1111 the king's army approached Rome. The Pope, finding that neither the Romans nor the Normans would help him, sent legates to Sutri to make terms. Even in his supreme distress he would not give up lay investitures or freedom of elections; but he offered to the king that if he would accept those cardinal conditions of papal policy, he would renounce for the Church all its feudal and secular property. It was a bold or rash attempt to save the spiritual rights of the Church by abandoning its temporalities, lands, and jurisdictions. Henry naturally accepted an offer which put the whole landed estates of the Church at his disposal, and reduced churchmen to live on tithes and offerings—their spiritual sources of revenue. Only the temporalities of the Roman see were to be excepted from this sweeping surrender.

On Sunday, 12th February, St. Peter's church was crowded to witness the hallowing of the Emperor by the Pope. Before

Tumult at
Henry's
Coronation.
the ceremony began the compact was read, and the Pope renounced in the plainest language all intervention in secular affairs, as incompatible with the spiritual character of the clergy. A violent tumult at

---

[1] See the life of David [d. (?) 1139], Bishop of Bangor, by the present writer, in the *Dictionary of National Biography*, vol. xiv. pp. 115-117.

once arose. German and Italian bishops united to protest vigorously against the light-heartedness with which the Pope gave away their property and jurisdictions, while carefully safeguarding his own. The congregation dissolved into a brawling throng. The clergy were maltreated, and the sacred vessels stolen. The coronation was impossible. The king laid violent hands on Pope and cardinals, and the mob in the streets murdered any Germans whom they happened to come across. After three days of wild turmoil, Henry quitted the city, taking his prisoners with him. After a short captivity, Paschal stooped to obtain his liberty by allowing Henry to exercise investitures and appoint bishops at his will. 'For the peace and liberty of the Church,' was his halting excuse, 'I am compelled to do what I would never have done to save my own life.' In return Henry promised to be a faithful son of the Church. On 13th April Paschal crowned Henry with maimed rites and little ceremony at St. Peter's. Canossa was at last revenged. Henry returned in triumph over the Alps, and solemnly interred his father's remains in holy ground at Speyer.

Henry's triumph made a deep impression on Europe. The blundering Pope had betrayed the temporal possessions of the clergy, and the necessary bulwarks of the freedom of the spiritual power. The event showed that there were practical limits even to papal infallibility. Paschal was as powerless to retreat from the position of Hildebrand, as he had been to renounce the lands of all prelates but himself. The clergy would not accept the papal decision. In France a movement to declare the Pope a heretic was only stayed by the canonist Ivo of Chartres declaring that the Pope, having acted under compulsion, was not bound to keep his promise. The Italians gladly accepted this way out of the difficulty. Paschal solemnly repudiated his compact. 'I accept,' he declared, 'the decrees of my master, Pope Gregory, and of Urban of blessed memory; that which they have applauded I applaud, that which they have granted I grant, that which they have condemned I condemn.'

Triumph of Henry over Paschal.

Paschal repudiates his concessions.

Even in Germany Henry found that he had gained nothing by his degradation of the Pope. The air was thick with plots and conspiracies. His most trusted councillors became leaders of treason. Adalbert, Archbishop of Mainz, his chief minister, formed a plot against him and was imprisoned. The Saxons rose once more in revolt under their new Duke Lothair of Supplinburg. Friesland refused to pay tribute. Cologne rose under its Archbishop, and Henry found that he was quite unable to besiege it successfully. The nobles who attended his wedding with Matilda of England at Mainz, profited by the meeting to weave new plots. Next year the citizens of Mainz shut up the Emperor in his palace while he was holding a Diet, and forced him to release their Archbishop.

Conspiracies against Henry in Germany.

Affairs in Italy were even more gloomy. In 1115 the Countess Matilda died, leaving all her vast possessions to the Holy See. If this will had been carried out, Paschal would have become the greatest temporal power in Italy. Henry therefore crossed the Alps in 1116, anxious, if not to save Matilda's allodial lands, to take possession of the fiefs of the Empire which she had held. In 1117 Henry occupied Rome and crowned his young English wife Matilda. Even in his exile Paschal had not learnt the lesson of firmness. He died early in 1118, before he had even definitely made up his mind to excommunicate Henry.

Death of the Countess Matilda, 1115, and of Paschal II., 1118.

The new Pope, John of Gaeta, a monk of Monte Casino, who took the name of Gelasius II., was forced to flee from Rome as the Emperor was entering it. Henry now took the decisive step of appointing a Pope of his own. Burdinus, Archbishop of Braga, was in some fashion chosen by a few cardinals, and took the name of Gregory VIII. Gelasius at once excommunicated both Antipope and Emperor. He soon managed to get back to Rome, whence, however, he was again expelled by the malignity of local faction rather than the

Gelasius II. (1118-1119).

The Antipope Burdinus.

influence of the Emperor. He now betook himself to Marseilles by sea, and, after a triumphant progress through Provence and Burgundy, held a synod at Vienne. On his way thence to Cluny he was smitten with pleurisy, reaching the monastery with difficulty, and dying there on 18th January 1119.

Guy, the high-born Archbishop of Vienne, was chosen somewhat irregularly by the cardinals who had followed Gelasius to Cluny. He had long been conspicuous as one of the ablest upholders of Hildebrandine ideas in the dark days of Paschal II. The son of William the Great, Calixtus II. Count of imperial Burgundy (Franche-Comté), (1119-1124). he was the kinsman of half the sovereigns of Europe. He was, moreover, a secular (the first Pope not a monk since Alexander II.), and accustomed to diplomacy and statecraft. He resolved to make an effort to heal the investiture strife, and with that object summoned a council to meet at Reims. Henry himself was Negotiations tired of the struggle. He practically dropped his for a Antipope, and gave a patient hearing to the agents settlement. of the Pope, who came to meet him at Strasburg. These were Hugh, Abbot of Cluny, and the famous theologian, William of Champeaux, now Bishop of Châlons. The two divines pointed out to Henry that the King of France, who did not employ investiture, had as complete a hold over his bishops as the Emperor, and that his father-in-law, Henry of England, who had yielded the point, was still lord over his feudal vassals, whether clerks or laymen. For the first time perhaps, the subject was discussed between the two parties in a reasonable and conciliatory spirit. Before the king and the divines parted, it was clear that a compromise on the lines of the English settlement was quite practicable.

On 20th October 1119, Calixtus II. opened his council at Reims. Louis VI. of France, who had married the Pope's niece, was present, and the gathering of prelates Council of was much more representative than usual. Next Reims, 1119. day the Pope went to Mouzon, a castle of the Archbishop

PERIOD II. K

of Reims, hoping to meet the Emperor.   But their agents
haggled about details, and mutual suspicion threatened to
break off all chance of agreement.   Deeply mortified, and

Breakdown   without having seen the Emperor, Calixtus
of the   went back to the council, where the old decrees
negotiations. against simoniacs and married clerks were renewed, and where a canon forbidding laymen to invest
a clerk with a bishopric or abbey was passed.   But this
canon marked a limitation of the Pope's claim.   While
Hildebrand had absolutely forbidden all lay investiture,
Calixtus was content to limit the prohibition to the investiture with the spiritual office.   Yet, before the council
separated, the excommunication of Emperor and Antipope
was solemnly renewed.   An agreement seemed to be further
off than ever.

No Pope ever stood in a stronger position than Calixtus
when in February 1120 he at last crossed the Alps.   He was

Triumph of   received with open arms by the Romans, and with
Calixtus in   more than ordinary loyalty by the Normans of
Italy, 1120.   the south.   The Antipope fled before him, and
was soon reduced to pitiful straits in his last refuge at Sutri.
At last he was captured, contemptuously paraded through
the Roman streets, and conveyed to prison, until, after peace
had been restored to the Church, he was released to end his
life obscurely in a monastery.

The Emperor saw that he had been too suspicious at
Mouzon, and again wished to retire with dignity from a con-

Negotiations   flict in which his prospects of complete triumph
renewed,   had long utterly vanished.   Things were now
1121.   going better in Germany.   In 1121 a Diet was
held at Würzburg, at which Henry made peace with Adalbert of Mainz and the Saxon rebels.   It was agreed to
refer the investiture question to a German council under
the Pope's presidency, and direct negotiations with Rome
were renewed.   The Pope's words were now exceedingly
conciliatory.   'The Church,' he said, 'is not covetous of

royal splendour. Let her enjoy what belonged to Christ, and let the Emperor enjoy what belonged to the Empire.'

On 8th September 1122 the council met at Worms. Calixtus, after some hesitation, did not attend himself, but sent Lambert, Bishop of Ostia, as his legate. Lambert was a citizen of Bologna, who had been arch-deacon of his native town, and had learnt from its rival schools of Canonists and Civilians [see pp. 217-220] the principles involved in both sides of the controversy. He soon turned his knowledge and skill to good account. The council lasted little more than a week. The Emperor at first stood out for his rights, but was soon persuaded to accept a compromise such as had been suggested previously at Strasburg. On 23rd September the final Concordat of Worms was ratified, which put an end to the investiture strife. Two short documents, of three weighty sentences each, embodied the simple conditions that it had cost fifty years of contest to arrive at. 'I, Henry,' thus ran the imperial diploma, 'for the love of God, the holy Roman Church, and of the lord Pope Calixtus, and for the salvation of my soul, abandon to God, the holy Apostles Peter and Paul, and to the holy Catholic Church all investiture by the ring and the staff, and I grant that in all the churches of my Empire there be freedom of election and free consecration. I will restore all the possessions and jurisdictions of St. Peter, which have been taken away since the beginning of this quarrel. I will give true peace to the lord Pope Calixtus and to the holy Roman Church, and I will faithfully help the holy Roman Church, whenever she invokes my aid.' The papal diploma was even shorter. 'I, Calixtus, the bishop,' said the Pope, 'grant to Henry, Emperor of the Romans, that the elections of bishops and abbots in the kingdom of Germany shall take place in thy presence without simony or violence, so that if any discord arise, thou mayst grant thy approbation and support to the most worthy candidate, after the counsel of the metropolitan and his suffragans. Let the prelate-elect receive from thee by thy sceptre the property and the immunities of his office, and let him fulfil the obligations to thee arising from these. In other parts of the Empire let the prelate receive his regalia six months after his consecration, and fulfil the duties arising from them. I grant true peace to thee and all who have been of thy party during the times of discord.'[1]

Less clear in its conditions than the English settlement, the Concordat of Worms led to substantially the same result.

Character of the compromise. The Emperor gave up the form of investiture, and public opinion approved of the temporal lord no longer trenching on the domain of the spirituality by conferring symbols of spiritual jurisdiction. But the Emperor might maintain that, if he gave up the shadow, he retained the substance. The Henries had not consciously striven for mere forms, but because they saw no other method of retaining their hold over the prelates than through these forms. The Pope's concessions pointed out a way to attain this end in a way less offensive to the current sentiment of the time. As bishops and abbots, spiritual men could not be dependent on a secular ruler. As holder of fiefs and immunities, the clerical lord had no more right to withdraw himself from his lord's authority than the lay baron. By distinguishing between these two aspects of the prelate's position, the Concordat strove to give Cæsar what was Cæsar's and God what was God's. The investiture question was never raised again. But in its broader aspect the investiture question was only the pretext by reason of which Pope and Emperor contended for the lordship of the world, and sought respectively to trench upon the sphere of the other. The Concordat of Worms afforded but a short breathing-space in that controversy between the world-Church and the world-State—between the highest embodiments of the spiritual and secular swords—that

[1] The text of the Concordat of Worms, and many other German constitutional documents, can be studied in Altmann and Bernheim's useful *Ausgewahlte Urkunden zur Verfassungsgeschichte Deutschlands im Mittelalter.*

was still to endure for the rest of the Middle Ages. Contemporary opinion, unapt to distinguish between shadow and substance, ascribed to the Papacy a victory even more complete than that which it really won. After all, it was the Emperor who had to yield in the obvious question in dispute. The Pope's concessions were less clear, and less definite. The age looked upon the Concordat as a signal triumph for the Roman Church. Henceforth the ideals of Hildebrand became part of the commonplaces of European thought. *Practical triumph of the Church.*

Neither Henry nor Calixtus long survived the Concordat of Worms. Calixtus died at Rome in December 1124, having previously held a council in the Lateran, where the Concordat was confirmed, and a vast series of canons drawn up to facilitate the establishment of the new order of things. He strove also to restore peace and prosperity in Rome, which had long lain desolate and ruinous as the result of constant tumults. Short as was his reign, it could yet be said of him that in his days there was such peace in Rome that neither citizen nor sojourner had need to carry arms for his protection. He had not only made the Papacy dominate the western world; it even ruled, if but for a time, the turbulent city that so often rejected and maltreated the priest whom all the rest of the world revered. *Death of Calixtus II., 1124.*

Henry V.'s end was less happy. The war had taught him that the real ruler of Germany was not himself but the feudal aristocracy. He planned, in conjunction with his English father-in-law, an aggressive attack on Louis VI. of France, but he utterly failed to persuade his barons to abandon their domestic feuds for foreign warfare. He fought one purposeless campaign as the ally of England. In May 1125 he died on his way back, at Utrecht, saddened, disappointed, and worn out before his time. He is one of the most unattractive of mediæval Emperors. Cold-blooded, greedy, treacherous, *Last failures and death of Henry V., 1125.*

violent, ambitious, and despotic, he reaped no reward from his treasons, and failed in every great enterprise he undertook. Yet despite his constant misfortunes, the strong, hard character of the last Salian Emperor did something to keep up the waning fortunes of the Empire, and the unity of the German kingdom.

CHAPTER VII

THE EASTERN EMPIRE AND THE SELJUKIAN TURKS
(912-1095)[1]

The Macedonian Dynasty—Constantine VII. and his Co-regents—Condition
of the Eastern Empire in the Tenth Century—The Conversion of the
Slavs—Break-up of the Mohammedan East—Period of Conquest and
Glory—Nicephorus Phocas and John Zimisces—The Russian War—
Basil II. and the Bulgarian War—Decline of the Macedonian House—
Zoe and Theodora—Cærularius and the Schism of East and West—Rise
of the Seljukians—Contrast of Turks and Arabs—Decline of the Eastern
Empire—Manzikert—Alexius Comnenus and his House—The last phase
of the Eastern Empire.

SITUATED on the borderland that divided two civilisations,
the unchanging Eastern Empire represented the East to the
Latins and the West to the Arabs and Turks. During the
first half of the tenth century there was a strange
contrast between the East Roman state and the
rest of the world. In the West the Empire of
Charles the Great had fallen, and few could yet
see that a new order was gradually evolving out
of the chaos into which the world seemed plunged. In the
East the Caliphate had ceased to represent the political
unity of Islam. A process of strife and disintegration had
broken up the Mohammedan no less that the Latin world.
Between these two seething and troubled regions, the

Contrast between the Eastern Empire and the rest of the world.

[1] The best English book on later Byzantine history is Finlay's *History
of Greece*, which covers the whole period. Oman's *Byzantine Empire*
('Story of the Nations') is a readable summary. Gibbon's *Decline
and Fall* must always be consulted. Schlumberger's *Un Empereur
byzantin au Xe siècle, Nicéphore Phocas*, and *L'Epopée byzantine à la fin
du Xe siècle*, present attractive aspects of the subject in a recent light.

Empire of Constantinople lived on its quiet, self-contained, stationary, orderly life. No vital dangers from without threatened its existence. Catholics and Mohammedans were alike too busy with their own affairs to make serious attacks upon its boundaries. The long-lived dynasty of the Macedonians continued to rule over a state that had little history. The inglorious calm bore witness to a standard of civilisation, order, and prosperity that, with all its faults, could be found nowhere else in the world.

Basil the Macedonian had founded, in 867, the ruling house, which was to reign at Constantinople for a hundred and ninety years. The long reign of his weak and pedantic son, Leo VI., the Philosopher (886-912), had attested the care and stability with which Basil had laid the foundations of the new dynasty. Under Leo's son Constantine VII., Porphyrogenitus (912-959), the same quietude that had marked Leo's time continued with hardly a break. A boy of seven when he was called to the throne, Constantine VII. showed, as he grew up, such lack of firmness and practical wisdom that his whole reign has been described as a long minority. Co-regents did most of the work of governing. For the first year his uncle, Alexander, Leo VI.'s brother, acted as joint-emperor. For seven years after his death (913-919) a commission of regency ruled, not too successfully, in the name of the little Emperor. Severe defeats from Simeon, king of the Bulgarians, made this rule unpopular. The grand admiral Romanus Lecapenus now became successively the prime minister, the father-in-law, the colleague, the master of Constantine. In December 919 Romanus, already Cæsar, was crowned joint-emperor with his son-in-law, and for twenty-five years he practically ruled the state as he would. Though aged, weak, and incompetent, Romanus managed to protect himself from numerous court conspiracies, and hoped to secure the permanence of his influence by associating three of his sons as colleagues in the Empire, and

The Macedonian dynasty.

Constantine VII., 912-959.

Romanus I., 919-945.

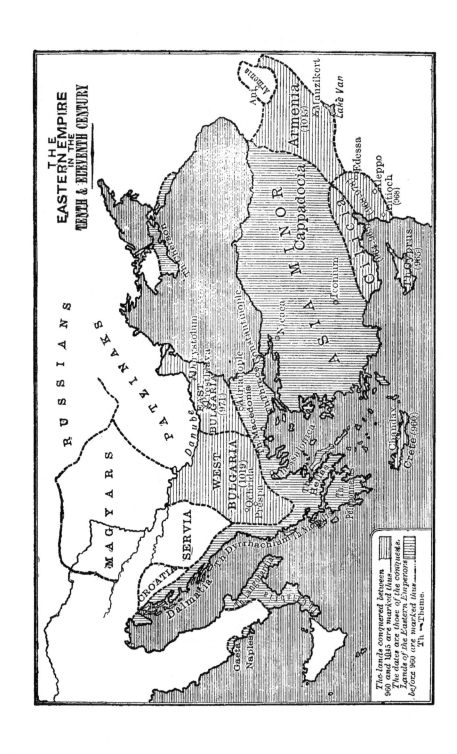

THE
EASTERN EMPIRE
IN THE
TENTH & ELEVENTH CENTURY

RUSSIANS

MAGYARS

PATZINAKS

Danube

Thessalon...

Adrystolum

EAST
BULGARIA
(971)

WEST
BULGARIA
(1019)

Ochrida

Presba

SERVIA

CROATIA

Dalmatia and Dyrrhachium

ITALY

Gaeta
Naples

Macedonia

Adrianople

Constantinople

Th. Macedonia

Salonica

Th.
Hellas

Th.
Peloponnesus

Cherbax

Crete (960)

ASIA MINOR

Cappadocia

Nicaea

Iconium

Armenia
(1015)

Manzikert

Lake Van

Edessa

Aleppo
(968)

Antioch
(968)

CILICIA
(965)

Cyprus
(965)

Anti-
Taurus

Armenia

The lands conquered between
960 and 1035 are marked thus
The dates are those of the conquests.
Lands of the Eastern Emperors
before 960 are marked thus
Th.—Theme.

procuring for another the patriarchate of Constantinople. But the quarrels of sons and father gave the friends of Constantine a chance of removing them all. The sons of Romanus drove their father into a monastery. The outraged public opinion of the capital involved the sons in the same fate. In 945, when already nearly forty years old, Constantine VII. became Emperor in fact as well as in name.

Constantine was a shy, nervous, studious man, who had amused himself, during his long exclusion from power, by dabbling in nearly every science and art. He painted pictures, composed music, designed churches, and wrote books on such different subjects as agriculture, veterinary science, history, geography, tactics, politics, and court etiquette. Weak and hesitating though he was, his good nature, amiability, love of justice and moderation made him a respectable ruler for quiet times. Under him the consolidation of the imperial despotism, under the hereditary rule of the Basilian house, was completed. The suppression of the legislative power of the senate, and the destruction of the old municipal system by Leo the Philosopher, had removed the last barriers to the autocracy of the Emperor. This despotism the well-drilled administrators carried out so well on the traditional lines, that it was no great matter that the Emperor himself was a bookish recluse. The *Basilica*, the revised code of law in Greek, now assumed its final form, and with the change which its introduction involved in the language of the law courts and statutes, the Latin tongue ceased to have any practical utility to the East Romans. The works of Constantine give us a picture of the Empire of his time. In his longest book he dwells with loving care on the elaborate and pompous court etiquette which environed the majesty of the Emperor, and struck awe into the hearts of the barbarians. In a more summary manner he wrote 'On the administration of the Empire,' and 'On the *Themes*' into which it was divided. In the latter book he described not

Sole rule of Constantine VII., 945-959.

Condition of the Empire in the tenth century.

merely the actual Empire, but districts like Sicily and Crete, which had long fallen into the hands of the Saracen, or, like the interior provinces of the Balkan peninsula, had been absorbed by Slavs and Bulgarians.

Asia Minor was now the chief stronghold of the Eastern Empire. The population had been recruited by Christian refugees from the Mohammedan lands farther east, and had therefore become more decidedly Oriental, but it was strenuous, industrious, and warlike. The whole of the peninsula was included in the Empire, save the south-eastern district of Cilicia between the Taurus and the sea. But the loss of Tarsus was more than compensated for by the inclusion of a larger portion of western Armenia within the Empire, by reason of the Armenians, despite their obstinate adherence to the Monophysite heresy, seeing in incorporation with the Empire their only chance of salvation from Islam. In the Balkan peninsula the districts actually ruled by the Emperor were much less extensive. The western and central parts were still 'Slavonia,' and even the Peloponnesus was largely peopled by Slavonic tribes, at best tributary, and often practically independent. But the settlement of the Magyars in Pannonia (895) had pushed the Bulgarians more to the south, and now not only were the lands between Danube and Rhodope Bulgarian, but this nation encroached largely on the Slavs in the lands south of the Balkans. The result left little for the Romans save long strips of coast territory. Nowhere in Europe did their power penetrate far inland. Adrianople was at best the border town of the Greeks. A few miles inland from Thessalonica the Bulgarian rule began. The Bulgarians separated the theme of Hellas, which included Thessaly and the lands south down to Attica, from the themes of Nicopolis and Dyrrhachium that crept along the coast of Epirus. Scattered scraps of islands and coastlands in Dalmatia almost connected the Empire with its Venetian dependency. The theme of Cherson included the south coast of the

Crimea, but this outpost of Greek civilisation was hardly more
directly ruled from Constantinople than Venice itself. The
lesser islands were still Greek, but Cyprus alone of the great
islands remained under the Empire, and that was soon lost.

Italy.   In south Italy there only remained the misnamed
theme of Lombardy, including the heel of the
boot, of which the capital was Bari, and the theme of Calabria,
cut off from its neighbour province by the Lombard princes
of Salerno, who held the low-lying grounds at the head of
the Gulf of Taranto. Such a widely scattered dominion was
hard to rule and harder to defend. But each theme was
under the government of a *strategos*, who subordinated the
civil to the military administration. A large standing army
of mercenaries—largely Norsemen—well drilled and equipped,
enabled the Greeks to cultivate their fields and carry on their
commerce in peace. The trade between east and west was
still entirely in Greek hands. Even an exhaustive fiscal system
could not cut off these sources of wealth. But if the Greek
Emperors taxed unwisely and unmercifully, they helped commerce by upholding the integrity of the coinage. The gold
Byzants of the Emperors were the common medium of ex-
change among merchants, and, amidst all the vicissitudes of
palace revolutions, were never seriously depreciated in value.
The manufactures of Greece still commanded the markets.

Constanti-   Constantinople was still the greatest city in the
nople.   world, and excited the astonishment of all the barbarians who visited it. Its administration, poor-law system, and
philanthropic organisations anticipated much that we are apt
to regard as exclusively modern. Liutprand, the Lombard
bishop, has left a record of the profound impression made on
him by its wonders. Even in the twelfth century, when its
splendours were somewhat decayed, it was still unique. The
Franks of the Fourth Crusade could not believe that there
was so rich a city, until they saw its high walls and strong
towers, gorgeous palaces, lofty churches, and vast extent.
Though Thessalonica was also a famous place of trade, the

interests of the capital were becoming so great as to absorb unduly those of the provinces. This was partly counteracted by the growth of a great landholding aristocracy, which approached the character of the feudal noblesse of the west, save that it never attained any political influence over the centralised despotism of the Basileus. Nor were the Letters and arts and literature forgotten. Constantine VII.'s Arts. example was followed by a crowd of men of letters, and the labour of compilers like Suidas have preserved for us much of what we know of more ancient times. A new school of romance writers showed more original genius. Painting, architecture, and all the arts wonderfully revived.

Constantinople now became again a source of civilisation to ruder peoples. The Servians and other Slavs called upon its help to protect them from the terrible Simeon The Con-of Bulgaria. In the ninth century, Methodius version of and Cyril had converted the Southern Slavs to the Slavs. Orthodox Christianity. In the tenth, Greek missions, radiating from the great monasteries on Mount Athos, secured the Christianising of Bulgaria. In the next century, the distant Russians received their faith from the same source. Thus Slavonic Europe became for the most part Orthodox rather than Catholic. Never was the influence of Constantinople more widely felt than in carrying out this great work.

The restful if inglorious age of Leo the Philosopher and Constantine Porphyrogenitus gave the Greek Empire time to recruit its energies for the more stirring times of their successors. From 959 to 1025 a period of conquest and military glory followed upon the quiet times that we have described. Before the change came over the spirit of the Eastern Empire, the best chances of aggression in west and north had slipped unnoticed away. During the reigns of Leo and Constantine, the Saxon kings of the Germans were building up a great state in Germany and Italy, and before long the growing material prosperity of Italy was to raise up commercial rivals who ultimately tapped the very springs of Byzantine trading supremacy. The consolidated and Christianised states of the barbarians on the north were less likely to send out bands of conquerors and marauders, but were harder to conquer than their heathen and savage fathers. But the east was sinking into worse confusion than ever. The old political and religious unity of Islam was a thing of the past. What spirit now re-

Changes in the Moham-medan East.
mained to the Mohammedan world was to be found in North Africa under the Fatimite Caliphs of Cairoan, or in Spain under the Ommeyad Caliphs of Cordova. While these rebels and schismatics still showed some remnants of the old conquering energy of Islam, the orthodox Abbasside Caliphs of Bagdad were sunk in indolence and decay. Their provinces successively revolted. The Bowides, sons of a Persian fisherman, captured Bagdad in 945, and ruled Persia and lower Mesopotamia for more than a century as the *Emirs-ul-Omra* of the puppets that they still allowed to pretend to act as successors of the Prophet. In Egypt and southern Syria, the Ikshidites, a Turkish dynasty, now established themselves. But the only Mohammedan power that now actually met the Eastern Empire on its south-eastern frontier was that of the Hamdanides, who about 930 occupied northern Mesopotamia and afterwards conquered northern Syria and Cilicia. This dynasty split into two and was represented by the Ameers of Aleppo and Mosul. The new Mohammedan states were all the precarious creations of adventurers' swords, and were generally at war with each other.

The divisions of the east gave the Emperors at Constanti-nople the opportunity which their predecessors had neglected

Romanus II., 959-963.
in the west. Under the son and successor of Constantine VII., Romanus II. (959-963), the work of reconquest began. Crete since the ninth century had been occupied by Spanish Moors, and had been the centre of piratical attacks on Greek commerce, that had threatened the

Conquest of Crete.
prosperity of the islands of the Ægean and the regularity of the food-supply of the capital. Even Leo and Constantine had made feeble efforts to subdue the

corsairs, but their expeditions against Crete had been utter failures. In 960 Romanus II. sent Nicephorus Phocas with a strong force to atone for the blunders of his predecessors. Within a year the capture of the Saracen stronghold of Chandax brought about the complete conquest of the island. The Saracens were enslaved or expelled, and missionary monks soon succeeded in winning back the Greek population to the faith of their fathers, which many had been forced to reject for the religion of their conquerors. Nicephorus followed up this great triumph by attacking the Hamdanad Ameer of Aleppo. He crossed the Taurus into Cilicia, and in another spirited campaign restored many strong places to the Empire.

In 963 Romanus II. was cut off prematurely, leaving his young widow Theophano to act as regent for the two infant sons, Basil II. (963-1025) and Constantine VIII. (963- 1028) who now became joint-emperors. But the triumphs of Nicephorus Phocas had won him such a position that in a few months he associated himself with them in the Empire and married their mother Theophano. By this ingenious combination of hereditary succession with the rule of the successful soldier, the quiet transmission of power was combined with the government of the fittest. For six years Nicephorus Phocas (963-969) ruled the Empire in the name of his two step-sons and soon procured for them new triumphs. His first measure was to improve the condition of the army, and with this object he piled up new taxes, and, almost alone among Greek Emperors, stooped to debase the coinage. A fierce soldier in a nation of monks and merchants, Nicephorus soon got into conflict with the Church, as well as the trading class. He issued a sort of law of mortmain to check the foundation of new monasteries, and kept important sees vacant to enjoy their revenues. At last in his zeal for war against Islam, Nicephorus wished the Church to declare that all Christians who died in war against the infidel were martyrs to the

Basil II., 963-1025, and Constantine VIII., 963-1028.

Nicephorus Phocas, 963-969.

Nicephorus' military reforms and quarrel with the Church.

Christian religion.   The Patriarch replied that all war was unchristian, and that a Christian who killed even an infidel enemy in war, deserved to be denied the sacraments.   The Emperor made himself hated by the mob of the capital by suppressing the costly shows and amusements which the court had hitherto provided for their diversion, while the officials were scandalised at his disgust for the childish ceremonies that hedged about his domestic life.   Conscious of his unpopularity, he fortified his palace and lived as much as he could in the camp, where he enjoyed unbounded popularity with the soldiers.

In a series of vigorous campaigns against the Ameer of Aleppo, the Emperor sought to consolidate his former efforts

His con- as general by winning back all Cilicia and
quests.   north Syria to the Empire.   In 964 and 965 he completed the conquest of Cilicia, sending the brazen gates of Tarsus and Mopsuestia to adorn the imperial palace at Constantinople.   In 965 Nicetas, one of his generals, reconquered Cyprus.   In 968 Nicephorus again took the field and overran northern Syria.   Aleppo, the residence of the Ameer, was easily captured ; the Ikshidite realm, now on the verge of dissolution, was overrun ; Damascus paid tribute to avoid destruction ; and Antioch was captured by assault on a snowy night in winter.

While thus occupied with the east, Nicephorus did not neglect the west.   He projected the famous marriage between

His western the future Emperor, Otto II. and Theophano, the
policy.   daughter of Romanus II. and his own step-daughter [see page 34], hoping thus to strengthen the Byzantine power in south Italy.   But the terms of the alliance were hard to settle, and no agreement could be arrived at during Nicephorus' lifetime.   Liutprand, Bishop of Cremona, sent to negotiate the match, left Constantinople in disgust, and vented his spleen in the famous, but not very flattering, account of Constantinople and its court to which we have already referred.   Soon hostilities broke out between Otto the Great

and Nicephorus in southern Italy, without any very permanent results. Nicetas, the conqueror of Cyprus, failed signally in an attempt to win Sicily from the Saracens. There were wars with the northern barbarians that produced equally little effect.

Nicephorus was a brave soldier, sprung from a stock of warlike Cappadocian landowners, who changed few of his habits even on the throne. He was cultured enough to write a book on the art of war, but he had neither the policy or pliancy for the intrigues of a despotic Oriental court. The uprightness he showed in preserving intact his step-sons' position as Emperors met with an evil requital from their mother. Theophano hated and feared her stern, uncouth, unsympathetic husband. She conspired with her lover, John Zimisces, nephew of Nicephorus, a dashing cavalry soldier and the most capable of his captains. On the night of 10th December 969 the Empress's woman admitted Zimisces and a select band of confederates into Conspiracy of the castle. They found the Emperor sleeping on Theophano. the floor after his soldier's fashion, and promptly stabbed him to death. The murderers at once proclaimed John Zimisces Emperor, and court and city alike accepted the results of the despicable intrigue that had robbed the Empire of its strongest man. John I. Zimisces reigned from 969 to 976. John I. The brutal treachery which gained him the throne Zimisces, was somewhat atoned for by the energy and vigour 969-976. he displayed in the possession of power. He was mean enough to make Theophano the scapegoat of his crime, and, instead of marrying her, shut her up in a monastery. After this he did little that was not commendable. By way of penance he devoted half his private fortune to the poor peasantry round Constantinople and to building a great hospital for lepers. Like Nicephorus, he studiously respected the rights of his young colleagues, the sons of Romanus II., and legiti- matised his rule by wedding their sister Theodora. The negotiations for the marriage of the other sister, Theophano,

with Otto the Saxon were now resumed and completed
in 972, Theophano taking with her to Germany Byzantine art and the temporary friendship of east and west.   John
The Russian abandoned the civil administration to the dexterous
war.   chamberlain Basilius, and soon found in the
Russian war an opportunity to revive the exploits of his uncle.
The valour of Rurik and his Vikings had, before this, united
the Slavs of the east into a single Russian state, of which the
centre was Kiev, and which, though constantly threatening
the Byzantine frontiers, had since the conversion of Olga,
baptized at Constantinople in the days of Constantine vii.,
began slowly to assimilate Byzantine Christianity and civilisation.   But Olga's son Sviatoslav (964-972) had refused to incur
the ridicule of his soldiers by accepting his mother's religion.
He was a mighty warrior who, in alliance with the Hungarians,
overran and conquered Bulgaria, and in 970 crossed the
Balkans and threatened Adrianople.   In 971 John Zimisces
took the field against him, and a desperate campaign was
fought in the lands between the Danube and the Balkans.
Like true sons of the Vikings, the Russians fought on foot in
columns, clad in mail shirts and armed with axe and spear.
John's army was largely composed of heavy cavalry, and its
most efficient footmen were slingers and bowmen.   In two
great battles at Presthlava and Dorystolum (Silistria), Russians
and Greeks fought under conditions that almost anticipate the
battle of Hastings, and in both cases the result was the same.
After long resisting the fierce charges of the Greek horsemen,
the close array of the Russians was broken up by a hail of
arrows and stones, and the lancers, returning to the charge,
rushed in and completed the discomfiture of the enemy.
After the second battle, Sviatoslav and the remnants of his
host stood a siege within Silistria, until a treaty was drawn up
by which they promised to go home, on being supplied with
enough corn to prevent them plundering by the way.   For
the future, they were to renew the old commercial treaties
and leave the Empire in peace.   Intercourse between Russia

and Constantinople was quickly renewed, and henceforth Russian or Norse mercenaries, the famous Varangians, began to form an important part of the imperial armies. Thus the Empire was relieved from the pressure of her most dangerous foe in the north, and again acquired the command of the interior of the Balkan peninsula. Bulgaria, already conquered by Sviatoslav, was reduced to obedience, while its titular king lived as a pensioner at Constantinople. Flushed with these brilliant successes, John again turned his arms against the Saracens of Syria, who had won back many of Nicephorus' conquests, including Antioch. He reconquered Antioch, though only with great difficulty; his capture of Edessa prepared the way for the occupation of the upper valley of the Euphrates; and many holy relics passed from Moslem to Orthodox custody. In the midst of his triumphs John died suddenly in 976, poisoned, it was said, by the crafty eunuch Basilius, who feared that his wealth had excited the Emperor's jealousy.

Basil II. (976-1025), the elder of Constantine VII.'s sons, was now twenty years of age when, under the guidance of Basilius he proceeded, after his brother-in-law's death, to govern as well as reign. But the over- Basil II.'s wealthy minister soon fell from power. Basil personal rule, soon showed the same austere Roman type of character as Nicephorus Phocas, and became a brave soldier, a skilful general, and a capable administrator. His chief object of internal policy was the repression of the great landholding families of Asia, which were the only barrier left against the imperial despotism; and, after a long struggle, he succeeded in accomplishing their ruin. Under the legitimate Basilian Emperor, the military glories of the fortunate adventurers were fully continued. The great event of his long The Bulgarian reign is the Bulgarian war. The occupation War. of Bulgaria by John I. was too rapid to be permanent, and, except in the lands between the Danube and Balkans, had been merely nominal. Under a new Bulgarian king, named Samuel, the unconquered regions of the west made a long and determined effort for freedom. Even the Slavs—the chief inhabitants of these regions—followed Samuel to the field; and by fixing his capital first at Prespa and afterwards at Ochrida, in the highlands bordering on Albania and Macedonia, he threatened alike Dyrrhachium and Thessalonica Year after year, Samuel's motley following plundered and devastated the rich plains of Thessaly and Macedonia. Even in the north all the Greeks could do was to hold Silistria, and a few fortresses, and keep a tight hold of the Balkan passes. In 981 Basil first took the field in person, but his early campaigns were but little successful. Samuel at last invaded southern Greece ; but though he devastated the Peloponnesus from end to end, he failed to capture any of the larger cities (996). On his way back, he was surprised by the Greek general Uranus, and escaped with infinite difficulty and the complete destruction of his army. Basil now took the offensive. In 1002 he captured Vidin, a triumph that resulted in the gradual reconquest of Bulgaria proper. But Samuel still held out long in the fastnesses of Mount Pindus. Bit by bit Basil won back the hill castles that were the centres of the Slavo-Bulgarian power. At last, in 1014, Basil gained a decisive victory, taking prisoner some 15,000 Bulgarians. The grim Emperor put out the eyes of all his captives, save that he spared one eye to every hundredth man, and sent the mutilated wretches back to their king at Ochrida under the guidance of their one-eyed leaders. Samuel, on seeing his subjects' plight, fell senseless to the ground, and died two days later. His brave son Gabriel continued the contest, but was soon murdered by his cousin Ladislas, who usurped the throne. In despair Ladislas took the bold step of besieging Dyrrhachium, hoping thus to open communications with Basil's enemies beyond sea ; but he perished in the siege, and with him fell the last hopes of the kingdom of Ochrida. In 1018 the work of conquest was completed, and Basil celebrated his victory by a splendid triumph at Constantinople. The populace greeted the relentless conqueror with the surname of 'Slayer of the Bulgarlans' [βουλγαροκτόνος]. Basil then turned his arms against the Armenians, but his success in pushing forward his eastern frontier at the expense of a Christian kingdom did not atone for the impolicy of weakening a natural ally against the Mohammedans. Conscious perhaps of this, he prepared to divert his arms against the infidel by a new expedition to Sicily. Death overtook him in the midst of his preparations, when he was sixty-eight years old, and had reigned for sixty-two years. No Emperor since Justinian had succeeded so well in enlarging the bounds of the Empire. But with him expired all the glories of the Macedonian dynasty.

Basil II. left no son, and his brother Constantine VIII. (1025-1028) therefore became sole Emperor. Though nominal Emperor since 963, Constantine had never taken any real part in political affairs, and he was now too old and careless to change his habits. He lived like an Oriental despot, secluded in his palace, amusing himself with musicians and dancing-girls, while six favourite eunuchs of the household relieved him from all cares of state. Great indignation was excited among the nobles, but Basil II. had humbled them too thoroughly for them to take any effective action. However, Constantine died in 1028, before he could do much harm. He was the last man of the Macedonian house, and his only heirs were his daughters Zoe and Theodora, under whose weak and contemptible rule the Basilian dynasty came to an end.

Sole rule of Constantine VIII., 1025-1028.

From 1028 to 1054 the husbands and dependants of Zoe governed the Byzantine Empire. First came Romanus III. (1028-1034), to whom she had been married at her father's deathbed. But Zoe was hard, greedy, and self-seeking, and allowed her husband little real share of power. On his death she married a handsome young courtier, Michael IV. the Paphlagonian (1034-1041), who, though an epileptic invalid,

Zoe and her husbands. Romanus III., 1028-1034.

did good work against the Saracens before his early death in 1041. His brother John the Orphanotrophos [minister of charitable institutions], a monk and a eunuch, who had procured Michael's marriage, conducted the internal government with great dexterity and cunning, but the time of his rule marks an epoch of deterioration in Byzantine finance. By constantly increasing the taxes, and devising more arbitrary and oppressive methods for their collection, he did much to sap the foundations of the industrial supremacy of the Empire.

Michael IV., 1034-1041.

It was thought necessary always to have a male Emperor. When Michael IV. died, Zoe, already more than sixty years of age, took three days to decide whether she should wed a third husband or adopt a son. She chose the latter course; but Michael V. (1041-1042), nephew of Michael IV., whom she raised to this great position, speedily proved ungrateful and unworthy, and was deposed, blinded, and shut up in a monastery. Having failed with her son, Zoe chose as her third husband Constantine Monomachus (an hereditary surname), who was soon crowned as Constantine IX. (1042-1054). The new Emperor was an elderly profligate, who had only consented to wed Zoe on condition that his mistress should be associated with her in the Empire. Their rule was most disastrous. It saw the expulsion of the Greeks from Italy by the Norman conquest of Apulia and Calabria. It saw the consummation of the fatal policy of weakening Armenia, at a moment when the rise of the Seljukian Turks was again making Islam aggressive. It witnessed the impolitic imposition of taxes on the eastern subjects and vassals, who had hitherto defended the frontiers with their swords, but who henceforth were discontented or mutinous. It saw the final consummation of the schism of Eastern and Western Churches.

Michael V., 1041-1042.

Constantine IX., 1042-1054.

The Synod of Constantinople in 867 [see Period I., pp. 453-4], following upon the quarrel of Pope Nicholas I. and the Patriarch Photius, had already brought about the open breach of the Orthodox East and the Catholic West. Despite new rivalries between the Greek and Latin missions to the Slavs and Bulgarians, efforts had been made from time to time to heal the schism, and Basil II. negotiated with Rome, hoping to persuade the Pope to allow 'that the Church of Constantinople was œcumenical within its own sphere, just as the Church of Rome was œcumenical throughout Christendom.' But in 1053 Michael Cærularius, the Patriarch of Constantinople foolishly shut up the Latin churches and convents and wrote to the Latin bishops, bitterly reproaching them with their schismatic practices, and taking new offence in the Latin use of unleavened bread in the Eucharist. Mutual excommunications followed, and, at the very moment when Christendom had most need of union, the schism of East and West became inveterate.

The Schism of the Eastern and Western Churches.

Zoe died in 1050, and Constantine IX. in 1054. On his death, Zoe's sister Theodora, the last of the Macedonians, became Empress. Though old, she was strong and vigorous, and her long incarceration in a cloister gave her monastic virtues that contrasted strangely with the dissolute habits of Zoe. During her reign of three years the Empire enjoyed at least peace and repose. Her death in 1057 ended not ingloriously the famous dynasty that had since the days of Basil I. held the imperial throne. A new period of trouble now sprang from disputed successions and weak Emperors, at a time when the growth of the Seljukian power threatened the very existence of the Empire.

Theodora, 1054-1057.

The Turkish or Mongol tribes of Central Asia had long troubled from time to time the tranquillity of Europe. Among them were Attila and his Huns, but these fierce marauders passed away without leaving any permanent traces of their influence. Of the same stock were the Magyars, who, in 895, finally settled in Pannonia, and the Bulgarians, who, as we have seen, had

Rise of the Seljukian Turks.

even earlier taken possession of a large part of the Balkan peninsula. But the Magyars and Bulgarians by accepting Christianity made themselves permanent members of the European commonwealth. While Mongolian invasions such as these disturbed from time to time the peace of eastern Europe, similar invasions had terrified all the civilised nations of Asia as far as the Chinese frontier. But it was the Caliphate in its decline that began to stand in the most intimate relations with the Turks. The growing anarchy of the Arab Empire offered to the Turks a career as mercenaries, and a field for plunder and devastation. As the reward of their services, the Caliphs gave them what they could conquer from the Christians on the eastern frontiers of the Empire. A large Turkish immigration soon peopled the marches of the Caliphate with the fierce warriors from the north. As the Caliphs declined in power, the Turkish condottieri chieftains grew discontented with their pay, and set up military despotisms on their own account. Many of the petty states that grew out of the dissolution of the Caliphate had, like the Ikshidites in Syria, Turkish lords, and were kept together by Turkish arms. Early in the eleventh century the period of transition was over. The Turks became converts to Islam, and religious enthusiasm bound together their scattered tribes and directed their aims. A great Turkish invasion plunged all Asia in terror. In the extreme east Turks or Tartars established at Peking a Manchurian kingdom for northern China (1004). In the very same year, Mahmoud of Ghazni set up a great Turkish state in Afghanistan and India. A generation later, the Turks of the house of Seljuk began to threaten the thrones of western Asia.

The fame of Seljuk, the founder of a united Turkish state in Central Asia, is almost mythical. Under his son, the Seljukian house became great by crossing the Oxus and effecting the conquest of Khorassan. Under his grandson Togrul Beg, the Seljukians became the greatest power in Asia. Togrul first broke up the power of the descendants of Mahmoud of Ghazni, and then attacked the Bowides, and conquered Persia. In 1055 he crowned his career by the occupation of Bagdad, where he was welcomed as the deliverer of the phantom Caliphs from the tyranny of their Bowide Ameers, and was solemnly invested by them with their temporal power. Henceforth Togrul, the Sultan of East and West, posed as the defender of the faith, and the protector of the successor of Mohammed.

After the conquest of Bagdad, Togrul Beg attacked Armenia and threatened the Byzantine frontiers. He died in 1063, and in the very next year Alp Arslan, his nephew and successor (1063-1072), completed, by the capture of Ani, the capital, the subjugation of the unhappy Armenians. The Georgians were next enslaved; and, master of the Christian outposts of the East Roman realm, Alp Arslan turned his arms against the Empire itself.

The occupation of the rich plains of Asia in no wise changed the character of the Turks. They remained as they had ever been, soldiers and nothing more. Their old religions had died away as they came into contact with Islam, and in embracing the Mohammedan faith they obtained religious sanction for their ferocity and greed. But they never, like the Arabs, entered into the spiritual side of the faith. They rather received and retained the new religion, as a faithful soldier keeps the word of command of his general. They had no eyes for the brilliant fascination of Arab civilisation, such as was at that very time attaining its highest perfection in Mohammedan Spain. They appropriated what had gone before, but they never assimilated it or added anything of their own. The statecraft of the Arabs had no more attraction for them than the poetry, the romance, the lawgiving, the architecture, or the busy commercial life of Semitic Asia. When they had conquered they carelessly stood aside, and contemptuously allowed their vassals to live on their old life, save when, in occasional fits of fury, they taught that they were masters by hideous

Contrast between Turks and Arabs.

violence or promiscuous massacres.   But their hardiness won
an easy triumph over the soft and effeminate Arabs, and was
soon to win fresh laurels at the expense of the lax and corrupt
Christians of the East.   It was a day of ill omen for East and
West alike when the capture of Bagdad made the Turkish
soldier the type of Mohammedan conquest.   In the centuries when the Arab was the typical representative of
Islam, the desolation of Africa and Syria showed how
great were the evils that followed in the wake of Mohammedan conquest of Christian lands.   But in East and West
alike the triumphs of the Turk were unmixed evils, and the
strife of East and West assumed a new aspect when a barbarous and unteachable soldier, mighty only in destruction,
became the chief agent of Eastern advance.   It was no
longer the continuance of the struggle between Eastern and
Western civilisation that was as old as Marathon.   Henceforth it was a strife between the only possible civilisation and
the most brutal and hopeless barbarism.   Yet the superior
military efficiency of the Turk put an irresistible weapon into
his hands.   Since the days of Leo the Isaurian and Charles
Martel, the relations of the Eastern and Western worlds had
been almost stationary.   A new wave of Eastern aggression
now set in, to be followed in its turn by a period of Western
retaliation.   The Seljukian attacks on Armenia and the
Empire brought about the Nemesis of the Crusades and the
Latin kingdoms of the East.

The period of revolution and confusion that had followed
the extinction of the Basilian dynasty made the Empire little
Decline of   able to resist the Turkish assault.   It is as weari-
the Eastern   some as unprofitable to tell in any detail of the
Empire.   purposeless palace intrigues and provincial revolts,
that set up and pulled down Emperors in the dreary years
that followed the death of Theodora.   The first successor of
Michael VI.,   the last of the Macedonians was of her own
1057.   designation.   Michael VI., surnamed Stratioticus
(1057), was an aged and incompetent soldier, who within a

year succumbed to a revolt of the Asiatic nobles, who seated on the throne one of the most powerful of their number, Isaac I., Comnenus (1057-1059), but the hopes excited by him were rudely dispelled by a disease that drove him into a monastery to die. Another great Cappadocian magnate, Constantine X., Ducas (1059-1067), was now made Emperor. He was a pettifogging financier, who disbanded part of his troops and disheartened the rest by miserable and disastrous economies. In his reign the Seljukian assaults first became formidable. On his death in 1067, his widow Eudocia acted as regent for their son, the boy Emperor Michael VII. (1067-1078). Eudocia chose a second husband and co-regent in Romanus Diogenes (1068-1071), a Cappadocian noble, who had won a high reputation for brilliancy as a soldier, but lacked the prudence and policy necessary to a general. Romanus at once took the field against the Seljukian hordes, who were now devastating Cappadocia with fiendish cruelty, and had just captured Cæsarea and plundered the shrine of St. Basil. But the heavy Greek cavalry, with their formal drill and slow traditional tactics, were only a poor match for the daring valour and rapid movements of the swift light horse that constituted the chief strength of the Turkish army. At first Romanus won easy triumphs as the scattered bands of marauders retreated before his troops, without risking a battle. Alp Arslan changed his plans and lured Romanus into the Armenian mountains, where he was suddenly attacked by the whole Seljukian power.

The decisive battle was fought in 1071 at Manzikert, an Armenian town, to the north of Lake Van, which the Sultan had captured in 1070, and which Romanus now sought to reconquer. The Emperor had already many difficulties from the mixed army of mercenaries, that had no heart for the cause and a strong dislike to

[Side notes: Isaac I., Comnenus, 1057-1059. Constantine X., Ducas, 1059-1067. Michael VII., 1067-1078. Romanus IV., Diogenes, 1068-1071. Battle of Manzikert, 1071.]

discipline. With great impolicy he divided his army, and
marched with but a fraction of it against Manzikert. The
city was soon retaken, but by this time the whole force of
the Seljuks had drawn near. It was the first pitched battle
between Turks and Greeks, and, having misgivings of the result,
Alp Arslan showed some willingness to treat. But Romanus
impatiently prepared for battle. The fight was long and
fierce, until at last the bad tactics of the Emperor and the
treachery of some of his generals gave the Turks a hardly
won victory. The Greek army was destroyed, and Romanus
was wounded and made prisoner. The defeat is the turning-
point of Byzantine history. The hardy mountaineers of
Cappadocia were unable to hold out much longer. With the
loss of the land which had given birth to Nicephorus and
Zimisces, to the Comneni, the Ducasii, and to Romanus
himself, the best part of the Empire surrendered to barbarism.
Within a few years all the interior of Asia Minor had become
Turkish. In the very year of Manzikert, the capture of
Bari by the Normans cut off the last town that had been
faithful to the East Romans in Italy.

Alp Arslan magnanimously allowed Romanus Diogenes to
ransom himself from captivity, but the discredited soldier
only returned to Constantinople to be dethroned and imprisoned by John Ducas, uncle of Michael VII. His eyes
were put out so roughly that he died a few days later. With
him perished the last of the heroes of the Eastern Empire.
Confusion and weak rule at Constantinople facilitated the
Turkish advance. Many provinces revolted, and famine
followed in the train of war. What revenue still flowed in was
spent upon court luxuries and popular games. The Turks burnt
the Asiatic suburbs of the capital, and in 1074 Michael VII.
made a treaty with Suleiman, the general of Malek Shah,
who had now succeeded Alp Arslan, by which he conferred
on him the government of all the imperial provinces which
were actually in his possession. Suleiman established himself
at Nicæa, the most westerly of his conquests, and soon

assumed the state of an independent prince. In 1078 Michael was dethroned, and meekly abandoned the Empire for the bishopric of Ephesus. His supplanter, Nice- Nicephorus phorus III. (1078-1081), was the most brutal, III., 1078-1081. lustful, and helpless of all the Emperors of this miserable time. Rebellions burst out on every side. At last Alexius Comnenus, a shrewd and wily soldier, whose sword had long protected the Emperor from other rebels, became a rebel himself. The army declared for him and chose him Emperor, and the treachery of some German mercenaries admitted him and his troops into the capital, which was brutally sacked. Nicephorus was driven into a monastery, and Alexius reigned in his stead.

With the new Emperor the worst troubles were over. Some sort of hereditary succession reappeared, and the Com-nenian dynasty long occupied the throne of the Alexius Eastern Empire. But the Empire was reformed Comnenus, on a narrower and less heroic mould. The ability 1081-1118. of Alexius was partly seen in his energy; but subtlety and deceit, which often took the shape of self-defeating cunning, were his favourite weapons, and in his dexterous The Com-pursuit of personal and family aims, he often lost nenian sight of broader issues. It was characteristic of dynasty and the transi-the later age of the Byzantine Empire that the tion to the founder of the new house should have the dis- last phase of similar characteristics of courage and craft, and the East that Alexius' literary daughter, Anna Comnena, in Empire. eulogising her father's exploits, regards his courage and craft as equally laudable. With him we enter that latest stage of East Roman history to which the term 'Byzantine' may not unreasonably be applied as a term of reproach, and which perhaps justifies the contempt with which Gibbon and the older writers regarded all stages of East Roman history. The Empire became more 'Greek' in the narrower sense, and with its restricted limits became in a sense stronger by being more national and less cosmopolitan. But it lived a smaller, meaner life.　Henceforth it stood on the defensive, equally afraid of the Turk in the east and the Frank in the west.　Its territory gradually fell away, its civilisation became as stereotyped as that of China, its Church more superstitious and ignorant, its people more slavish and degraded.　It is no small praise to Alexius and his successors that they had the skill to keep some sluggish life in the inert mass, and, amidst the greatest difficulties, offer a brave and constant resistance for two more centuries to the greatest foes of civilisation that the world has seen in modern days.

At home, the first years of Alexius' reign were occupied in putting down the nobles and restoring the centralised despotism

Alexius and the East. of the Macedonians.　A whole series of rebellions was successfully suppressed, and order was restored even to the finances, though at the price of an unwonted depreciation of the currency that further imperilled the declining trade of the Greeks.　Another trouble was found in the growth of the fantastic heresies of the Paulicians and Bogomilians, which Alexius stamped out with the rigour of a monk.　Meanwhile, Alexius fought hard against the Seljukian Turks, and for the time prevented their further advance.　But the death of Malek Shah in 1092, and the struggles of his children for the succession, did more to remove the terror of Turkish conquest than the arms and diplomacy of Alexius. Alexius had also to fight against the Slavs, and the Patzinaks of the north, and to face grave trouble from the west.　With the conquest of Bari in 1071, Robert Guiscard and his

Alexius and Robert Guiscard. Normans had absorbed the last of the Byzantine dominions in Italy.　Robert now resolved to cross the Straits of Otranto and win fresh booty and dominions from a foe that, since Manzikert and Bari, seemed predestined to speedy destruction.　Only fifteen years before, William the Norman had crossed the English Channel and won a great kingdom from a warlike usurper.　In 1081 another Norman duke crossed another narrow strait, and sought to win the crown and kingdom of another successful soldier-prince. Robert laid siege to Dyrrhachium [Durazzo], the chief centre of the Byzantine power on the Adriatic, and Alexius hastened to its succour. The bad generalship of the Greeks made easy the victory of the invaders. The Varangian heavy-armed infantry of the imperial guard vigorously withstood for a time the charge of the feudal cavalry from the west. But as at Hastings the Norman archers broke up the enemy's ranks, so that the best troops of Alexius were defeated before the rest of the Greek army could take the field. These latter were soon put to flight, and Alexius rode off from the scene of his defeat. Dyrrhachium surrendered, and the Normans crossed the mountains into Macedonia and Thessaly. Italian politics [see pages 135-136] took Robert back to Italy, but his son Bohemund efficiently filled his place. Alexius now called upon his cunning to remedy the disasters that had arisen from his courage. By avoiding general engagements and carrying on a destructive petty warfare, he managed to wear out the Normans. In 1084 he brilliantly raised the siege of Larissa, and Bohemund returned to Italy. In 1085 the death of Robert Guiscard relieved Alexius of any immediate fear of Norman aggression.

The war with the Normans had taught the Eastern Empire to know and to fear the warriors of the West. Within ten years of the end of the struggle with the Guiscards, Alexius sent envoys to the West imploring Latin help against the Turks, and in 1095 his ambassadors appeared before Urban II. Before long, East and West seemed likely to unite to urge a holy war against the Turks. With the preaching of the First Crusade a new epoch set in for the Byzantine Empire.

The appeal for Western help.

GENEALOGY OF THE MACEDONIAN DYNASTY.

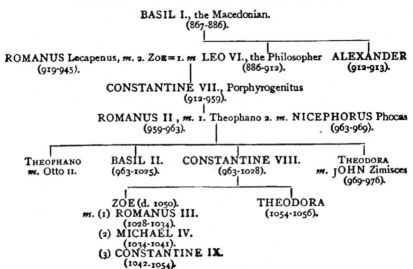

BASIL I., the Macedonian.
(867-886).

ROMANUS Lecapenus, *m.* 2. ZOE = 1. *m* LEO VI., the Philosopher　ALEXANDER
(919-945).　　　　　　　　　　　　　　　　(886-912).　　　　　　(912-913).

CONSTANTINE VII., Porphyrogenitus
(912-959).

ROMANUS II , *m.* 1. Theophano 2. *m.* NICEPHORUS Phocas
(959-963).　　　　　　　　　　　　　　　(963-969).

THEOPHANO　　　BASIL II.　　CONSTANTINE VIII.　　THEODORA
m. Otto II.　　(963-1025).　　(963-1028).　　　　*m.* JOHN Zimisces
　　　　　　　　　　　　　　　　　　　　　　　　(969-976).

ZOE (d. 1050).　　　　　　THEODORA
m. (1) ROMANUS III.　　(1054-1056).
(1028-1034).
(2) MICHAEL IV.
(1034-1041).
(3) CONSTANTINE IX.
(1042-1054).

CHAPTER VIII

THE EARLY CRUSADES

AND THE LATIN KINGDOM OF JERUSALEM (1095-1187)[1]

Early Pilgrimages to Palestine — The Turkish Conquest — Causes of the Crusades—Urban II. and the Council of Clermont—Leaders of the First Crusade—Alexius and the Crusaders—Results of the Crusade—Organisation of the Kingdom of Jerusalem and its dependent States — The Military Orders—Rise of the Atabeks—Fall of Edessa—The Second Crusade—Decline of the Kingdom of Jerusalem—Power of Saladin—Fall of Jerusalem.

THE piety of the Middle Ages, ever wont to express its spiritual emotions in concrete shape, had long found in pilgrimages to holy places a favourite method of kindling its religious zeal and atoning for past misdeeds. Of all pilgrimages, the most meritorious was that to the sacred spots where Christ had lived His earthly life and where the Christian faith first arose. From the days of St. Jerome, Jerusalem was the chief centre of holy travel; and from the days of Helena, the mother of Constantine, faithful Christians had sought to identify and consecrate the exact places of the Lord's birth, suffering, and resurrection. A great Christian

Early Pilgrimages to Palestine.

---

[1] The best short book on the Crusades in English is Archer and Kingsford's _The Crusades_ ('Story of the Nations'). Kugler, _Geschichte der Kreuzzüge_ (Oncken's Series), is a fuller but dry survey of the whole subject. H. von Sybel's _History and Literature of the Crusades_ (translated from the German) is one of the earliest of modern critical works. Mr. Archer's article in the _English Hist. Review_, iv. 89-105, determines some points. Gibbon's Chapters LVIII. and LIX. should always be read. Rohricht's _Geschichte des Konigreichs Jerusalem_ is invaluable for the internal history.

Basilica, built by Helena's pious care, marked the site of the
Holy Sepulchre, and men believed that divine agency had led
to the discovery of the True Cross on which Jesus had suffered.
As long as the Roman Empire remained in its integrity, pilgrimages to the Holy Land were safe and easy. Even the conquest
of Syria by the Caliph Omar did not make them impossible.
A noble mosque—the mosque of Omar—was built on the site
of the Jewish Temple, but the custody of the Holy Sepulchre
and the other sacred spots remained in Christian hands, and
the places themselves were treated with respect and reverence
by the tolerant Arabs, to whom Jerusalem was a city as venerable as to the Jew or Christian. All through the early Middle
Ages the swarm of pilgrims continued. The risks of the
journey through the lands of Islam increased the merit of
the act. But with the break-up of the great Caliphate, the
holy places became for the first time dangerous to the
Christian wayfarer. In the second third of the tenth century
Jerusalem was ruled by the fanatical Ikshidites (934-969),
but in 969 the Fatimite Caliphs of Cairoan conquered
Egypt and Syria, and for a time pilgrimages again became
easy. The Fatimites were Shiites, and their dissensions from
the orthodox Sunnites made them perforce tolerant of other
creeds. Only the mad Caliph El Hakim (996-1021), who
contemplated the destruction of the Holy Sepulchre, stayed
for a time the influx of the faithful. The religious revival that
flowed from Cluny, and the greater peacefulness of western
Europe, led to a vast throng of pilgrims during the seventy
years that succeeded El Hakim's death. The fierce Fulk
the Black of Anjou thrice visited the holy places. Robert,
Duke of Normandy, abandoned his son William to go on
pilgrimage in 1035. In 1064 Archbishop Siegfried of Mainz
headed a band of 7000 penitents to Jerusalem. The conversion of the Hungarians under St. Stephen again opened up
the land route through the Danube valley and the Greek Empire, which men preferred to the stormy sea swarming with
Saracen pirates.

The growth of the Seljukian power again stopped the flow of Christian pilgrims to Jerusalem. Here as elsewhere the Turkish period of conquest marked the beginning of the worst of evils for the once Christian lands of the East. Asia Minor, the centre of the East Roman Empire, became a desolate waste ruled by Turkish plunderers. In 1076 the expulsion of the Fatimites from Jerusalem left the custody of the holy city to the Turks. The legend of Peter the Hermit expresses the indignation of western Europe when the few wanderers who got back told terrible tales of wrongs suffered and blasphemies witnessed from the infidel lords of the Sepulchre of Christ. But the stories of pilgrims, though they did much to kindle the indignation of Europe against Turkish rule in Palestine, did not of themselves account for the movement to redeem it. The preaching of Peter the Hermit, fruitful though it was, is not in authentic history the cause of the First Crusade. The Crusades were the work of the Popes at the instigation of the Eastern Emperor

Though, after the death of Malek Shah, the Seljukian monarchy split up into many rival powers, the danger of Turkish advance was still great. The direct rule of the Seljuks was henceforth limited to Persia, while Sultans of Seljukian blood established themselves lords of Kerman, Syria, and Roum. The Seljuks of Syria now ruled the Holy Sepulchre. The descendants of Suleiman, the conqueror of Nicæa, carved out a separate power in the inland parts of Asia Minor, called the kingdom of Roum [*i.e.* Rome], whose capital Nicæa was not one hundred miles from Constantinople, and whose limits extended to the waters of the Sea of Marmora. Some fragments of the Armenian race profited by this break-up to re-establish their freedom in the mountains of the Taurus. But Kilidj Arslan, the Sultan of Roum, was almost as threatening to Alexius as Alp Arslan had been to earlier Emperors. Fear of the lords of Nicæa, rather than a zeal for the holy

places, led Alexius to apply for help to the West, and rouse
the Westerns to defend the Greek Empire, by dwelling on
the desolation of Jerusalem.

There was no strong political power in western Europe to
which Alexius could appeal.   The Empire was drifting asunder
under the rule of Henry IV., and France was hopelessly
broken up into a mass of feudal states, hardly recognising
the authority of Philip I.   The Roman Church alone
was sufficiently vigorous and representative to help him.
Already Michael VII. had sent similar requests to Gregory
VII., who had caught eagerly at the prospects of a holy
war against the Turks, but the expulsion of Islam was
so united in his mind with the necessity of ending the
Greek and Armenian schisms, that it was not an unmixed
evil to the Eastern Empire that the Pope was too much
occupied at home to embark seriously upon the undertaking.   Yet it is a fact of no small significance that Gregory,
who created the mediæval Papacy, was also the first Western
to whom a Crusade seemed a practicable thing.   His ally,
Robert Guiscard, shared his eastern projects, but the campaign
at Durazzo showed how little the fierce Norman distinguished between the schismatic and the infidel.

Alexius' envoys appeared before Urban II. at the Council of
Piacenza, and at Clermont a few months later the active French
Urban II. Pope preached with extraordinary force and
and the fervour a holy war against the infidel.   The vast
Council of crowd received the Pope with unmeasured en-
Clermont, thusiasm.   'It is the will of God,' resounded from
1095. churchman and layman alike the answer to Urban's appeal.
Thousands pledged themselves to fight against Islam, and
Urban himself distributed the crosses which the armed pilgrims
were to bear as their special badge, and which gave the holy
wars the name of Crusades.   Preachers, like Peter the Hermit,
stirred up the passion of the multitude, and before the
lords and knights were ready, huge swarms of poor pilgrims
gathered together in northern France and the Rhineland,

under the leadership of Peter himself and of a French knight called Walter the Penniless. These disorganised hordes either perished on the long land journey through Hungary and Greece, or fell easy victims to the first encounter with the Turks of Roum, but their misordered zeal showed how the movement had touched the heart of Europe.

The great kings of the West took no part in the First Crusade. The Emperor and the King of France had incurred the papal anathema, the King of England was a profligate blasphemer, and the Kings of Spain had enough crusading work at their own gates. The highest class that was affected by the Pope's preaching was that of the feudal magnates of the second rank, and especially the barons of France and the adjacent French-speaking Lotharingia and Burgundy. These were the lands which had been the chief home of the Cluniac movement, and this was the class to which the Pope looked for allies in his struggle against the mighty kings of the earth. The most dignified potentate to take the cross was Raymond of Saint-Gilles, Count of Toulouse and Marquis of Provence, the greatest of the lords of southern France. Of the north French magnates, Hugh, Count of Vermandois, King Philip's brother, was the highest in rank and position. After him came Stephen, Count of Blois and Chartres, the son-in-law of William the Conqueror, and the father of an English king and of a line of Counts of Champagne and Blois. Robert, Duke of Normandy, left the care of his dominions to his more astute brother, and accompanied his brother-in-law. His cousin, Count Robert II. of Flanders, the son of an old pilgrim to Jerusalem, followed in his father's footsteps. Of the princes of the Empire the most important was Godfrey, Duke of Lower Lorraine, the son of the Count of Boulogne, and Ida, sister of the Duke Godfrey of Lower Lorraine who had so zealously supported the cause of Henry IV. In 1089 the Emperor had granted Godfrey his uncle's duchy, yet he is better known as Godfrey of Boulogne, and still oftener, through a curious misnomer, as

The leaders of the First Crusade.

Godfrey of Bouillon. His brothers Eustace and Baldwin, and his nephew Baldwin the younger, followed him to the Crusade. But the strongest of the Crusaders was Bohemund, the Italian Norman, the old enemy of Alexius Comnenus, who, after his father Robert Guiscard's death, being only possessed of the little lordship of Otranto, hoped to win eastern lands for himself. Other Crusaders besides Bohemund. had an eye on possible principalities to be conquered from the infidel. But with him went his nephew Tancred, a more chivalrous character. No great number of the higher clergy went on the Crusade. Conspicuous among them was the Pope's legate, Adhemar of Monteil, Bishop of Le Puy en Velay.

The Crusaders levied their followers in their own way, and went at different times and in different directions to

Alexius Comnenus and the Crusaders.

Constantinople, which Bishop Adhemar had indicated as their meeting-place. As swarm after swarm of mail-clad warriors marched through his dominions to his capital, Alexius Comnenus became very anxious as to their attitude to the Greek Empire. His hope had been to get an auxiliary Western force of knights, but the vast throng of Frankish chivalry, that had obeyed Pope Urban, alarmed him excessively, especially when he found his old enemy Bohemund among them. There was real danger lest the Crusaders should turn their arms against Constantinople instead of Nicæa and Antioch, and realise by force Hildebrand's ideal of a union of the churches, before the attack was made on the infidel. Greed and religious zeal combined to inspire them to turn against the opulent and schismatic capital. But the craft and ingenuity of Alexius served him in good stead, and in the end he persuaded all the leaders to take oaths of fealty to him, hoping thus to retain the overlordship of any districts they might conquer from the Turks. He then gave them facilities for crossing into Asia.

The Crusaders now entered into infidel ground. Nicæa, the capital of Kilidj Arslan, was taken in June 1097, and

next month the army of the Sultan was defeated at Dory-
læum. These successes secured Asia Minor. After a long
and painful march the Taurus was crossed, and The march
in June 1098 Antioch was forced to surrender. through
Even after that the Christians were in a sorry Asia, and the
conquest of
plight from famine, and were almost blockaded in Jerusalem,
their new conquest by the army of Corbogha, 1097-1099.
Ameer of Mosul. The Bishop of Le Puy died, and after his
moderating influence was removed, disputes broke out,
especially between the Normans and the south French.
Many of the Crusaders, chief among whom was Stephen of
Blois, went home in despair. But the fancied discovery of
the Holy Lance, with which the Roman soldier had pierced
the side of Christ, revived the fainting energies of the
Crusaders, though at first the Normans declared that the
'invention' was a fraud of a chaplain of Raymond of
Toulouse. Corbogha was defeated in a great battle, and at
last the Christians entered the Holy Land. The divisions of
Islam facilitated their progress. A month after the capture
of Antioch, the Fatimites of Egypt had conquered Jerusalem,
which nevertheless resisted vigorously. Finally, on 15th July
1099, Jerusalem was stormed and, amidst hideous scenes of
carnage, the remnant of the crusading army attained its goal.
A new victory at Ascalon in August secured southern Palestine
from Egyptian assault.

The whole fate of the East seemed changed by the First
Crusade. The Sultanate of Roum was hemmed up in the
central and eastern parts of Asia Minor, while Results of
Nicæa and perhaps a third of Asia Minor went the Crusade.
back to the rule of Alexius. The little Armenian lordships of
the Taurus grew into a new Armenian kingdom in Cilicia,
strong enough to keep Turks and Saracens at bay. The Christians predominated in Syria, whence they soon threatened both
the Fatimites of Egypt and the Seljukian dynasty in Persia.
The Latin lordship of Edessa crossed the Euphrates, and
formed in the upper valley of that river a permanent check

to the lords of Mosul.   Despite national jealousies, and the still deeper ill-will of Catholic and Orthodox, Christianity had acted with wonderful unity of purpose, while Islam could not forget its petty feuds even in the face of the enemy. The exploits of Leo the Isaurian and Nicephorus Phocas were more than outdone by Alexius and his Western allies. Never since the days of Heraclius had the old limits of Rome's power in the East been so nearly maintained.

It remained to provide for the government of the conquered provinces.   All Syria was portioned among the victorious Latins.   Godfrey of Boulogne accepted the

The early difficulties of the Frankish conquerors. government of Jerusalem ; but he refused to wear a crown of gold in the city where Christ had worn a crown of thorns, and contented himself with the modest title of Baron and Advocate of the Holy Sepulchre.   Bohemund, the Norman, ruled northern Syria as Prince of Antioch, and Baldwin, brother of Godfrey, became Count of Edessa.   But these chieftains had at first so few followers that they held little more than the cities and castles that they garrisoned.   Up to Godfrey's death in 1100, the hold of the Christians on southern Syria was very slight.   Jaffa was their only port, and the road from Jaffa to Jerusalem was beset with Saracen brigands, and marked by ruined villages and unburied bodies.   At Antioch, Bohemund was in even worse straits.   In 1100 he was taken prisoner by the Turks, who next year besieged Antioch, where Tancred with difficulty defended the Christian cause.   Meanwhile a new crusade, mostly from Aquitaine, Germany, and Italy, had been almost annihilated in Asia Minor by long marches, thirst, hunger, and the arms of the Turks.   With the remnants, Raymond of Toulouse conquered Tripoli, and established himself in middle Syria. Meanwhile Bohemund was released, on an Armenian prince paying his ransom.   He then joined with Baldwin of Edessa on a distant expedition against Harran, but was badly beaten and forced in despair to return to Europe, where he again attacked his old enemy the Greek Emperor. Failing at a new siege of Durazzo, Bohemund was forced to become the vassal of the Eastern Basileus for Antioch. Baldwin of Edessa, a prisoner since the battle of Harran, made terms with the Ameer of Mosul, and joined with him in waging war against the Normans of Antioch. Yet, if the Crusaders were divided, the infidels were equally at cross-purposes. A constant stream of fresh pilgrims reinforced the scanty armies of the Latins, and their military superiority, both in pitched battles and in building and defending castles, stood them in good stead. Financial help came from the keen-witted Italian traders of Pisa, Genoa, and Venice, who found in the Latin conquests new outlets for their commerce, and who were now winning the trade of the Levant from the Greeks. Baldwin of Edessa, called after Godfrey's death to succeed him at Jerusalem, did not share his scruple against bearing the title of king, and showed such skill, both as warrior and statesman, that he became in a very real sense the founder of the kingdom of Jerusalem. Bit by bit the Saracens were expelled from the open country, and within the generation succeeding the First Crusade, an ordered political system was set up among the Latin principalities of Syria.

Under Baldwin I. (1100-1118) the crusading state attained its limits and its organisation. His nephew and successor, Baldwin II. (1118-1130), called like his uncle from Edessa to Jerusalem, was also a man of courage and character. Dying without sons, his daughter Millicent's husband, Fulk, Count of Anjou (1130-1143), became the next king. Under him the Latin state reached its zenith, and gave him no reason to repent his preference for his Eastern kingdom rather than his Western county. After him, his son by his first wife, Geoffrey (the father of our Henry II.), became Count of Anjou, while, unluckily for Jerusalem, his two sons by Millicent, Baldwin and Amalric, were mere children. With them the decline begins.

The crusading lords, accustomed only to the forms of

government that prevailed at home, reproduced in the Latin states of Syria the strict feudalism of western Europe. Feudalism required a nominal head, and the King of Jerusalem

Organisation of the kingdom of Jerusalem and its dependent states. stood to the Latin princes as the King of early Capetian France stood to his vassals, having outside his own dominions nothing more than a vague supremacy over three great feudatories ruling over substantially independent states. The Prince of Antioch and the Counts of Tripoli and Edessa thought they had made a great concession in acknowledging his superiority at all, and were constantly at war with each other and with their suzerain. But each of the four Frankish princes had, like their Western counterparts, by no means unrestricted authority, even within their own peculiar territories. All four states were divided into fiefs, whose holders exercised the regalian rights that seemed proper to a baron. Within the kingdom of Jerusalem proper there were twelve such lordships, four of which were the 'great baronies' of Jaffa-Ascalon, Kerak-Montreal, Galilee, and Sidon. These in turn had their feudatories, and the powerful lordship of Ibelin, though but a mesne tenancy, overshadowed the double county of Jaffa and Ascalon. Beyond the royal domain, which centred round the capital and the towns of Tyre and Acre, the Kings of Jerusalem had little real authority. For the administration of their realm a customary code grew up, which, in days when the Latin lordships had waned almost to nothing, was embodied in the Assizes of Jerusalem, more valuable as an ideal picture of a perfect feudal state than as a description of what really prevailed at any one time in Syria. Being an artificial creation, the Latin state was more fully feudal than the kingdoms of the West, where the system had grown up naturally, and where there were still survivals of older forms of polity. Each lord held by the tenure of constant military service, and every effort was made to prevent the accumulation of fiefs in the same hands lest it should diminish the military

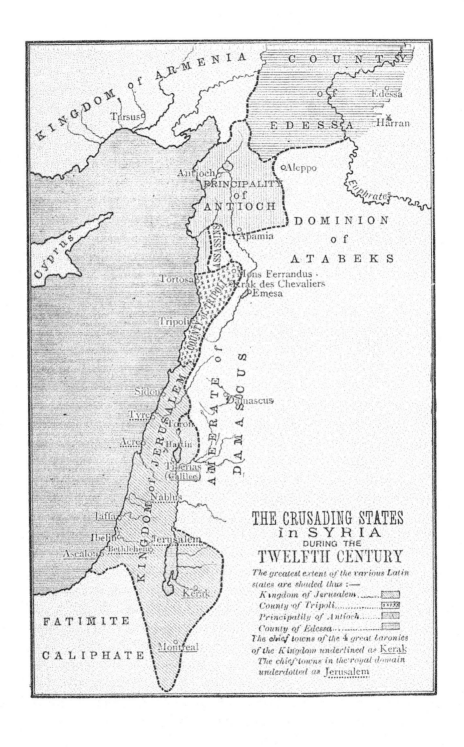

KINGDOM of ARMENIA

Tarsus

C O U N T Y

of Edessa

E D E S S A

Harran

Antioch

PRINCIPALITY

of

ANTIOCH

Aleppo

Euphrates

DOMINION

of

ATABEKS

Apamia

Cyprus

ASSASSINS

Tortosa

Mons Ferrandus

Krak des Chevaliers

Emesa

COUNT of TRIPOLI

Tripoli

Sidon

Tyre

AMIRATE of DAMASCUS

Damascus

KINGDOM of JERUSALEM

Acre

Toron

Hattin

Tiberias

(Galilee)

Nablus

Jaffa

Ibelin

Bethlehem

Jerusalem

Ascalon

Kerak

FATIMITE

CALIPHATE

Montreal

THE CRUSADING STATES
in SYRIA
DURING THE
TWELFTH CENTURY

The greatest extent of the various Latin
states are shaded thus :—
Kingdom of Jerusalem......
County of Tripoli............
Principality of Antioch......
County of Edessa............
The chief towns of the 4 great baronies
of the Kingdom underlined as Kerak
The chief towns in the royal domain
underdotted as Jerusalem

forces of the kingdom. There were the usual feudal officers of state, seneschal, constable, marshal, chamberlain, chancellor, and the rest. There were the great feudal Council of the Realm, and local courts presided over by hereditary viscounts. But the Franks were ever a small minority of warriors, rulers, priests, and, in the towns, traders. The priests and barons were practically all French or French-speaking, and the tongue of northern France became the ordinary language of the Latin East, while 'Frank' became the commonest name by which Greeks and Arabs, Turks and Armenians, alike designated the Western settlers. It was a proof of the commercial importance of the land that customs duties became from the beginning a chief source of revenue. The only non-French element was the Italian commercial colony, which lived in separate quarters in the towns under governors and laws of its own. Venetians settled largely in the kingdom of Jerusalem, where the Marseilles merchants had exceptionally an enclosed factory of their own in the capital. Genoese mainly occupied the fiefs of Antioch and Tripoli. Pisa was already rather crowded out by her younger rivals. Through Italian hands the commerce between West and East almost exclusively passed. In the country, Syrian peasants, mainly of the Orthodox faith, tilled the lands of their Latin and Catholic masters, and like the Mohammedans and Jews, paid taxes from which the Franks were exempt. The paucity of numbers of the Franks led to extreme care being devoted to building castles and fortifying towns. The feudal stronghold became bigger, harder to take, and more elaborate than ever it had been in the West, and to this day there remain ruins of eastern castles that rival in dignity and strength Coucy, Carnarvon, or Caerphilly. Even in the desert beyond Jordan, the remnants of a vast fortress like Kerak shows how real and solid was the crusading state. Side by side with the Latin state went the Latin Church. Catholic bishops and priests were brought in everywhere, and the various sects of Oriental Christians—Greeks, Armenians,

Nestorians, and the rest—shared in a common condemnation as schismatics, though at first common interests and common enemies kept the churches better together than might have been expected. Churches and monasteries grew up beside the new castles. The Holy Sepulchre was soon enclosed in a newer and grander sanctuary. The mediæval ideal—half martial, half ascetic—never had so fair a chance of development as in this land of Christians, forced to fight for their lives against Islam. It found its most characteristic expression in the martial monasticism of the military orders. For the present all looked well. Besides the constant crowd of pilgrims, there was a permanent population growing attached to its new home, which with strange quickness of sympathy, was adopting the conditions of Eastern life, and not seldom intermarrying with Syrians, Armenians, and Greeks. 'God has poured the West into the East,' boasted the chronicler Fulcher of Chartres. 'We who were Westerns are now Easterns. We have forgotten our native land.'

When the Latin kingdom was still young, a knight from Burgundy, named Hugh de Payens, made the journey to Jerusalem. Seeing that poor pilgrims were still The Military exposed to great hardships and dangers, he formed Orders. a society, with eight knights like-minded with himself, devoted to the protection of distressed wayfarers. The grant of a house near Solomon's Temple led to the brethren The Templars. being called the Knights of the Temple, and so successful did the new movement become that St. Bernard, then omnipotent in the Latin world, interested himself in it, and drew up a rule for it, which, in 1128, was authorised by Honorius II. It was a new departure in the history both of war and of religion. The knights took the threefold monastic vow of poverty, chastity, and obedience; and in time of peace ruled their life after the fashion of the canons regular, that were becoming so popular in the West [see pp. 204-207]. Their main business of protecting pilgrims soon grew into a general duty of war against the infidel. Ascetic, austere, living the lives of monks, taught to regard hunting, games, and personal adornment as frivolous and worldly, they were, as their panegyrist says, 'lions in war, lambs in the house.' To Christians they were monks, to Islam they were soldiers. 'They bear before them a banner, half-white, half-black : this they call Beauséant, because they are fair and friendly to the friends of Christ, to His enemies stern and black.'

The needs of poor pilgrims had led the citizens **of** Amalfi to set up a hospital at Jerusalem for their refreshment, in the The Knights days when Palestine was still ruled by the Fatimite of St. John. Caliphs. This institution, dedicated to St. John the Baptist, was revived and reorganised by its master Gerard after the Latin conquest. Gerard's successor, Raymond of Le Puy, struck by the success of the Templars, obtained about 1130 the Pope's permission to convert this charitable foundation into a military brotherhood like that of Hugh de Payens. Before long the Hospitallers, or Knights of St. John, vied with the Templars in their numbers, wealth, and importance. At later times other military orders were founded, such as the Teutonic Order [founded in 1197], the struggling little English community of the Knights of St. Thomas of Acre [1231], and the three famous military orders of Spain. But in the Holy Land no other order ever took the position that was soon attained by the Templars and the Knights of St. John. Enormous estates gradually accrued to them in every country in Europe, and their houses in the West became recruiting stations, whence a regular supply of knights and servitors, vowed to a perpetual crusade, kept alive the forces of the Latin kingdom. A papal grant of 1162 exempted the Templars from all ecclesiastical jurisdiction, save that of the Grand Master and the Pope. Like Cluny or Citeaux, each order formed an organised unity, ruled in the last instance by General Chapters, whose power controlled even that of the Master of each order. In the East each order formed **a** new little state, with castles, soldiers, revenues, and government of its own. Often in conflict with the kings and each other, the two chief orders nevertheless formed the most permanent and indestructible element in the Latin kingdom. It was due to their well-drilled enthusiasm that the Latin East could still hold its own against the Saracen and Turk.

The organisation of the Latin East was hardly completed when the period of decline set in. Much of the success of the First Crusade had been due to the antagonism Rise of the of Turk and Arab, and the break-up of the Atabeks. Seljukian kingdom. In the generation following, a new danger arose in the growth of a consolidated Mohammedan state in Syria. Imad-ed-din Zangi was a Turk whose father had been a trusted follower of Malek Shah, and who, after a stormy youth, had been, in 1127, made governor, or Atabek, of Mosul. In the course of the next fifteen years Zangi destroyed all the rival Mohammedan powers in northern Syria and Mesopotamia, and then turned his arms against Edessa, the remote crusading county that encroached upon his territories and threatened his capital. Jocelin of Courtenay, who ruled Edessa after Baldwin became King of Jerusalem, opposed him by a vigorous resistance, but Jocelin's son, Jocelin II., was a cowardly voluptuary, who left Edessa almost undefended. In 1144 Zangi conquered Edessa, Fall of and put the Frankish garrison to the sword. The Edessa, 1144. whole county was speedily overrun, and the Latin East experienced its first great disaster.

The fall of Edessa filled Europe with alarm, and St. Bernard, then in the plenitude of his influence, preached a new crusade with extraordinary fervour, and won over the two foremost princes in Christendom. Louis VII., St. Bernard and the King of France, had already taken the Crusader's Second vow to expiate an early crime of violence [see Crusade. page 284], but his barons, and his minister Suger, urgently dissuaded him. At Easter, 1146, St. Bernard appeared before a great gathering at Vezelai, and amidst scenes that recalled the first enthusiasm at Clermont, all ranks took the cross from the hands of the great Cistercian. After preaching the crusade over northern France, Bernard went to Germany, and at Christmas, in the cathedral at Speyer, overcame by his eloquence the hesitation of Conrad III.

Two large armies were now equipped. Conrad and his Germans were first on the march, and travelling by way of Crusade of Hungary and Bulgaria, were well received by the Conrad III. Greek Emperor, Manuel Comnenus, whose wife, Bertha of Sulzbach, was Conrad's sister-in-law. Unwilling to wait for the arrival of the French, Conrad started at once to march by way of Nicæa and Iconium to Syria, a route that led him through the heart of the kingdom of Roum, where the light-armed Turkish horsemen perpetually assailed his ill-disciplined and unwieldy squadrons, who were overwhelmed by the same fate that befel the Crusaders of 1101 [September 1147]. A mere remnant escaped with Conrad to Crusade of Nicæa, where the French, under Louis VII., had Louis VII. at last assembled. To avoid the dangers of the upland plateau, the French proceeded southward along the coast of Asia Minor as far as Ephesus, whence they ascended the valley of the Maeander into the interior, in order to avoid the rugged shores of Caria and Lycia. They were at once exposed to constant Turkish attacks. Conrad, who started with them on a second attempt, soon lost heart, and returned to Constantinople. When the wearied army at last reached the little port of Attalia in Pamphylia [February 1148], the leaders resolved to borrow ships from the Greeks, and effect the rest of their journey by sea. But so small a number of ships was forthcoming, that only the knights were enabled to embark. The rest of the army was forced to resume its dangerous land march, and few indeed ever reached their destination.

In March 1148 Louis VII. and his wife, Eleanor of Aquitaine, landed at Antioch with the little band of knights, that now alone represented the two greatest military powers of Christendom. He hurried at once to the south, where he was joined by Conrad III., who had now reached Acre by sea. It was unwisely resolved to march against Damascus, though its ruler was the chief enemy of Noureddin, Zangi's son and successor, and would have willingly stood aside had the attack been concentrated on the conquerors of Edessa. As it was, Mosul and Damascus made common cause, and the attack on the latter city proved an utter failure. Conrad at once went home, and Louis followed him a year later. The result of the Second Crusade was to promote the unity of Islam, and to divert the enemy from the north to Jerusalem, where the Christian position was weakest.

The thirty years succeeding the Second Crusade were a period of fair but somewhat stationary prosperity for the Latin East. The long minority of Baldwin III. (1143-1163) was a great calamity in itself, but his mother, Millicent, was a capable regent, and Baldwin, when he grew up, proved a vigorous warrior both against the Egyptians and Noureddin, while his affability, generosity, and bright ready wit made him the most popular of all his line. By his marriage with Theodora, daughter of the Emperor Manuel, Baldwin III. did something to promote active co-operation between the Greeks and the Latins against Islam, and his death in 1163 was a great loss to the Latin kingdom. Amalric I., his brother (1163-1174), also married a Byzantine wife, and even visited Constantinople. But with all his policy he failed to unite effectively the Christian forces, or to check seriously the growth of the power of Noureddin, and with his death the decline of the kingdom rapidly set in. His son and successor, Baldwin IV. (1174-1185), began to reign as a boy of twelve, and as he grew up proved a hopeless leper. On his death another child, Baldwin V. (1185-1186), his sister Sibyl's son by her first husband, succeeded, but he died the next year. The crown was now disputed between Guy of Lusignan, Sibyl's second husband, and Raymond, Count of Tripoli, who had acted as regent for the leper king. In the short but sharp civil war that followed, the last hopes of the kingdom perished.

A state ruled in turn by a leper, a child, and an intriguing

The Kingdom of Jerusalem between the Second and the Third Crusades.

woman was in no fit state to carry on a perpetual struggle for existence, and the disorders of the royal house were only typical of the disorganisation of the realm.   There was always a corrupt element among the Crusaders.   A momentary religious enthusiasm could not change the nature of the criminals and desperadoes, who had sought a refuge in the East from the errors they had committed in the West.   But even the descendants of the warrior saints lamentably degenerated under the fierce sun of Syria, and the luxury and moral corruption of Oriental life.   The best and bravest perished in the ceaseless wars against the infidel, and the crusading lordships were constantly diminishing in numbers, and too often a single heiress, an imbecile or a minor, represented a great aggregation of fiefs, formerly owned by many warriors able to make head personally against the Turks.   Things were almost worse with the Franks in the towns, whose frequent intermarriage with native women led to a mixed race called 'Pullani,' with Eastern habits and ways of thought.   Under these circumstances the military orders became indispensable. Their castles were always commanded by grown men accustomed to affairs, and from their numerous commanderies throughout Christendom came a succession of warriors, whose strength had not been sapped by an almost tropical climate.

The physical and moral decline of the Latins was made more fatal by their divisions.   The princes of Antioch and their Armenian neighbours stood apart from the states of southern Syria, and the Greek Empire was increasingly hostile.   While Roger of Sicily repeated the policy of Robert Guiscard and Bohemund, and the Italian allies of the Crusaders robbed the Empire of its trade, real co-operation against Islam was impossible.   Within the crusading realm there was constant strife.   The Templars quarrelled with the Hospitallers, the French with the Provençals, English, and Germans, and the Genoese with the Pisans and Venetians. The new-comers from the West quarrelled with the older settlers.   Among the baronial houses hereditary feuds arose, as in every feudal country. The purely feudal organisation of the kingdom made a strong central power impossible, and nothing but a vigorous despotism, like that of Henry II. in England, could have long kept the motley state together. As time went on, the relations between the Franks and their Eastern subjects grew worse, and neither the unwarlike Armenian nor the slavish Syrian was of any avail to supplement their armies. It speaks well for the energy of such parts of the polity as remained sound, that a century was still to elapse before the crusading kingdoms entirely disappeared.

The growth of a great Moslem monarchy in Syria was the last and worst of the many misfortunes of the Latin Christians. After Zangi's death in 1146, Noureddin had carried the power of the Atabeks to much loftier heights. He *Growth of* captured Damascus, and pushed his dominions to *the power* the sea-coast, thus isolating Antioch from Tripoli *of Saladin.* and Jerusalem. In 1171 his nephew, Saladin, conquered Egypt, and practically put an end to the schismatic Caliphate of the Fatimites. Noureddin died in 1174, recognised even by the Christians as a 'just man, wise and religious, so far as the traditions of his race allowed.' His sons were quite unable to hold their own against their cousin. In a few years the lord of Cairo and Alexandria soon became also the lord of Aleppo and Damascus. The Latins were enclosed by a single united Moslem state, ruled by a generous soldier and a crafty statesman.

After Guy's coronation, most of the Frankish barons accepted him as king, though Raymond of Tripoli, indignant at his usurpation, intrigued with Saladin. Next year the pillage of a Mussulman convoy by the lord of Kerak gave Saladin a pretext for proclaiming a holy war against the *The Battle* Christians, and invading the kingdom of Jerusalem. *of Hattin* On 4th July 1187 a great battle was fought at *and the* *fall of* Hattin, in which Saladin won a complete victory, *Jerusalem,* King Guy was taken prisoner, and the True Cross *1187.* fell into the infidels' hands. On 2nd October Jerusalem fell, and Tyre, Tripoli, and Antioch alone succeeded in driving Saladin from their walls. Thus the great kingdom of the Franks of Syria was reduced to a few towns near the sea-coast, and a few sorely beleaguered castles. 'The Latins of

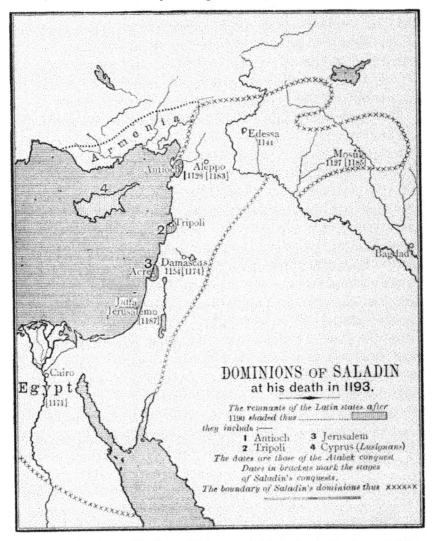

DOMINIONS OF SALADIN
at his death in 1193.

The remnants of the Latin states after
1190 shaded thus
they include :—
1 Antioch   3 Jerusalem
2 Tripoli   4 Cyprus (*Lusignans*)
The dates are those of the Atabek conquest
Dates in brackets mark the stages
of Saladin's conquests.
The boundary of Saladin's dominions thus ×××××

the East,' said William of Tyre, 'had forsaken God, and God now forsook them.' Unless Europe made another such effort as Urban II. had made, the crusading state would soon disappear altogether.

GENEALOGY OF THE EARLY KINGS OF JERUSALEM.

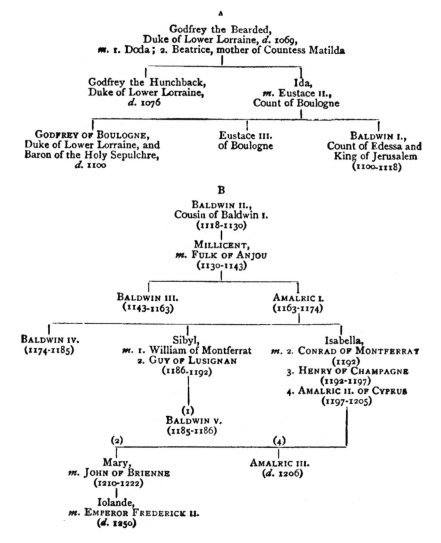

A

Godfrey the Bearded,
Duke of Lower Lorraine, *d.* 1069,
m. 1. Doda ; 2. Beatrice, mother of Countess Matilda

Godfrey the Hunchback,
Duke of Lower Lorraine,
d. 1076

Ida,
m. Eustace II.,
Count of Boulogne

GODFREY OF BOULOGNE,
Duke of Lower Lorraine, and
Baron of the Holy Sepulchre,
d. 1100

Eustace III.
of Boulogne

BALDWIN I.,
Count of Edessa and
King of Jerusalem
(1100-1118)

B

BALDWIN II.,
Cousin of Baldwin I.
(1118-1130)

MILLICENT,
m. FULK OF ANJOU
(1130-1143)

BALDWIN III.
(1143-1163)

AMALRIC I.
(1163-1174)

BALDWIN IV.
(1174-1185)

Sibyl,
m. 1. William of Montferrat
2. GUY OF LUSIGNAN
(1186-1192)

Isabella,
m. 2. CONRAD OF MONTFERRAT
(1192)
3. HENRY OF CHAMPAGNE
(1192-1197)
4. AMALRIC II. OF CYPRUS
(1197-1205)

(1)
BALDWIN V.
(1185-1186)

(2)

(4)

Mary,
m. JOHN OF BRIENNE
(1210-1222)

AMALRIC III.
(*d.* 1206)

Iolande,
m. EMPEROR FREDERICK II.
(*d.* 1250)

CHAPTER IX

THE MONASTIC MOVEMENT
AND THE TWELFTH CENTURY RENASCENCE [1]

Aspects of the Hildebrandine Movement—The new Religious Orders—Bruno
and the Carthusians—The Beginnings of the Cistercians and Robert of
Molême—The Charter of Charity—The Canons Regular—Norbert and
Prémontré—The Military Orders—Influence of St. Bernard—The Speculative Revival—Beginnings of Scholasticism—Abelard and his influence—
Abelard and Bernard—Popular Heresies—Peter de Bruys—The Poor
Men of Lyons—The Albigenses—The Legal Revival—Irnerius and the
Civil Law—Gratian and the Canon Law.

WITH all their importance, the Crusades were only one aspect
of the great religious and intellectual movement that heralded
the twelfth century throughout the length and
breadth of Western Europe, and was as directly
a result of the triumph of the Hildebrandine
ideal as the new theories themselves were an
emanation from the Cluniac revival. Beginning with the
strenuous careers of Gregory VII. and Urban II., this new spirit

Various aspects of the Hildebrandine movement.

---

[1] Besides the dry pages of Möller and Gieseler, reference can be made
to Montalembert's picturesque *Monks of the West,* and Maitland's *Dark
Ages,* while J. H. Newman's *Lives of English Saints* tells the story of
some of the monastic heroes with rare sympathy and power. An idea of
the monastic life can be got from good biographies, such as Church's *Life
of St. Anselm,* or Morison's *Life of St. Bernard.* Poole's *Illustrations of
the History of Mediæval Thought,* and Rashdall's *Universities of the
Middle Ages* (chap. ii. 'Abelard and the Renaissance of the Twelfth
Century,' and chap. iv. §§ 1 and 2) give admirable accounts of the intellectual movements of the time. Hardwick's *History of the Christian
Church in the Middle Ages* is a succinct one-volume summary of general
Church history.

at once began to work powerfully on Europe, and reached its height in the days of peace that succeeded the end of the Investiture Contest.

A monastic revival succeeded, as it preceded, the reformation of the Papacy. At first the movement was on the old lines, and Cluny still maintained its reputation, and increased its number of offshoots. But the 'Congregation of Cluny' was too unelastic to be capable of indefinite expansion, and its influence was perhaps widest felt in those houses which adopted its ideal without giving up their ancient Benedictine independence. Conspicuous among such was Hirschau, a convent situated on the north-eastern slopes of the Black Forest, in Swabia, where Abbot William introduced the rule of Cluny in 1077, and which immediately became a centre of monastic reformation in southern Germany, though the congregation of Hirschau never attained the organisation or permanence of that of Cluny.

The weak point of the Cluniac system was that everything depended upon the abbot. Under the unworthy Pontius (1109-1125), whom kinship to Paschal II. had brought to the headship of Cluny at an exceedingly early age, discipline declined, the old simplicity disappeared, and the abbot, whose virtues were those of a feudal noble rather than a true monk, wasted his energies in conflicts with the Bishop of Macon, who, in spite of papal exemptions, strove to reform the declining house as diocesan. But under the famous abbot, Peter the Venerable, Cluny again became a power in Europe, though its old influence was never restored. Younger houses, organised on newer lines, divided among themselves the reverence once felt for it, and even Peter of Cluny was overshadowed by Bernard of Clairvaux.

The times were still so stormy, and secular life so rough, that the impulse which drove pious minds into the cloister was as strong as ever. The feudal anarchy that still prevailed in France, perhaps continued to give that country the leading part, both in spreading hierarchical ideas and in Further bringing about further monastic revivals. **The** development great question for the new race of monastic re- of the congrega. formers was how to keep up the spirit of the tional idea. older rule while avoiding its dangers. Cluny had not quite solved the problem, though the congregational idea, the more disciplined austerity, and the admission of *conversi* or lay brothers, were steps capable of wider development. How to avoid the wealth, pride, and idleness that came from success was a still harder problem. The importance of the new orders that arose in the end of the eleventh and the early years of the twelfth century depended upon the skill with which the founders answered these fundamental questions.

The first new order was the order of Grammont. Its founder, St. Stephen, an Auvergnat noble, settled in 1076 Order of with a few companions at Muret, north of Grammont. Limoges, though after his death the house was removed to the bleak granitic plateau of the neighbouring Grammont. A large number of daughter houses grew up in Aquitaine, Anjou, and Normandy, all of which, after the Cluniac fashion, were subject to the prior of Grammont. St. Stephen's wish was to follow no fixed definite system, but to be content with the Gospel rules of poverty, humility, and long-suffering, and his successors embodied this aspiration in a form of life which forbade the order to possess land, cattle, or churches, to exclude seculars from its services, and allowed it, if no alms came, to beg for sustenance. This was a remarkable anticipation of the chief characteristic of the mendicant orders of the thirteenth century, but it did not prevent the early decay of these disorderly idealists. A stern fixed rule was necessary to a mediæval monastery.

A happier fate attended St. Bruno, the founder of the Carthusians. A German from Cologne, Bruno, became scholasticus of the famous chapter school at Reims, where he numbered Urban II. among his disciples. Driven with disgust from Reims by the violence of Archbishop Manasses, he hid himself in a wild mountain valley near Grenoble in Dauphiny, the site of the still famous Grande Chartreuse, where he gathered round him a band of hermits living in separate cells. Bruno was called to Rome by his old pupil Urban II.; but the love of retirement soon took him to Calabria, where he founded another Charterhouse, and died in 1101. Charterhouses now grew up, though not very rapidly, all over Europe, and the order took its final shape in the statutes of 1258. The possession of land, forbidden by Bruno, was strictly limited, as were all other sources of wealth. Ruled by a general chapter, the order followed up still further the idea of the congregation. But the special characteristic of the Carthusians was the union of the hitherto separated cœnobitic and eremitic ideals. The Carthusian belonged to an order and convent, with its common church and other buildings; but instead of living without privacy in common dormitory and refectory, he lived in a separate cell a life of meditation, study, and silence, while the *conversi* practised agriculture. The Carthusian life was novel; but the magnificent churches and buildings of the order show that it took a deep root. Better than many of the purely cœnobitic orders, the Carthusians maintained their purity with few traces of the inevitable decay that beset most monastic types when the enthusiasm of the founders had abated. Another order, that of Fontevrault, founded by the Breton, Robert of Arbrissel (1100), was distinguished by combining monasteries for men and women in one establishment after the primitive plan, and by making the abbess superior of the whole community, since Robert reverenced in her the representative of the Virgin. Outside France this order had no great importance.

The most important influence among the new orders

undoubtedly fell to the Cistercians, who rose rapidly from humble beginnings to a unique position.   In 1075 a monk

The
Cistercian
Order and
Robert of
Molême. named Robert founded a small convent at Molême in northern Burgundy, where he strove to carry out with absolute literalness and fidelity the rule of St. Benedict.   The monks found the austerities of their abbot so painful that they rebelled, and in 1098 Robert left Molême in despair, accompanied by the few zealots, conspicuous among whom was the Englishman Stephen or Harding.   The little band settled down at Citeaux, between Dijon and Châlon, a desolate spot which derived its name from the surrounding pools of standing water.   There was founded the famous abbey, which was to give its name to a new departure in monastic history.   At first the brethren lived in excessive poverty and isolation.   But the fame of their holiness gradually brought them adherents, and from 1113, when the young Burgundian nobleman, Bernard of Fontaines, applied for admission with thirty of his kinsmen, the growth of Citeaux was rapid.   The monastery overflowed, and swarm after swarm of monks established daughter houses elsewhere.   In 1115 Bernard himself, whose strong will and saintly character had won for him in two years a leading position, led one of these migrations to Clairvaux, of which house he became abbot. Stephen the Englishman was now abbot of Citeaux, and showed a capacity for organisation which soon made the single poor monastery that he ruled the mother of a great order.   In 1119 he obtained Calixtus II.'s approval for the

Carta
Caritatis,
1119. famous 'Charter of Charity,' the constitution which he had devised for Citeaux and its daughter houses.   The movement soon spread like wild-fire, and hundreds of Cistercian monasteries were founded throughout Christendom.

The leading characteristics of the Cistercians marked the new order clearly off from its fellows.   Starting from their first principle of absolute asceticism, they pushed the doctrine of self-renunciation as far as human capacity allowed.   They rejected soft and costly garments, lived on the plainest and simplest food, and would not tolerate splendour even in their churches, where, instead of gold and silver crosses, they contented themselves with painted wood. The very vestments of their priests were of coarse stuff without gold, or silver, or costly embroidery. Their churches and monasteries were built as simply as was possible. Towers and belfries were rejected as useless luxuries. Choosing for their abode remote valleys and wildernesses far from the haunts of men, they carefully avoided the proximity to town-life, which was a stumbling-block in the way of the older orders. Even the cure of souls was prohibited as likely to lead the monks into the world and its sins, and to celebrate Masses for money was denounced as simony. Thus the old Benedictine rule was upheld, and the monk reminded that he was no clerk but a pious recluse, whose business was to save his own soul. For the occupation of the brethren labour was enjoined ; and a large number of *conversi* carried on the hard agricultural work that soon made the wilderness blossom like a garden, and filled with sheep the downs and deserts. It thus resulted that the Cistercians, despite their principles, had considerable influence in promoting the civilisation of the regions in which they settled. The interconnection of their houses made it easy for them to spread a tendency or an idea from land to land, as when they transmitted the first rudiments of Gothic architecture from its north French home to Italy.[1] While wealth and idleness were thus kept at bay, elaborate efforts were made to keep watch over backsliders. While the example of Cluny had led all the great monasteries to strive to get from the Pope exemption from episcopal authority, Cîteaux ostentatiously professed canonical obedience to the Bishop of Châlon, and every daughter house was founded with the consent of the diocesan, to whom its abbot submitted himself as a subject. Moreover, the constitution sketched in

[1] See on this subject Enlart's *Origines de l'Architecture gothique en Italie* (Bibliothéque de l'Ecole française de Rome).

the 'Carta Caritatis' provided within the order itself means for perpetual visitation and reproof of weaker brethren, that was far more effective than episcopal control. Like the Cluniacs, the Cistercians formed a congregation over which the Abbot of Cîteaux exercised the powers of a king. But an elaborate series of checks on the abbot's power imparted an aristocratic or popular element to the government of the new order. The abbots of the four first daughters of Cîteaux [La Ferté (founded 1113), Pontigny (1114), Clairvaux (1115), and Morimond (1115)], and the General Chapter of the abbots of the order, while liable to be visited and corrected by their superior, had the power of correcting, administering, and depriving the head of the order himself. The monasteries were to be visited yearly. Each new house was affiliated to the earlier one from which it had sprung, and the mother-house exercised a special watchfulness over it. So different did the Cistercians feel themselves from other regulars that they significantly discarded the black garment of the Benedictines in favour of a coarse white dress, from which they got the name of the white monks. Their elaborate organisation gave them a corporate feeling and unity of purpose to which few other orders could aspire. They represent the last and most complete effort to give real effect to the ideal of St. Benedict, by enjoining an austerity even beyond that of Benedict, and by an elaborate organisation to which his rule for a single house was quite a stranger.

Other new orders started on a different purpose. Various hospital orders, which laid special stress on the care of the sick and suffering, were set up for those who sought salvation in good works for the world, rather than in isolation from human intercourse. But the great contribution of the twelfth century towards bridging over the great gulf between clerk and monk was the institution of the so-called Austin Canons, The Canons or Canons Regular. It was agreed that the higher Regular. life was the monastic life, and that the secular priest, possessing private property, living in his own house and immersed in worldly affairs, stood on a lower plane than the regular, but the cure of souls was left to the secular clergy, and it was no part of the Hildebrandine ideal to neglect the pastoral work of the Church. Hence came a movement for reforming the secular clergy by making them live the life of a monk, while they carried on the duties of a clerk. It was impossible to enforce monastic life on the isolated and ignorant parish clergy, among whom it was hard work enough to enforce the new obligation of celibacy. The great colleges and cathedrals, served by many priests, offered an easier and more fruitful field for reform.

In the fifth century St. Augustine of Hippo had sought to establish a 'monastery of clerks in the bishop's household.' In the days of the Carolingian reformation, Bishop Chrodegang of Metz had, in the spirit of the great African father, set up a rule of life, by which canons of a cathedral should live in common along with their bishops. In Hildebrand's days Peter Damiani appealed to the example of St. Augustine as the ideal pattern for the cathedral clergy. Many chapters were reformed, and from the twelfth century onwards a sharp distinction was drawn between 'regular canons,' subject to a rule of life, and 'secular canons' of the old-fashioned sort. The great property and the political influence of the cathedral chapters made it hard to keep out of them members of the great territorial families, who looked on their prebends as sources of income, and who soon found a regular life too austere, so that few cathedrals became permanently served by them. But new churches of Regular Canons, where there were no secular traditions to interfere with the strictness of their rule, began to rise up all over Christendom. The general name of 'Austin Canons' suggested that the whole of the class strove to realise the old ideal of St. Augustine.

Various congregations of Regular Canons were now set up, conspicuous among which was that of the Victorines, whose abbey of St. Victor in Paris became, as we shall see, a prominent

centre of conservative theology.   But it was the establishment
of the Premonstratensian congregation by Norbert of Xanten
which gave the Austin Canons so great a position in Christen-

Norbert and   dom that they almost rivalled the Cistercians in
the Premon-   popularity.   Norbert was a man of high family, who,
stratensians.   after having held canonries of the old-fashioned
sort at his native town and at Cologne, gave up the world
and wandered as a preacher of penitence throughout Gaul,
carefully avoiding intercourse with clerks or monks.   In 1120
he settled in a desert place in the forest of Coucy, not far
from Laon, where the bishop was his friend, and established
there a house of Canons Regular, calling the spot Prémontré
[Pratum Monstratum], in the belief that the site had been
pointed out to him by an angel.   The rule of Prémontré soon
became famous, and its canons, clad in the white garment of
the Cistercians, showed, by their energy and zeal, that clerks
bound by a rule could live lives as holy as monks and do as
much pastoral work as seculars.   As an 'order of clerks' they
exercised cure of souls, preached, taught, and heard confessions, and where possible made their churches parochial.   In
1126 Norbert became Archbishop of Magdeburg.   Finding
the secular chapter utterly opposed to his policy, he planted a
new colony of Premonstratensians hard by in the collegiate
church of St. Mary (1129).   Through his influence the Premonstratensians took the leading share in the civilising and
Christianising of the Slavonic lands beyond the Elbe.   In a
later chapter we shall see how Norbert soon became the
Emperor Lothair's chief adviser and helper.   Before his death
his order had spread throughout Western Christendom.   While
Cîteaux had for its ambition the perfection of an ancient
system, Prémontré made a new departure in religious history.
Later regular orders have in nearly all cases striven to carry
out the ideal of Norbert, of combining the religious life with
that pastoral care, which to the older type of monasticism was
but a subtle and attractive form of that worldliness which
they were pledged to avoid.   Within Norbert's own lifetime

the rule of the Austin Canons received a very great accession
to its strength. The military orders of the Latin East all
lived when at peace the life, and took the vows The Military
of Austin Canons, while the older military orders Orders.
of Spain [Calatrava, 1158, Alcantara, 1152] stood in close
connection with the Cistercians. [See chapter xx.]

The great development of new orders had a many-sided
influence on the character of the twelfth century. The monks
and the Regular Canons were everywhere the best Influence of
servants of the Papacy, while their international the new
organisation was a new link between the national orders on the
churches. The local jealousy of Roman influence, twelfth
the aspirations of the bishops to an independent century.
position, were energetically withstood by the enthusiasm of
the young orders. Their asceticism and zeal for good works
won for them the passionate attachment of the laity, and
stimulated the sluggish seculars to greater activity and holiness. Their influence over public opinion was enormous.
Not Louis of France or Conrad of Germany, but Norbert
of Magdeburg and Bernard of Clairvaux, were the real leaders
of European thought towards the middle of the twelfth
century.

The practical authority of Norbert was mainly limited to
Germany, but the influence of Bernard, confined to no class or
country, proved something almost unique in the
whole of Christian history. While Bernard lived St. Bernard.
the simple and self-denying life of a Cistercian in his
Burgundian monastery, his activity took in the whole of
Christendom. His correspondence was enormous, his works
numerous and varied, and his authority hardly questioned.
Through his influence the white robe of the Cistercians became familiar in the remotest valleys of Christendom, and
the simple and struggling order, which he had joined but a
few years before, attained a world-wide celebrity. Every sort
of dispute and difference was brought before his tribunal.
The rulers of Church and State flocked to the rude huts of

Clairvaux as to an oracle. In his frequent journeys throughout France, the Rhineland and Italy, he was welcomed as Pope or Emperor was never welcomed. It was Bernard who drew up the rule for the Knights Templars, who ended the papal schism of 1130, and procured the recognition of Innocent II. as Pope. Innocent II. set the example of deference to his authority which subsequent Popes obsequiously continued, till at last a simple Cistercian became Pope Eugenius III., merely because he was the friend of Bernard. Bernard joined with Norbert in reprobating the rationalism that sprang from the teaching of an Abelard or Gilbert de la Porrée or Arnold of Brescia, and strove with sublime unreasonableness to put down the new questioning spirit. More open heresy, like that of Peter de Bruys, found in him an equally implacable foe. He upheld every doctrine of hierarchical power, and scrupled not to rebuke kings and emperors if they gainsaid him. He rekindled the crusading spirit when it seemed growing cool, and persuaded the two greatest princes of Christendom to set forth on the ill-fated Second Crusade. Stern, unyielding, rigid, dogmatic, blind to all things which in his view did not immediately promote the kingdom of God, Bernard represents the very triumph of the older monastic spirit with its completeness of self-renunciation, its terrible asceticism, its strange and almost inhuman virtues. Even in his own day, his spirit was not that of the whole Church, and bold voices were found to lament his obstinacy, his narrowness, his obscurantist hatred of secular learning. But with all his faults he is a great and noble figure, and as the supreme representative of a dying type, his career marks a transition to a newer, brighter and more progressive world, than the gloomy realm over which he had reigned so long as unquestioned sovereign. Yet it shows that the days of brute force were over, when a simple monk, whose singleness of purpose and zeal for righteousness were never so much as questioned, could rule with such astounding power over the minds of men. Even more than the authority of the great Popes, the power of Bernard supplies a striking justification of the universal monarchy of the Church of the twelfth century.

From the religious revival there sprang a revived interest in literature and speculation. Monastic life was strictly conservative, and the old doctrine of Gregory the Great, that secular literature was unworthy the attention of a good Christian, was the position *The literary and specula-tive revival.* of St. Bernard himself. But the monks were at least interested in theology; and not even Bernard's influence could prevent pious souls from seeking in nature and literature the justifica-tion of the ways of God to man. As the necessary preliminary of theological study, the 'seven arts' of the old-fashioned 'Trivium' and 'Quadrivium' had again to be cultivated. Monastic schools once more stimulated the intel-lectual interest of Europe. Many of the greater houses became centres of education. So far back as the tenth century monks like St. Bruno of *Its relation to the monastic movement.* Cologne and Gerbert of Aurillac had restored the Carolingian educational discipline, which had fallen into ruin in the dark days of barbarian invasion and internal anarchy. German cloisters, like St. Gallen and Reichenau, became famous for their learning. Cluny forged the theories that Hildebrand wielded. Lanfranc of Bec made the Norman monastery one of the great centres of dialectical and theological study in northern Europe. Side by side with the cloister schools were the schools of the great cathedrals, such as that of Reims, where Gerbert taught. In these the teachers were partly seculars, and there was perhaps more freedom and breadth of interests than in the purely monastic academies. When the revival of speculation brought out differences of opinion, Berengar, the scholasticus of the cathedral school of Tours, used the weapon of logic to attack the newly formulated doctrine of transubstantiation. It was Lanfranc, the monk of Bec, that employed all the resources of his skill to demolish the arguments of the hardy heretic. But though Berengar was first condemned by Leo IX. in 1050, it was not until

1078 that Gregory VII. practically settled the controversy by insisting upon his complete retraction. So slow were the methods against heresy in times when its danger was hardly realised.

In the next generation two distinct tendencies present themselves. Anselm of Aosta, Lanfranc's successor alike at Bec and Canterbury, defended the traditional position of the Church with a wider learning and deeper insight than his predecessor. Anselm has been called both the last of the fathers and the first of the schoolmen. But while his motive was the same as that of the later schoolmen, his methods were somewhat different, and his enduring fame is not for the acuteness of his dialectic, so much as for his broad insight into the deeper problems of philosophy and his anticipation of positions that were not fully taken up until the reign of scholasticism was over. The Realism of which he was the upholder was part of the earlier tradition of the ecclesiastical schools. Much more epoch-making, though not in itself altogether original, was the Nominalism of Roscelin, the true parent of scholastic philosophy. While Anselm only saw in philosophy the way of justifying the Church's teaching, Roscelin's logical nominalism led him to deny the possibility of the Trinity in Unity and teach undisguised Tritheism. But he argued as a logician and not as a divine, and in 1092 acquiesced in the recantation which was presented to him by a council at Soissons. From the controversies of Anselm and Roscelin all the later intellectual activity sprang.

The transition to the scholastic philosophy.

Anselm and Roscelin.

Early in the twelfth century there were many schools and masters scattered through central Europe and particularly in northern Gaul. Of one of the least of these schools and scholars it could be said that 'clerks flocked from divers countries to hear him daily; so that if thou shouldst walk about the public places of the city and behold the crowds of disputants, thou wouldst say that the

Activity of the schools.

citizens had left off their other labours and given themselves to philosophy.'[1]   There was no order or method in study. Any one could teach who had learnt under an accredited master and had received the Church's licence.   The students followed the masters, and the centres of study fluctuated as reputations were made and destroyed.   But at this period there were three chief schools in northern France, all closely connected with the cathedrals of the respective towns.   The teaching of Anselm of Laon (a scholar of St. Anselm) made that city a great centre of theological lore.   The dialectical renown of William of Champeaux brought crowds of students to the cathedral schools of Paris.   The literary enthusiasm of the Breton Platonist, Bernard Sylvester, and of his successor, William of Conches, made the cathedral school of Chartres 'the most abundant spring of letters in Gaul.'[2]

Peter Abelard (1079-1142), a Breton from Palais, near Nantes, was the most striking manifestation of the new spirit. He was the eldest son of a gentleman of good estate, but he early renounced his inheritance, and devoted himself with extraordinary enthusiasm to study.   He first learnt dialectic under Roscelin at Loches, near Tours, and afterwards under William of Champeaux at Paris.   But his sublime self-confidence and acute sceptical intellect speedily brought Abelard and him into conflict, both with the novel Nominalism his influence. of Roscelin and with the old-fashioned extreme Realism of William of Champeaux.   He soon despised and strove to supplant his masters.   While William of Champeaux taught with declining authority at the cathedral school, and afterwards in the Abbey of St. Victor, his audacious disciple gathered an opposition band of pupils round him in neighbouring towns, and finally on the hill of Ste. Geneviève, where he became so famous, that William retired in disgust to his

---

[1] Poole, *Illustrations of the History of Mediæval Thought*, p. 106, quotes the local chronicle's account of the teaching of Odo of Cambrai at the Abbey of St. Martin's, Tournai.

[2] See on this subject Clerval, *Les écoles de Chartres au moyen âge*.

bishopric of Châlons. Abelard's acuteness, rhetorical skill, and attractive personality, soon drew to Paris crowds of students, who gave the city a unique position among the schools of Europe. The Conceptualism, which he perhaps learnt from Aristotle, seemed more scientific than Realism, and less revolutionary than Nominalism. But it is not so much what he taught, as the spirit in which he taught, that gave Abelard his position in history. His method was essentially rationalistic. He based his orthodoxy on its reasonableness. 'A doctrine is not to be believed,' he is reported to have said, 'because God has said it, but because we are convinced by reason that it is so.' Moved by religious zeal as well as greed for applause, he went to Laon to study theology under Anselm, but very soon came to despise his teacher, whom he denounced as a phrase-monger. 'Anselm kindled a fire,' he said, 'not to give light but to fill the house with smoke.' He forsook the pretender's school, and at once proceeded to prove the audacious thesis that a man could learn theology without a master. He was soon back at Paris, where his teaching attracted greater crowds than ever, until the tragic conclusion of his relations with Heloisa drove him to take the monastic vows at Saint-Denis. Even in the cloister he was restless and insubordinate. He published a treatise on the Trinity, which was denounced by the aged Roscelin as savouring of Sabellianism, and burnt at a Council at Soissons in 1121. He left Saint-Denis after rousing the fury of his fellow-monks by demonstrating the unhistorical character of the accredited legend of St. Dionysius the Areopagite, their imaginary founder. After some years spent in his new monastery of the Paraclete in Champagne, Abelard sought absolute retirement as abbot of St. Gildas de Rhuys, in the **Abelard and** wildest part of his native Brittany. But he fled at **St. Bernard.** last from the savage monks of St. Gildas, and again appeared as a teacher in Paris. As the incarnation of the new critical spirit, he had long been obnoxious to the stout upholders of ecclesiastical tradition like Norbert and Bernard.

Bernard now denounced him, and induced the bishops, who registered his will, to assemble in council at Sens to condemn his heresies (1141). Despairing of justice from such a body, Abelard appealed to the Pope. But Innocent II. was as much under Bernard's influence as the French bishops, and condemned him to lifelong confinement in a monastery. Abelard fell sick at Cluny while on his way to Rome, and obtained from Peter the Venerable a sympathy and kindness that stood in strong contrast to Bernard's inveterate hostility. He was received into the Cluniac fold, and made some sort of recantation of his heresies. In 1142 he died at Châlon. The spirit of his teaching did not die with him. The schools of Paris retained the fame with which he had first invested them. While the Regular Canons of St. Victor made their abbey the home of traditional theology tempered by mysticism, the secular school of the cathedral retained the spirit of inquiry and criticism which secured for it a permanence of influence that not even the patronage of St. Bernard could give to the school of St. Victor. If the stigma of heresy was attached to some of Abelard's disciples, others became lights of orthodoxy without any great departure from Abelard's doctrines. Arnold of Brescia, denounced by St. Bernard as the armour-bearer of the Goliath of misbelief his master, incurred by his rash entrance into politics the fate of a heretic who was also a rebel [pages 239-243 and 250]. But Peter the Lombard (died 1160), was not only Abelard's pupil, but a pillar of orthodoxy, bishop of Paris, and author of that *Book of Sentences* which was the accredited text-book of all later scholasticism. Gilbert de la Porrée (died 1154), a disciple of the humanistic school of Chartres, and bishop of Poitiers, was denounced by St. Bernard as a heretic. In 1148 Pope Eugenius, a creature of Bernard's, presided at a council at Reims to deal with Gilbert's errors. But the very cardinals refused any longer to follow Bernard's leading. When Gilbert escaped uncondemned, the new theology had

The Schools of Paris.

Change in the character of Scholasticism after Abelard.

won its way to a recognised position in the Church. With its wider diffusion, the new learning lost the character of revolt which in Abelard's time was associated with it. It became more systematic, more specialised, less original. The discovery of the whole of Aristotle's *Organon*, in the latter part of the century, crushed the critical spirit by the weight of its authority. The conflict of studies drove out the liberal pursuit of literature in favour of specialised dialectic and theology, while the majority showed most favour to bread-winning studies like the canon and civil laws. The dialectic of Paris prevailed over the humanism of Chartres. But if some of the first freshness of the new birth was thus lost, the end of the century saw the scholar class a recognised element in the European commonwealth. So numerous were the 'masters' who taught in the Paris schools that they formed themselves into guilds or corporations, from which the germ of the University of Paris and of all other transalpine universities grew.

Monasticism and philosophy combined to strengthen the Church, but the spirit of revolt that had been conquered in the schools now took more popular shapes. All through the eleventh century there were found wandering teachers of strange doctrines. From the beginning of the twelfth century Popular definitively heretical sects were crystallising round heresies. different principles of innovation. For more than twenty years an unfrocked priest, Peter de Bruys, taught with Peter de powerful effect in Dauphiny and Provence. He Bruys. was an enthusiast like the old Montanists, rejecting all forms, discipline, and tradition, in favour of the living spirit, and denouncing the sacerdotal system and many of the most treasured dogmas of the Church. In 1137 or 1138, Peter was burnt alive at Saint-Gilles by the mob, whose fury he had excited by making a bonfire of crosses and pious emblems. But his followers kept together after his death, under the guidance of Henry, an outcast monk of Cluny. Peter the Venerable wrote against the Petrobrusians, and St. Bernard saw in the popularity of the young sect the malign influence of the spirit of Abelard. 'The Catholic faith,' he lamented, 'is discussed in the streets and market-places. We have fallen upon evil times.' His energy secured the conversion of many of the Petrobrusians. The remnant joined themselves to the new sect of the Waldenses or Vaudois.

Peter Valdez, a rich merchant of Lyons, gave up all his property, and began about 1177 to wander about the country preaching repentance and the imitation of the Apostles. He procured the translation of the Bible into the vulgar tongue, and soon began to gather followers. After a few years of toleration he *Peter Valdez and the 'Poor Men of Lyons.'* was excommunicated in 1184 by Pope Lucius III. Thus cut off from the orthodox, Peter joined the Petrobrusians and became more frankly heretical. Before his death in 1197, his followers were to be found in Bohemia, in Lorraine, in southern France, in Aragon, and in northern Italy. These 'Poor Men of Lyons,' as they were called, rejected all priestly ministration, and included in one sweeping denunciation prayer for the dead, six of the seven sacraments, military service, and property. But grave differences soon broke them up into hostile sects. The Lombards sought to organise themselves separately from the Church, while the French were content to remain a school within the Church. The wise policy of later Popes allowed the more moderate to combine their own way of thinking with acceptance of the Church's authority, and they remained for the most part humble-minded quietists, whose highest aspiration was to live in peace.

Other sects assumed a more dangerous complexion than the Poor Men of Lyons. From the eleventh century onwards, obscure bodies of heretics appear under the names of Manicheans, Paulicians, Cathari, Bulgarians, Patarini, and Publicani. Their strength was at first in the Rhineland, whence they infected the north of France. Finally they

found a more sympathetic field in southern France, where heresy had long flourished in various forms. The origin
The Mani-
chean sect. of these sects is obscure. The ancient opinion that they were direct descendants of the ancient Gnostics and Manichees cannot be upheld, and it is difficult even to prove their affiliation with the Paulicians and Bogomili of the Balkan peninsula, whose heresy had troubled the Eastern Empire in the days of the Macedonian and Comnenian dynasties. Their doctrines are as hard to define as their origin, and we have for the most part to rely upon the statements of their enemies. But it is clear that they represent neither a definite sect nor an organised body of heretical doctrine. Like the early Gnostics, they indicate a vague general tendency rather than any precise teaching, and differed widely among each other. The more thorough-going of them were dualists like the Manichees, believing that there existed two equal and co-eternal deities, the one evil and the other good. The rest seem to have held the modified dualism of the Bogomili, admitting the good principle to be the only God, and the author of the New Testament, and regarding the evil principle as a fallen spirit, the creator of the world, the source of the Old Testament revelation, essentially the Demiurgus of the Gnostics. The practical teaching of these heretics was as various as their doctrine. They utterly despised all things of the flesh, and from this contempt flowed moral doctrines both ascetic and antinomian. They distinguished sharply between the elect and the reprobate. They rejected the authority both of the Church and of the State. Instead of the ordinary offices of the Church, they had a sort of spiritual baptism called *Consolamentum*, which was reserved to the perfect believers. Apart from their religious heresies, they were frankly hostile to the whole order of society.

The south of France soon swarmed with these innovators,
The
Albigenses. who took the name of Albigenses, Albigeois, from one of their strongholds, the town of Albi on the Tarn. Besides the avowed heresies, a general spirit of revolt

against the Church seized alike upon lords and people. Before the end of the century, the Albigenses had obtained a firm hold over the county of Toulouse and its dependencies, and defied the efforts of the Church to root them out. Elsewhere the speculations of the twelfth century had no very prolonged vitality. A few burnings of leaders, a crusade of energetic preaching, and a dexterous effort to turn the undisciplined zeal of the heretic into more orthodox channels, were generally enough to prevent their further progress. The offspring of vague discontent, twelfth century heresy took as a rule such vague and fantastic shapes that it almost condemned itself. After all, the spirit of Henry of Cluny or Peter Valdez was not very different from that of Norbert or Robert of Arbrissel. But however ill-regulated, it was another sign that the human mind had awakened from the sleep of the Dark Ages. If the popular heretics could not reason, they could at least feel.

We have still to deal with one of the great intellectual forces of the twelfth century. The revival of the scientific study of law, which grew up alongside the new *The revival* birth of dialectic and philosophy, had almost as *of the study* powerful an influence as these studies in stimu- *of law.* lating intellectual interests, and had practical results of an even more direct and palpable kind. The study of Roman Law had never been quite forgotten, especially in Italy. The revival of the Roman Empire by the Ottos, the development of the power of the secular state all over Europe, the growth of ordered municipal government in southern Europe, and particularly in Italy, all contributed to make this study more popular, more necessary, and more universal. But side by side with the development of the civil power the even greater growth of the ecclesiastical authority set up a law of the Church in rivalry with the law of the State. The legal revival was thus two-sided. There was a fresh interest in both the Civil Law, which Rome had handed down, and in the Canon Law, which had slowly grown up in the ecclesiastical courts.

The same age that witnessed the work of Irnerius saw the publication of the *Decretum* of Gratian.

The early Middle Ages had an almost superstitious reverence for the written law of Rome. Its decisions were still looked upon as eternal and universally binding, even when practically it had been superseded by a mass of fluctuating feudal custom. In Italy the elementary texts of the Roman Law had always been studied, and its principles always upheld in the courts. The eleventh century battle of Papacy and Empire became before long a conflict of political principles and theories. Both sides sought weapons in the legal treasures of ancient Rome. Accordingly the eleventh century saw flourishing schools of law at Pavia, at Ravenna, and perhaps at Rome. Early in the twelfth century the fame of Irnerius led to the establishment of a still greater school of law at Bologna, already the seat of flourishing schools of dialectic and literature, and where the teaching of law had already been begun by Pepo. Irnerius was a jurist in the service of the Countess Matilda, who, at her request, lectured on the laws of Justinian, and particularly the Pandects, at Bologna. The fact that he was afterwards in the service of Henry v. shows that both the papal and imperial powers agreed in welcoming his work. But with the appearance of Irnerius upholding the election of a schismatic Pope in 1118, the new school of Civil Lawyers became frankly imperialist, looking upon the law as furnishing an armoury of texts, from which the divine rights and universal claims of the Roman Emperor could be deduced, though also treating it as an intellectual discipline, and almost as a literary exercise. Wealth, honour, and political importance were showered on men, who possessed at once the key to theoretical knowledge and to success in practical life. Even earlier than at Paris, the law schools of Bologna became organised and permanent. Before the end of the century, the crowds of mature foreign students who flocked to hear the famous successors of Irnerius had

[margin note: Irnerius and the revival of Civil Law.]

set up the student-university of Bologna, whose establishment is as much of an epoch in the history of European thought as that of the university of masters at Paris.

The Church had long had its own courts and its own law ; but the victory of the Hildebrandine system gave a new importance to the Courts Christian and to the Canon Law which they upheld. It was the aim of the Church reformers to draw a hard and fast line between Church and State, and to bind together the scattered and often antagonistic corporations, out of which the Church was constituted, into a single self-governing, self-sufficing, independent body, of which the Pope was the absolute monarch. All through the eleventh century efforts were made by leading ecclesiastical lawyers to do for the law of the Church what was already being done for the law of the State. Italy witnessed most of these attempts, but the canonists of Germany and Gaul were not behindhand, and the most famous of the early compilations, which appeared in 1115, was the work of a north-French churchman, Ivo, Bishop of Chartres, a pupil of Lanfranc of Bec. But these preliminary efforts were superseded by the *Decretum*, or more accurately the *Concordantia discordantium Canonum*, of Gratian, which probably appeared in 1142. Gratian was a monk of the new order of Camaldoli, living in a convent at Bologna. The book which he published was a text-book, the effort of a private student, with no other authority than what it could command from its own merits. But its merits were such that it swept all its predecessors out of the field, and soon won something of the authority that belonged to a definite codification of previous ecclesiastical jurisprudence. It appeared at the right place and at the right moment. From that time onwards the study of Canon Law stood side by side with that of the Civil Law at Bologna, and the town of Irnerius and Gratian became the intellectual centre of the great controversies of Church and State, which then distracted Europe. Before long the Canon

Law became as elaborate and comprehensive a system as that Civil Law, which it copied, developed and sometimes reacted against. The canonists became a band of specialists, separated from the civilians on the one hand and the theologians on the other. Just as the practical advantages of the study of Civil Law called away the votaries of the unprofitable secular study of literature, so did the practical uses of Canon Law divert active and ambitious churchmen from the academic study of theology. Law became the attractive science as well for ardent ecclesiastics as for men of the world. If it involved less speculative activity than the studies it superseded, it had the advantage of helping to bridge over the gulf between the little world of isolated students and the broad world of everyday life. As the revival of dialectic renewed men's interests in abstract science, so did the revival of law broaden men's practical interests. If in the long-run it gave weapons to Empire as well as to Papacy, the first result was to complete the equipment of the hierarchy for the business of ruling the world. While the civilian's Empire was a theory, the canonist's Papacy was a fact. As living head of a living system, the Pope became a constant fountain of new legislation for the Canon Law, while the Civil Law remained as it had been in Justinian's time, with little power of adaptation to the needs of a changing state of society.

The new movements strengthen the Church. Stimulated by the religious revival and the monastic movement, victorious over nascent heresy, yet invigorated by the new activity of human thought, protected by the enthusiasm which had brought about the Crusades, a state within the state, with her own law, her own officers, and her own wonderful organisation, the Church of the twelfth century stood at the very height of her power, and drew fresh strength, even from the sources that might well have brought about her ruin.

CHAPTER X

Origin of the Hohenstaufen—Election of Lothair II. and consequent rivalry of Welf and Weiblingen—The reign of the Priests' Emperor—Norbert and Albert the Bear—Lothair and Italy—Roger unites Sicily and Naples—Honorius II.—Schism of Innocent II. and Anacletus—Lothair's privilege to the Church—Election of Conrad III.—His contest with the Guelfs—The Eastward march of German civilisation—Final triumph of Innocent II.—Roger's organisation of the Norman kingdom—Growth of municipal autonomy in northern and central Italy

Two thousand feet above the sea, on the very summit of one of the northern outliers of the rugged Swabian Alp that separates the valley of the upper Neckar from that of the upper Danube, stood the castle of Hohenstaufen, that gave its name to the most gifted house that ever ruled over the mediæval Empire. The hereditary land of the family lay around, and a few miles east, nearer the Neckar valley, lies the village of Weiblingen from which came the even more famous name of Ghibelline. The lords of this upland region were true Swabian magnates, who were gradually brought into greatness by their energy and zeal in supporting the Empire. In the darkest days of his struggle with the Church, Henry IV. had no more active or loyal partisan than Frederick of Buren or Hohenstaufen, whom he married to his daughter Agnes, and upon whom he conferred the duchy of Swabia. It was after the ancient fashion that the

Origin of the Hohen-staufen.

[1] To the books enumerated in chapter i. may now be added, Busk's discursive but detailed *Mediæval Popes, Kings, Emperors and Crusaders, from 1125 to 1268.* Bernhardi's *Lothar von Supplinburg* and *Konrad III* deal specially with the two reigns covered in this chapter.

new Duke of Swabia should find his chief enemy in the Duke of Bavaria. But besides many a bitter feud with the papalist house of Welf or Guelf, Frederick had to deal with no less formidable enemies within his own duchy. The same dis-integrating influences that were affecting all Germany were at work in Swabia. Berthold of Zähringen, a mighty man in the upper Rhineland, sought to attain the Swabian duchy by zealous championship of the papal cause. After long fighting with the Staufer, the lord of Zähringen was able to effect a practical division of the duchy. In 1097 he was allowed all ducal rights in those Swabian lands between Rhine and Alps, which in a later age became the centre of the Swiss confederation. He did not lose even the title of duke, so that with the Dukes of Zähringen as effective rulers of Upper Swabia, the Hohenstaufen influence was limited to the north. The first Hohenstaufen Duke of Swabia had, by the Emperor's daughter, two sons, whose names were

Frederick
and Conrad.
Frederick and Conrad. These nephews of Henry v. were always marked out by their uncle as his successors. They inherited as a matter of course the private possessions of the Salian house. They had already given proof that they were worthy of a high destiny. Frederick, the elder, succeeded to his father's duchy of Lower Swabia. He was now thirty-five years old, strong, courageous, ambitious, and well conducted. He had further strengthened his position by marrying Judith, daughter of Henry the Black, the Guelfic Duke of Bavaria (died 1126), a match which seemed likely to bridge over the natural antagonism of the two great southern 'nations' of Germany. Conrad, the younger brother, had obtained from his uncle the duchy of Franconia. All south Germany might well seem united in support of Frederick's succession to the Empire. But the hierarchical party feared lest the traditional attitude of the Staufer might imperil the triumph of the Church. The feudal nobles were alarmed lest too vigorous a ruler might limit their independence. The Saxons as ever were opposed

to a southern Emperor, likely to renew the Salian attack upon their national liberties.

Saxony was still almost as vividly contrasted to the rest of Germany as in the days when it gave Henry the Fowler and Otto the Great to save the kingdom, that the last degenerate Frankish rulers had brought to the verge of rum. Despite many defeats and constant attacks, it was as free, restless, strong and warlike as ever. In the later years of Henry v.'s reign a new and vigorous duke had restored and reorganised its fighting power. Lothair of Supplinburg was the son of that Count Gerhard who had fallen in battle against Henry iv. on the banks of the Unstrut. By his marriage with Richenza, niece of Egbert of Meissen, and grand-daughter of Otto of Nordheim, he had acquired the Saxon duchy, which under his hands had lost nothing of its ancient character. While the Dukes of Swabia had yielded the jurisdiction of the south to the Dukes of Zähringen, while Franconia was hopelessly split between rival houses, Lorraine divided between upper and lower Lorraine, and the Margraves of the East Mark, who had already the power and were soon to have the title of Dukes of Austria, had cut deep into the integrity of the Bavarian duchy, while in all the duchies alike a swarm of counts and barons had absorbed most of the effective attributes of sovereignty, Saxony alone maintained its unity and independence. Whatever the encroachments of the feudal principle, the Saxon duke still headed and represented a nation proudly conscious of its greatness and fiercely resentful of all southern influence. Lothair had grown old in long and doubtful struggles against Henry v., and the Emperor had never ventured to deprive his unruly subject of his duchy. The Duke had found his position much strengthened, since the setting-up of a Danish archbishopric at Lund in 1104 had barred the prospects of the Archbishop of Bremen obtaining that northern patriarchate that Adalbert had of old desired, and had in consequence destroyed the importance of the chief ecclesiastical makeweight

The Saxon Duchy and Lothair of Supplinburg.

to his authority. He was no servile friend of the hierarchy, but, after the Saxon fashion, he wished well to the Church, as the best check upon the power of the imperialistic south. Long experience had made him cautious, moderate, and politic. He was the strongest noble in Germany.

In August 1125 the German magnates met together at Mainz to chose their new king. The antagonism of the nations was so fierce that, while Saxons and Bavarians encamped on the right bank of the Rhine, Swabians and Franks took up their quarters on the opposite side of the stream. A committee of forty princes, ten chosen from each of the four nations, was set up to conduct the preliminary negotiations, and if possible, to agree upon a candidate. Frederick of Swabia, Lothair of Saxony, and Leopold of Austria were all proposed as candidates. The craft of Adalbert of Mainz, as ever the foe of Henry v. and his house, prevented the election of the Staufer, by representing to the princes that Frederick's choice would be interpreted as a recognition of an hereditary claim. For the first time since the election of Conrad II., the magnates had a free hand, and they could not resist the temptation to use it. Adalbert isolated Frederick by breaking up his new alliance with the Guelfs. Conrad of Franconia was away on Crusade. The alliance of Saxons and Bavarians, backed up by the skill of Adalbert, the zeal of the Papalists and the enthusiasm of the Rhineland, led to the election of Lothair.

Election of Lothair II., 1125.

Lothair II. reigned from 1125 to 1138. He was already sixty years old, at his accession, but he ruled with energy and vigour. By marrying his only daughter, Gertrude, to Henry the Proud, son of Duke Henry the Black, he united his fortunes with those of the house of Guelf, and prepared the way for that union of Saxony and Bavaria which had long been the Guelfs' dream. In these days the struggle of the rival families of Welf and Weiblingen, of Guelf and Ghibelline, first brought out the famous antagonism that in

The reign of Lothair II., 1125-1138.

The Hohenstaufen subdued.

later times was extended over the Alps, and grew from a strife of hostile houses to a warfare of contending principles, and finally degenerated into the most meaningless faction fight that history has ever witnessed.

Lothair deprived Frederick of Swabia of part of the Salian lands inherited from Henry v. This was the signal of war between Swabian and Saxon, Weiblingen and Welf. In 1127 Conrad, the younger Hohenstaufen brother, was set up as anti-king, and in 1128 crossed the Alps in quest of the imperial crown and the heritage of the Countess Matilda. Milan welcomed him, and crowned him with the Iron Crown. But the Pope, Honorius ii., excommunicated him, and he could make no way south of the Apennines. Meanwhile King Lothair and his son-in-law, Henry the Proud, took possession of the Rhenish towns that were the Hohenstaufen strongholds, and devastated Swabia with fire and sword. In 1134 Frederick gave up the contest, and next year Conrad also made his submission. Lothair showed politic magnanimity and left them their hereditary possessions.

In a Diet at Bamberg in 1135 Lothair proclaimed a general peace for Germany. To Saxons and churchmen his reign was a golden age. 'It is with right,' wrote a contemporary annalist, 'that we call Lothair the father of his country, for he upheld it strenuously and was always ready to risk his life for justice's sake.' 'He left behind him,' said another, 'such a memory that he will be blessed until the end of time: for in his days the Church rejoiced in peace, the service of God increased, and there was plenty in all things.' He has been accused of sacrificing the greatness of the Empire for the sake of immediate advantages. But there is little evidence that he was ever false to the Concordat of Worms, and it is hard to condemn a prince who, by accepting the ideas of the rights of the Church that found favour at the time, was able to put down domestic strife, and allow his people to advance in civilisation and power.

(marginal note: Lothair and German Civilisation.)

PERIOD II.

As the true heir of the Ottos, Lothair occupied himself with extending German political supremacy and culture into Scandi-

The Slavs and the Danes.

navian and Slavonic lands. His earlier efforts against the Bohemians were not successful, but even before peace was restored in Germany, he forced King Niel of Denmark and his son Magnus to do homage and pay tribute. He turned his arms against the neighbouring Slavs, and brought back to his obedience the chiefs of the Wagrians and the Abotrites. Duke Boleslav of Poland recognised him as his lord, and agreed to hold Pomerania and Rügen as fiefs of the Empire. Duke Sobeslav of Bohemia and King Bela II. of Hungary referred their disputes to his arbitration. At his court were seen the envoys of the Eastern Emperor and of the Venetians. Everywhere his influence was recognised.

Lothair busied himself greatly with the revival of religion in his rude Saxon duchy, and with the extension of Christianity

Norbert and Albert the Bear.

and German political influence amidst the heathens and half-heathens beyond the limits of his Empire. Side by side with the soldiers of Albert the Bear, Margrave of the North Mark, went the Christian missionaries and revivalists. At the bidding of the Emperor, Norbert left Prémontré, and became Archbishop of Magdeburg, and founded there a new house that became the second great centre of Premonstratensian ideas. Through his influence secular canons were removed from most of the cathedrals of eastern Saxony and the Marches, and replaced by Premonstratensians. Norbert wished to make Magdeburg the centre of missions to the East and a patriarchate over Polish and Wendish Christianity. New bishoprics were founded in Poland and half-heathen Pomerania, and the Polish Archbishop of Gnesen lost for a time his metropolitical power. For a time the ideas of Adalbert of Bremen were again in the ascendant, and the Pope restored the rights of Bremen over Lund and the churches of Scandinavia. From Bremen Vicelin brought Christianity to the conquered Wagrians and Abotrites. The fortress of Siegburg, built by Lothair on the Trave, both assured his supremacy and protected the famous monastery that grew up at its walls.

The alliance between Lothair and the Papacy did not involve the abdication of any imperial rights in Italy, but the pressure of German affairs put Italy somewhat in Lothair and the background. A great series of changes was Italy. now being brought about in Italy. In the north and centre the communal revolution was, as we shall soon see, in full progress. In the south the Norman power was being consolidated, while a fresh schism soon distracted the Papacy.

Since the conquest of Sicily from the Mohammedans by Roger, the youngest brother of Robert Guiscard, the chief Norman lordship of southern Italy had been Union of divided between the two branches of the house of Sicily and Tancred. Roger ruled Sicily as its count until Apulia by his death in 1101, when he was succeeded by Roger, 1127. his son and namesake, Roger II., a child of four. Meanwhile the stock of Robert Guiscard bore rule in Calabria and Apulia. Roger, son of Robert, was Duke of Apulia from his father's death in 1085 to his own decease in 1111. His son and successor, William, was a weakling, and upon his death without issue in 1127, the direct line of Robert became extinct. Roger of Sicily had now long attained man's estate, and had shown his ability and energy in the administration of his county. After his cousin's death, he at once got himself accepted as Duke of Apulia and Calabria by the mass of the Norman barons, and then directed his resources towards conquering the states of southern Italy that were still outside the power of his house. With the subjugation of the rival Norman principality of Capua, and of the republics of Amalfi and Naples, the unity of the later kingdom of Naples and Sicily was substantially established.

Since 1124 Lambert, Bishop of Ostia, the Bolognese lawyer who had ended the Investiture Contest, had held the papal throne, with the title of Honorius II., but he failed to show the decision of character necessary to dominate the unruly local factions of Rome, or to resist the usurpations of the Count of Sicily. The union of Apulia and Sicily threatened the Italian balance, but Honorius strove in vain to form a league of Italian princes against Roger. In 1128 he was forced to accept Roger as lord of Apulia. The Norman soon scorned the titles of count and duke, which had contented his predecessors, and soon had an opportunity of gratifying his ambition to become a king.

Honorius II., 1124-1130.

On the death of Honorius II., the cardinals with due observance of all proper forms, chose as their Pope Peter Pierleone, a former monk of Cluny, who took the name of Anacletus II. But nothing could be less Cluniac than this Cluniac Pope, the son of a Jewish banker who had turned Christian, and made a great fortune at Rome during the Investiture Contest. The house of Pierleone had taken a considerable place among the great families of Rome, and one of the worst troubles of Honorius II. had been its violent opposition to his rule. Peter had shamelessly used his father's money to buy over the majority, and the worst and best motives led to the questioning of his election. The houses of Corsi and Frangipani, who had had the ear of the last Pope, were dismayed at the triumph of the head of the rival faction. The strong hierarchical party had no faith in the Jewish usurer's son. Accordingly, five cardinals offered the Papacy to Gregory, Cardinal-deacon of St. Angelo, who took the name of Innocent II., and was at once hailed as the candidate of the stronger churchmen. But in Rome he found himself powerless. He fled to Pisa, and thence to Genoa, Provence, Burgundy, and France. Anacletus meanwhile reigned in Rome and Italy, where, by granting the title of king to Roger of Sicily, he secured the support of the Normans.

Schism of Innocent II. and Anacletus, 1130.

Anacletus and Innocent both appealed to Lothair. But the real decision of their claims rested with Bernard of Clairvaux

Bernard had no faith in the splendour and pride of Cluny, and showed little respect for the forms of a papal election. He quickly perceived that the interests of the hierarchy were involved in recognising Innocent, and with characteristic enthusiasm declared for his cause, and soon won over France and its king.   Like Urban II., Innocent II. traversed France, crowned Louis VII. at Reims, and presided over a synod at Clermont.   England, Castile, Aragon followed France in recognising him.   Norbert accepted eagerly the guidance of St. Bernard, and prevailed upon Lothair to recognise Innocent.

Italy alone resisted, and Lothair crossed the Alps to win Italy for Innocent, and receive from him the imperial crown. Germany took little interest in his expedition, and the scanty band that followed him was almost exclusively Saxon.   Innocent availed himself of his coming to return to Italy, and enter into the possession of the long-contested inheritance of the Countess Matilda.   In April 1133, Lothair and Innocent entered Rome.   But Anacletus held the Leonine city and the castle of St. Angelo, and Innocent could only get possession of the Lateran, where he crowned the Emperor on 4th June.   Four days later Innocent II. issued a diploma of privilege to Lothair, in which the Pope, 'not wishing to diminish but increase the majesty of the Empire, granted the Emperor all his due and canonical rights, and forbade the prelates of Germany laying hands on the temporalities [regalia] of their offices, except from the Emperor's grant.'   An agreement was also arrived at with regard to the inheritance of the Countess Matilda. Lothair consented to receive Matilda's fiefs from the Pope, and to pay tribute for them.   At his death they were to go to Henry of Bavaria, his son-in-law.   By thus appearing before the world as receiving from the Pope rights which he could well claim as his own, Lothair secured for his family estates that might otherwise have gone to the Hohenstaufen.   But the Papalists were much exalted at the submission of the

Side notes: Lothair in Italy. / His coronation and issue of privileges to the Church, 1133.

Emperor. A German chronicler tells how Innocent caused a picture to be painted, in which the Pope was represented sitting on a throne, and the Emperor humbly receiving the crown from his hands. Two insolent verses inscribed beneath it told how the king had come to the gates of Rome, and had sworn to protect the privileges of the city, and how he became the man of the Pope who gave him the crown.[1]

Innocent had still much trouble with the Antipope, and his chief supporter, Roger of Sicily. He soon withdrew from
Rome to Pisa, where, in 1134, he held a synod,
which Bernard left Clairvaux to attend. But not
even the animating presence of the saint could
make Anacletus and Roger submit. Innocent
was forced to continue at Pisa until, in 1136, Lothair crossed the Alps a second time to help him. On this occasion the Emperor came with an army, and St. Bernard's fervid denunciations of the Norman tyrant, who alone upheld to any purpose the schismatic cause, gave the expedition the character of a crusade. Lothair performed exploits, said Otto of Freising, in Calabria and Apulia such as no Frankish king had done since the days of Charles the Great. He captured some of the chief Norman towns, such as Bari and Salerno, while the fleets of Pisa made precarious the communication between Calabria and Sicily. Roger, after striving in vain to bribe the Emperor into retreat, did not scruple to arm his Saracens against the two lords of the Christian world. He retreated into the mountains of Calabria, while the Pope and Emperor united in deposing him and conferring Apulia on Reginald, a prominent Norman baron of that region. But at the moment of victory Innocent and Lothair quarrelled. Both claimed to be the suzerains of Apulia, and both claimed the sole right of investing the new duke with his office. After a hot dispute,

Lothair and the Normans of Sicily, 1136-7.

---

[1] ' Rex venit ante fores, jurans prius Urbis honores,
Post homo fit papæ, sumit quo dante coronam.'
Ann. Colon. Max. s.a. 1133, in Pertz, *Mon. Hist. Germ. SS.* vol. xvii. ;
Ragewinus, *Gesta Fred. Imp. ib.* xx. 422.

they agreed to hand over jointly to Reginald the banner, which was the symbol of his dignity; but before long Lothair hurried home, disgusted with his Papal ally, and leaving Anacletus again in possession of Rome. The fatigues of war and travel told upon him, and he died at a Tyrolese village on 4th December 1137, saved only by death from entering upon the footsteps of the Salian enemies of the Church.

Henry the Proud, Duke of Bavaria, aspired to succeed his father-in-law, having, besides large hereditary possessions, the duchies of Bavaria and Saxony, while his Election of enjoyment of the heritage of Matilda gave Conrad III., him an equally important position in northern 1138. Italy and Tuscany. He boasted that his authority stretched from the North Sea to the Mediterranean. But the arrogance which gave him his nickname deprived him of personal popularity, and his extraordinary resources made his accession disliked by all who feared a strong monarchy, while the Church party, that had procured the election of Lothair, was now alienated from him. The result of all this was that the same circumstances that had led to Lothair's being made king in 1125, resulted, in 1138, in the rejection of his son-in-law. Adalbero, Archbishop of Trier, a creature of Innocent II., played, in the vacancy of both Mainz and Cologne, the part which Adalbert of Mainz had so cleverly filled on the previous occasion. He summoned the electoral diet to meet in his own town of Coblenz. Though Saxony and Bavaria sent no representatives, the magnates of Swabia and Franconia gathered together at the appointed spot. Frederick, Duke of Swabia, was no longer a candidate, but, on 7th March, his younger brother, Conrad, the old enemy of Lothair, was chosen king.

The struggle of Welf and Weiblingen soon broke out anew. Henry delivered up the imperial insignia, and Contest of offered to acknowledge Conrad, if confirmed in Conrad with his possessions; but the new king would not the Guelfs. accept these terms, and before long deprived Henry of both his duchies. The margrave, Albert the Bear, who, like Henry the Proud, claimed descent from the Billung stock, was made Duke of Saxony, and Leopold of Austria, Conrad's half-brother, received Bavaria. Civil war inevitably followed. All Saxony rallied round the Guelfs, and Albert was driven from his new duchy. But in October 1139, Henry the Proud was carried off by a sudden attack of fever, and a child ten years old succeeded. With the help of his brother Frederick and the faithful Rhineland, Conrad invaded Saxony in 1140, and won a victory at Weinsberg that secured him his throne, but did not ensure the reduction of the Saxons. Next year the death of the Austrian Duke of Bavaria made compromise more easy. In February 1142 a treaty was signed at Frankfurt, by which the Saxons recognised Conrad as king, and Conrad admitted the young Henry the Guelf to the duchy of Saxony. Before long Gertrude, his mother, married Henry, the Count Palatine, brother of Leopold of Austria, and another half-brother of Conrad, who next year received his brother's duchy of Bavaria. Thus the great struggle ended in a compromise, in which, if Conrad retained the throne, Saxony and Bavaria still remained under the influence of the house of Guelf.

Conrad was a gallant knight, liberal, attractive, and popular, but he had little statecraft, and no idea how best to **The Second** establish his position. The preaching of the **Crusade,** Second Crusade soon called him from the dull and **1147.** ungrateful work of ruling the Germans to adventures more attractive to his spirit of knight-errantry. At Christmas 1146 he took the cross from Bernard of Clairvaux in the cathedral of Speyer. Next spring he proclaimed a general peace, and procured the coronation of his little son Henry as joint king. Between 1147 and 1149 he was away from Germany on Crusade. With him went his gifted nephew Frederick, who, in 1147, had succeeded on the death of his father, the elder Frederick, to the Duchy of Swabia. The Crusade was a failure, and the long absence of the monarch still further increased the troubles of Germany.

The crusading spirit rose so high under Bernard's preaching that those who could not follow Conrad to the Holy Land organised fresh Crusades against the heathen who, despite the work of Norbert and Lothair, still closely fringed the Empire on the east. The Saxons naturally took a prominent share in this Crusade. But the rivalry of Albert the Bear and Henry of Saxony, whom men now began to style Henry the Lion, prevented any very immediate results flowing from these movements. Yet the definitive conversion of Pomerania, and the acquisition by Albert of Brandenburg, were important steps forward in the Germanisation of the lands between Elbe and Oder. From the victories of Albert the Bear begins the history of that Mark of Brandenburg, which in nearly every after-age was to take so prominent a part in German history. In later years, when the strong rule of Frederick Barbarossa kept local feuds within bounds, Albert the Bear and Henry the Lion vied with each other as pioneers of German civilisation in the north-east. At the moment it was enough for Henry the Lion to consolidate his power in Saxony. When Conrad came back from Syria he found that Count Welf, a kinsman of Henry the Lion who had returned early from the Crusade, had raised a rebellion. When this was suppressed, Henry the Lion again claimed Bavaria and prepared for revolt. The young King Henry, in whose name the country had been ruled during his father's absence, now died prematurely, and on 15th February 1152 Conrad followed him to the tomb.

The east-ward advance of the German kingdom.

Never did the affairs of Papacy and Empire run in more separate courses than during the reign of Conrad III. While Europe as a whole paid unquestioning obedience to the Papal power, the last period of the Pontificate of Innocent II., and nearly the whole of the reigns of his immediate successors, were occupied in sordid struggles with the Roman nobility, with disobedient neighbours, and with rebellious vassals. After the retreat of Lothair over the Alps, Innocent II.

was again left, in 1137, to contend against the Antipope
and his partisans. His position was, however, stronger
than it had been, and he was able to maintain himself in
Rome, despite Anacletus' continued presence in the castle
of St. Angelo. But the loss of the imperial presence was soon
far more than balanced by the arrival of a man whose support
outweighed that of kings and princes. In the spring of 1137
Bernard crossed the Alps, resolved to make a last desperate
effort to root out the remnants of the schism that he had
laboured against for seven years. He reached Rome, and
instead of falling back on his usual methods of violent and
indiscriminate denunciation, he prudently had recourse to
private conferences with the few despairing partisans of the
schismatic Peter. There is perhaps no more convincing testi-
mony to Bernard's powers of persuasion than his victory
over the rude Roman barons and greedy self-seeking priests,
who upheld the Antipope through family tradition or through
fear of losing their revenues. He had talked many of them
over when the opportune death of the Antipope in January
1138 precipitated his inevitable triumph. The schismatics
chose a new Antipope, who took the name of Victor iv.,
but his policy was to negotiate terms of surrender, not to
prolong the division. In a few weeks Bernard persuaded
him to surrender his dignity to Innocent. Bernard at once
returned to Clairvaux, the crowning work of his life successfully accomplished.

In April 1139 Innocent ii. consummated his triumph by
holding a General Council in the Lateran, which was attended
by a thousand bishops. This second Lateran
Council was reckoned by the Westerns as the
Tenth General Council. It removed the last
traces of the schism, and re-enacted more formally
the canons already drawn up in the Pope's presence at
the Council of Reims of 1131. It is significant of the
future that the Council condemned the errors of Arnold of
Brescia.

The Second
General
Lateran
Council,
1139.

Innocent thus restored the Papacy to its old position in things spiritual, but not even St. Bernard could give him much help against Roger of Sicily.   After the quarrel of Pope and Emperor, the Norman king speedily won back his position in Apulia and Calabria, and even *Innocent II. and Roger of Sicily.* at the very end of the schism his influence had forced Monte Casino, the mother of all Western monasticism, to acknowledge Anacletus.   Spiritual weapons were useless against Roger. No sooner, therefore, was the council over than Innocent took the field in person against his rebellious vassal.   The fate of Leo IX. was speedily repeated.   The papal army was no match against Roger's veterans, and Innocent, shut up in San Germano, was forced to yield himself prisoner.   Roger showed the head of the Church the same respect which Robert had shown his predecessor.   But the Pope could only win back his liberty by confirming to the Norman all the advantages which he had formerly wrested from the weakness of Anacletus. The treaty of Mignano again restored the old alliance between the Papacy and the Italian Normans.   Roger did homage to Innocent for Sicily, Apulia, and Capua.   A great south Italian kingdom was thus definitely legalised which, in the varied changes of subsequent history, obstinately maintained its unity with itself and its separateness from the rest of the peninsula.

Roger governed the state which he had founded with rare ability and energy.   He was a true Norman, and many features of his character suggest a comparison between him and William the Conqueror.   He now showed as much capacity in statecraft as he had previously shown as a warrior.   Fierce, relentless, and unforgiving, he ruthlessly crushed the barons that *The organisation of the kingdom of Sicily under Roger I., 1127-1154.* had profited by the period of struggle to consolidate their independence, and built up a well-ordered centralised despotism, that was able to give examples in the art of government to Henry of Anjou.   With rare sympathy and skill, he permitted the motley population of his new kingdom to live their old lives under their old laws.   The Saracens of Sicily that had faithfully supported him in the days of his adversity, continued in their former abodes, occupying separate districts in the cities, worshipping without hindrance in their mosques, and still governed in the petty matters of every-day life by their own judges after the laws of Islam. The Byzantine Greeks, still numerous in the towns of Calabria, enjoyed similar immunities for their schismatic worship, and still followed the Roman law. Arabic and Greek were equally recognised with Latin as official languages in the public acts, and Roger's coins bore Arabic devices. The court of the king took a character of Eastern pomp and luxury that anticipated the times of Frederick II. A Greek general led Roger's armies, and a Greek churchman, who wrote a book against the Roman primacy, shared with Arab physicians, geographers, and astronomers the patronage of the Norman king. The very monuments of art show the same strange juxtaposition of the stern romanesque of Neustria with the mosaics of the Byzantines, and the brilliant decorations of Arabic architects. Roger made Naples and Sicily one of the best-governed states in Europe, and with the happy quickness of sympathy and readiness to learn and borrow, which was the best mark of the Norman genius, combined elements the most diverse and unpromising into a happy and contented whole.

Despite his energy at home, Roger pursued an active external policy. He remained a faithful but an unruly ally of the Papacy. **Roger's later wars.** Like Robert Guiscard he turned his ambition against Constantinople, and Europe saw the strange spectacle of Manuel Comnenus allied with Conrad III. in withstanding the aggressions. But Roger's most important wars were those against the Saracens, whom he pursued into Africa. His first and most permanent conquest was Malta, which remained until the sixteenth century a part of **Conquest of North Africa.** the Sicilian realm. The Mohammedan princes of North Africa recognised him as their lord and opened their ports to his merchants. In 1146 his admiral conquered Tripoli, and in 1148 Roger himself led a large expedition to Africa. After the capture of Tunis, the whole coast line from Cape Bon to Tripoli was subject to the Norman king, who boasted that the African obeyed him as well as the Apulian, the Calabrian, and the Sicilian. After a long reign, he died in 1154, with the reputation of one of the greatest kings of his time.

While southern Italy settled down into a well-ordered state, a very different process was at work in the north, where the feudal nobility had never been strong, and the towns had always been important. As the contest between Papacy and Empire became chronic, the general tendency was for the feudal nobility *Growth of municipal autonomy in Lombardy.* to uphold the Empire, and the townsmen the cause of the Church. As in the days of the early Church, each Italian town of any importance was the seat of a bishop, who became the natural leader of the citizens in their struggle against the rustic nobility. This tendency was particularly strong in Lombardy, where the logic of facts and lavish grants of imperial privilege had conferred on the bishops the power of the ancient counts, or had subordinated the imperial officers under the episcopal authority. In Lombardy therefore the municipal revolution broke out, though it soon spread to all northern and central Italy.

The municipal government of Lombardy grew up gradually and almost imperceptibly under the shade of the episcopal power. The townsfolk became more numerous and more wealthy. The inland cities became great seats of manufacturing industry, important market centres, or, like Bologna and Padua, famous for their schools. The towns on or near the sea found even greater prosperity through foreign trade. The necessity of common action in business, no less than juxtaposition in common residence behind strong walls, brought together the citizens in a common unity of feeling. The very subordinate agents of the bishops' power supply the rudiments of a common organisation. The eleventh century very commonly saw the citizens in revolt against their episcopal protectors

Milan, when on the side of its archbishop, had been strong enough to enable Aribert to wage war against the Emperor himself [see pages 58, 59]. In the next generation Milan and its archbishops were generally at war. The quarrel of Pope and Emperor made it easy for the dexterous townsmen to play the ecclesiastical and the temporal authority against each other, and Popes and Emperors alike were prepared to bid heavily for its support. Thus the 'regalia,' which the bishops had usurped from the counts, passed in some way from them to the citizens. By the beginning of the twelfth century the great towns of the north had become self-governing municipalities.

At the head of the municipal organisation stood the *consuls*, the chief magistrates of the town, varying widely in numbers, authority, and method of appointment, but everywhere the recognised heads of the city state. The consulate, which began in Italy towards the end of the twelfth century, was in its origin a sworn union of the citizens of a town bent upon obtaining for themselves the benefits of local autonomy, Private, and often, like the North French *Commune*, rebellious in its early history, the consulate in the end obtained the control of the municipal authority. With its erection or recognition begins the independent municipal organisation of the Italian cities.[1] Besides the ruling consuls was a council, or *credentia*, of the 'wise men' of the city, acting as a senate. Beyond these governing bodies was the *communitas*, meeting on grave occasions in a common *parlamentum* or conference. The local life of the municipalities was intensely active, but there were fierce jealousies and perpetual faction fights between the different orders of the population. The even more violent local hatred of

---

[1] On the whole subject of the constitution of the Italian towns see Hegel, *Geschichte der Stadteverfassung von Italien* (1847), Heinemann, *Zur Entstehung der Stadteverfassung in Italien* (1896), whose views Hegel contests; or for their more general history, Lanzi, *Storia dei communi italiani* (1881-1884), and Sismondi's old-fashioned *Histoire des Républiques Italiennes*.

neighbouring cities made common action almost impossible, and led to constant bloody wars. But despite these troubles, the Lombard cities grew in wealth, trade, numbers, and reputation.

The Tuscan cities followed at a distance the example of their northern neighbours. It was their chief concern to wrest municipal privileges from the feudal mar- The Tuscan quises, who had up to this point ruled town cities. and country alike. Even more conspicuously than the inland towns, the maritime cities attained wealth and freedom. Pisa, Genoa, and Venice obtained, as we have seen, a great position in the East from the time of the First Crusade. While Venice stood apart, proud of its dependence on the Eastern Emperor, the life of the other maritime cities was much the same as that of the inland towns, save that it was more bustling, tumultuous, and varied. Before the end of eleventh century, Pisa and Genoa had driven the Saracens out of Corsica and Sardinia, and set up their own authority in their stead.

The free, restless life of the Italian commune offered a splendid field for the intellectual revival which we have traced in the preceding chapter. Side by side with the development of Italian municipalities, went the growth of the famous schools of Italy. The Italian scholars were for the most part townsmen, laymen, and lawyers. While the students north of the Alps became a little cosmopolitan aristocracy of talent, living in a world of their own, and scarcely influenced by the political life around them, the Italian students easily became politicians and leaders of men. Abelard led no revolt save against the tyranny of authority and teachers of obsolete doctrine. His chief Italian disciple became the first educated popular leader known to the mediæval world. With the influence of Arnold of Brescia the gulf between the new life of action and the new life of speculation was bridged over.

Arnold of Brescia was born in the town from which he

took his name.   At Paris he became an ardent disciple and
personal friend of Abelard.   Returning to his native city,

Early life of
Arnold of
Brescia.

he became provost of a foundation of Canons
Regular, and a conspicuous influence both in the
spiritual and political life of the town.   He had the
love of novelty, the restless vanity, the acute sceptical intellect
of his brilliant teacher.   He preached that priests were to live
on the tithes and free offerings of the faithful, that bishops
were to renounce their 'regalia,' and monks their lands,
and the laity only were to rule the state.   Under his
leadership, Brescia, like the other Lombard cities, cast off
the bishop's rule, but Innocent II. took up the bishop's
cause, and, as we have seen, the Lateran Council of 1139
deprived Arnold of his benefice and banished him from Italy.
He again crossed the Alps, stood by the side of Abelard
at the Council of Sens, and returned to Paris, and taught
at Abelard's old school on Mont Ste. Geneviève.   But his
doctrine of apostolic poverty was too extreme to please the
ambitious clerks who thronged the Paris schools, and he was
pursued by the inveterate malice of Bernard, who persuaded
Louis VII. to drive the heretic from France.   Arnold retired
to Zürich, whence he soon wandered, preaching, through the
valleys of upper Swabia, protected against Bernard's anger by
the papal legate Cardinal Guido, his old Paris comrade.
The abbot of Clairvaux was furious with the cardinal.
'Arnold of Brescia,' he wrote, 'whose speech is honey, whose
doctrine poison, the man whom Brescia has vomited forth,
whom Rome abhors, whom France drives to exile, whom
Germany curses, whom Italy refuses to receive, obtains thy
support.   To be his friend is to be the foe of the Pope and
God.'   In 1145 Arnold returned to Italy with Guido, and
was reconciled to the Church.   With his arrival in Rome
to work out his penance, the last and greatest period of his
career begins.

The end of the Pontificate of Innocent II. was marked by
the beginning of a fierce fight between the Pope and the city

of Rome. The old Roman spirit of opposition to the Pope had been revived by the long struggle of the typically Roman Anacletus, and what had been accomplished in The last Milan and Brescia seemed no impossible ideal years of for the Romans. In 1143 the Romans, enraged Innocent II. at the refusal of Innocent to destroy the rival city of Tivoli, set up a Commune, at the head of which was a The Roman popular Senate, to exercise the power hitherto in revolution. the hands of the noble consuls or the Pope himself. Before long they chose as 'Patrician' Giordano Pierleone, a kinsman of Anacletus. Innocent II. died at the very beginning of the struggle. His successor, Celestine II., reigned Celestine II., only from September 1143 to March 1144, and 1143-4, was powerless to withstand the Commune. The Lucius II., next Pope, Lucius II., put himself at the head Eugenius III., of the nobles, went to war against it, but was 1145-1154. slain while attempting to storm the Capitol (February 1145). This time the timid cardinals went outside their own number, and chose Eugenius III., the abbot of the Cistercian convent of Tre Fontane in the Campagna, a man whose chief recommendation was the ostentatious patronage of St. Bernard, and who was a simple and timid monk quite unversed in statecraft. Immediately after his election Eugenius fled from Rome, and after some temporising he crossed the Alps in 1147, leaving the Roman republic triumphant. He remained absent till 1148, mainly engaged in furthering the work of Bernard.

Arnold of Brescia now abandoned his spiritual exercises and put himself at the head of the Roman revolution. All Rome listened spellbound to his eloquence while Arnold of he preached against the pride and greed of the Brescia and cardinals, and denounced the Pope as no shep- Rome. herd of souls, but a man of blood and the torturer of the Church. His hope was now to free Rome permanently from all priestly rule, to reduce the clergy to apostolic poverty, and to limit them to their purely spiritual functions. Rome was to be a free municipality subject only to the Emperor,

PERIOD II. Q

who was to make the city the centre and source of his power, like the great Emperors of old 'We wish,' wrote the Romans to Conrad III., 'to exalt and glorify the Roman Empire, of which God has given you the rule. We would restore it as it was in the days of Constantine and Justinian. We have restored the Senate. We strive with all our might that Cæsar may enjoy his own. Come over and help us, for you will find in Rome all that you wish. Settle yourself firmly in the City that is the head of the world, and, freed from the fetters of the clergy, rule better than your predecessors over Germany and Italy.' But Conrad, intent on his crusading projects, paid no heed to the Roman summons.

Bernard saw as keenly as Arnold of Brescia how the political influence and wealth of the Church were in danger

Arnold of Brescia and St. Bernard. of overshadowing its religious work. 'Who will permit me to see before I die,' he wrote to Eugenius, 'the Church of God so ordered as it was in the old days, when the Apostles cast their nets to fish for souls and not for gold and silver?' But he recognised in Arnold's policy an attack on the influence of the Church, not merely an assault on its worldly possessions and dignities. He carried on the war against Arnold with more acerbity than ever. Eugenius again passed over into Italy to measure swords with the Roman republic. When personal intercourse ceased, Bernard sent to the Pope his book *De Consideratione*, in which he warned the Papacy to follow the Apostles and not Constantine, and lamented the danger lest the avarice of lordship and apostolate should prove fatal to it. It is strange how nearly the arch-enemies Arnold of Brescia and Bernard approached each other, both in their ideas and in their way of life. Both lived like ascetics. Both hated the pomp and show of priestly dignity, and wished to keep the Church apart from the world. Yet the pupil of Abelard was the apostle of the lay spirit; and the last of the fathers was the greatest pillar of that sacerdotal autocracy, whose dangers to spiritual life he so fully realised.

Eugenius now accepted the new constitution of the City, and was content to act as the spiritual chief of his diocese. But even on these conditions a prolonged stay in Rome was impossible. In 1150 the conflict was renewed. But the death of King Conrad, two years later, put an end to the state of things that had prevailed since the end of the Investiture Contest. Conscious that under his hands the imperial power had suffered some diminution, Conrad on his deathbed bade his friends pay no regard to the claims of his infant son, but secure the succession to his well-tried nephew Frederick. The year after, Bernard of Clairvaux, the wielder of the Church's might, followed the king to the tomb. We now enter into a new period, when the changed relations of Church and State correspond to a mighty development of the economical and industrial powers of the people of western Europe. The imperial power was to be renewed, and, as in the days of the Saxon Emperors, was to save the Papacy from its Roman enemies, only to enter again into fierce conflict with it for the rule of the world. The quiet period, during which each country was free to work out its own development, and during which, in the absence of great rulers, the dominating influences were those of the leaders and opponents of the new religious movement, is succeeded by another period, when the chief interest again shifts back to politics. The age of Bernard and Abelard is succeeded by the age of Frederick Barbarossa and Henry of Anjou.

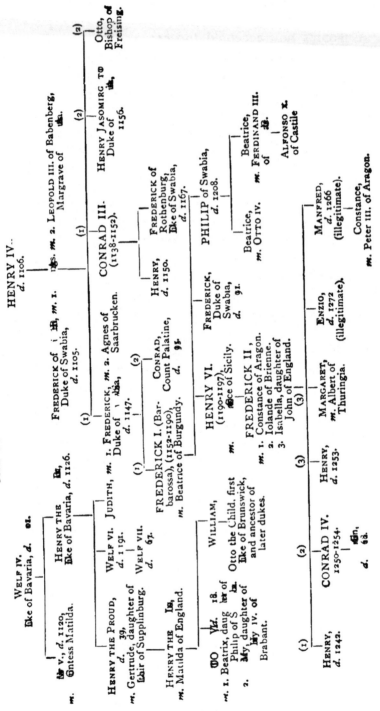

THE GUELFS AND THE HOHENSTAUFEN.

CHAPTER XI

Election and Policy of Frederick I.—Frederick and Adrian IV.—Fall of Arnold of Brescia—Frederick's early German Policy—The Burgundian Marriage and the Diet of Besançon—Breach with the Papacy—Frederick's Second Italian Journey—Diet of Roncaglia and Destruction of Milan—Alexander III. and the Antipopes—The Lombard League—Battle of Legnano—Peace of Constance—Frederick and Germany—Fall of Henry the Lion—Division of the Saxon Duchy—Union of Sicily with the Empire—The Lateran Council and the last days of Alexander III.—His Successors—Urban III. and Frederick—The Crusade and Death of Frederick—His Personality and Character.

'IT is the cardinal principle of the law of the Roman Empire,' wrote Otto of Freising, 'that the succession depends not upon hereditary right, but on the election of the princes.' According to this precept the magnates of Germany met in March 1152 at Frankfurt to appoint a successor to Conrad III. Some of the barons of Italy attended the assembly. 'There were,' wrote Otto, 'two mighty houses in the Roman Empire, one that of the Henrys of Weiblingen, the other that of the Welfs of

Election of Frederick I., 1152.

---

[1] Among the modern authorities for this period may be quoted Prutz's *Kaiser Friedrich I.*, Reuter's *Geschichte Alexanders des Dritten und der Kirche seiner Zeit*, and Ficker's *Forschungen zur Reichs- und Rechtsgeschichte in Italien.* Giesebrecht's great work, unluckily, ends with the fall of Henry the Lion. Raumer's *Geschichte der Hohenstaufen* is quite antiquated. A full account of Frederick's Italian struggle is to be found in English in Testa's *History of the War of Frederick I. against the Communes of Lombardy* (1877). Otto of Freising is a first-rate original chronicler.

Altorf. The one was wont to furnish mighty emperors, the other puissant dukes. These families, jealous of each other, had been long accustomed to disturb the tranquillity of the commonwealth by their feuds, but in the days of Henry v. Frederick, the duke, representative of the royal stock, had married the daughter of Henry, Duke of the Bavarians, the representative of the ducal family. The offspring of this union was Duke Frederick, and the princes, regarding not only the energy and valour of the young duke, but considering that he shared the blood of both houses, and like a corner-stone could bind the two together, chose him as their king that thus with God's blessing he might end their ancient quarrel.'

The new king was well worthy of the general confidence which he inspired. Already thirty years of age, he had *Frederick's* abundantly displayed rare gifts both as a states-*policy.* man and as a general. He had administered his duchy of Swabia with energy and success. He had combined loyalty to his uncle Conrad with friendship for his cousin Henry the Lion, and his mediation had saved Duke Welf vi. in the time of his greatest disaster. His exploits on the Crusade had spread abroad his fame, and the few survivors who had reached home in safety recognised that they owed their lives to his courage and policy. He was admired for his kingly bearing and fair proportions, for the chivalry and generosity of his character, for his independent attitude towards the Church, for the subtle policy so rarely combined with the simple virtues of the hero of romance.

Frederick threw himself, with all the passionate ardour of his character, into the difficult task of restoring the waning glories of the Empire. For the thirty-seven years of life that remained to him, he never faltered in his task. To him Germany and Italy were but two sections of the Holy Roman Empire whose rights and dignities he strove with all his might to uphold. 'During all his reign,' wrote a chronicler, 'nothing was nearer his heart than re-establishing the

Empire of Rome on its ancient basis.' To him every right that had been exercised by Justinian or Constantine, by Charlemagne or Otto the Great, was literally his right as the lawful successor of these mighty rulers. He has been very truly described as an 'imperialist Hildebrand,' and Hildebrand himself had not a more lofty consciousness of his high purpose and divine mission to establish God's kingdom on earth. But he was no dreamer like Otto, 'the wonder of the world.' He strove to realise his lofty ideals with shrewd practical wisdom and businesslike command of details. The great jurists of Bologna, who constantly stood round his throne, not only taught him that the Emperor was lord of the world, and that the will of the prince had the force of law, but illustrated to the most minute detail the individual prerogatives of his office. His German subjects re-echoed these sentiments, and his uncle, Bishop Otto of Freising, taught that to the Emperor belonged the protection of the whole world. When bitter experience showed him that all his strength and all his faith were of little avail in setting up again a polity which the age had outlived, he had perforce to distinguish between his position as German King and Roman Emperor, and apply one method in breaking down the turbulent feudalism of his northern kingdom and another in checking the growing spirit of municipal independence in the lands beyond the Alps. In Italy his path seemed strewn with disasters, and even in Germany he obtained no very brilliant success. But if he failed, his was one of the most magnificent failures in history, a failure which did not prevent him from handing on his power almost unimpaired to his son. With all his faults, Frederick remains the noblest embodiment of mediæval kingship, the most imposing, the most heroic, and the most brilliant of the long line of German princes, who strove to realise the impracticable but glorious political ideal of the Middle Ages.

Frederick from the first directed his attention to Italy, and in March 1153 concluded a treaty with the fugitive Eugenius III.

at Constance. By this he agreed to make no peace with Roger of Sicily without the approval of the Curia, and to reduce The settle-ment of Germany, 1152-1154. the rebellious City to obedience to the Pope, in return for the promise of the imperial crown and papal support against his enemies. But Frederick was too wise to hurry across the Alps before he was assured of the obedience of Germany, where from the moment of his coronation he went on progress, receiving the homage of his vassals and seeking to appease ancient feuds. The loyalty of Henry the Lion was rewarded by the formal grant of the duchy of Bavaria, while Frederick's own duchy of Swabia was granted to his cousin Frederick of Rothenburg. Berthold of Zähringen, a possible rival for this position, was conciliated by his appointment as rector or viceroy in Burgundy. Henry, Archbishop of Mainz, paid the penalty of his solitary opposition to Frederick's election by his deposition from his archbishopric on a charge of wasting the lands of his see. Even beyond the limits of Germany, the Scandinavian and Slavonic princes were taught that there was again an Emperor, and the disputed succession to Denmark was settled by Frederick's mediation, and the king, Svend, who owed his throne to Frederick's action, submitted to become his feudal dependant. But after two years the outlook in Italy became so threatening that Frederick was compelled to leave his Frederick's first Italian visit, 1154-55. German work half undone and hurry across the Alps with a small force hastily collected. Aecompanied by Henry the Lion, and the Bavarian palatine, Otto of Wittelsbach, and only 1800 knights, he crossed the Brenner in October 1154 and appeared in the plain of Lombardy. He held his Diet at Roncaglia near Piacenza, and received the homage of the barons and cities of Italy. Milan held sullenly aloof, but small as was Frederick's following, the destruction of Tortona (Easter, 1155), an ally of Milan, taught the Italians that the Emperor was to be feared. After receiving the Lombard crown at Pavia, Frederick marched through Tuscany to Rome.

The condition of the Papacy was still critical, though the persistence of Eugenius III. had broken the back of the Roman opposition, and Arnold of Brescia had already begun to lose influence among the fickle Romans. But Eugenius III. had died on 8th July 1153, and his successor, the mild Anastasius IV., dwelt continuously in Rome until his death, after a reign of less than a year and a half, on 3rd December 1154. The next Pope, Adrian IV., was the only Englishman who ever occupied the throne of St. Peter. The son of a poor man, Nicholas Breakspear had adopted the life of a wandering scholar, and had worked his way up to the head- Adrian IV., ship of the house of Canons Regular of St. Rufus, 1154-1159. near Valence on the Rhone. His stern rule excited the hostility of the canons whose complaints to Eugenius III. first attracted the Pope's notice to him. In 1146 he was made cardinal-bishop of Albano, and was soon afterwards sent on an important legation to Scandinavia, in the course of which he freed the northern churches from their dependency on Germany, by setting up the new archbishopric of Trondhjem. Soon after his return he was elected to the Papacy. Adrian IV. was a man of high character, sound learning, and kindly disposition. He fully felt the responsibility of his great office, declaring that 'the Pope's tiara was splendid because it burnt like fire.' His pontificate began amidst street-fights in which a cardinal was slain; but Adrian took the strong measure of laying Rome under interdict, and the inconstant citizens, whose gains were decreased by the refusal of pilgrims to visit a city under the Pope's ban, made their submission to him and drove out Arnold of Brescia, who spent the short remainder of his life as a wandering fugitive. But William, the new King of Sicily, devastated Campania, and threatened to march on Rome. In his despair, Adrian renewed with Frederick the Treaty of Constance, and went out to Nepi to meet him. The good understanding was almost destroyed when Frederick refused to hold the bridle of the Pope's horse and assist him to dismount, and the alliance was only renewed

by Frederick's submission, which was rendered necessary by
the sullen hostility of the Romans to Frederick and Adrian
alike. On 18th June Adrian crowned Frederick

**Coronation
of Frederick,
18th June
1155.**

Emperor in St. Peter's, hastily and almost secretly,
for fear of the Romans, who, on hearing of it,
rushed to arms. Frederick could only hold
his ground by hard fighting, and soon lack of provisions
forced him to flee from Rome, taking the Pope with
him. The fierce heat of the Italian summer had already
decimated Frederick's little army, and he now resolved to recross the Alps, leaving Adrian to his fate. The only act of

**Death of
Arnold of
Brescia.**

power that had followed the reconciliation of Pope
and Emperor was the execution of Arnold of
Brescia, who had been taken prisoner in Tuscany
by the Emperor, and having been handed over to the cardinals, was condemned and executed as a heretic. His
dead body was burnt at the stake. 'His ashes,' says Otto
of Freising, 'were thrown into the Tiber, that his relics
might not be worshipped by the obstinate populace.' Arnold's
work, the Roman Commune, lived after him, and Adrian,
after the Emperor's departure, was forced to make terms
with it.

On recrossing the Brenner, Frederick began anew the task
of reconciling Germany, which had been interrupted by his

**Troubles
in Germany.**

Italian journey. Fierce feuds had burst out all over
Germany, and in particular the quarrels of Arnold,
the new Archbishop of Mainz, with Hermann, Count Palatine
of the Rhine, had laid waste the Rhineland. The establishment of Henry the Lion as Duke of Bavaria had been bitterly
resented by Frederick's uncle, Henry of Austria, called, from
his favourite oath, 'Henry Jasomirgott,' who still waged
fierce war against his rival for the possession of his former
duchy. But the return of the Emperor was soon marked by
good results, and from the measures taken to appease the
aggrieved feudatories sprang a new departure in the territorial
history of Germany. In September 1156 he ended the

rivalry of Henry the Lion and Henry of Austria by investing the latter with Austria, erected into a new duchy absolutely independent of Bavaria, and itself indivisible, hereditary in the house of Babenberg even in the female line, and exempt from many of the burdens usually imposed on the great fiefs. In the creation of the duchy of Austria, Frederick prepared the way for the more sweeping changes in the same direction which followed the fall of Henry the Lion in 1180. Leaving the control of northern and eastern Germany to Albert the Bear and the two Henrys, Frederick attempted to consolidate his own dynastic power in the south-west. He punished the disorderly Count Palatine Hermann for his attacks on Mainz, by depriving him of his possessions. These he granted to his half-brother Conrad, his father's son by his second marriage, and already possessor of the hereditary Salic estates round Worms, the Palatinate of the Rhine. Conrad united these two districts to form a new territorial power, that had for its centre the recently-founded castle and town of Heidelberg, and was the starting-point of the later Palatinate. In 1156 Frederick married Beatrice, the heiress of Renaud of Macon, Count of Burgundy.[1] This match immensely strengthened the imperial power in that Middle Kingdom where it was always weak, and moreover materially extended the domains of Frederick in that region where his influence was already strongest. His direct sway now stretched from the Swabian uplands across the middle Rhine to the Vosges, and thence south to the neighbourhood of Lyons. Such an accession of power necessarily brought about the end of the nominal Zähringen rectorate, but Frederick bought off Duke Berthold by lands and privileges beyond the Jura. It was only by freely sacrificing his sovereign rights that Frederick was able to persuade the magnates of Germany to promise him such adequate support in his

The Duchy of Austria established, 1156.

Frederick's marriage and Burgundian policy.

---

[1] On Frederick's relations to the Middle Kingdom, see Fournier's *Royaume d'Arles et de Vienne, 1138-1378.*

projected expedition into Italy as would enable him to cross the Alps as a conqueror and not as a suppliant. For the moment his policy seemed extremely successful. Besides conciliating Germany, he had won back Burgundy. He had conciliated Duke Vratislav of Bohemia, who had refused him homage, by allowing him to crown himself king. He had forced King Boleslav IV. of Poland to recognise his overlordship by a brilliant invasion that got as far into Poland as Gnesen. Svend of Denmark was still his obedient vassal. Henry II. of England wrote acknowledging in general terms the supremacy of the Emperor over all his dominions. In his chancellor Rainald of Dassel, he found a zealous and able chief minister. 'In Germany,' wrote Ragewin, the continuator of Otto of Freising, 'there was now such an unwonted peace that men seemed changed, the land a different one, the very heaven had become milder and softer.' Frederick's early glory culminated

Diet of Besançon, 1157. in the brilliant Diet at Besançon, the chief town of his wife's inheritance, in October 1157, where 'all the earth,' exclaimed Ragewin, 'filled with admiration for the clemency and justice of the Emperor, and moved both by love and fear, strove to overwhelm him with novel praises and new honours.' This Diet witnessed a hot dispute between Frederick and the Papacy.

Ever since Frederick's sudden withdrawal from Rome, his relations with Adrian IV. had been exceedingly strained. Both

Alliance of Adrian IV. and the Normans. claimed to be lord of the world, and neither could agree as to the respective limits of their power. For a moment the common fear of the Italian communes and alarm at the revolutionary heresy of Arnold might unite them in a temporary truce. The pressing danger once over, they fell back into their natural relations of watchful hostility. When Frederick withdrew from Italy, he had neither reduced Rome to the obedience of the Pope, nor had chastised the forays of the new King William of Sicily. Adrian soon found that he would have to fight for his own hand. He cleverly formed a league with the feudal barons of Apulia, who were ripe for revolt against their over-powerful sovereign. He negotiated with the Greek Emperor, Manuel I., who was willing to fight William, if the Pope would grant him three Neapolitan seaports. Alarmed at such a formidable coalition, William became the Pope's vassal, and received in return the investiture of Apulia and Sicily. Adrian IV. thus renewed the policy of Leo IX. and Innocent II., and now further strengthened himself by an agreement with the Romans. By accepting the Roman Commune, he was allowed again to take up his residence in the City. Without the least help from Frederick, Adrian had turned the chief enemies of the Holy See into allies.

Frederick bitterly resented the Pope's alliances with William and the Romans, which he regarded as breaches of faith. Adrian feared the increased power of Frederick, Quarrel of and had a more tangible grievance in Frederick's Frederick imprisonment of the Swedish Archbishop of Lund, and Adrian. an old friend of Adrian's in the days of his northern mission. He accordingly sent the most trusted of his advisers, Roland Bandinelli of Siena, Cardinal and Chancellor of the Roman Church, to state his grievances to the Emperor at the Diet of Besançon. Roland's first salutation of the Emperor The Cardinal was threatening. 'The Pope,' he said, 'greets you Roland at as a father and the cardinals greet you as brothers.' Besançon. Frederick was irritated at the new and unheard-of claim of the cardinals to rank as the equals of Cæsar. But he was still more annoyed at the recitation of a papal letter, which boasted that the Pope had conferred many benefits on the Emperor.[1] The Latin phrase (*conferre beneficia*) used by Adrian might bear the technical sense of granting a feudal benefice from a lord to a vassal, and Rainald the Chancellor took care to

---

[1] 'Debes erim ante oculos mentis reducere . . . qualiter imperialis insigne coronae libentissime *conferens*, benignissimo gremio suo tuae sublimitatis apicem studuerit confovere . . . sed si majora *beneficia* de manu nostra excellentia tua suscepisset . . . non immerito gauderemus.' Ragewinus, *Gesta Frederici Imperatoris*, in Pertz, *Scriptores*, xx. 421.

translate it in that sense to the illiterate magnates. The fiercest indignation burst out, which rose to fever heat when Cardinal Roland answered the objectors by inquiring, 'From whom then does the Emperor hold the Empire if not from the Pope?' In answer to the Pope's implied claim of feudal supremacy, the Emperor circulated a declaration of his rights throughout the Empire. 'The Empire is held by us,' he declared, 'through the election of the princes from God alone, who gave the world to be ruled by the two necessary swords, and taught through St. Peter that men should fear God and honour the king. Whosoever says that we received the imperial crown from the lord Pope as a benefice goes against the Divine command and the teaching of Peter, and is guilty of falsehood.' Early next year Adrian was forced to explain that he had used 'beneficium' in its general sense of 'benefit' and not in its feudal sense of 'fief.' A complete breach was thus prevented, but the ill-will still smouldered on and soon found a chance of bursting out again into flame.

In July 1158 Frederick, at the head of a great army, crossed the Alps for the second time. 'The arrogance of the Milanese,' *Frederick's* he declared, 'has long caused them to raise their *Second* heads against the Roman Empire, and is now *Italian* disturbing all Italy. We have therefore resolved *Journey,* to turn against them all the forces of the Empire.' *1158-1162.* Lombardy was divided into two rival leagues, which bitterly hated each other. While Brescia, Crema, Parma, Piacenza, and Modena followed the league of Milan, Pavia headed a second confederacy, which included Lodi, Como, *Submission* and Cremona, which fearing the power of Milan, *of the* gave its support to the Emperor. After a fierce *Lombard* resistance Milan also made its submission, and *Towns.* promised to submit to the Emperor the ratification of the appointment of their consuls.

Flushed with his easy triumph, Frederick held in November a second Diet at Roncaglia. The most famous civilians of

Bologna attended and declared the imperial rights so vigorously that Frederick took their order under his special protection, and gave doctors of laws the privileges of knights. Diet at It was announced that the Emperor had resolved Roncaglia. to take all his royal rights back into his own hands. The pleasure of the prince had the force of law, and no length of prescription could justify usurpation. But the Emperor was willing to reinvest both the lay and ecclesiastical lords and the towns with rights to which they had a lawful title. Nevertheless, the supreme magistrates of the towns were to be in all cases appointed by the king with the assent of the citizens. Instead of the aristocratic consulate, it was henceforth a main object of Frederick's policy to establish a *podestà* as the supreme governor of each town. This representative of the imperial power was generally a stranger, with no interest or sympathy in the town that he ruled, and universally detested as an intruder and a despot. Immediately after the dissolution of the Diet, Rainald of Dassel and Otto of Wittelsbach went round to the various Lombard cities to set up *podestàs*. Milan, disgusted at the Emperor's ignoring the terms of their former capitulation, refused to receive its *podestà*, and broke into revolt. Other cities followed its example—one of which, Crema, was carried by assault by Frederick after a terrible siege. Milan held out for three years, and had to face the whole of Frederick's power, until at last famine forced it to open its gates. Frederick hardened his heart to the prayers of the Milanese, and made a great favour of allow-ing them their lives. The chief men of the city destruction were kept as hostages; the walls and defences of Milan. were destroyed; and the ancient inhabitants were forbidden to dwell in the open village that now represented the city of St. Ambrose, where a few ancient churches, conspicuous among which was the Basilica of the patron saint, alone arose amidst the ruins. The relics of the three Magi of the East were secured by Rainald of Dassel for his own church at Cologne, of which they have ever since remained the chief glory. The municipal independence of Italy seemed extinct. The Emperor was king as well as overlord.

The Church witnessed with extreme alarm the growing fortunes of the Emperor. Adrian IV. showed his ill-will by putting obstacles in the way of the appointment of imperial nominees to vacant bishoprics, and Frederick retaliated by reverting in his correspondence with the Pope to a more ancient but less respectful form of address. In great disgust Adrian encouraged Milan to resist, and got ready for an open breach. He hoped to form an Italian league against the Emperor, and did not scruple to invoke the aid of the schismatic Manuel against the orthodox Frederick. But, on 1st September 1159, he was cut off by a sudden illness in the midst of his preparations. The next Pope was that Cardinal Roland whose zeal at Besançon had even outrun the zeal of Adrian himself. Roland assumed Alexander III. the significant name of Alexander III. ; and during 1159-1181. his unusually long pontificate of nearly twenty-two years, he continued his predecessor's policy with such energy that the strife of Pope and Emperor was soon renewed with all its old intensity.

Frederick's friends among the cardinals, finding themselves powerless to oppose Alexander's election, fell back on the old weapon of schism. On the same day (7th September 1159) that the majority of the cardinals elected Alexander, the imperialist minority of the Sacred College, stirred up by the The Anti- indefatigable Otto of Wittelsbach, declared that pope Victor their choice had fallen on the Cardinal Octavian, IV. who assumed the name of Victor IV. Frederick returned from the reduction of the Lombard cities to hold a council at Pavia to decide between the rival claims, and boasted that he was following the examples of Constantine, Charles, and Otto. Alexander utterly refused to submit his claims to a body convoked under the sanction of the temporal sword. 'No one,' he declared, 'has the right to judge me, since I am the supreme judge of all the world.' Though the synod of Pavia declared that Victor was the canonical Pope, Alexander, driven out of Rome within a few days of his election, was nevertheless looked up to as rightful Bishop by the greater part of the Christian world. In 1160 a synod of bishops subject to Louis VII. and Henry II. met at Toulouse and declared for Alexander. But the lawful Pope upheld his position with great difficulty in Italy. Alexander During the first three years of his pontificate he in France. maintained his court at Anagni and Terracina. In January 1162 he took ship to Genoa, whence after the fall of Milan, a few weeks later, he fled to France. Secure of the friendship of the two chief kings of the West, Alexander now quietly waited until the time was ripe for his return to Italy. In 1163 he held a council at Tours, within the dominions of Henry of Anjou, in which he excommunicated the Antipope and his supporters, among whom Rainald of Dassel, now Archbishop-elect of Cologne, was specially mentioned.

In 1162 Frederick returned to Germany; but not even the presence of the Emperor could keep the German prelates firm in their adhesion to the Antipope. Many of the clergy and most monks were on Alexander's side, or at least strove to avoid open hostility to Frederick by demanding a General Council to heal the schism. The whole Cistercian and Carthusian orders worked hard for Alexander's interest, and many of their leaders joined the growing band of Italian and German fugitives that swelled the court of the exiled Pontiff in Gaul. The death of the Antipope during Frederick's third visit to Italy, in 1164, did not end the breach. Rainald of Dassel procured the election of a new Antipope in the Cardinal Guy of Crema, who styled himself Paschal III. In 1165 Frederick held a Diet at Würzburg, where he pro- The Anti-mulgated the severest laws against the champions pope of Alexander, while the Emperor and his barons Paschal III. bound themselves by oath never to recognise Alexander or any of his followers as Pope. Rainald of Dassel strove hard to bring over Henry of England to support the schismatic Pope; but Henry, already involved in his struggle with Thomas of

Canterbury, was too prudent to confuse his local quarrel with his primate with the general conflict of Pope and Emperor. The new Antipope formally announced the canonisation of Charles the Great, and Frederick went in great state to Aachen, where the bones of the great Emperor were solemnly translated to a golden shrine, while Frederick adorned the round Carolingian chapel with the magnificent candelabrum that is still one of its chief ornaments. But in the same year (1165), Alexander III. was encouraged, by the hostile attitude of the Lombards to Frederick, to venture back into Italy, and by November was again in possession of Rome, whence he fulminated excommunication against the Emperor.

Even after the fall of Milan, the north Italian cities still gave Frederick trouble. In 1164 the towns of the March **Renewal of** of Verona, among them Verona, Vicenza, Padua, **the Town-** and Treviso, rose in revolt against their new **leagues in** **Lombardy,** *podestàs*, and formed a league for the preservation **1164.** of their liberties. By holding in force the narrow gorge of the Adige to the north of Verona (La Chiusa di Verona), they hoped to prevent the return of Frederick to Italy by his usual route. Venice, already the open enemy of Frederick, actively supported the league of Verona. On the news of Frederick's excommunication, the Lombard cities began to revive. Milan was rebuilt and re-fortified, and the schismatic bishops were chased away. It was high time for the return of the Emperor, and in November 1166 Frederick entered upon his fourth Italian expedition. Fearing to fight the Veronese league at Chiusa, he descended into Lombardy by the Val Camonica. Open resistance seemed stifled by the enormous German host that followed the Emperor; and **Frederick's** Frederick, hurrying through the disaffected dis- **fourth Italian** trict, marched straight on Rome. After a fierce **journey,** siege Frederick captured Rome, and was again **1167-1168.** crowned by the Antipope Paschal (1st August 1167), while Alexander fled, disguised as a pilgrim, to seek shelter with the friendly Normans at Gaeta. A terrible plague now swept away the victorious army of Frederick, and the Lombard cities, profiting by his misfortunes, formally renewed their league. Among the victims of the pestilence were Rainald of Cologne, the indefatigable chancellor, and the Emperor's two cousins, Frederick of Rothenburg, Duke of Swabia, and the warlike young Welf VII., son of Welf VI. of Bavaria. Frederick, with the remnants of his army, had the utmost difficulty in effecting his retreat to Lombardy. The Papalists boasted that God had cut off the host of Frederick as of old He had destroyed the army of Sennacherib before the walls of Jerusalem.

The Lombard league took its final shape in the beginning of 1168, when Frederick was refreshing his exhausted forces at Pavia. The members pledged themselves to The Lombard aid each other against all those who would make League, 1168. war against them, or would exact anything more from them than had been customary. They also appointed rectors, chosen from among the consuls of the several cities, for the management of federal affairs. Fear of the Emperor had now destroyed even the jealousies of neighbouring and rival cities, and the league now included all the towns of the northern plain, from Milan to Venice, and from Bergamo to Bologna. Lodi itself now made common cause with its old enemy Milan, and even the obstinate imperialists of Pavia grudged to the beaten Emperor the protection of its walls. All the approaches to the northern Alpine passes were blocked by the confederate cities, and the Emperor could only get home by a long detour through the uplands of Montferrat and Piedmont. In the spring of 1168 Frederick made his way to Susa, and thence over the Mont Cenis. After his departure, new accessions increased the Lombard league, and Alexander III. sent it his blessing. In the spring of 1168 Foundation of the league founded a new city in a marshy dis- Alessandria, trict, on the banks of the Tanaro, and called it 1168. Alessandria in honour of its patron. Vast earthworks and a strong castle made their creation an impregnable fortress, calculated to hold out as long as provisions remained. The town soon prospered : the Pope erected it into a bishopric, and settlers from all sides made it a busy centre of trade. The foundation of Alessandria pushed the league's territory more to the westwards, into the region where the feudal potentates were still strong, and where cities like Asti, Vercelli, Novara, were now emboldened to join it. Moreover, the city protected the high road from Milan to Genoa which gave Lombardy access to the sea, and blocked the descent of German armies from the Burgundian passes as effectively as the league had already blocked the northern valleys of the Alps.

For the next six years the Lombard league was suffered to live in peace. On the death of the Antipope Paschal in 1168, The Antipope a new pretender was set up, called Calixtus III. Calixtus III. But for all practical purposes Italy was independent of the Emperor. Frederick's last partisans in north Italy, the citizens of Pavia, and the Counts of Montferrat and Biandrate, were constrained to submit to the league. In Germany the ecclesiastical opposition grew under the guidance of the Archbishop of Salzburg, and Alexander became more and more generally recognised. Renewed efforts to win over Henry of Anjou to support the Antipope were unsuccessful, and the humiliation of the English king after Becket's murder was a lesson to Frederick of the abiding might of the Church to control princes. The growing power of Henry the Lion excited the fears of the smaller Frederick's barons and the jealousy of the Emperor. But fifth Italian Frederick sought to avert the inevitable conflict journey, in order that he might revenge himself on the 117 -1177. revolted Lombards. Meanwhile his agents strove to gain friends for him in central Italy, where the removal of all external control had fiercely divided the towns of Tuscany and Romagna. In 1174 Frederick made his fifth expedition to Italy. But the small army which he led in September over Mont Cenis was mainly composed of his personal vassals, the stronger princes remaining at home. Nevertheless, a revival of the imperial party followed the reappearance of the Emperor in Italy. After destroying Susa and capturing Asti, Frederick vigorously besieged the new city of Alessandria—the city of straw, as the imperialists called it. Meanwhile Christian, Archbishop of Mainz, won important successes for the Emperor in Tuscany and Romagna, but failed at the siege of Ancona. The siege of Alessandria lasted till April 1175, when the rectors of the league came to its relief. Both armies prepared for battle at Montebello, but at the very moment of the conflict negotiations were entered upon, at the instance of the Cremonese. Yet Frederick would not accept the hard conditions of the Lombards—the recognition of their liberties, acknowledgment of Alexander as lawful Pope, and the incorporation of Alessandria as a member of the league. The 'Peace of Montebello' was accordingly broken, and both sides prepared to fight to the end.

Frederick drew fresh reinforcements from Germany for the campaign of 1176; but Henry the Lion refused to come, and a personal interview between him and Frederick at Chiavenna did not induce him to change his purpose. Nevertheless, with the help of his Italian friends, Frederick was still at the head of a gallant army, while the warlike Christian of Mainz kept the Normans in check by invading Apulia. The northern campaign opened when Frederick left Pavia and joined the force, which was now brought from Germany, at Como. His plan of campaign was to attack Milan from the north with his Germans, while the men of Pavia assaulted their rival from the south. But the Milanese anticipated this combination by marching out of the city with their caroccio, hoping to find the German army before it could join the Pavese. On 29th May the confederates approached the imperial army near Legnano, about seventeen miles north-west of Milan, in the plain that stretches from the river Olona westwards to the Ticino. The caroccio was put in the centre of the army, and protected by

The battle of Legnano, 1176.

a select band styled the ' Company of Death,' who had sworn
either to conquer or never return.   The fierce charge of the
mail-clad German knights broke the left wing of the Lombard
army, and Frederick, who here commanded in person, cut his
way through the fugitives to the caroccio.   For a moment
the cause of the league seemed undone.   But the Emperor
was unhorsed in the struggle, and the rumour soon spread
that he had fallen.   The 'Company of Death' defended its
sacred charge with self-sacrificing devotion, and gradually a
panic fell on the imperialists.   Before nightfall Frederick's
army was hopelessly broken, and the Emperor gained
Pavia, almost unattended, with the utmost difficulty.   But
the citizen-soldiers went home, and did not follow up their
victory, and Cremona with other towns became so jealous of
the success of Milan that they prepared to make separate
terms with the Emperor.   Frederick himself had grown
weary of the struggle; and the Archbishops of Cologne and
Magdeburg, who had brought the last army from Germany,
declared that they would no longer support the Emperor, and
urged him to reconcile himself with Alexander.   In October
Frederick reluctantly broke the ill-fated oath of Würzburg, and
sent Christian of Mainz and other German prelates to Anagni
to conclude peace with the Pope.   He still hoped to detach
Alexander from the Lombard cities, and resume hostilities
against them after he had been reconciled to the Church.
Alexander refused to betray either the cities or his older ally,
William of Sicily, and Frederick reluctantly brought himself
to accept the hard terms of the victors.   In March 1177
The Peace of Alexander and his cardinals journeyed to Venice
Venice, 1177. to be near the negotiations.   It seemed as if all
Italy were banded together against the Emperor, and as if
instead of resisting lawful authority, the papal alliance represented an Italian national party banded together against
foreign invaders from beyond the Alps.   Frederick yielded on
all substantial points.   He was restored to the communion of
the Church, and on 24th July 1177 was suffered to enter

Venice to make his submission to Alexander. Frederick was conducted in great state to the Piazza, where the Pope, surrounded by cardinals and prelates, waited for him in the portico of St. Mark's. 'Then,' says a contemporary, 'he was touched by the spirit of God, and, abandoning his imperial dignity, threw himself humbly at the feet of the Pope.' Alexander, with tears in his eyes, raised his fallen enemy, and gave him the kiss of peace. It was exactly a hundred years since Henry iv. had gone to Canossa.

In August the Peace of Venice settled the details of Frederick's reconciliation with the Papacy. All the lands usurped from the patrimony of St. Peter were to be restored. The Pope and Emperor promised mutual aid against each other's enemies, and were lavish in vows of future friendship. A truce was secured for the Lombards, the Normans, and even for Manuel Comnenus, while the detailed conditions of a final settlement were slowly adjusted under the mediation of the papal legate. In August 1178 the Antipope Calixtus renounced his pretensions, and, though a few obstinate schismatics sought still to carry on the line of Antipopes, their nominee was soon forced into a monastery. The permanent treaty with the Lombards was finally signed on June 1183 at Constance. By it the Emperor granted to the cities of the Lombard league all the royal rights (*regalia*) which they ever had, or at that moment enjoyed. The cities were allowed to build fortifications, to continue their league, and make such other combinations as they wished. They had complete jurisdiction over their own members, could levy troops, coin money, and exercise practically all regalian rights. The imperial *podestàs* disappeared, and henceforth the *podestà* was but a foreign judge called in by the citizens, in the hope that his strangeness to local factions would make him an impartial magistrate. The only clauses which upheld the supremacy of the Emperor stipulated that the consuls should receive imperial confirmation, that a right of appeal should

End of the schism in the Papacy, 1178.

Peace of Constance, 1183.

lie to the imperial court, and that the Emperor should still have a claim to receive the *fodrum* as a contribution to his military expenses. Such rights as thus remained to the Emperor were henceforth exercised by legates and vicars, very careless of their absent master. For all practical purposes, the Treaty of Constance made the Lombard republics self-governing city-states. The barest over-lordship henceforth alone remained to him who in past generations had aspired to be their effective master. The Empire was by no means destroyed by this great blow, but henceforth Italy and Germany have each their independent development.

After the peace, Frederick's main occupation lay in Germany. During the Emperor's Italian troubles the power of
Frederick and Henry the Lion had gone on increasing. In
Germany. the north in particular, Henry had renewed the ancient policy of extending the German race at the expense of the Slavs. Using his Saxon duchy as the basis of his operations, he completed the Germanisation of the lands between the Elbe, Baltic, and Oder, that, despite the work of the Ottos, and Lothair and Albert the Bear, were still largely Slavonic and heathen. So solid was his power, that disasters in Italy, such as in the days of the Ottos had led to a Slavonic reaction in the north-east, had no influence in retarding the march of German conquest. Before long, the vastness of Henry's resources and the stability of his policy threw the exploits of Albert the Bear into the shade. In alliance with the young Valdemar I of Denmark, Henry carried to a completion the long process of the conquest of the half-heathen tribes beyond the Elbe, and grudged his reluctant ally a share in the spoils of war. The warlike Abotrites were at last subdued and forced to profess Christianity, and the fortress and bishopric of Schwerin was estab-
Henry the lished by Henry in their midst, along with
Lion and the numerous colonies of Saxons and Flemish settlers.
Marks. Henry was as great a founder of towns as Otto the Great. Lübeck, founded in 1143 by his dependant,

Count Adolf of Holstein, and the first German town on the Baltic, owed its existence to his energy. The bishoprics of Mecklenburg and Pomerania claim him as their founder. Cistercian and Premonstratensian missionaries crushed out the last remnants of heathenism, and trade followed strong rule. In 1168 Henry married Matilda, the daughter of Henry of Anjou, an alliance that established a warm and permanent connection between the Guelfic house and the English throne.

Henry the Lion sought to rule within his duchies with the same autocratic power with which he governed his border conquests. The local nobles and prelates saw   Henry the in his policy a design against their franchises, and   Lion and his combined to offer him a vigorous resistance.   duchies. Albert the Bear, who had never lost hope of regaining Saxony, opposed him even in the Marks. In 1166 the princes of Saxony, headed by Rainald of Dassel and the Archbishop of Bremen, went to open war against Henry, but the personal intervention of the Emperor restored peace in the Diet of Würzburg. The Lion's northern allies were equally alarmed at his triumphs; and Valdemar of Denmark, irritated by his requiring a share in the recent Danish conquest of Rügen, became his enemy, but was soon obliged to crave his forgiveness, and Valdemar's son and successor, Canute VI., married Henry's daughter Gertrude. In 1170 the death of the restless Margrave Albert relieved Henry from the most dangerous of his opponents. His position was now so strong that he was able, between 1170 and 1172, to go on pilgrimage to the Holy Land, where he was received with great honour, and whence he brought back many relics, which he enshrined in the stately churches at Brunswick of which he was the founder. Though shorn of the East Mark by the creation of the new duchy of Austria, Henry was still able to exercise almost as great an influence on the Germanisation of the south-west as on the same process in the north-east. It was the age of German colonisation, when, from the overpeopled lands of the Netherlands and old Saxony, adventurers sought a fresh home in the lands newly won to civilisation. German colonists in Meissen and in the lands ruled by Czech and Magyar, owed their position to Henry. In Bavaria itself he was the founder of the city of Munich.

It was inevitable that Frederick should look with suspicion upon so powerful and restless a vassal, especially as, even before the Chiavenna interview, Henry had ceased to take part in promoting the imperial designs on Italy. But as long as Frederick's main object was the subjection of the Church and the Lombards, the support of Henry was indispensable to him. However, after the Peace of Venice the condition of affairs was altered. Henceforth the Emperor's best hopes of success, both in Germany and Italy, lay in the support of the great ecclesiastics who had so long opposed Henry in Saxony. It was now Frederick's policy to strengthen his position in North Germany by alliances with the local magnates, both ecclesiastical and lay, who were eager to join with the Emperor in breaking down the power of their autocratic duke.

After the peace with the Church, Bishop Ulrich of Halberstadt, who had been expelled as a partisan of Alexander, came back to his see. Henry, who, during his absence, had administered the possessions of the bishopric, refused to surrender them to him. Philip of Heinsberg Archbishop of Cologne, formed a close alliance with Bishop Ulrich. The allies excommunicated the duke, and devastated his lands in Westphalia. Meanwhile Frederick left Italy in the summer of 1178, and after receiving the crown of the Middle Kingdom at Arles, reached Speyer in October, where Henry the **Fall of** Lion visited him and complained bitterly of the **Henry the** treatment he had received from the confederated **Lion, 1180.** bishops. A Diet was summoned to meet at Worms in January 1179, to consider the feud, but Henry did not appear, and the elaborate complaints of his vassals remained unanswered. In the summer the Emperor visited Saxony, but Henry again refused an interview at Magdeburg, where new complaints were laid before the Emperor. A little later, a private interview between king and duke led to no result. Henry neglected the third and last opportunity of formally appearing before Frederick, and despairing of the Emperor's justice, devastated the Saxon bishoprics with fire and sword, and called in his old enemies the Slavs to invade German territory. In January 1180 a Diet was held at Würz-

burg. For the fourth time Henry refused to appear, and the sentence of banishment and the loss of his fiefs was given against him. Henry declared that as a Swabian he had a right to be tried by the magnates of Swabia alone, and strove to fight for his inheritance, but had little success. He hoped great things from his foreign friends, but no help came either from his father-in-law, Henry of England, his old ally, Valdemar of Denmark, or his more recent associate, the young Philip II. of France. In the summer of 1181 the Emperor easily conquered Saxony. In November the once mighty duke was forced to crave pardon at Erfurt. Frederick treated him kindly, and restored to him Brunswick, Lüneburg, and most of his allodial possessions. But at the prayer of the assembled magnates he reaffirmed his sentence of banishment, and of the deprivation of his duchies. The exiled duke retired to Normandy and England, where his father-in-law, Henry II., treated him with marked consideration. By a pilgrimage to St. James of Compostella, he sought to do penance for his violence to the churches. His political career seemed at an end. .

The vacant duchies of the Guelfs were disposed of on conditions that mark an epoch in the territorial development

Division of the Saxon duchy. of Germany. Saxony, the last stronghold of the sentiment of the ancient four peoples of Germany, now underwent the same fate that had fallen to Bavaria earlier in Frederick's reign. The western parts, including the vast dioceses of Cologne and Paderborn, were erected into the new duchy of Westphalia, and granted to the Archbishop of Cologne, Frederick's ally. The lands between the Weser and the Elbe went to the chief of the lay enemies of the Guelfic house. Bernard of Anhalt, the son of Albert the Bear, received this district, along with the ducal title, but only on condition that the counties and bishoprics that in Henry the Lion's days had been directly dependent on the Saxon duke, should henceforward hold immediately of the Empire. In the south the aged Welf VI. had quite withdrawn from politics, and Otto of Wittelsbach, Count-Palatine of Bavaria, the strenuous upholder of Frederick's policy in Italy, was before long invested with the duchy of Bavaria, over which his descendants still bear rule. The fall of the Guelfs, the one family strong enough to rival the throne, compensated in some measure for Frederick's failures in Italy. By the partition of Saxony and Bavaria, the

Diet of Mainz, 1184. last danger to the monarchy from the national duchies was removed. In the great Diet of Mainz, held in 1184, the glories of the Diet of Besançon were renewed, after which the Emperor went over the Alps for his sixth and last visit to Italy. So strong did Frederick still feel himself, that he yielded to the importunities of Henry of England, and allowed Henry the Lion to return to Germany.

Misfortunes followed Frederick's fresh intervention in Italy. On his way he concluded, at Augsburg, a treaty (October 1184), which ranks as the greatest of his diplomatic triumphs. In 1169 his eldest son, Henry, had been crowned King of the Romans at Aachen, when still a child. He was now becoming his father's active fellow-worker. By the Treaty of Augsburg it was arranged that the young king should marry Constance of Sicily, the daughter of King Roger, and the aunt and heiress of the childless William II. From this sprang the ultimate union of the Hohenstaufen with the Sicilian royal house, and the conversion of southern Italy, hitherto the chiefest strength of the papal power, into the strongest bulwark of the Swabian Empire. Nor was this Frederick's only success in Italy. The league of northern cities had broken asunder after the fear of his strong hand was removed. In 1181 the former imperialist towns—Cremona, Pavia, Lodi, Bergamo, Como—separated themselves from the confederation, and formed a league, bitterly opposed to Milan and her allies. Frederick also took advantage of the feuds of Tuscany and Bologna to build up a party there, and by lavish grants to Pisa and Lucca he secured, though at vast cost, powerful friends in middle Italy.

Union of Sicily with the Empire.

Revival of Frederick's power in Italy.

The Papacy had lost the great man who had so long upheld its fortunes. Alexander III.'s last important act was the assembling, in March 1179, of the third General Council of the Lateran, where the law was promulgated that a valid election to the Papacy required the votes of two-thirds of the cardinals present in the conclave. He died on 30th August 1181, full of years and honours. His five immediate

The Lateran Council, 1179. Death of Alexander III., 1181.

successors did not reign long enough to make any real mark, and were much hampered by their strife with the Romans. Lucius III. (1181-1185) the first of the series,

Lucius III., 1181-1185.

was still Pope when Frederick paid his sixth visit to Italy. In November 1184 Pope and Emperor met at Verona, where Lucius refused to consent to Frederick's proposal that his son, the young King Henry, should be crowned Emperor during his own lifetime. Under Urban III. (1185-1187), Lucius' successor, a new quarrel

Urban III., 1185-1187.

between Pope and Emperor seemed imminent. The immediate pretext of this was a double election to the Archbishopric of Trier, where the imperialist choice of Rudolf of Wied had been opposed by the appointment of the ambitious Archdeacon Folmar by the hierarchical party. Urban III. consecrated Folmar archbishop, and a powerful coalition against Frederick was formed, including

Threatened renewal of quarrel between Empire and Papacy.

besides Folmar, Philip, Archbishop of Cologne, and Henry the Lion, but recently back to his German estates, whose father-in-law, Henry of England, and son-in-law, Canute VI. of Denmark, promised their assistance. But Frederick had still the upper hand, and his ancient enemies in Italy and Germany were now foremost in supporting him. While Cremona joined the Pope, Milan concluded a close alliance with the Emperor, and the marriage of King Henry and Constance was celebrated within the walls of the once rebellious city. After the marriage, a threefold coronation ceremony took place, in which Frederick received the crown of Burgundy, Henry that of Italy, and Constance the queen's crown of Germany. Henceforth the ancient title of Cæsar was revived in Henry's favour, in the same sense as that in which Diocletian had designated the Cæsar to be the assistant and successor of the imperial Augustus. In Italy the young Henry devastated the lands of the Papalists. In Germany, where the bishops supported Frederick, Philip of Cologne, abandoned by his English allies, was utterly

defeated. Urban persisted in his opposition, and was preparing to excommunicate the Emperor, when the fatal news
of the collapse of the Christian power in the East came as a
thunderclap. A few days later Urban died (20th October
1187), and his successor Gregory VIII. (October-December
1187) strove to unite Europe in a new Crusade, Gregory
and dying after a few weeks, the next Pope, VIII., 1187.
Clement III (1187-1191) removed the chief cause of the dispute by depriving Folmar of his archbishopric, Clement III.,
and by promising to crown Henry. Henry the 1187-1191.
Lion atoned for his new treason by a new exile. The
younger son of Frederick, Frederick, now received the duchy
of Swabia, in succession to Frederick of Rothenburg. Peace
was thoroughly restored, and the power of the Emperor
established on a firmer basis than ever. In Italy order was
again secured. Since the death of Alexander III., the Popes
had mainly lived in northern Italy, but in 1188 Clement III.
was restored to Rome. His successor Celestine III. (1191-
1198) lived peacefully in the capital, but the Senate still
ruled Rome and not the Pope.

Once more master of Germany and Italy, the old Emperor
showed his imperial position in its most ideal aspect by
putting himself at the head of a great European
movement. In 1187 Saladin conquered Jerusalem Crusade and
death of
from the Christians, and a mighty crusading Frederick,
impulse ran for a third time throughout Europe. 1190.
At Easter 1188, Frederick once more took the Cross, and
leaving the Cæsar Henry as regent, left Germany in May 1189.
In June 1190 he perished in Cilicia, without having ever
reached his goal.

Ragewin, the biographer of Frederick, minutely describes
his person and character. His stature was not above the
middle height, but his frame was elegant and Frederick's
well proportioned. Flowing yellow hair curled character.
over his brow and almost concealed his ears, and his close-
cropped reddish beard gave him his familiar surname of

Barbarossa.   His eyes were clear and bright, his nose well shaped, and his whole countenance joyous and merry.   His throat and neck were somewhat thick.   His milk-white skin easily reddened, not through anger but from modesty.   His gait was firm and regular, and his habit of body vigorous. His voice was clear and full.   He enjoyed excellent health but for chronic attacks of fever.   He was chaste, honourable, just and religious.   He was assiduous at divine worship, devout in his behaviour in church, and very respectful to the clergy, regularly putting aside a tenth of his income for pious and charitable objects.   A mighty warrior, he only rejoiced in battle because victory was the best means of assuring peace. He was zealous in his attention to public business, and kept in his hands the whole strings of his policy.   He delighted in hunting, and was able to lay aside his royal state in hours of recreation without loss of dignity.   He was fond of reading history, especially the story of his great predecessors in the Empire.   Speaking eloquently in German, he could understand Latin better than he could talk it.   Simple but never negligent in his personal habits, he wore the ordinary German dress.   He spent much money on buildings, especially in restoring ancient palaces in Germany and Italy.   His greatest ambition was to restore the Roman Empire to its pristine glory.   During his reign both Germany and Italy enjoyed a prosperity and peace to which they had long been strangers. Agriculture flourished : commerce took a mighty impetus : the towns became wealthy and self-governing, and secured for themselves as strong a position as the barons and bishops within the political system of feudalism.   A German national literature attested the growth of German national consciousness.   The *Niebelungenlied* took its modern form, and its heroes, by their strange medley of chivalry and violence, well represent the ideals of the age.   The *Minnesinger* began their songs, and the rhymed *Kaisercronik* brought home to all the mighty deeds of former Emperors.   In later times, when the seeds of disunion sown by the great Emperor's policy had brought forth their fruits, men looked back to the age of Barbarossa with admiration and longing. A strange legend ultimately grew that Frederick was not dead but sleeping, and that in due time he would again appear to restore peace and justice, and again realise in his own person the Kingdom of God on earth.

PERIOD II.

CHAPTER XII

FRANCE, NORMANDY, AND ANJOU, AND THE BEGINNINGS
OF THE GREATNESS OF THE CAPETIAN MONARCHY
(1108-1189)[1]

Contrast between French and German History—Character and Policy of
Louis VI.—Suger—The Conquest of the Royal Domain — Louis VI.'s
relations with Normandy, England, Blois, and Aquitaine—Louis VI.'s
dealings with the Church and the Towns : Character of Louis VII.—The
first ten years of his reign—Divorce from Eleanor of Aquitaine—Rise of
Blois and Anjou—The Rivalry of Louis VII. and Henry II.—Progress of
the Monarchy under Louis VII.—The early years of Philip Augustus—
Death and defeat of Henry II.

WHILE the imperial rulers of Germany lavished their resources
on the pursuit of impossible ideals, the kings of France
worked up their way from small beginnings to the
possession of great power. In the beginning of
the twelfth century there could be no effective
comparison between the insignificance of Philip I.
and the grandeur of Henry IV. even in the
moments of his worst difficulties. Before the century was
out, the power of Philip Augustus was worthy to rival that
of Henry VI., and a few years later triumphed in the field
over all the forces of the German Empire.

> Contrast
> between the
> course of
> French and
> German
> History.

[1] Besides M. Luchaire's *Institutions Monarchiques*, his *Louis VI. le
Gros, Annales de sa vie et de son règne* and his *Etudes sur les actes de
Louis VII.*, are of capital importance for this period. Hirsch's *Studien zur
Geschichte Ludwigs VII. von Frankreich*, and Delisle's *Catalogue des Actes
de Philippe Auguste*, well illustrate the latter part of the chapter. Hutton's
short *Philip Augustus* ('Foreign Statesmen Series') is a readable
summary, while W. Walker's *On the Increase of the Royal Power in France
under Philip Augustus* is also useful. Miss Norgate's *England under
the Angevin Kings* is fullest for the struggle of France and Anjou.

The reign of Louis VI. (1108-1137) marks the first and most important stage in this development. The only son of Philip I. and Bertha of Holland, Louis was born in 1081 and brought up in the abbey of Saint-Denis, which he left in 1092, on receiving from his father the investiture of the Vexin, where he learnt his first experience in war and statecraft while defending his appanage against William Rufus. About the end of the century he was associated with his father as king-designate, and for the next eight years the premature infirmities of Philip I. gave Louis a large share of power. On Philip's death in July 1108, he was at once crowned king at Orleans.

In person Louis was very like his father, with his great height, pale face, and the excessive corpulence that neither constant activity in the field nor unwearied labours in the chase could subdue, and which gave him his almost contemporary surname of the Fat. Like his father also, he was greedy and sensual. But with all his faults, he had acquired at Saint-Denis the softness and mildness of disposition which was his most essential characteristic. He was, moreover, just, loyal, and upright, ever preferring to reach his aims by simple and direct means rather than by craft and treachery. 'A mighty athlete and an eminent gladiator,' as his biographer calls him, he was constantly engaged fighting from youth upwards, and never abandoned his military habits, though at the age of forty-six he was too bulky to be able to mount on horseback. His nobles disliked him, as the Normans disliked Henry I., for his love of men of low condition. He was no knight-errant, but a shrewd practical warrior, ever bent on maintaining or increasing his power, and making the chief object of his activity the abasement of the barons of the royal domain and the protection of the poor and the weak from their high-handed violence. He also carefully watched the overgrown power of the great feudatories. Unlike his father, Louis kept on good terms with the Church, posing as the protector of churchmen from the brutality and greed of the lay baronage. He was ever mindful of the monks, and never lost his love for the home of his youth. His famous

Suger. minister Suger became, in 1122, Abbot of Saint-Denis, and the relations of king and minister went back to the days when Louis abode within the great abbey where Suger, a boy like himself, was being prepared for the religious vocation. A man of humble origin, small and mean appearance, and with wretched health, but restless, indefatigable, clear-sighted and politic, Suger's brain suggested a subtle policy such as the rough soldier-king delighted to follow. Suger accompanied his master in all his travels, and kept so constantly at court that the zealots reproached him with neglecting the administration of his abbey. In Louis' later years the influence of St. Bernard induced the statesman-monk to make the reform of the discipline of Saint-Denis one of his main objects of attention. But he never lost his influence over Louis, and to his interest in the strong Church party must be largely attributed the direction of Louis' ecclesiastical policy. After the king's death, Suger wrote his biography, and gave us the clearest notion of the life and work of the first Capetian king who approached greatness.[1]

There was a real danger of the hereditary domain of the Capetians slipping away as completely from the control of the house of Capet as the more remote regions

The conquest of the royal domain. which only acknowledged the king as suzerain. The proprietor of the strong tower of Montlhéry could block the road between Paris and Orléans, and the bishops and abbots of the Isle de France, the most faithful supporters of the crown, had to witness the constant aggressions of a swarm of petty tyrants. It was an everyday thing for the local lord to take up his quarters in a monastery, with his greedy following, steal the wine, corn, and cattle of the hosts, and pollute the cloister with orgies and bloodshed. Conspicuous among these high-born brigands

---

[1] *Vie de Louis le Gros*, par Suger. Ed. Molinier in Picard's Collection de textes pour servir à l'étude et à l'enseignement de l'histoire.

were Hugh of Le Puiset, the tyrant of the rich plains of La Beauce, and Thomas of Marle, a member of the house of Coucy, and the cruellest and most able of the barons of the royal domains. Louis VI. ever gladly responded to the complaints of a bishop or abbot against a baronial oppressor. He led countless expeditions against the barons of the Isle de France ; expeditions which were individually unimportant, but which in the aggregate completely revolutionised the position of the monarchy within its domain. He was as a rule successful, though his task was complicated by his insignificant enemies rallying to their support more formidable foes, such as the King of England or the Count of Blois, the most rebellious representatives of the great feudatories. Confident of the support of the clerks, the townsfolk, and the lesser people, the king was able, by his vigour and persistence, to crush the most formidable of his enemies. Hugh du Puiset, after repeated defeats, was forced to betake himself to the Holy Land. Thomas de Marle died a defiant captive of the prince that he had so often disobeyed. Louis' numerous campaigns kept clear the roads that united the royal towns, such as Paris, Orléans, Bourges, Sens, Beauvais, Mantes, Etampes, Senlis, Noyon, Montreuil. Before his death the baronage of the domain had learnt that the king was no mere suzerain, but an effective ruler. Moreover, Louis' triumphs in war enabled him largely to dispense with the disloyal assemblies of magnates who had claimed to direct his policy. The power of the state fell into hands that Louis could trust, like Suger and the bishops. Among laymen the barons were superseded by warriors and men of business, whose whole occupation was in the royal household. Three brothers of the family of Garlande had among the knights of the court the same pre-eminence that Suger had among the clerks ; and the fourth Garlande, Stephen, though tonsured, succeeded two of his brothers as royal seneschal, and was the only cleric who ever held that knightly office.

The establishment of the royal authority over the royal

domain was but analogous to the process which was going
on all over France, and making the chief feudatories of the
Louis VI. crown centres of stronger and better organised
and the great patrimonies.   Each of the leading states of France
feudatories. had become more self-centred, more concentrated
within its own resources.   As a natural consequence their
relations with each other and with the crown assumed a
different character.   Each fief lived its own life apart,
and followed a different course of development.   Of all
the French kings Louis VI. had the least frequent dealings
with the great vassals of the crown.   What relations he
had remind us rather of international than of domestic
relations.

In 1106 Henry I. of England became Duke of Normandy
by the defeat of his brother Robert at Tinchebrai, and
Louis VI. Louis VI. had to contend for the greater part of
and Henry I. his reign against him.   Before long, two strong
coalitions were formed under Louis and Henry.   Louis
supported the rebellious barons of Normandy, who hoped to
make Robert's son, William Clito, their duke, and ultimately
found more powerful allies in Baldwin VII. of Flanders and in
Bertrada's son by Fulk le Réchin, Fulk v., Count of Anjou.
After Baldwin's death, Louis VI. secured the succession to
Flanders for Charles of Denmark, whose brief reign of
peace, justice, and benevolence secured for him the title
of Charles the Good.   Charles's murder in 1127 filled Europe
with horror.   Louis prevailed on the Flemings to accept
William Clito as their next count, and to him Thierry of
Alsace became a rival claimant.   The Clito died in 1128
after destroying his prospects by his folly, and Louis was
now forced to recognise Thierry.   All through his reign
he thus exercised a real influence over the course of Flemish
affairs.

Henry of England was equally active on his side.   Besides his Breton vassals, he could rely upon the special
enemies of Louis, the barons of the Isle de France.   He

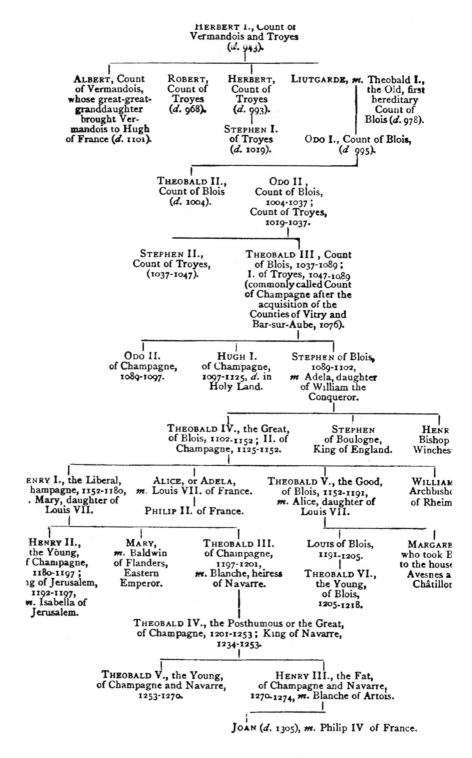

HERBERT I., Count of
Vermandois and Troyes
(*d.* 943).

ALBERT, Count
of Vermandois,
whose great-great-
granddaughter
brought Ver-
mandois to Hugh
of France (*d.* 1101).

ROBERT,
Count of
Troyes
(*d.* 968).

HERBERT,
Count of
Troyes
(*d.* 993).

STEPHEN I.
of Troyes
(*d.* 1019).

LIUTGARDE, *m.* Theobald I.,
the Old, first
hereditary
Count of
Blois (*d.* 978).

ODO I., Count of Blois,
(*d* 995).

THEOBALD II.,
Count of Blois
(*d.* 1004).

ODO II ,
Count of Blois,
1004-1037 ;
Count of Troyes,
1019-1037.

STEPHEN II.,
Count of Troyes,
(1037-1047).

THEOBALD III , Count
of Blois, 1037-1089 ;
I. of Troyes, 1047-1089
(commonly called Count
of Champagne after the
acquisition of the
Counties of Vitry and
Bar-sur-Aube, 1076).

ODO II.
of Champagne,
1089-1097.

HUGH I.
of Champagne,
1097-1125, *d.* in
Holy Land.

STEPHEN of Blois,
1089-1102,
m Adela, daughter
of William the
Conqueror.

THEOBALD IV., the Great,
of Blois, 1102-1152 ; II. of
Champagne, 1125-1152.

STEPHEN
of Boulogne,
King of England.

HENR
Bishop
Winches

ENRY I., the Liberal,
hampagne, 1152-1180,
. Mary, daughter of
Louis VII.

ALICE, or ADELA,
m. Louis VII. of France.

PHILIP II. of France.

THEOBALD V., the Good,
of Blois, 1152-1191,
m. Alice, daughter of
Louis VII.

WILLIAM
Archbishc
of Rheim

HENRY II.,
the Young,
f Champagne,
1180-1197 ;
g of Jerusalem,
1192-1197,
w. Isabella of
Jerusalem.

MARY,
m. Baldwin
of Flanders,
Eastern
Emperor.

THEOBALD III.
of Champagne,
1197-1201,
m. Blanche, heiress
of Navarre.

LOUIS of Blois,
1191-1205.

THEOBALD VI.,
the Young,
of Blois,
1205-1218.

MARGARE
who took B
to the house
Avesnes a
Châtillor

THEOBALD IV., the Posthumous or the Great,
of Champagne, 1201-1253 ; King of Navarre,
1234-1253.

THEOBALD V., the Young,
of Champagne and Navarre,
1253-1270.

HENRY III., the Fat,
of Champagne and Navarre,
1270-1274, *m.* Blanche of Artois.

JOAN (*d.* 1305), *m.* Philip IV of France.

became a warm partisan of Thierry of Alsace, and intrigued with the Flemish townsfolk, who were seldom on good terms with their counts. Above all he had the power-

Louis VI. and the House of Blois.

ful support of his nephews, Theobald IV., Count of Blois, surnamed the Great, and of his younger brother Stephen, who through his wife had become Count of Boulogne, and was later to become King of England. Theobald the Great was a much abler man than his brother, and the most rancorous and persistent of Louis VI.'s foes among the leading feudatories. In 1125 he once more united the counties of Blois and Champagne, so that he could attack his suzerain both from the south and from the east. But the most powerful combinations of twelfth century diplomacy proved singularly weak when brought into action. Almost ceaseless war was waged between Louis and Theobald, and the struggles of Louis and Henry were only less constant. The desolating, unending, purposeless, and unskilful warfare of the twelfth century was utterly fruitless in results. It was enough for Louis that, despite some defeats, he held his own fairly well.

Before the end of Louis' reign new complications ensued. In 1128, finding the hostility of Anjou a chief obstacle in the

Louis VI. and Aquitaine.

way of his plans, Henry I. married his widowed daughter and heiress, the Empress Matilda, to Geoffrey, the son and heir of his old enemy Fulk of Anjou. The way was thus prepared for the Angevin Empire of Henry II., though the refusal of England to accept Matilda as Henry's successor in 1135 seemed for the moment to remove any imminent danger. While England received Stephen, Geoffrey of Anjou established himself a few years later as duke of Normandy. Soon after, Stephen's brother, Theobald of Blois, made his peace with Louis. More-over, two years later Louis negotiated another alliance that seemed to offer even greater prospects to the heir to the French throne. On Good Friday 1137 William X., Count of Poitou and Duke of Aquitaine, died on pilgrimage. He was

the last male of his house, and his daughter Eleanor succeeded peaceably to his great inheritance. William had
wished that his daughter should marry Louis the Young,
the eldest surviving son of his suzerain. In a few months
the marriage was effected. The vast domains of Eleanor
in Poitou, Saintonge, and Guienne at once doubled the
domain of the crown, and made the young Louis immediate
lord of most of the great barons between the Loire and the
Pyrenees. But so long as the interests and feelings of south
and north were so absolutely different, it was no great gain
to a king, who had only just secured the overthrow of the
feudal castles of the Seine and Oise, to begin in his old age
a similar but more hopeless struggle on the Charente and the
Dordogne.

While Philip I. kept both Rome and Cluny in check, his
son became the stalwart champion of the rights of the Church.
It was his friendship for the Church that con-　Louis VI.
quered the Isle de France and made it possible　and the
for Suger to serve two such different masters as　Church.
Louis VI. and St. Bernard. Louis VI. restored the strong
alliance with the Papacy that prepared the way for the time
when the French king could boast that he was 'the eldest son
of the Church.' He ardently supported Innocent II. against
Anacletus, welcomed Innocent to his dominions, and attended
the Council of Sens in 1131. Nevertheless he did not
scruple to show priests and monks that he meant to be
master in his own kingdom, making bishops as well as barons
respect the royal justice, and never relaxing his rights over
ecclesiastical appointments. Even when Suger was chosen
abbot by the over-zealous monks of Saint-Denis, who had
neglected to wait for the King's authorisation to elect, Louis,
though he confirmed the election, put in prison the monks
who brought him the news of their brethren's unconstitutional
haste. Louis quarrelled with leading bishops like Ivo of
Chartres and Henry of Sens. Indignation at Louis' treatment
of his bishops drew Bernard from his retreat to denounce a

king who 'persecuted not so much bishops, as the zeal for justice, and the habit of religion which he finds in them.' But these examples of friction were exceptional. If the clergy would but accept his authority, they could have no better friend than Louis VI. And besides his alliance with the Church, Louis VI. drifted gradually into an alliance with the lesser people, which reminds us of the constant champion-ship by the Norman kings of England of the popular as against the feudal party. The better peace that now prevailed throughout France made town life, trade and com-merce, possible on a larger scale than in the rough times The of absolute feudal anarchy. The communal communal movement was now beginning in northern movement France, and though the king was far from being, as the older historians make him, the 'enfranchiser of the communes,' he was at least not fiercely hostile to the less revolutionary sides of the new movement.[1] He issued a large number of charters to towns and villages under ecclesiastical control, which, though meant to help the Church, also tended to help forward the municipal move-ment. Even more than this, his zeal to uphold sound justice was an incalculable boon to his people. The simple peasants saw in the good king a wonder-worker and a thaumaturgist, and were ready to give almost divine honours to the prince whom they celebrated as 'the Justiciar.'

Ill health and anxiety wore out the health and spirits of Louis. His last days were full of trouble. He desired to retire to the home of his youth clad in the Benedictine garb, but he was too ill to be able to realise his wish. He died at Paris almost in the odour of sanctity, lamenting with his last breath that it was not the lot of man to combine the energy of youth with the experience of age.

Louis VII., surnamed the Young, the eldest of the five sons that Adelaide of Maurienne bore to her husband, had already,

---

[1] See on this subject Luchaire's *Les Communes françaises à l'époque des Capétiens directs.*

when a child nine years old, been crowned at Reims by Innocent II. He was still in his new Aquitanian domains when his father's death gave him the exclusive Character of rule over France. Suger and the other ministers of Louis VII. the old king did their best to carry on still further the policy which had so much improved the position of the French monarchy. But Louis VII. was very unworthy to continue the work of his strong and vigorous father. He is praised by the chroniclers for his honesty, simplicity, and benevolence. He was a fair soldier, but his love of peace made him reluctant to assume the sword, and his weakness and indecision of character often led him into deceit and double-dealing. The chief positive trait in his disposition was a rigid and monastic piety, which kept his private life pure, but led to scruples of conscience and hesitation in conduct that not a little unfitted him for the rude tasks of kingship. The feudal party soon realised his weakness, and Suger found that the work of Louis the Fat had to be done over again. If the petty lords of the Isle de France were still kept in check, the independent great vassals soon began to enlarge their pretensions. It was a time of feudal reaction all over Europe. The weak Stephen had succeeded Henry I., 'the lion of righteousness,' in England. Conrad III., the slave of the Church, had replaced the capable but limited Lothair of Supplinburg. Under Louis VII. the same tendencies manifested themselves in France. It speaks well for Louis VI. and Suger that it was a period of stagnation rather than of positive reaction in the fortunes of the French monarchy.

The first ten years of Louis VII.'s reign were filled with petty and purposeless wars. In his zeal to assert the rights of his wife, Louis spent much time south ·of the Loire to the neglect of his more immediate interests in northern France. Besides useful but not very fruitful efforts to carry out in Eleanor's domains the policy of his father in the Isle de France, Louis led, in 1141, an expedition against the Count of Toulouse, The first ten years of Louis VII., 1137-1147.

Alphonse Jordan, who had refused the homage claimed from him to the Duke of Aquitaine. The city of Toulouse offered him a vigorous and successful resistance, and the first direct action of a descendant of Hugh Capet in Languedoc did not increase the prestige of the royal power. Nor were affairs in the north much more favourable. All his monastic virtues did not prevent him quarrelling with Innocent II., who had consecrated Peter de la Châtre to the archbishopric of Bourges despite the strenuous efforts of the king to prevent his election (1141). As Louis would not yield, Innocent excommunicated him, declaring that he was a child who had to be taught the lesson of not resisting the authority of the Church. Bernard re-echoed the thunders of the Pope, though Suger remained true to his master. Graver danger set in when Theobald of Champagne, who up to this point had remained on good terms with Louis, took up the cause of Peter de la Châtre, and gave him a refuge within his dominions. Louis indignantly went to war against Theobald and invaded Champagne. In the course of the campaign that ensued the king captured Vitry by assault. In the midst of the tumult the church, packed with fugitive townspeople, was set on fire, and more than a thousand men, women, and children were believed to have perished in the flames. Louis, terribly shocked at the sacrilege and slaughter, soon sought peace both with the Church and with Theobald, and allowed Peter de la Châtre to take possession of his see. Vitry was restored to Theobald, and Celestine II., who had now succeeded the truculent Innocent, made no difficulty in absolving Louis (1144). But the massacre at Vitry still weighed on the king's conscience, and led him to seek expiation by taking the crusader's vow. In 1147 Louis and Eleanor set out for the Second Crusade. The disasters and miseries of that fatal expedition have

The Second Crusade, 1147-1150. been already chronicled [see pages 191-193]. In 1150, Louis came back humiliated and defeated. During his absence the aged Suger had striven with all his might to uphold the royal authority, though he had disapproved of the king's crusading project, and never ceased to urge upon him the necessity of a speedy return. His fears were more than justified, for all the spirits of disorder took advantage of Louis' absence to disturb the realm. It was proposed to depose Louis in favour of his brother Robert, Count of Dreux. The return of the discredited king was quickly followed by the death of Suger (1152). With him expired the last hope of carrying on the work of national development at which he had so long laboured. To the first great error of the Crusade Louis now added his second mistake of repudiating his wife. In both cases the king put his personal feeling above the interest of his house and realm. As his absence on crusade led to a new wave of feudal anarchy, so his divorce helped on the growth of the great Angevin power, which was, for the rest of his life, to put an insurmountable obstacle in the way of the development of the French monarchy.

The relations between Louis and Eleanor had long been strained. After many years of barrenness, the two children which, as it was believed, came to the pair as the result of the prayers of St. Bernard, were both girls, and Louis ardently desired a son and successor. There was, moreover, a strange contrast of character between the weak, pious, and shifty king and the fierce, imperious, and ambitious queen. New grounds of dispute arose during the Crusade, when Eleanor strove to divert the French host from their projected march to Jerusalem in order that its presence might support her uncle Raymond of Antioch in his schemes for the aggrandisement of his principality. The relations of husband and wife became so bad that Suger wrote imploring the king to conceal his anger against the queen. After their return to France nothing but the influence of Suger prevented a breach. Soon after his death, the question of divorce was formally raised. St. Bernard, still omnipotent over Louis' mind, approved the step. In March 1152 a church council held at Beaugency annulled the marriage

Divorce of Louis VII. and Eleanor of Aquitaine, 1152.

on the ground of consanguinity. Eleanor withdrew to her
own dominions, which were now again separated from the
French crown. Anxious to do all in her power to spite her
former husband, she offered herself in marriage to young
Henry of Anjou. At Whitsuntide their marriage at Poitiers
exposed the French monarchy to the gravest danger. So

The rise of   long as the chief fiefs were held by separate and
the House   rival houses it was not impossible for the crown
of Blois.   to hold its own against them, but an aggregation
of several great fiefs into the same hands might easily set up a
rival power whose forces could overbalance the scanty strength
of the king. The union of Chartres, Blois, and Champagne
under Theobald the Great had been the gravest obstacle to
the plans of Louis VI. The establishment of Theobald's
younger brother in Boulogne, Normandy, and England would
have been even more dangerous but for the incompetence of
Stephen. Side by side with the union of several fiefs under the
house of Blois, was the union of Anjou, Maine, and Normandy,
brought about by the policy of Henry I. in marrying his
daughter, the Empress Matilda, to Geoffrey, the son of Fulk
of Anjou. These two amalgamations neutralised each
other, when the accession of Stephen to England and Normandy brought the old interests of Blois and Anjou into
fierce antagonism, and for a time neither side won a preponderating position over the other. Though Matilda the
Empress failed to conquer England, her husband established
himself in Normandy, and in 1144 received from Louis VII.
the formal investiture of the duchy. In 1149 Geoffrey and

The growth   Matilda handed over their Norman claims to their
of Anjou.   son Henry, now sixteen years old. In September
1151 the death of Geoffrey made Henry Fitz-Empress (so the
young prince was commonly described) sole lord of Normandy,
Anjou, Maine, and Touraine. Anjou now rapidly prevailed
over Blois. Young as he was, Henry had already a character
and a policy. After his marriage with Eleanor he had
a position in France far stronger than that of King Louis

himself; from the Somme to the Pyrenees, from the Bay of Biscay to the mountains of Auvergne, Henry and Eleanor ruled directly or indirectly over the fairest half The Empire of France. Two years later, the death of Stephen of Henry II. made Henry King of England. In 1158 Henry added to his possession the county of Nantes and re-enforced the old Norman claims of overlordship over Duke Conan of Brittany. Later he secured the hand of Constance, Conan's daughter and heiress, for his second son Geoffrey, who in 1171 peacefully succeeded his father-in-law as Duke of Brittany. Henry was equally successful in realising the many pretensions of Eleanor over the lands of south-western France. In 1158 Eleanor's claims to overlordship over the county of Toulouse led Henry to lead an expedition against Count Raymond v., who had succeeded his father Alphonse in 1148, and by his marriage with Constance, sister of Louis vii., and widow of Eustace of Boulogne, King Stephen's son, had united himself against the Angevin with the houses of France and Blois. The personal intervention of King Louis saved Raymond from absolute submission, though the peace transferred Cahors and the Quercy from Toulouse to the duchy of Aquitaine. In 1173 Henry accomplished his purpose. Henceforth the county of Toulouse, with its dependencies the Rouergue and the Albigeois, became, by Raymond's submission, recognised dependencies of Aquitaine. With equal energy Henry pressed his claims to overlordship over Berri, where his aggressions were particularly unwelcome by reason of the large strip of royal domain which ran from Bourges southward. Henry also revived successfully the old Aquitanian claim to the overlordship of Auvergne, while his alliance with the rising house of Maurienne, now Counts of Savoy, gave him some command of the upper Rhone valley and the chief passes over the Alps. The extraordinary ability of Henry made his commanding position the more formidable. He was no mere feudal chief like the Counts of Blois, but a statesman capable of building up a mighty empire.

After the consolidation of the Angevin Empire, Louis had to watch narrowly the actions of a vassal more powerful

Rivalry of Louis VII. and Henry II.
than himself. Before long war became almost chronic between him and Henry. It was not that constant efforts were not made to secure peace and alliance. Henry married his eldest son to Louis' daughter, Margaret, receiving as her marriage portion the long-coveted possession of the Vexin. In 1162 Louis VII. and Henry again made common cause in favour of Alexander III. against the Antipope [see page 257]. During his exile in France Alexander frequented the dominions of Henry as much as he did those of Louis. It was in Henry's town of Tours that the council assembled that excommunicated the Antipope. Henry seemed too strong to make direct resistance of much avail.

Before long Henry II. fell into his quarrel with Archbishop Thomas of Canterbury, which gave Louis an opportunity of adding to his rival's difficulties, by giving as much support as he could to his enemies. After Thomas's death Louis found an even better way of effecting this purpose by forcing Henry to divide his dominions among his sons, and then fomenting the discord that soon burst out between Henry and his wife and children. In 1170 the young Henry, Louis' son-in-law, was crowned joint king with his father, after the French fashion. Geoffrey was already Duke of Brittany, and in 1172 Richard, the third son, was enthroned Duke of Aquitaine, and betrothed to Alice, Louis VII.'s younger daughter. Louis soon persuaded the vain and weak Henry III.—so he was often styled —to make common cause with him against his father. In

The War of 1173 and 1174.
1173 a well-devised conspiracy burst forth against the power of Henry II. The feudal party in England and Normandy, the King of Scots, and Henry's discontented vassals in Britain, made common cause with Louis VII. and the younger King Henry against the arch-enemy of the Capetian house. The vassals of France, who feared Henry more than Louis, joined the confederacy,

and at their head were Geoffrey of Brittany and Richard of Aquitaine, and even Queen Eleanor herself. Among Louis' greater vassals Philip of Alsace (son of Thierry of Alsace), Count of Flanders, entered into the league. So did the sons of Theobald the Great—Henry the Liberal, Count of Champagne, and Theobald v., the Good, Count of Blois, both married to Louis VII.'s daughters. The representative of the younger branch of Blois, the Count of Flanders' brother, who ruled Boulogne as the husband of King Stephen's daughter Mary, also took up the hereditary policy of his house. The good luck and the genius of Henry prevailed over Louis and his associates, and in 1174 peace was patched up on conditions that left matters much as they had been before the war. Eleanor of Aquitaine, captured as she was endeavouring to escape to her divorced husband's court, was the chief sufferer. She was immured in a prison, from which she hardly escaped during the rest of Henry II.'s life.

In the last seven years of his life Louis VII. made no sensible advance against Henry II., but though beaten in the field, he had broken up the unity of the Angevin power, and could still count upon the support of the sons of his enemy. His reign ended as ingloriously as it had begun. Nevertheless, the constant interest of the king in the policy of the remotest parts of the monarchy was a step forward in the royal operations. The intervention of Louis in Toulouse, in Auvergne, in Burgundy, though not always successful, marked an advance over the incuriousness and indifference of his father's reign in matters not directly concerning the domain. He even looked beyond his kingdom into the Arelate, where Barbarossa's coronation in 1178 was a source of inquietude to him. Moreover, Louis VII.'s constant friendship for the Church stood him in good stead in his dealings with his remoter vassals. His pilgrimages to distant shrines, to St. James of Compostella, to the Grande Chartreuse, and to the

Progress of the Monarchy under Louis VII.

new shrine of St. Thomas at Canterbury, spread his fame.
The younger monastic orders, especially the Cistercians and
the Carthusians, were his enthusiastic friends, and the
unostentatious and timid support of a crowd of bishops
and abbots gave Louis VII.'s reign its peculiar position in
history. The chronicler tells us how, in Louis VII.'s days,
war was rare, and the realm ruled peacefully and strenuously;
many new towns established, and ancient ones increased;
many forests were cut down; and divers orders of religion
marvellously multiplied in various parts of the land.

Louis VII. was thrice married. His first two wives brought
him daughters only. Eleanor of Aquitaine's children, Mary
and Alice, became the wives of the two brothers,

*Family, old
age, and
death of
Louis VII.*

Henry of Champagne and Theobald of Blois.
Constance of Castile, Louis' second wife, was the
mother of Margaret, afterwards wife of the young
king, Henry III., and of another Alice, long betrothed to his
brother, Richard of Aquitaine. Fourteen days after Constance's
death, Louis VII. married his third wife, Alice or Adela of
Champagne, sister of his sons-in-law, Henry the Liberal
and Theobald the Good. For five years they had no
children, and Louis, fearing the division of his kingdom
between his daughters, longed earnestly for a son. He
visited Cîteaux, and threw himself on his knees before the
General Chapter that was in session, and only rose when he
had been assured that God would soon answer his prayers.
In August 1165 the long-wished-for son was born at Paris,
amidst heartfelt rejoicings, and was christened Philip, but soon
became known by the surnames 'Godgiven' and 'Augustus.'
When Philip was only fourteen years old, Louis VII. was
stricken with paralysis. On All Saints' Day 1179, he was
crowned joint-king at Reims by his mother's brother, Archbishop William of Blois. In September 1180 the old king
died, and Philip Augustus became sole King of France.

In the first ten years of the reign of Philip II., the fierce
factions that had raged round the death-bed of Louis VII.

were continued. The chief influences to which the boy-king was exposed were those of Philip of Flanders, and of the house of Blois. Philip of Alsace had shown more than the usual energy and skill of a feudal prince in his administration of Flanders. He is celebrated in Flemish history as the founder of ports and cities, the granter of charters of liberties, the maker of canals, the cultivator of sandy heaths and barren marshes, the strong administrator, the vigilant upholder of law, the friend and patron of poets and romancers. He also laboriously built up a great family connection, from which he hoped to establish a power such as might rival the aggregated fiefs of Blois or Anjou, and might well have anticipated the later unions of the Netherlands under the Bavarian and Burgundian houses. Himself lord of Flanders and Artois, Philip became, by his marriage with Isabella of Vermandois, the descendant of Hugh the Great the Crusader, Count of Amiens and Vermandois. His nephew Baldwin was Count of Hainault. His brother Matthew and his niece Ida were in succession Count and Countess of Boulogne. Moreover, Philip was the most trusted counsellor of the old age of Louis VII., and the godfather of Philip Augustus. Just before Louis' death his influence was confirmed by the marriage of his niece, Isabella of Hainault, to the young king. Being childless, he promised that after his death Artois should go to his niece and her husband.

The early years of Philip Augustus, 1180-1189.

The house of Blois had hoped much from the accession of a king whose mother was a Champenoise. But Philip of Flanders chased Adela of Champagne from the court, and showed a fierce hostility to her brothers. Theobald of Blois and Henry of Champagne were forced to make alliance with their old enemy, Henry of Anjou. William of Reims, disgusted that the Archbishop of Sens was called upon to crown the new queen, strove to act once again the part played by Thomas of Canterbury when the younger Henry was crowned by Roger of York. War seemed imminent between

the two Philips, and a strong coalition that included the houses
of Blois and Anjou, and a vast swarm of smaller feudatories,
who rejoiced that the reign of a boy of fifteen bade fair to
give them a chance of striking an effective blow against the
power of their suzerain. But Philip of Flanders pressed his
advantages too far. A natural reaction from the overbearing
Count of Flanders soon drove King Philip towards his mother
and her family. Henry of Anjou's mediation patched up
peace between Philip II. and his mother's kinsfolk, and
enabled him to shake off his dependence on Philip of
Flanders.

Peace did not last very long. For a short time Henry II.
was on good terms with the French king, and strove to per-
suade him to associate himself with the declining fortunes of
Henry the Lion, and swell the coalition against Frederick
Barbarossa. But Philip II. gave the deposed Saxon no
effective help, and before long the old relations were restored.
In 1183 Philip was again backing up the rebellious sons of
Henry II. against their father, though the sudden death of
Henry, the young king, quickly brought this struggle to an end.
In the next year, 1184, Philip went to war against Philip of
Flanders, who on the death of his wife, Isabella of Vermandois,
in 1183, had kept possession of her lands, which Philip II. had
declared forfeited. So fierce a struggle seemed imminent that
the Count of Flanders was glad to get the support of the house
of Blois, which had now again drifted into opposition to the
king. At the same time he called in the Emperor as a counterpoise against his other suzerain. But Philip of Flanders was
afraid to face the great host which the French king now
turned against him. He sought the intervention of Henry II.,
who, in November 1185, personally negotiated the peace of
Aumâle, by which the Vermandois was added to the royal
domain, and the promise of Artois and the Somme towns at
the Count's death was renewed. It was the first real triumph
of the young king's reign.

Flushed by his success against Flanders, Philip II. soon

fell again into hostilities against Henry II. He clamoured
for the restoration of the Vexin, the marriage portion of his
sister Margaret, widow of Henry the younger, but finally

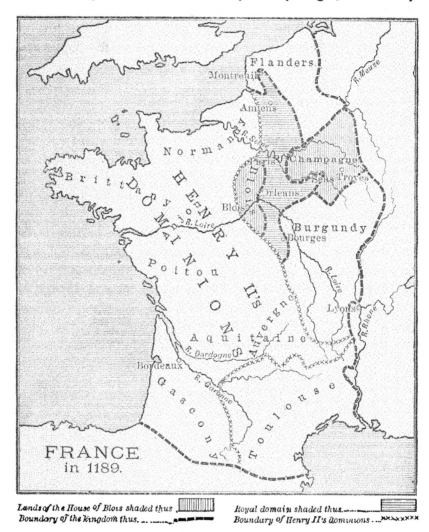

Lands of the House of Blois shaded thus ▯▯▯▯▯▯   Royal domain shaded thus ▭▭▭
Boundary of the Kingdom thus. ▬▬▬▬▬   Boundary of Henry II's dominions ⤫⤫⤫⤫⤫⤫

allowed it to remain in the English king's hands as the
future portion for his other sister Alice, the promised bride of
Richard of Aquitaine. But he still intrigued actively with
Henry's disloyal sons. In 1186 Geoffrey of Brittany went to

Paris to plot new designs against his father, but was cut off by fever when still the French king's guest. Projects of crusade delayed for a time the weaving of the network of intrigue. But in 1189 Philip again found Richard at war against his father. A sharp campaign was fought, which resulted in the complete defeat of Henry II., who on 4th July 1189 was forced to make a complete submission at Colombières, and died two days afterwards. It was the second great triumph of Philip's reign. Though the Angevin heritage passed unimpaired to Richard, the new king was not statesman enough long to keep together so precarious an inheritance. Henceforth the advantage was increasingly on Philip's side. The call to the Third Crusade postponed the inevitable struggle between them. But the historian of France may well pause at the death of Henry II. The period of struggling and waiting was now almost over. In the later and more brilliant portion of his reign, the conqueror of Philip of Alsace and Henry of Anjou had to gather in the fruits of his victories. Yet the future position of France was already assured in the year that saw the death of the most resourceful of her enemies.

Marginal notes:

Defeat and death of Henry II., 1189

The call to the Third Crusade, 1187-1189.

CHAPTER XIII

THE THIRD CRUSADE AND THE REIGN OF HENRY VI.[1]
(1187-1197)

Europe in 1187—Preparations for the Third Crusade—Crusade and Death of
Frederick Barbarossa—Destruction of the German Army—Crusade of
Philip II. and Richard I.—Truce with Saladin—The Reign of Henry VI.
—Henry's Coronation and first Italian journey—First attack on Apulia—
German troubles—Captivity of Richard I.—Conquest of Apulia and
Sicily—The Hereditary Empire and the Conquest of the East—Death of
Henry.

In the second half of the twelfth century limits had already
been set to the worst forms of feudal anarchy, and strong
and well-ordered states ruled by powerful kings
had replaced the chaos of the Dark Ages.
Frederick Barbarossa, if no effective lord of the
world, exercised a very real authority over
Germany, and even over Italy. Louis VI. and Louis VII. had
put the resources of the French monarchy on a solid basis,
and Philip Augustus was now preparing the way for still
greater triumphs. Henry II. had bound together his vast but
heterogeneous empire so firmly that the power of Anjou was
able to survive the blind knight-errantry of his successor.
Even in the remoter parts of Europe the same tendency

The state of Europe after the fall of Jerusalem.

---

[1] To the authorities mentioned in chapter viii., may be added for the
Third Crusade, the *Itinerarium Regis Ricardi* (Rolls Series), with
Dr. Stubbs' Introductions, Ambroise's *Estoire de la guerre sainte*, ed. G.
Paris, and Archer's useful, though popular, *Crusade of Richard I.* Toeche's
Kaiser Heinrich VI. is the standard modern authority for Henry VI.'s reign;
some of its results are usefully criticised in Bloch's *Forschungen zur Politik
Kaiser Heinrichs VI. in den Jahren* 1191-1194.

manifested itself towards the growth of strong monarchies. The kingdoms of the east and north, barely redeemed from barbarism, saw rulers like Valdemar of Denmark and Ottocar of Bohemia. The kingdoms of divided Spain, the Norman dominion of Sicily, show the universal drift of the tide. Even the greater feudatories of the larger kingdoms were making themselves centres of an authority that was not far from being national. States like Toulouse and Provence, representing the growing national feeling of the south French nation; opulent and manufacturing Flanders, cutting itself apart from France and Germany alike, and even mere dynastic powers, like the house of Champagne and Blois, show how authority was becoming concentrated into few hands. If the unity of the German kingdom was still rather illusory, the dukes, counts, and margraves, who ruled over its larger subdivisions, were making themselves, like the great French feudatories, centres of a local feeling and of a local order, which, in days when the strongest king's arm did not reach very far, were real securities for peace and prosperity.

When the terrible news that Jerusalem was once more in the hands of the infidel spread throughout Europe, the result of this development was seen in the shape taken by the movement to re-establish the Christian power in the East. In the eleventh century the Popes had preached, organised, and directed the Crusades. A hundred years later the Papacy had certainly not declined in influence. But it was no longer the only strong power in Europe. Absolutely it was what it had been in the days of Gregory and Urban. Relatively it was much less, since instead of a Henry IV., or Philip I., or a William Rufus, it had to deal with a Barbarossa, a Philip Augustus, a Henry of Anjou. Even the leadership of the Church, as St. Bernard's career shows, was not necessarily given to the reigning Pope. While the First Crusade was the work of Urban II., and the Second Crusade sprang from the efforts of St. Bernard, the Third Crusade was due to the prompt action of the great kings of Europe, and above all to Frederick Barbarossa. In the First Crusade the leadership of the Christian host fell to the lesser feudal princes, like the Count of Toulouse or the Count of Flanders. In the Second Crusade the Emperor and the King of France took the lead, but they went with insufficient resources, and left their dominions in disorder and anarchy. In the Third Crusade the three chief monarchs of Europe appeared at the head of well-equipped and fairly disciplined armies. However little successful they were, their failure was as much due to their taking with them on their pilgrimage their Western rivalries, as to their military insufficiency for their task. In each case they left their dominions well cared for and well governed, and in no case did their long absence from their homes stop the orderly development of their states.

The absorption of the Western monarchs on their own territorial aggrandisement seemed for a time to lessen the force of the crusading impulse, and certainly during the thirteenth century led to the gradual decay of the crusading ideal. Europe was now breaking up slowly but surely into the great nations of modern times, and was inevitably losing a good deal of her consciousness of unity in the process. Even Frederick Barbarossa, filled as he was with his dreams of reviving the power of Rome, had been, as we saw, obliged to adopt a different policy in Germany and Italy, and had attained his greatest successes in proportion as he acted most fully as a German national king. To kings like Philip Augustus and Henry of Anjou, the Empire was a mere name, and they were conscious of no lord over them save God Himself. Such unity of feeling as remained in Europe was rather the result of common chivalrous and martial ideals, and the steady and persistent international influence of the Catholic Church, than of any ideal unity of the Christian state under the Roman Emperor. The kings of the West had too much work at home to give them much leisure to look abroad. If ambition, restlessness, or principle compelled them to take interest in the affairs of their neighbours, they had not yet attained sufficient strength to make their intervention a reality.

It was harder to bring about a combined European movement in the days of Barbarossa than it had been in the days of Urban II. But the news that the infidel was once more lording it over the Holy Sepulchre so profoundly stirred up the mind of Europe that all difficulties in the way of continued action were rapidly surmounted, and within three years of the fall of Jerusalem the best organised of the Crusades was already started. The Papacy proved true to its noblest traditions. It was universally believed that the fall, or the prospect of the fall, of the Holy City had proved Urban III.'s death-blow. His successors, the enthusiastic Gregory VIII. and the conciliatory Clement III., strove, at great sacrifices, to heal the feuds of Pope and Emperor, and to assuage the rivalries of the monarchs of Europe, so that all might turn their resources to the Holy War. Within a few weeks of the receipt of the fatal news, orders were issued from Rome, calling on the faithful to unite to free Jerusalem from the infidel, enjoining public fasts and prayers, and offering ample indulgences and spiritual encouragements to such as would take the cross. The Cardinals talked of living on alms, and devoting their property to the Crusade, while they wandered through Europe, preaching the Holy War. Italy, so little moved as a rule by the crusading impulse, and so accustomed to make a heavy profit from the necessities of Northern and Western pilgrims, was all aglow with enthusiasm. The first succour sent to the East came from a Norman fleet from Naples and Sicily, which took up the work of Bohemund. William of Sicily turned to the succour of Antioch and Tyre the army which he had collected to attack Constantinople. Not much behind the Sicilians were the Scandinavian peoples, who were now for the first time brought within the range of the crusading movement. If Norway, torn asunder by civil war, contributed

(Marginal note:) Preparations for the Third Crusade, 1187-1189.

but few Crusaders, thousands took the cross in Sweden and Denmark. But the individual efforts of the smaller states soon subordinated themselves to the action of the three greatest princes of Europe. Richard of Aquitaine was the first of Western rulers to take the cross in 1187. His father and Philip of France received the cross from the Archbishop of Tyre in the early part of 1188. But though England and France could agree to levy a 'Saladin tithe,' to equip the crusading host, the hostility of their sovereigns postponed the Crusade until after Henry II.'s death. When, in 1189, Philip Augustus and Richard Cœur de Lion made themselves the leaders of the Third Crusade in the West, Frederick Barbarossa, with his German host, was already on his march for the East. Round these three monarchs goups the history of the Crusade.

Frederick Barbarossa was the first to start. In the spring of 1189, the German Crusaders gathered together at Ratisbon. Great pains were taken to provide money and equipment as well as men, and every precaution to avoid the swarm of unarmed pilgrims and penniless fanatics, who had destroyed the discipline and military efficiency of earlier crusading armies. In May the German host started on the dangerous land route through Hungary, Greece, and Asia Minor. The friendship of Bela III. of Hungary made the first part of the journey easy. Much time was wasted through the treachery of the Eastern Emperor, Isaac Angelus, yet Isaac dared not face the open hostility of the Germans, and at last made his submission. Winter was now at hand, and Frederick thought it prudent to rest at Adrianople. In March 1190 the Germans resumed their march. April saw them in Asia, on the borders of the kingdom of Roum, where Kilidj Arslan proved as plausible and as treacherous as Isaac. But, like Isaac, the Sultan feared provoking their direct hostility, and after many delays and difficulties, the Christian army was allowed to proceed. By June the Crusaders were descending the passes

Crusade and death of Frederick Barbarossa, 1089-1191.

of the Taurus into Cilicia, then part of the Christian kingdom of Armenia. On reaching the banks of the Salef, the old Emperor, against the advice of his followers, sought refreshment and the shortening of his journey by swimming over the river. But the swift current swept him away, and the sorrowful warriors could only rescue his lifeless body from the stream.

Up to this point the German expedition had been decidedly successful. But the utter consternation that fell upon it after the Emperor's death did more for Islam than the tricks of Kilidj Arslan and the deserts and defiles of Asia Minor. Many knights hastened to the coast and took ship home. Duke Frederick of Swabia, Barbarossa's second son, assumed the command of the dispirited remnant, which, after resting a while in the friendly land of the Armenians, entered Syria. The reins of discipline were now hopelessly relaxed. The army broke up into

Destruction of the German Army.

various bands, and the disconnected fragments were so severely handled by the Saracens that German slaves were cheap for many a day in every market of Syria. Duke Frederick at last reached Antioch, where he buried the perishable parts of his father's body in the church of St. Peter. The plague now decimated the much tried host, and only a miserable remnant followed Duke Frederick to join in the siege of Acre. Before long the Duke of Swabia died, and the Germans were now so utterly demoralised that they lost the sacred bones of their Emperor, which they had preserved in the hope of giving them a worthy tomb in the Church of the Holy Sepulchre. The great German army was of less account in Palestine than the scattered bands that came from Lower Germany by sea and finally got to Acre after doing good service against the Moors in Spain, or the little host that had sailed from Brindisi under the Landgrave Louis of Thuringia, and also reached Syria in safety.

The German Crusade had already been undone when the kings of France and England met at Vézelai and marched thence to Marseilles. A gallant army accompanied them, conspicuous among the leaders of which were Hugh, Duke of Burgundy, Theobald v. of Blois (the son and successor of Theobald the Great), Henry II., Count of Champagne (the Count of Blois' nephew), and Philip of Alsace, the aged Count of Flanders. In September 1190 both kings had reached Sicily, where they passed the winter, detained by the critical state of the island. William the Good had died in November 1189, and his throne should have passed to his aunt Constance's husband, the new king of the Romans, Henry VI. But the rule of the northerners was not popular in Sicily. Despite the efforts of Walter Archbishop of Palermo to keep the Sicilian grandees true to their oaths, the national party, headed by the chancellor Matthew, passed over Constance, and gave the throne to Tancred, Count of Lecce, a young, vigorous, warlike, and popular prince. Tancred was a bastard son of Duke Roger, King Roger's eldest son, who had died before his father. As the determined foe of the Hohenstaufen, Richard bore no ill-will to Tancred, and, with a little more statecraft, would have seen the wisdom of gaining his friendship. But Richard often neglected policy for adventure, and was perhaps seized by a wild desire to conquer Sicily. Tancred had rashly imprisoned King William's widow, Joanna, who was Richard I.'s sister, and had deprived her of her dowry. On Richard's arrival, King Tancred released the lady, but still kept her lands. But Richard took Messina by storm, 'quicker than a priest could chant matins,' and forced Tancred to surrender his sister's portion. He stayed in Sicily all the winter, and at the time of the spring passage, Richard and Philip set sail for the Holy Land. On the way Richard conquered Cyprus, then ruled by the Comnenian prince Isaac, who was called Emperor of Cyprus, and had won an ill name for his ill-concealed alliance with Saladin and his bad treatment of Frankish pilgrims.

Marginal notes:
Crusade of Philip Augustus and Richard I., 1190-1192.

Tancred of Sicily and Isaac of Cyprus, 1189-1191.

The affairs of the Christians in Palestine seemed utterly desperate. Guy of Lusignan [see pp. 193-195], who had Capture of been released by Saladin on promising to relin- Acre, 1191. quish the crown, had been absolved from his oath by the clergy, and now again called himself King of Jerusalem, though Conrad of Montferrat held Tyre against him, and the Christians were hopelessly divided. Nevertheless Guy, with the help of the first Crusaders, had undertaken the siege of Acre, the most important of the Saracen conquests after Jerusalem itself. But the Saracens, who came to the relief of Acre, were themselves strong enough to besiege the besiegers, who were soon in a terrible plight. The constant arrival of fresh Crusaders, and the need of dividing Saladin's army to deal with Barbarossa, enabled Guy to hold his own until the spring of 1191, when Saladin renewed his blockade. In despair Guy hurried to Cyprus and begged for Richard's help. Philip reached the camp in April, and Richard early in June. Saladin now retired, and the siege of Acre was renewed. In July the standard of the Cross again floated over its walls.

The Western army had taken with them to Palestine their national jealousies, and the quarrels of the rival claimants for the throne of Jerusalem brought these animosities to a crisis. Philip looked upon Richard with deadly hatred as his most formidable rival, and Richard's insulting repudiation of his long-plighted faith to Alice, Philip's sister, and his marriage with Berengaria of Navarre at Cyprus, would have irritated a colder man than the French king. Conrad Rivalry of of Montferrat was urged by the great nobles of Guy of Palestine to claim the throne, since Sibyl and her Lusignan and Conrad children were already dead, and Guy's title to of Mont- the throne had entirely disappeared. Isabella, ferrat. Sibyl's younger sister, now repudiated her husband, Henfrid of Toron, married Conrad, and transferred to him her claims to the succession. While these disputes were raging the army remained inactive, but at last a compromise was patched up by which Guy kept the royal title but shared his power with Conrad, who was appointed his successor. No sooner was this done than Philip Augustus started home. Freed from his presence Richard marched against the infidel, and performed prodigies of valour. But his army was breaking up through sickness, death, and desertion. Many of the French had gone back with Philip. The plague had carried off Theobald of Blois and Philip of Alsace. Hugh of Burgundy, who died in Palestine in 1193, and Henry of Champagne, were now the chief French Crusaders. Despite the arrangement between Guy and Conrad their rivalry burst out afresh, and Conrad became so strong that Richard acknowledged him king. Soon after, Conrad's murder by the emissaries of the 'Old Man of the Mountain' renewed the troubles, though they were for a time satisfactorily settled when Isabella, Conrad's widow, married Henry of Champagne, who was now accepted as king, both by Henry of the Crusaders and the Syrian Franks. Richard Champagne magnanimously compensated Guy by handing King of Jerusalem, over Cyprus, where the house of Lusignan reigned 1192. as kings until the latter part of the fifteenth century. At length the war with Saladin was renewed. But the Crusaders were decimated with sickness and weary of their enterprise, while the elaborate courtesies, now exchanged between the Christian and Mohammedan armies, showed that the long intercourse of Frank and Saracen had destroyed the bigotry and acerbity that had marked the earlier dealings Truce with of the two hosts. In September 1192 a truce Saladin, and was made by which Jaffa was left in Christian end of the Third hands and free access to Jerusalem was allowed Crusade, to pilgrims, though the Holy City remained ruled 1192. by the Mohammedans. In October Richard left Palestine, and next year Saladin died. With the passing away of the two mighty antagonists the great epoch of the Crusades ended. Even before this the Third Crusade had shown that a Europe, broken up into rival states, whose kings carried their animosities

with them even when they fought as soldiers of the Cross,
was less capable of upholding the Frankish power in the
East than even the tumultuous throngs of feudal chieftains
and adventurers, who had first established it. Yet the Third
Crusade had given a new lease to the Christian power in Syria.
Acre now became what Jerusalem had been in the twelfth
century, and the Latin kingdom of Cyprus afforded a good
basis for future operations against the infidel, and bound the
East and West together as they had never been bound before.
If the Third Crusade marked the end of the heroic period, it
made easy the regular flow of bands of armed pilgrims, every
spring and autumn passage, on which the future destinies of
the Latin East depended.

The short but most important reign of Henry VI. brings out
Henry VI., clearly that intimate interconnection of all Western
1190-1197. and Eastern politics which the Crusade had already
strikingly illustrated. The puny frame and delicate constitution of the young king stood in marked contrast to the physical strength and vigour of his father. But his strong features
expressed sternness and determination, and his mental gifts
and character were in no wise inferior to those of Barbarossa.
He was as good a general, as active and strenuous a politician,
as the old king. His policy shows a daring originality to
which his father could make no claim. But the broader,
nobler sides of Barbarossa's character were but little represented in that of his son. He carried out ambitious schemes
with cold-blooded selfishness, ruthless cruelty, and greedy
treachery. Yet his general objects were far-reaching, and not
wanting in nobility, and he ever showed a rare self-restraint.
The inheritor of his father's great work, the husband of the
heiress of Sicily, Henry had visions of a power which was not
limited to Germany and northern Italy. He dreamt of an
Empire as universal as the Empire imagined by Otto III.
Like Otto, he strove to make Italy rather than Germany the
centre of his power. Like Otto also, he reigned too short a
time to carry out his ideals. But, unlike Otto, he strove to

realise his ambitions in a thoroughly practical and masterly way. In his reign of eight years he had only one failure.

From the moment that the departure of Barbarossa had left King Henry the virtual ruler of Germany, grave difficulties encompassed his administration. Henry Return of the Lion returned, Lübeck opened its doors to Henry the its founder, and was soon in a position to dispute Lion, 1190. the supremacy of Saxony with the bishops and barons who had divided his ancient powers. In the summer of 1190, the mediation of the Archbishops of Cologne and Mainz concluded the Treaty of Fulda, by which the king allowed Henry the Lion's restoration, and gave him half the revenues of Lübeck. It was worth while to buy off opposition when the news of the recognition of Tancred by the Pope required Henry's immediate presence in Italy to vindicate the claims of his wife Constance to the Sicilian throne. Hardly less alarming was the news of the long sojourn of Richard of England in Messina, and of his treaty with the usurper Tancred. It seemed as if Richard, the brother-in-law of Henry the Lion, and the strenuous supporter of the Guelfs, was becoming the bond of union between the enemies of the Hohenstaufen in northern Germany and southern Italy. The news of Barbarossa's death now further complicated the position.

Early in 1191 Henry VI. crossed the Alps to Italy. The mutual rivalries of the Lombard cities made it improbable that he would have much difficulty with the Henry VI.'s north. He prudently sought the friendship Coronation of both the rival leagues, whose feuds were now and first Italian distracting Lombardy. He won the support of journey, Pisa and Genoa, which alone had fleets strong 1191. enough to convey him to Sicily. In his anxiety to isolate Tancred, he strove to conciliate Clement III, who had been allowed to live in Rome on the condition of recognising the autonomy of the city. But in March 1191 the Celestine III., pacific Clement died, and his successor, the 1191-1198. Roman Cardinal Hyacinth, who took the name of Celestine III., was a weak and petulant old man of more than eighty years of age, who feared both the union of the Empire and Sicily, and an open breach with Henry.

Henry demanded his coronation as Emperor, and Celestine strove to defer it by postponing his own consecration as Pope. Henry now marched to the neighbourhood of Rome, and took possession of Tusculum, which, in its bitter hatred of the Romans, had implored for an imperial garrison. He resolved to hasten his coronation by winning over the Romans, and with that object he treacherously handed over Tusculum to them. The Romans wreaked a hideous vengeance on their hated enemy. Tusculum was so absolutely demolished that no later attempt was ever made to repeople it. In later times Frascati, lower down the hill, became a populous town ; but the ruins of Tusculum still testify to the completeness of the Romans' vengeance. Henry's stroke of policy met with immediate success. On April 14th Celestine was consecrated, and next day he crowned Henry and Constance.

Triumphant over the Papacy, Henry now marched against Tancred. At first he was conspicuously successful, and Naples alone still held out for Tancred. It was besieged by Henry on the land side, while the galleys of Pisa and Genoa blocked all access to it by sea. The strenuous resistance of Naples soon shattered the Emperor's hopes. The Sicilian admiral, Margarito, drove away the Pisans, and re-opened communication between Naples and Sicily. The south Italian summer brought plague and fever into the German host. A fierce national reaction against the Northerners swept through southern Italy. Baffled and beaten, Henry raised the siege and returned to Germany.

Failure of the attack on Apulia, 1191.

Henry of Brunswick, the eldest son of Henry the Lion, who had accompanied the Emperor to Italy as a hostage, escaped from the imperial camp, and established an alliance between Tancred and the Guelfs. During the king's absence in Italy, Henry the Lion had broken the Peace of Fulda, and was waging war against his Saxon enemies. On the king's return to Germany, a struggle between the Guelfs and the Hohenstaufen seemed inevitable. However, Henry VI. still made it his main object to conquer Naples and Sicily, and Henry the Lion was too old and too fearful of fresh banishment to risk everything once more. Accordingly, negotiations were entered into between the two, and a reconciliation seemed likely to ensue. But the German magnates were more afraid of the Guelfs than the Emperor, and pressed him to go to war against Henry the Lion. At last, in 1192, Henry took the field against the Guelfs. A new complication followed. There had been a disputed succession to the see of Liége, which had given Henry a chance to annul the two rival elections, and appoint Lothair of Hochstaden as bishop. It was a glaring violation of the Concordat of Worms, and a direct defiance of the spiritual power. The stronger of the wronged claimants, Albert of Brabant, appealed to the Pope, and obtained his recognition. Unable to get hallowed as bishop by his own metropolitan at Cologne, Albert went to Reims, to seek consecration from a foreign prelate. Three knights, vassals of Liége and servants of the Emperor, followed Albert to Reims, and murdered him, in November 1192. A great sensation was created by the dastardly deed, which in many ways recalled the murder of St. Thomas of Canterbury twenty-two years before. But Henry managed to escape direct ecclesiastical censure, though the murderers afterwards received fiefs from him in Italy. However, the barons of the Rhineland, already disaffected· at Henry's masterful policy, and resenting his neglect of the magnates for his faithful officials, took the opportunity to revolt, and, joining the rebellious Guelfs, raised up a formidable opposition to the Emperor, and talked of transferring the crown to their leader, the Duke

Marginal notes:

Renewed German troubles, 1191-1194.

The Saxon troubles and the Liége succession, 1192.

The revolt of the Rhineland, 1193.

of Brabant. But fortune was on Henry's side At the same
time as the news of the rebellion came the joyful tidings that

Richard of England, returning in disguise from
the Holy Land, had been captured by Leopold,
Duke of Austria, who brought a series of charges
against him, and handed him over to the
Emperor. Philip of France, and John, Richard's brother,
pressed the Emperor to keep the captive as long as he could,
and Richard remained more than two years in prison, but
the delay was due to his unwillingness to accept the hard
conditions imposed upon him. At last Richard was forced
to agree to the Emperor's terms, and in June 1193 purchased
his release in the Treaty of Worms. Richard was forced to
pay a vast ransom and to renounce his alliance with Tancred.
But the hardest condition was the surrender of the English
crown to the Emperor, which in February 1194 Henry
formally handed back to Richard as a fief of the Empire.
Some compensation was given to Richard's wounded feelings by a grant to him of the kingdom of Arles, which
had some importance as a fresh declaration of hostility
against Philip of France. Moreover, Henry cleverly used
Richard to procure peace in Germany. Henry the Lion
yielded to his brother-in-law's pleadings, and again made
his submission. Even the barons of the lower Rhine
were not unmoved by his appeals. Richard's departure
left Germany at peace with the Emperor, and his ransom
made easy a fresh expedition against Tancred.[1] Henry of
Brunswick, Henry the Lion's eldest son, was married to a
cousin of the Emperor, Agnes, daughter of Conrad, Count
Palatine of the Rhine, and the Emperor's uncle. The Emperor promised him the succession to the Palatinate, and

*Captivity
and ransom
of Richard I.,
1192-1194.*

---

[1] Among the numerous treatises written in Germany on the political
significance of Richard I.'s captivity may be mentioned, besides Toeche
and Bloch, Kindt's *Grunde der Gefangenschaft Richards I. von England*,
and Kneller's *Des Richards Lowenherz deutsche Gefangenschaft*. Com-
pare *English Historical Review*, viii. 334-336, and ix. 746

Henry promised to join in the Sicilian expedition. In 1195 Henry the Lion ended his long and turbulent career. The Emperor was now free to turn his attention to Italy. His self-restraint and his good luck had carried him over his difficulties in Germany. His greatest merit was that, however proud he was of his mighty position, he never left out of sight the necessity of subordinating all minor aims to his desire to win Naples and Sicily. His moderation against Henry the Lion, his reconciliation with Richard, his rejection of the tempting offers of France, and his vast concessions to the German nobles, now attained their object.

During Henry's absence in Germany, the imperial cause in Italy had declined. Nevertheless Henry had kept up constant communications with his Italian partisans, and had observed a very careful policy with regard to the Lombards. He has often been accused of striving to restore his father's schemes of supremacy in Italy by violating the Treaty of Constance and seeking again the abasement of the Lombards. But the charge is no more just than the one of extravagant hostility against the Guelfs. As a matter of fact, Henry strove to postpone all other troubles in order to get his hands free to secure his wife's inheritance. He saw that Lombardy, after Constance, had fallen back into her ancient feuds, and that two leagues, one headed by Milan, the other by Cremona, had arisen, both equally indifferent to the Empire, and both equally willing to invoke its aid to crush the local enemy. Henry strove to make treaties with both confederacies, while he cheerfully replenished his coffers from the treasuries of both Milan and Cremona, and did his best to end the war. He established his brother Philip in Tuscany. Genoa and Pisa again provided him with ships. The Norman kingdom, isolated from its wonted allies, had to meet him single-handed, save for the timid support of Celestine III.

Tancred prepared manfully for the struggle. He obtained in 1192 the formal investiture of Apulia and Sicily from

Celestine III. He procured the coronation of his young son Roger as joint-king, and negotiated a marriage for him with Irene, daughter of the Greek Emperor Isaac Angelus. He strenuously and successfully held his own against the Emperor's lieutenants. But all his hopes were destroyed by the young King Roger's death, and soon after Tancred himself died. The national party set up his eldest surviving son as King William III., but in May 1194 Henry again reached Italy, and invaded the defenceless south. There was a mere show of resistance. By November Palermo was in the hands of the Emperor, and on Christmas Day he received the Sicilian crown in the cathedral. The young King William was sent, blinded and mutilated, to die obscurely in a German convent. The last upholders of the national power, including the Admiral Margarito, soon perished in gloomy dungeons. The very family of Tancred now secured its patrimonial possessions by a timely recognition of the rival. At Easter 1195 Henry was able to return to Germany, leaving Constance as regent, with the tried court official, Conrad of Urslingen, now Duke of Spoleto, as her chief adviser. The officials from the lower German nobility, who had served Henry so well in Germany, were intrusted with the administration of his new inheritance, and soon abased the great Norman houses.

Conquest of Apulia and Sicily, 1194.

Never was an Emperor stronger since the days of Charlemagne. All Italy was directly under his rule. The Pisan and Genoese fleets conquered Corsica and Sardinia in his name. His troops occupied the patrimony of St. Peter, and his officer Markwald of Anweiler was lord of Ancona and Romagna. His alliance with the Roman Senate kept Celestine III. from doing any mischief. Germany was obedient. The King of England was his vassal, and the heir of the Guelfs his follower and supporter. To add to his triumph, Constance, the day after his coronation at Palermo, bore him the long-prayed-for heir, the future Frederick II., called Frederick and Roger after his two famous

Henry's triumph and further projects, 1194-1197.

grandfathers. Before long the kings of the East sought his friendship and support. The Lusignan King of Cyprus boasted that he was the vassal of the Latin Empire. The King of Armenia received his ambassadors. Henry's brother, Philip of Swabia, now made Marquis of Tuscany and lord of the inheritance of the Countess Matilda, married young Roger's widow Irene, an alliance that made Isaac Angelus the close connection of his Western rival. Three great ambitions henceforth possessed Henry's soul. He would make the Empire hereditary in his own house, and unite for ever the German and the Sicilian thrones. He would rule Europe from Italy as a centre. He would make himself lord of the East, setting on foot a Crusade that would conquer the schismatic Greeks, and establish the Latin power in the whole East under his control. Wild as his schemes seemed, his extraordinary successes made them not altogether visionary.

On returning to Germany, Henry sought to persuade the princes to agree that the Empire, like the French monarchy, should henceforth descend from father to son. The heredi-At the Diet of Würzburg, in April 1196, more than tary Empire. fifty of the princes agreed to his proposals. But the strenuous opposition of Adolf, Archbishop of Cologne, and the conservative magnates of Saxony taught Henry that it was no time to persevere in an unpopular request. He contented himself for the moment with procuring the election of the two-year-old Frederick Roger as German king at Frankfurt, and in winning over many of the German nobles to his Eastern projects.

Before the end of 1196 Henry was again in southern Italy. The very Pope was now on his side. Celestine, delighted at the prospect of a new Crusade, forbore to press Henry to discharge the long-deferred homage which every Sicilian king had paid to the Papacy. During his absence the tyranny of the German officials had proved too grievous to be borne, and a formidable Sicilian conspiracy had been formed against them. Henry now stamped out all opposition with incredible brutality and harshness. Fresh from the hideous tortures of his victims, Henry now threw himself with all his might into his schemes of Eastern conquest.   The new Greek Emperor, Alexius III., was summoned to surrender all provinces east of Thessalonica as part of the Sicilian inheritance, and cheerfully agreed to pay a heavy tribute to avert the threatened attack. Meanwhile a vast swarm of German warriors had collected in

The Con-   Sicily and Apulia under the pretence of the new
quest of   Crusade.   In September the first ships sailed
the East.   from Messina to Acre.   But in the moment of the

realisation of his ambitions a sudden fever cut down the great

Death of   Emperor.   On 28th September Henry VI. died at
Henry VI.,   Messina when he was only thirty-two years of age.
1197.   Before his ashes were laid beside his Sicilian

ancestors in the cathedral at Palermo, his brilliant schemes were hopelessly shattered.

CHAPTER XIV

EUROPE IN THE DAYS OF INNOCENT III. (1198-1216)[1]

Character and theories of Innocent III.—The Sicilian Succession and the Minority of Frederick II.—The Subjection of Rome and the Patrimony of St. Peter—Innocent and Germany—Rivalry of Philip of Swabia and Otto of Brunswick—Innocent and Philip Augustus—The Pope as Feudal Lord—Otto IV. and Frederick II.—The Crusades—Innocent's Religious Position—The Lateran Council.

AFTER the great Emperors came the great Pope. Within four months of the death of Henry VI., Celestine III. had been succeeded by Innocent III., under whom the visions of Gregory VII. and Alexander III. at last became accomplished facts, the papal authority attained its highest point of influence, and the Empire, raised to such heights by Frederick Barbarossa and Henry VI., was reduced to a condition of dependence upon it.

Election of Innocent III., 1198.

The new Pope had been Lothaire of Segni, a member of the noble Roman house of Conti, who had studied law and theology at Paris and Bologna, and had at an early age won for himself a many-sided reputation as a jurist, a politician, and as a writer. The favour of his uncle, Clement III., had made him Cardinal before he was thirty, but under Celestine III. he kept in the background, disliked by the Pope, and

---

[1] Hurter's *Geschichte Papst Innocenz III.*, which can also be read in a French translation, though rather an old-fashioned book, gives a full account of the period covered by this chapter. Milman's *Latin Christianity*, vol. v., will be found useful as far as it goes. The imperial history is treated in detail by Winkelmann, *Philipp von Schwaben und Otto IV. von Braunschweig*.

himself suspicious of the timid and temporising old man. But on Celestine's death on 8th January 1198, Lothaire, though still only thirty-seven years of age, was at once hailed as his most fitting successor, as the strong man who could win for the Church all the advantages that she might hope to gain from the death of Henry VI. Nor did Innocent's Pontificate belie the promise of his early career.

Innocent III. possessed a majestic and noble appearance, an unblemished private character, popular manners, a disposi-

Character and theories of Innocent III. tion prone to sudden fits of anger and melancholy, and a fierce and indomitable will. He brought to his exalted position the clearly formulated theories of the canonist as to the nature of the papal power, as well as the overweening ambition, the high courage, the keen intelligence and the perseverance and energy necessary to turn the theories of the schools into matters of everyday practice. His enunciations of the Papal doctrine put claims that Hildebrand himself had hardly ventured to advance in the clearest and most definite light. The Pope was no mere successor of Peter, the vicegerent of man. 'The Roman pontiff,' he wrote, 'is the vicar, not of man, but of God Himself.' 'The Lord gave Peter the rule not only of the Universal Church but also the rule of the whole world.' 'The Lord Jesus Christ has set up one ruler over all things as His universal vicar, and as all things in heaven, earth and hell bow the knee to Christ, so should all obey Christ's vicar, that there be one flock and one shepherd.' 'No king can reign rightly unless he devoutly serve Christ's vicar.' 'Princes have power in earth, priests have also power in heaven. Princes reign over the body, priests over the soul. As much as the soul is worthier than the body, so much worthier is the priesthood than the monarchy.' 'The *Sacerdotium* is the sun, the *Regnum* the moon. Kings rule over their respective kingdoms, but Peter rules over the whole earth. The *Sacerdotium* came by divine creation, the *Regnum* by man's cunning.' In these unrestricted claims to rule over

Church and State alike we seem to be back again in the anarchy of the eleventh century. And it was not against the feeble feudal princes of the days of Hildebrand that Innocent III. had to contend, but against strong national kings, like Philip of France and John of England. It is significant of the change of the times, that Innocent sees his chief antagonist, not so much in the Empire as in the limited localised power of the national kings. When Richard of England had yielded before Henry VI., the national state gave way before the universal authority of the lord of the world. But Innocent claimed that he alone was lord of the world. The Empire was but a German or Italian kingdom, ruling over its limited sphere. Only in the Papacy was the old Roman tradition of universal monarchy rightly upheld.

Filled with these ambitions of universal monarchy, Innocent III.'s survey took in both the smallest and the greatest of European affairs. Primarily Innocent's work was that of an ecclesiastical statesman, and entrenched far upon the authority of the state. We shall see him restoring the papal authority in Rome and in the Patrimony, building up the machinery of papal absolutism, protecting the infant King of Sicily, cherishing the municipal freedom of Italy, making and unmaking kings and emperors at his will, forcing the fiercest of the Western sovereigns to acknowledge his feudal supremacy, and the greatest of the Kings of France to reform his private life at his commands, giving his orders to the petty monarchs of Spain and Hungary, and promulgating the law of the Church Universal before the assembled prelates of Christendom in the Lateran Council. Nevertheless, the many-sided Pontiff had not less near to his heart the spiritual and intellectual than the political direction of the universe. He had the utmost zeal for the extension of the Kingdom of Christ. The affair of the Crusade was, as we shall see, ever his most pressing care, and it was his bitterest grief that all his efforts to rouse the Christian world for the recovery of Jerusalem fell on deaf ears. He was strenuous in upholding orthodoxy against the daring heretics of Southern France. He was sympathetic and considerate to great religious teachers, like Francis and Dominic, from whose work he had the wisdom to anticipate the revival of the inner life of the Church. As many-sided as strong, and successful as he was strong, Innocent III. represents the culmination of the papal ideal of the Middle Ages, and represents it worthily and adequately.

Even before Innocent had attained the Chair of Peter, the worst dangers that had so long beset the successors of Alexander III. were over. After the death of Henry VI. the Sicilian and the German crowns were separated, and the strong anti-imperial reaction that burst out all over Italy against the oppressive ministers of Henry VI. was allowed to run its full course The danger was now not so much of despotism as of anarchy, and Innocent, like Hildebrand, knew how to turn confusion to the advantage of the hierarchy.

Innocent III. and Italy.

No real effort was made to obtain for the little Frederick the crowns of both Germany and Sicily. Constance, freed from her husband's control, sensibly changed her policy. Her keen sympathies with her father's inheritance had made her an unwilling spectator of the harshness and cruelty of his German soldiers and ministers. While Philip of Swabia, her brother-in-law, hurried to Germany to maintain, if he could, the unity of the Hohenstaufen Empire, Constance was quite content to secure her son's succession in Naples and Sicily by renewing the homage due to the Pope, by renouncing the ecclesiastical privileges which Urban II. had once granted to Count Roger [see page 139], and promising a yearly tribute. Having thus obtained the indispensable papal confirmation, Constance ruled in Naples as a national queen in the name of the little Frederick. She drove away the German bandits who had made the name of her husband a terror to her subjects. Markwald of Anweiler left his Apulian fiefs for Romagna. But the Pope

The Sicilian Succession and the minority of Frederick.

joined with Constance in his hostility to the Germans. Without Innocent III.'s strong and constant support she could hardly have carried out her policy. Recognising in the renewal of the old papal protection the best hopes for the independence of Sicily, Constance, on her death in 1198, called on Innocent III. to act as the guardian of her son. Innocent loyally took up her work, and struggled with all his might to preserve the kingdom of Frederick against his many enemies. But the contest was a long and a fierce one. No sooner was Constance dead than the Germans came back to their prey. The fierce Markwald, driven from Romagna by the papal triumph, claimed the regency and the custody of the king. The Saracens and Greeks of Sicily, still numerous and active, joined the Germans. Walter, Bishop of Troja, chancellor of Sicily, weaved deep plots against his master and his overlord. But the general support of the Church gave Innocent a strong weapon. Roffrid, Abbot of Monte Casino, a tried friend of Henry VI., declared for Innocent against Markwald, who in revenge besieged the great monastery, until a summer storm drove him baffled from its walls. But the purchased support of Pisa gave Markwald the command of the sea, and Innocent had too many schemes on foot and too little military power at his command to be able to make easy headway against him. At last Innocent had reluctant recourse to Count Walter of Brienne, the French husband of Tancred's daughter Albina, and now a claimant for the hereditary fiefs of Tancred, Lecce and Taranto, from which, despite Henry VI.'s promise, he had long been driven. For almost the first time in Italian history, Frenchmen were thus called in to drive out Germans. But it was then as afterwards a dangerous experiment. Walter of Brienne and his small French following invaded Apulia, and fought hard against Diepold of Acerra, another of King Henry's Germans. Meanwhile Markwald, now in open alliance with the Bishop

Death of Constance, 1198.

Innocent's guardianship and the expulsion of the Germans.

Markwald and Walter of Brienne.

of Troja, made himself master of Sicily, and regent of the young king. His death in 1202 removed the most dangerous enemy of both Innocent and Frederick. But the war dragged on for years in Apulia, especially after Diepold had slain Walter of Brienne. The turbulent feudal barons of Apulia and Sicily profited by this long reign of anarchy to establish themselves on a permanent basis. At last Innocent sent his own brother, Richard, Count of Segni, to root out the last of the Germans. So successful was he that, in 1208, the Pope himself visited the kingdom of his ward, and arranged for its future government by native lords, helped by his brother, who now received a rich Apulian fief. It was Innocent's glory that he had secured for Frederick the whole Norman inheritance. It was amidst such storms and troubles that the young Frederick grew up to manhood.

In central and northern Italy, Innocent III. was more speedily successful than in the south. On Philip of Swabia's return to Germany, Tuscany and the domains of the Countess Matilda fell away from their foreign lord, and invoked the protection of the Church. The Tuscan cities formed themselves into a new league under papal protection. Only Pisa, proud of her sea power, wealth, and trade, held aloof from the combination. It seemed as if, after a century of delays, the Papacy was going to enjoy the inheritance of Matilda, and Innocent eagerly set himself to work to provide for its administration. In the north the Pope maintained friendly relations with the rival communities of the Lombard plain. But his most immediate and brilliant triumph was in establishing his authority over Rome and the Patrimony of St. Peter. On his accession he found his lands just throwing off the yoke of the German garrisons that had kept them in subjection during Henry VI.'s lifetime. He saw within the city power divided between the Præfectus Urbis, the delegate of the Emperor, and the Summus Senator, the mouthpiece of the Roman commune. Within a month

[margin note: Innocent and the inheritance of Matilda.]

[margin note: The subjection of Rome and of the Patrimony of St. Peter.]

the Prefect ceased to be an imperial officer, and became the servant of the Papacy, bound to it by fealty oaths, and receiving from it his office. Within a year the Senator also had become the papal nominee, and the whole municipality controlled by the Pope. No less complete was Innocent's triumph over the nobility of the Campagna. He drove Conrad of Urslingen back to Germany, and restored Spoleto to papal rule. He chased Markwald from Romagna and the march of Ancona to Apulia, and exercised sovereign rights even in the most remote regions that acknowledged him as lord. If it was no very real sway that Innocent wielded, it at least allowed the town leagues and the rustic nobility to go on in their own way, and made it possible for Italy to work out its own destinies. More powerful and more feared in Italy than any of his predecessors, Innocent could contentedly watch the anti-imperial reaction extending over the Alps, and desolating Germany by civil war.

Despite the precautions taken by Henry VI., it was soon clear that the German princes would not accept the hereditary rule of a child of three. Philip of Swabia aban- Innocent III. doned his Italian domains and hurried to and Germany, anxious to do his best for his nephew. Germany. But he soon perceived that Frederick's chances were hopeless, and that it was all that he could do to prevent the undisputed election of a Guelf. He was favoured by the absence of the two elder sons of Henry the Lion. Henry of Brunswick, the eldest, the Count Palatine of the Rhine, was away on a Crusade, and was loyal to the Hohenstaufen, since his happy marriage with Agnes. The next son Otto, born at Argenton during his father's first exile, had never seen much of Germany. Brought up at his uncle Richard of Anjou's court, Otto had received many marks of Richard's favour, and looked up to the chivalrous, adventurous king as the ideal of a warrior prince. Richard had made him Earl of Yorkshire, and had invested him in 1196 with the county of Poitou, that he might learn war and statecraft in the same rude school in which Richard had first acquainted himself with arms and politics. Even now Otto was not more than seventeen years of age. Richard himself, as the new vassal of the Empire for Arles and England, was duly summoned to the electoral Diet, but his representatives impolitically urged the claims of Count Henry, who was ruled ineligible on account of his absence. Thus it was that when the German magnates at last met for the election, on 8th March 1198, at Mühlhausen, their choice fell on Philip of Swabia, who, mindful of the third century Emperor, Philip the Arabian, took the title of Philip II.

Election of Philip of Swabia, March 1198.

Many of the magnates had absented themselves from the Diet at Mühlhausen, and an irreconcilable band of partisans refused to be bound by its decisions. Richard of England now worked actively for Otto, his favourite nephew, and found support both in the old allies of the Angevins in the lower Rhineland and the ancient supporters of the house of Guelf. Germany was thus divided into two parties, who completely ignored each other's acts. Three months after the Diet of Mühlhausen, another Diet met at Cologne and chose Otto of Brunswick as King of the Romans. Three days afterwards the young prince was crowned at Aachen.

Counter-election of Otto of Brunswick, June 1198.

A ten years' civil war between Philip II. and Otto IV. now devastated the Germany that Barbarossa and Henry VI. had left so prosperous. The majority of the princes remained firm to Philip, who also had the support of the strong and homogeneous official class of *ministeriales* that had been the best helpers of his father and brother. Nevertheless, Otto had enough of a party to carry on the struggle. On his side was Cologne, the great mart of lower Germany, so important from its close trading relations in England, and now gradually shaking itself free of its archbishops. The friendship of Canute of Denmark and the old Guelf tradition combined to give him his earliest and greatest success in the north. It was the interest of the baronage to prolong a struggle which secured their own independence at the expense of the central authority. Both parties looked for outside help. Otto, besides his Danish friends, relied on his uncle Richard, and, after his death, on his uncle John. Philip formed a league with his namesake Philip of France. But distant princes could do but little to determine the result of the contest. It was of more moment that both appealed to Innocent III., and that the Pope willingly accepted the position of arbiter. 'The settlement of this matter,' he declared, 'belongs to the Apostolic See, mainly because it was the Apostolic See that transferred the Empire from the East to the West, and ultimately because the same See confers the imperial crown.' In March 1201 Innocent issued his decision. 'We pronounce,' he declared, 'Philip unworthy of Empire, and absolve all who have taken oaths of fealty to him as king. Inasmuch as our dearest son in Christ, Otto, is industrious, provident, discreet, strong and constant, himself devoted to the Church and descended on each side from a devout stock, we by the authority of St. Peter receive him as king, and will in due course bestow upon him the imperial crown.' The grateful Otto promised in return to maintain all the possessions and privileges of the Roman Church, including the inheritance of the Countess Matilda.

Philip of Swabia still held his own, and the extravagance of the papal claim led to many of the bishops as well as the lay magnates of Germany joining in a declaration that no former Pope had ever presumed to interfere in an imperial election. But the swords of his German followers were a stronger argument in favour of Philip's claims than the protests of his supporters against papal assumptions. As time went on, the Hohenstaufen slowly got the better of the Guelfs. With the falling away of the north, Otto's cause became distinctly the losing one. In 1206 Otto was defeated outside the walls of Cologne, and the great trading city was forced to transfer its obedience to his rival. In 1207 Philip became so strong that Innocent was constrained to reconsider his position, and suggested to Otto the propriety of renouncing his claims. But in June 1208 Philip was treacherously murdered at Bamberg by his faithless vassal, Otto of Wittelsbach, to whom he had refused his daughter's hand. It was no political crime but a deed of private vengeance. It secured, however, the position of Otto, for the *ministeriales* now transferred their allegiance to him, and there was no Hohenstaufen candidate ready to oppose him. Otto, moreover, did not scruple to undergo a fresh election which secured for him universal recognition in Germany. By marrying Beatrice, Philip of Swabia's daughter, he sought to unite the rival houses, while he conciliated Innocent by describing himself as king ' by the grace of God and the Pope.' Next year he crossed the Alps to Italy, and bound himself by oath, not only to allow the Papacy the privileges that he had already granted, but to grant complete freedom of ecclesiastical elections, and to support the Pope in his struggle 'against heresy. In October 1209 he was crowned Emperor at Rome. After ten years of waiting, Innocent, already master of Italy, had procured for his dependant both the German Kingdom and the Roman Empire.

Despite his preoccupation with Italy and Germany, the early years of Innocent's pontificate saw him busily engaged in upholding the papal authority and the moral order of the Church in every country in Europe. No consideration of the immediate interests of the Roman see ever prevented him from maintaining his principles even against powerful sovereigns who could do much to help forward his general plans. The most conspicuous instance of this was Innocent's famous quarrel with Philip Augustus of France, when to vindicate a simple principle of Christian morals he did not hesitate to abandon the alliance of the ' eldest son of the Church ' at a time when the fortunes of the Papacy were everywhere doubtful. Philip's first wife, Isabella of Hainault, the mother of the future Louis VIII.,

Innocent III. and Philip Augustus.

had died in 1190, just before her husband had started on
his Crusade.   In 1193 Philip negotiated a second marriage
with Ingeborg, the sister of Canute vi., the power-   Ingeborg
ful King of Denmark, hoping to obtain from his   of Denmark.
Danish brother-in-law substantial help against England and
the Empire.   Philip did not get the expected political
advantages from the new connection, and at once took a
strong dislike to the lady.   On the day after the marriage
Philip refused to have anything more to do with his bride.
Within three months, he persuaded a synod of complaisant
French bishops at Compiègne to pronounce the marriage void
by reason of a remote kinship that existed between the two
parties.   Ingeborg was young, timid, friendless, helpless,
and utterly ignorant of the French tongue, but King Canute
took up her cause, and, from her retreat in a French convent, she appealed to Rome against the wickedness of the
French king and clergy.   Celestine iii. proved her friend,
and finding protestations of no avail, he finally quashed
the sentence of the French bishops and declared her the
lawful wife of the French king.   But Philip persisted in
his repudiation of Ingeborg, and Celestine contented himself
with remonstrances and warnings that were utterly disregarded.   In 1196 Philip found a fresh wife in   Agnes of
Agnes, a lady of the powerful house of Andechs-   Meran.
Meran, whose authority was great in Thuringia, and whose
Alpine lordships soon developed into the county of Tyrol.
Innocent at once proved a stronger champion of Ingeborg
than the weak and aged Celestine.   He forthwith warned
Philip and the French bishops that they had no right to
put asunder those whom God had joined together.   'Recall
your lawful wife,' he wrote to Philip, 'and then we will hear all
that you can righteously urge.   If you do not do this, no power
shall move us to right or left, till justice be done.'   A papal
legate was now sent to France, threatening excommunication
and interdict, were Ingeborg not immediately reinstated in
her place.   For a few months the Pope hesitated, moved no

doubt by his Italian and German troubles, and fearful lest his action against a Christian prince should delay the hoped-for Crusade.   But he gradually turned the leaders of the French clergy from their support of Philip, and at last, in February 1200, an interdict was pronounced forbidding the public celebration of the rites of the Church in the whole lands that owed obedience to the King of France.

Philip Augustus held out fiercely for a time, declaring that he would rather lose half his lands than be separated from

Agnes.   Meanwhile he used pressure on his

The Interdict over France, 1200-1201.

bishops to make them disregard the interdict, and vigorously intrigued with the Cardinals, seeking to build up a French party in the papal curia. Innocent so far showed complacency that the legate he sent to France was the king's kinsman, Octavian, Cardinal-bishop of Ostia, who was anxious to make Philip's humiliation as light as possible.   His labours were eased by the partial submission of Philip, who in September visited Ingeborg, and promised to take her again as his wife, and so gave an excuse to end the interdict.   Philip still claimed that his marriage should be dissolved ; though here again he

Partial submission of Philip, 1201.

suddenly abandoned a suit which he probably saw was hopeless.   The death of Agnes of Meran in July 1201 made a complete reconciliation less difficult.   Next year the Pope legitimated the children of Agnes and Philip, on the ground that the sentence of divorce, pronounced by the French bishops, gave the king reasonable grounds for entering in good faith on his union with her.   Ingeborg was still refused the rights of a queen, and constantly besought the Pope to have pity on her forlorn condition.   The Pope was now forced to content himself with remonstrances.   Philip declared that a baleful charm separated him from Ingeborg, and again begged the Pope to divorce him from a union, based on sorcery and witchcraft.   The growing need of the French alliance now somewhat slackened the early zeal of Innocent for the cause of the queen. But no real cordiality was possible as long as the strained relations of Ingeborg and Philip continued. At last in 1213, in the very crisis of his fortunes, Restitution of Philip completed his tardy reconciliation with Ingeborg, his wife, after they had been separated for twenty 1213. years. Henceforth Philip was the most active ally of the Papacy.

While thus dealing with Philip of France, Innocent enjoyed easier triumphs over the lesser kings of Europe. It was his ambition to break through the traditional The feudal limits that separated the Church from the State, overlordship and to bind as many as he could of the kings of the of Europe to the Papacy by ties of political Papacy over Portugal, vassalage. The time-honoured feudal superiority Aragon, and of the Popes over the Norman kingdom of Sicily England. had been the first precedent for this most unecclesiastical of all papal aggressions. Already others of the smaller kingdoms of Europe, conspicuous among which was Portugal, had followed the example of the Normans in becoming vassals of the Holy See. Under Innocent at least three states supplemented ecclesiastical by political dependence on the Papacy. Sancho, King of Portugal, who had striven to repudiate the former submission of Affonso I., was in the end forced to accept the papal suzerainty. Peter, King of Aragon, went in 1204 to Rome and was solemnly crowned king by Innocent. Afterwards Peter deposited his crown on the high altar of St. Peter's and condescended to receive the investiture of his kingdom from the Pope, holding it as a perpetual fief of the Holy See, and promising tribute to Innocent and his successors. In 1213 a greater monarch than the struggling Christian kings of the Iberian peninsula was forced, after a long struggle, to make an even more abject submission. The long strife of Innocent with John of Anjou, about the disputed election to the see of Canterbury, was fought with the same weapons which the Pope had already employed against the King of France. But John held out

longer.   Interdict was followed by excommunication **and**
threatened deposition.   At last the English king surrendered
his crown to the papal agent Pandulf, and, like Peter of
Aragon, received it back as a vassal of the Papacy, bound
by an annual tribute.   Nor were these the only kings that
sought the support of the great Pope.   The schismatic
princes of the East vied in ardour with the Catholic princes
of the West in their quest of Innocent's favour.   King
Innocent   Leo of Armenia begged for his protection.   The
and the   Bulgarian Prince John besought the Pope to
lesser
monarchs of   grant him a royal crown.   Innocent posed as a
Europe.   mediator in Hungary between the two brothers,
Emeric and Andrew, who were struggling for the crown.
Canute of Denmark, zealous for his sister's honour, was his
humble suppliant.   Poland was equally obedient.   The Duke
of Bohemia accepted the papal reproof for allying himself
with Philip of Swabia.

Despite his vigour and his authority, Innocent's constant
interference with the internal concerns of every country in
Europe did not pass unchallenged.   Even the kings who
invoked his intercession were constantly in conflict with him.
Beside his great quarrels in Germany, France, and England,
Innocent had many minor wars to wage against the princes of
Europe.   For five years the kingdom of Leon lay under interdict because its king Alfonso had married his cousin, Berengaria of Castile, in the hope of securing the peace between the
two realms.   It was only after the lady had borne five children
to Alfonso that she voluntarily terminated the obnoxious
union, and Innocent found it prudent, as in France, to legiti-
mise the offspring of a marriage which he had denounced as
incestuous.   Not one of the princes of the Peninsula was
spared.   Sancho of Navarre incurred interdict by reason of
his suspected dealings with the Saracens, while the marriage
of his sister with Peter of Aragon, the vassal of the Pope,
involved both kings in a contest with Innocent.   Not only
did the monarchs of Europe resent, so far as they were

able, the Pope's haughty policy.   For the first time the
peoples of their realms began to make common cause with
them against the political aggressions of the Papacy.   The Papacy
The nobles of Aragon protested against King   and the
Peter's submission to the Papacy, declared that   people.
his surrender of their kingdom was invalid, and   Innocent's
prevented the payment of the promised tribute.   policy.
When John of England procured his Roman overlord's condemnation of Magna Carta, the support of Rome was of no
avail to prevent his indignant subjects combining to drive
him from the throne, and did not even hinder Louis of
France, the son of the papalist Philip II., from accepting
their invitation to become English king in his stead.   It was
only by a repudiation of this policy, and by an acceptance of
the Great Charter, that the Papacy could secure the English
throne for John's young son, Henry III., and thus continue
for a time its precarious overlordship over England.   For
the moment Innocent's iron policy crushed opposition, but
in adding the new hostility of the national kings and the
rising nations of Europe to the old hostility of the declining
Empire, Innocent was entering into a perilous course of
conduct, which, within a century, was to prove fatal to one of
the strongest of his successors.   The more political the papal
authority became, the more difficult it was to uphold its
prestige as the source of law, of morality, of religion.   Innocent himself did not lose sight of the higher ideal because
he strove so firmly after more earthly aims.   His successors
were not always so able or so high-minded.   And it was as
the protectors of the people, not as the enemies of their
political rights, that the great Popes of the eleventh and
twelfth centuries had obtained their wonderful ascendency
over the best minds of Europe.

The coronation of Otto IV. did not end Innocent's troubles
with the Empire.   It was soon followed by an open breach
between the Pope and his nominee, from which ultimately
developed something like a general European war, between

a league of partisans of the Pope and a league of partisans of Otto. It was inevitable that Otto, as a crowned Emperor, should look upon the papal power in a way very different from that in which he had regarded it, when a faction leader struggling for the crown. Then the support of the Pope was indispensable. Now the autocracy of the Pope was to be feared. The Hohenstaufen *ministeriales*, who now surrounded the Guelfic Emperor, raised his ideals and modified his policy. Henry of Kalden, the old minister of Henry VI., was now his closest confidant, and, under his direction, it soon became Otto's ambition to continue the policy of the Hohenstaufen. The great object of Henry VI. had been the union of Sicily with the Empire. To the alarm and disgust of Innocent, his ancient dependant now strove to continue Henry VI.'s policy by driving out Henry VI.'s son from his Sicilian inheritance. Otto now established relations with Diepold and the other German adventurers, who still defied Frederick II. and the Pope in Apulia. He soon claimed the inheritance of Matilda as well as the Sicilian monarchy. In August 1210 he ocenpied Matilda's Tuscan lands, and in November invaded Apulia, and prepared to despatch a Pisan fleet against Sicily. Innocent was moved to terrible wrath. On hearing of the capture of Capua, and the revolt of Salerno and Naples, he excommunicated the Emperor and freed his subjects from their oaths of fealty to him. But, despite the threats of the Church, Otto conquered most of Apulia and was equally successful in reviving the imperial authority in northern Italy.

Quarrel of Innocent with Otto IV., 1210.

Innocent saw the power that he had built up so carefully in Italy crumbling rapidly away. In his despair he turned to France and Germany for help against the audacious Guelf. Philip Augustus, though still in bad odour at Rome through his persistent hostility to Ingeborg, was now an indispensable ally. He actively threw himself into the Pope's policy, and French and Papal agents combined to stir up disaffection against

Election of Frederick II., 1212.

Otto in Germany.   The haughty manners and the love of the young king for Englishmen and Saxons had already excited disaffection.   It was believed that Otto wished to set up a centralised despotism of court officials, levying huge taxes, on the model of the Angevin administrative system of his grandfather and uncles.   The bishops now took the lead in organising a general defection from the absent Emperor. In September 1211 a gathering of disaffected magnates, among whom were the newly made King Ottocar of Bohemia and the Dukes of Austria and Bavaria, assembled at Nurnberg.   They treated the papal sentence as the deposition of Otto, and pledged themselves to elect as their new king Frederick of Sicily, the sometime ward of the Pope.   It was not altogether good news to the Pope that the German nobles had, in choosing the son of Henry VI., renewed the union of Germany and Sicily.   But Innocent felt that the need of setting up an effective opposition to Otto was so pressing that he put out of sight the general in favour of the immediate interests of the Roman see.   He accepted Frederick as Emperor, only stipulating that he should renew his homage for the Sicilian crown, and consequently renounce an inalienable union between Sicily and the Empire.   Frederick now left Sicily, repeated his submission to Innocent at Rome, and crossed the Alps for Germany.

Otto had already abandoned Italy to meet the threatened danger in the north.   Misfortunes soon showered thick upon him.   His Hohenstaufen wife, Beatrice, died, and her loss lessened his hold on southern Germany.   When Frederick appeared, Swabia and Bavaria were already ready to welcome the heir of the mighty southern line, and aid him against the audacious Saxon.   The spiritual magnates flocked to the side of the friend and pupil of the Pope.   In December 1212 followed Frederick's formal election and his coronation at Mainz by the Archbishop Siegfried.   Early in 1213 Henry of Kalden first appeared at his court.   Henceforward the important class of the 'ministeriales' was divided. While some remained true to Otto, others gradually went back to the personal representative of Hohenstaufen.

Otto was now thrown back on Saxony and the lower Rhineland. He again took up his quarters with the faithful citizens of Cologne, whence he appealed for help to his uncle, John of England, still under the papal ban. With English help he united the princes of the Netherlands in a party of opposition to the Pope and the Hohenstaufen. Frederick answered by a closer and more effective league with France. Even before his coronation he had met Louis, the son of Philip Augustus, at Vaucouleurs. All Europe seemed arming at the bidding of the Pope and Emperor.

The papal and imperial leagues, 1213.

John of England now hastily reconciled himself to Innocent, at the price of the independence of his kingdom. He thus became in a better position to aid his excommunicated nephew, and revenge the loss of Normandy and Anjou on Philip Augustus. His plan was now a twofold one. He himself summoned the barons of England to follow him in an attempt to recover his ancient lands on the Loire. Meanwhile, Otto and the Netherlandish lords were encouraged, by substantial English help, to carry out a combined attack on France from the north. The opposition of the English barons reduced to comparative insignificance the expedition to Poitou, but a very considerable army gathered together under Otto, and took up its position in the neighbourhood of Tournai. Among the French King's vassals, Ferrand, Count of Flanders, long hostile to his overlord Philip, and the Count of Boulogne, fought strenuously on Otto's side; while, of the imperial vassals, the Count of Holland and the Duke of Brabant [Lower Lorraine] were among Otto's most active supporters. A considerable English contingent came also, headed by Otto's bastard uncle, William Longsword, Earl of Salisbury. Philip himself commanded the chivalry of France, leaving his

son Louis to fight against John in Poitou. On 27th July
the decisive battle was fought at Bouvines, a few miles south-
west of Tournai. The army of France and the Battle of
Church gained an overwhelming victory over the Bouvines,
league which had incurred the papal ban, and 1214.
Otto's fortunes were utterly shattered. He soon lost all his
hold over the Rhineland, and was forced to retreat to the
ancient domains of his house in Saxony. His remaining
friends made their peace with Philip and Frederick. The
defection of the Wittelsbachers lost his last hold in the south
of Germany, and the desertion of Valdemar of Denmark
deprived him of a strong friend in the north. John withdrew from continental politics to be beaten more decisively
by his barons than he had been beaten in Poitou or at
Bouvines. By the summer of 1215, Aachen and Cologne
had opened their gates to Frederick, who repeated his
coronation in the old chapel of Charlemagne. Before Otto's
death in 1218 his power was confined to Brunswick and the
region of the Harz. His brother Henry delivered The fall of
up the imperial insignia to the conqueror, and the Guelfs
received a confirmation of his hereditary estates. triumph of
In 1235 the establishment of the Duchy of Innocent.
Brunswick-Lüneburg, in favour of the Guelfic house, secured
for it a permanent position among the territorial powers of
northern Germany. The higher aspirations of the descendants of Henry the Lion perished for ever on the fatal field
of Bouvines.

Frederick II. was now undisputed King of the Romans, and
Innocent III. had won another great triumph. By the
Golden Bull of Eger (July 1213) Frederick had already renewed the concessions made by Otto to the Church, and
promised obedience to the Holy See. In 1216 he pledged
himself to separate Sicily from the Empire, and establish his
son Henry there as king, under the supremacy of the Church.
But like his other triumphs, Innocent's victory over the
Empire was purchased at no small cost. For the first time,

a German national irritation at the aggressions of the Papacy began to be distinctly felt. It found an adequate expression in the indignant verses of Walter von der Vogelweide, protesting against the priests who strove to upset the rights of the laity, and denouncing the greed and pride of the foreigners who profited by the humiliation of Germany.

Amidst all the distractions of Western politics, Innocent III. ardently strove to revive the crusading spirit. He never succeeded in raising all Europe, as several of his predecessors had done. But after great efforts, the eloquent preaching of Fulk of Neuilly stirred up a fair amount of enthusiasm for the crusading cause, and, in 1204, a considerable crusading army, mainly French, mustered at Venice. It was the bitterest disappointment of Innocent's life that the Fourth Crusade [see chapter xv.] never reached Palestine, but was diverted to the conquest of the Greek Empire. Yet the establishment of a Catholic Latin Empire at Constantinople, at the expense of the Greek schismatics, was no small triumph. Not disheartened by his first failure, Innocent still urged upon Europe the need of the holy war. If no expedition against the Saracens of Syria marked the result of his efforts, his pontificate saw the extension of the crusading movement to other lands. Innocent preached the Crusade against the Moors of Spain, and rejoiced in the news of the momentous victory of the Christians at Navas de Tolosa [see chapter xx.]. He saw the beginnings of a fresh Crusade against the obstinate heathen on the eastern shores of the Baltic. But all these Crusades were against pagans and infidels. Innocent made a much greater new departure when he proclaimed the first Crusade directed against a Christian land. The Albigensian Crusade, which can more profitably be described when we deal with the development of the French monarchy [see chapter xvii.], succeeded in destroying the most dangerous and widespread popular heresy that Christianity had witnessed since the fall

Innocent III. and the Crusades.

Extension of the crusading idea.

of the Roman Empire, and Innocent rejoiced that his times saw the Church purged of its worst blemish.   But in extending the benefits of a Crusade to Christians fighting against Christians, he handed on a precedent which was soon fatally abused by his successors.   In crushing out the young national life of southern France the Papacy again set a people against itself.   The denunciations of the German Minnesinger were re-echoed in the complaints of the last of the Troubadours.   Rome had ceased to do harm to Turks and Saracens, but had stirred up Christians to war against fellow-Christians.   God and His Saints abandon the greedy, the strife-loving, the unjust, worldly Church.   The picture is darkly coloured by a partisan, but in every triumph of Innocent there lay the shadow of future trouble.

Crusades, even against heretics and infidels, are the work of earthly force rather than of spiritual influence.   It was to build up the great outward corporation of the Church that all these labours of Innocent mainly tended.   Even his additions to the Canon Law, his reforms of ecclesiastical jurisdiction, dealt with the external rather than the internal life of the Church. The criticism of James of Vitry, that the Roman Curia was so busy in secular affairs that it hardly turned a thought to spiritual things, is clearly applicable to much of Innocent's activity.   But the many-sided Pope did not ignore the religious wants of the Church.   His Crusade against heresy was no mere war against enemies of the wealth and power of the Church.   The new tendencies that were to transform the spiritual life of the thirteenth century were not strange to him.   He favoured the early work of Dominic: he had personal dealings with Francis, and showed his sympathy with the early work of the poor man of Assisi [see chapter xviii.].   But it is as the conqueror and organiser rather than the priest or prophet that Innocent made his mark in the Church.   It is significant that, with all his greatness, he never attained the honours of sanctity.

Towards the end of his life, Innocent held a General Council in the basilica of St. John Lateran. A vast gather-

The Fourth General Lateran Council, 1215.

ing of bishops, heads of orders, and secular dignitaries gave brilliancy to the gathering and enhanced the glory of the Pontiff. Enthroned over more than four hundred bishops, the Pope proudly declared the law to the world. 'Two things we have specially to heart,' wrote Innocent, in summoning the assembly, 'the deliverance of the Holy Land and the reform of the Church Universal.' In its vast collection of seventy canons, the Lateran Council strove hard to carry out the Pope's programme. It condemned the dying heresies of the Albigeois and the Cathari, and prescribed the methods and punishments of the unrepentant heretic. It strove to rekindle zeal for the Crusade. It drew up a drastic scheme for reforming the internal life and discipline of the Church. It strove to elevate the morals and the learning of the clergy, to check their worldliness and covetousness, and to restrain them from abusing the authority of the Church through excess of zeal or more corrupt motives. It invited bishops to set up free schools to teach poor scholars grammar and theology. It forbade trial by battle and trial by ordeal. It subjected the existing monastic orders to stricter superintendence, and forbade the establishment of new monastic rules. It forbade superstitious practices and the worship of spurious or unauthorised relics. The whole series of canons sought to regulate and ameliorate the influence of the Church on society. If many of the abuses aimed at were too deeply rooted to be overthrown by mere legislation, the attempt speaks well for the character and intelligence of Pope and Council. All mediæval law-making, civil and ecclesiastical alike, was but the promulga-tion of an ideal, rather than the issuing of precepts meant to be literally executed. But no more serious attempt at rooting out inveterate evils was ever made in the Middle Ages than in this Council.

The formal enunciation of this lofty programme of reform brought Innocent's pontificate to a glorious end.   The Pontiff devoted what little remained of his life to hurrying on the preparations for the projected Crusade, which was to set out in **1217**.   But in the summer of **1216** Innocent died at Perugia, when only fifty-six years old.   If not the greatest, he was the most powerful of all the Popes.   For nearly twenty years the whole history of Europe groups itself round his doings.

Death of Innocent III. 16th July 1216.

CHAPTER XV

THE BYZANTINE EMPIRE IN THE TWELFTH CENTURY,
THE FOURTH CRUSADE, AND THE LATIN EMPIRE
IN THE EAST (1095-1261) [1]

The Comnenian dynasty and Alexius I.—Decay of the Empire—The end of
the Comneni—The Angeli—The mustering of the Fourth Crusade—The
Conquest of Zara—The First and Second Captures of Constantinople—
The Partition and Organisation of the Latin Empire—The Greek Revival
—Rivalry of Constantinople and Thessalonica—The Latin Emperors—
Michael Palæologus and the Fall of the Latin Empire—The Franks in
the Peloponnesus.

THE Comnenian dynasty, finally established by Alexius I.
[see chapter vii.], ruled for more than a century over the

The Comnenian dynasty.
Roman Empire in the East. We have already
noticed the most stirring episodes of its external
history, in tracing the dealings of the Comnenian
Emperors with the Seljukian Turks, with the passing
Crusaders, with the permanent Latin garrison in Syria, and
with the Norman rulers of Apulia and Sicily, who strove
to make southern Italy the starting-point for a Norman
conquest of the Balkan Peninsula. It remains now to
describe briefly the internal history of the Eastern Empire
during the twelfth century, as a necessary preliminary to the
understanding of the collapse of the Greek power in 1204.

The combination of strength and duplicity, which constituted the practical ability of Alexius Comnenus, had saved

Alexius I., 1081-1118.
the Byzantine state from the ruin with which it
had been threatened. But the rescue of the
Empire had been accomplished at no small cost. The

---

[1] To the authorities mentioned under Chapter VII. may now be added
Pears' *Fall of Constantinople, being the Story of the Fourth Crusade.*

Crusaders had allowed Alexius to resume possession of a large share of Asia Minor, but the constant presence of Latins in the East was a permanent danger to him, both from their superior military capacity and their fierce Catholicism. The Eastern Empire sank into the condition of stagnation, which it was to retain for the rest of its existence. The low cunning and trickery of Alexius are glorified by his literary daughter Anna as the highest resources of civilisation when face to face with the barbarian Franks. Such methods might save the state, but they could hardly adapt it to meet the new conditions which Western activity in the East had brought about.

The military danger of the Frankish powers was not the worst result of the Crusades on the Byzantine Empire. Even more important was the sapping of its sources of wealth and the decay of its commercial prosperity, as the consequence of the development of the trade of the Italian republics, like Pisa, Genoa, and Venice, who really reaped nearly the whole material advantages of the Crusades. Acre and other Syrian ports began to supersede Constantinople as the great meeting-places of Eastern and Western trade. The skill and energy of the Italian merchants transferred the commerce of the Levant from Greek to Western hands. Since the loss of the rich agricultural districts of Asia Minor, the commerce of Constantinople was the one really solid source of Byzantine prosperity. The revenue of the imperial exchequer now began to fall off, and the disastrous expedients of Alexius to restore it made permanent ruin more certain. In the hope of making the Bosporus and Golden Horn as attractive to the Italian traders as the waters of the Levant, Alexius sought to entice the Venetians back to his ports by giving them exemption from customs dues (1082). The Venetians were established in a special quarter of Constantinople, exempt from the jurisdiction of the Greek authorities, with its Catholic church, its walls, and its magistrates. The

Internal decay of the Eastern Empire.

Pisans had privileges less extensive but still considerable. Such concessions made the Italians easily able to undersell the native merchants and to establish their factories on an almost independent basis. But it was unlikely that the shrewd Venetians would be content with what they had got. Their settlement within the Empire as traders only paved the way to the time when they aspired to establish themselves as rulers. It was a strange turn to make arbiters of the destiny of the Empire those Venetians who had in former times protected themselves from Western Cæsars by parading their dependence on the Emperor at Constantinople, and whose city bears to this day the abiding impress of Byzantine art. The strong Comnenian Emperors postponed the danger for a time, but when the Empire was again divided between rival claimants, it was as natural to the Venetians as it was to the English and French in India to take advantage of the decay of an ancient but stagnant civilisation to turn from their factories and counting-houses to play the part of conquerors and rulers.

It is one of the innumerable proofs of the vitality of the East-Roman system that this result came so slowly and succeeded so imperfectly. The latter part of the reign of Alexius seemed to revive the former glories of the Eastern Empire. The dynasty was firmly settled on the throne; the foreign enemies driven away or reduced to insignificance; the internal decay was too gradual to be readily perceived. On his death John II., in 1118 Alexius handed on to his son an empire 1118-1143. enlarged and peaceful. John II. Comnenus (1118-1143), called John the Good, was one of the best of Byzantine rulers. As vigorous a ruler and a better soldier than his father, his private character, stainless in its morals, was marked by qualities, such as frankness, generosity, and mercy, which rarely adorned the throne of the Eastern Cæsars. He reigned undisturbed by revolts or conspiracies, save those of his sister Anna, the historian, and his brother Isaac, and these foes within his household received from him a generous forgiveness that they did nothing to deserve. John was mostly occupied in his constant campaigns on the frontiers, fighting the Patzinaks of the lower Danube, the Hungarians and the Servians in Europe, and the Seljukian Turks and the Armenians in Asia. Master of Cilicia, he forced Raymond of Antioch to acknowledge his supremacy. Only his death in Cilicia, due to an accident in the hunting field, prevented his invasion of the Latin kingdom of Syria. Had he seriously grappled with the reform of administration and the finances, he might have inaugurated a new period of prosperity. But his effort to shake off the commercial supremacy of Venice involved him in a long and unsuccessful war with the rulers of the sea, which he was glad to end by restoring the Venetians to their former privileges, and by recognising them as lords of some of the Greek islands. Even as it was, John the Good did much to arrest decay.

Manuel I. Comnenus (1143-1180), John's son and successor, was a worthy heir to the military talents of his father. But his violent passions sullied his private life, Manuel I., and his extravagance, ostentation, and vanity took 1143-1180. away from the lustre of his domestic administration. He was one of the most Western in temperament of all the Greek sovereigns. He was proud of his prodigious personal strength, of his handsome person, and of his skill in all chivalrous exercises. He was the only Greek Emperor who could surpass the most famous knights of the West in the mimic war of the tournament. He had the spirit of a knight-errant, suggesting Richard Cœur de Lion rather than the sly and demure Oriental. When he had safely extricated himself from the perils of the Second Crusade [see page 192], he plunged into a series of wars in which he sought personal glory rather than the welfare of his Empire. There were strange tales of his wonderful personal adventures and hairbreadth escapes from Patzinaks and Turks. He introduced Western tournaments into Constantinople, had a truly Frankish ardour for crusading, re-armed his troops after the Western fashion with ponderous shields and heavy lances, and eagerly sought to connect himself by marriage with the great royal houses of the West. His first wife Bertha—called Irene to satisfy Greek susceptibilities—was a sister-in-law of the Emperor Conrad III., and his second wife was a princess of Antioch. His daughter married in succession the brother of the King of Hungary and the son of the Marquis of Montferrat. His son, Alexius, was wedded to the daughter of Louis VII. of France. His influence extended over all the Danubian states as far as the German frontier. His wars, if not always politic, were often successful. He defeated the strenuous attempts of King Roger of Sicily and his son William the Bad [see page 236] to invade his Empire. He waged a long and not inglorious war with Venice, and even when unable to destroy her privileges did something to counterbalance them by calling in rival Italian traders, such as the Genoese. When beaten by the Seljuks, he was able to negotiate an honourable peace. But his wastefulness brought the financial disorders to a crisis, and his utter neglect of routine threw the obsolete administrative system into confusion. Yet with all his faults he was a brilliant personality, and with his death the good fortune of the Comnenian dynasty came to an end.

Alexius II. (**1180-1183**), the son of Manuel, was a boy twelve years old, and his mother, Mary of Antioch, strove to carry on
Alexius II., 1180-1183. the government in his name. Her incapacity gave an opening for intrigues of the members of the royal house, and, two years later, Andronicus Comnenus, cousin of Manuel, displaced the Empress and became the guardian of Alexius with the title of Cæsar. As soon as he
Usurpation of Andronicus, 1183-1185. was secure of power, Andronicus murdered his ward, married his widow, Agnes of France, and made himself sole Basileus. Andronicus was a strong and brave soldier, but overweeningly ambitious, wantonly cruel, and already infamous by a long caieer of brutality and treachery. His success in gaining power was greater than his success in retaining it. Rebellions broke out in the provinces. Cyprus

shook itself free from his rule under the local Emperor Isaac
Comnenus, who finally succumbed to Richard of England
[see page 301]. Even the reign of terror which marked his
rule did not check the plots of the angry nobles. The
Normans again invaded Macedonia, and captured Thessalonica. So hateful did Andronicus become that a very small
incident sufficed to bring his power to an end. During his
absence from Constantinople, one of his ministers ordered
the arrest of an incapable and cowardly noble named Isaac
Angelus. Driven to despair at the prospect of the torments
meted out for Andronicus' victims, Isaac plucked up courage
to resist, and took refuge in St. Sophia's. The mob of Constantinople arose in revolt, declaring that it would have 'no more
old men or men with forked beards as Emperors.' End of the
Andronicus hurried back, but all classes deserted Comneni.
him. He was tortured to death by the mob, and Isaac
Angelus was declared his successor. With him the glorious
house of Comnenus ingloriously expired (1185).

The reign of Isaac Angelus ushered in a worse period of
degradation. Even the brutality of Andronicus had been
in some measure redeemed by its strength, but Isaac II.,
under his weak and contemptible successor the 1185-1195.
Empire suffered from the worst results of incompetence. The
Emperor lavished his revenues in building churches and
palaces, in collecting relics and sacred icons, in ministering to
the luxury and vanity of a crowd of parasites and dependants.
He put the administrative offices up for sale, and allowed
their purchasers to recoup themselves by oppressing the pro-
vincials. His ten years' rule was full of military disasters.
The imposition of a new tax was followed by the revolt of
the Bulgarians, who had lived as peaceful subjects of the
Empire since their conquest, two hundred years previously,
by Basil II. [see pages 163-165]. In a short time the whole of
Bulgaria had shaken off the yoke of Constantinople, and the
mercenary arms of Conrad of Montferrat. The efforts of
Isaac, who took the field in person against the rebels, were

powerless to win back a warlike and united people. The loss of Bulgaria was not the only humiliation of Isaac's reign. We have already seen how the Third Crusade dealt roughly with his power, how Frederick Barbarossa, provoked by his treachery, forced him to make an abject submission, and how Richard of England permanently turned Cyprus into a feudal Frankish kingdom, utterly unconnected with the Empire. Isaac had also to buy off the attacks of the Sultan of Roum by the payment of tribute.   In the midst of all these disasters his wretched government was abruptly ended by a palace conspiracy, formed against him by his elder brother Alexius, while he was absent engaged in the Bulgarian war.   Isaac hurried back to Constantinople, only to be deposed, blinded, and immured in a monastery (1195).

Alexius III. Angelus (1195-1203), was as wasteful, as profligate, and as incompetent as his brother, pillaging his sub-

Alexius III., jects to reward the conspirators who had helped

1195-1203.   him to the throne.   Rebellions broke out in the provinces, and the Venetians and Pisans fought out their feuds in the streets of the capital.   The efforts to reconquer Bulgaria proved abortive, and the Turks of Roum again threatened the heart of the Empire.   The utter feebleness of the Byzantine power tempted the Emperor Henry vi. to re-enact the part of Robert Guiscard and Roger.   His death postponed, without averting, the danger of Western conquest. Philip of Swabia was the brother-in-law of the deposed Isaac, and welcomed his son Alexius, when he escaped in a Pisan ship from his ill-guarded prison.   The Venetians, though loaded with privileges, clamoured for more.   It was just at the moment when the anarchy of Constantinople had reached its height that the army of Crusaders, collected from all Europe by the zeal of Innocent iii. and the preaching of Fulk of Neuilly, appeared at Venice, waiting to take ship thence in the vessels of the republic for the Holy Land.

The golden age of the Crusades was now over.   The difficulties that limited the success of the Third Crusade

now prevented even the undertaking of a new one on the same grand lines. The long efforts of Celestine III. to start a new Crusade had borne little fruit. Fulk of Neuilly began his preaching very soon after Innocent III.'s accession to the Papacy, and the new Pope warmly supported him. But none of the great princes of Europe responded to his call. It was not until 1201 that the beginnings of a crusading army was gathered together under leaders more of the status of the heroes of the First Crusade than of those of the Second or Third. Theobald III., Count of Champagne, was not deterred by his brother Henry's death from striving to redeem his brother's lost kingdom. Among the lords of Champagne that attended him was his marshal, Geoffrey of Villehardouin, who has left us a famous account of the expedition. Among Theobald's companions of high rank were his kinsman Louis, Count of Blois, and his sister Mary, who accompanied her husband, Baldwin IX., Count of Flanders, Baldwin's brothers Eustace and Henry, and Simon of Montfort, soon to become famous as the leader of the Albigensian Crusade. Theobald of Champagne was appointed general-in-chief, and it was resolved to attack Egypt, as the real centre of the Ayoubite power. Early in 1201, ambassadors of the Crusaders, conspicuous among whom was Villehardouin, appeared at Venice to negotiate with the Republic as to their means of transport. After lengthened negotiations a treaty was concluded between them and Henry Dandolo, the blind and aged, but still ardent, subtle, and active Doge. It was agreed that the Venetians should provide the necessary transports, with provisions for a year, and a convoy of fifty galleys. But in return, the Frankish Crusaders agreed to pay Venice the vast sum of 85,000 marks of silver, and to divide all conquests and booty equally between themselves and the Venetians. It was characteristic of the Italian seafaring republics to drive hard bargains with the Crusaders, and Dandolo had little concern for the Holy War, though he had infinite zeal for the interests

The muster-ing of the Fourth Crusade, 1198-1202.

of Venice. As soon as the Crusaders began to collect by the lagoons to embark for Egypt, he aspired to use them as soldiers of the Republic rather than of the Church. The appearance of the fugitive Alexius in Italy already suggested the idea of diverting the expedition against Constantinople.

There were still long delays. The death of the Count of Champagne left vacant the supreme command, and, after several attempts to fill it up, the Crusaders appointed as their chief the North Italian Boniface of Montferrat, brother of Conrad of Montferrat, and a scheming and unscrupulous adventurer. He was soon approached by King Philip of Swabia, who urged upon him the claims of the young Alexius, his kinsman. The Hohenstaufen monarch and the Doge of Venice now combined to recommend the Crusaders to undertake the restoration of Isaac Comnenus, as a preliminary to their attack on the infidels. Even at this early stage it is more than likely that the Venetians had formed a deliberate design to divert the Crusade, and had perhaps even an understanding with the Saracens to that effect.

When the spring of 1202 came, the passage from Venice was still unaccountably delayed. Many of the Crusaders The capture had spent all their resources during their long of Zara, 1202. stay, and the leaders were quite unable to pay the Venetians the huge sum they had promised. Dandolo now proposed that they should acquit themselves of part of their debt by helping Venice to conquer the maritime town of Zara, an old enemy of the Republic, and the haunt of pirates that preyed on its trade. Zara belonged to the King of Hungary, who had also taken the cross. But the spirit of adventure and love of booty was stronger among the Franks than zeal for the Holy War. Despite the protests of Simon of Montfort against the turning aside of a crusading army to fight a Catholic and crusading prince, it was agreed to accept Dandolo's suggestion. In October, the Crusaders at last left the Lido. In November Zara fell, after a short siege, into the hands of the united Venetian and Frankish host. The Pope vigorously denounced the forsworn soldiers of the Cross. But the Venetians paid no heed, and the Franks very little, to his fulminations. The season was now too late to make a start, and the army took up winter quarters in Dalmatia. Alexius now appeared in person in the crusading camp, and his glittering offers were greedily accepted. The Crusade turned against Constanti-nople, 1203. Boniface of Montferrat thought more of his own advantage than of the sacred cause. The pious scruples of the Count of Flanders were finally allayed. In the early summer of 1203, the Crusaders made sail for the Ægean. The fatal results of the decay of the Greek marine now made themselves clearly manifest. Alexius iii. was the first ruler of Constantinople who had to defend his capital, without having the command of the sea. With next to no resistance, the Venetians and Franks passed through the Dardanelles, and encamped at Scutari. The land-attack on Constantinople was beaten off, but the Venetians, headed by the blind old Doge, stormed the sea-wall, and burnt the adjacent ports of the city. The incapable and cowardly Emperor fled in alarm to Thrace, whereupon the army took the blind Isaac out of prison, and restored him to his throne, but invited his son Alexius to share it with him (July 1203).

The Crusaders had made an easy conquest, but their main feeling was one of disgust that the premature surrender of the city had deprived them of a chance of a richer plunder than their imaginations had ever conceived before they saw the wonders of the New Rome. They settled down for the next winter in the suburbs of the capital, while Isaac and Alexius iv. left no stone unturned to satisfy their clamour for their pay. When First capture of Constanti-nople Restoration of Isaac Angelus and Alexius IV., July 1203. the Emperors were reduced, in their efforts to appease the Latins, to plunder the churches of their jewels and reliquaries, and impose odious taxes on their subjects, the mob of

to regard itself as all-powerful, rose in revolt against them, and murdered all the Latins within reach. Isaac, unnerved Revolution in Constantinople. by captivity, died suddenly, it was said, of fright. Alexius IV. was strangled. A strong Alexius V., Feb. 1204. and daring adventurer, Alexius Ducas, surnamed Murzuphlus from his shaggy eyebrows, was proclaimed the Emperor Alexius v. (February 1204). The house of Angelus thus quitted history even less gloriously than the house of Comnenus.

It was but a revolution in the capital, and the provinces hardly recognised the usurper. But Alexius v. threw a Second capture and sack of Constantinople, April 1204. new energy into the defences of Constantinople, and the Crusaders found that they must either retire discomfited, or capture the city for a second time. After two months of preparations, they advanced in April to the final assault. This time they limited their attack to the sea-wall. The first effort was a failure, but a few days later a second onslaught admitted them into a corner of the city. There was still a chance for the Greeks, if they had had courage to stubbornly defend the city street by street. But the mercenary soldiers would not fight, and Alexius v., despairing of further resistance, fled from the capital, though he soon fell into the hands of the Crusaders, who put him to death. Constantinople now belonged to the Franks, and a hideous three days of plunder, murder, lust, and sacrilege, at last satisfied them for the moderation they had been forced to show upon the occasion of the first conquest. The priceless relics of ancient art were barbarously destroyed : the very churches were ruthlessly pillaged, and the city of Constantine was robbed for ever of that unique splendour that had made it for ages the wonder of the world.

The cry of indignation, that had already broken out when the Crusaders turned aside to besiege Zara, was renewed on their abandoning their campaign against the infidel to conquer a Christian city. But the feebleness of the opposition showed that the crusading spirit was dying, and even Innocent III., who was bitterly grieved at the failure of the Crusade, found consolation in the hoped-for collapse of the Greek schism, and made his peace with the Latin conquerors of Constantinople. The victorious Westerns now proceeded to the division of the spoil. The Venetians and

The partition and organisation of the Latin Empire, 1204-1261.

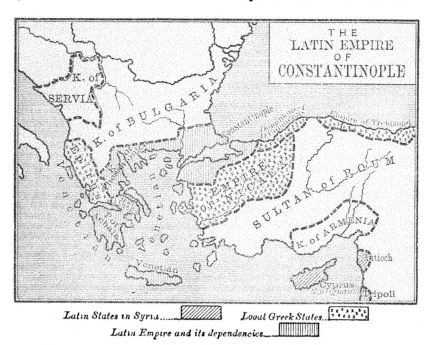

Latin States in Syria...... Loval Greek States...
Latin Empire and its dependencies__

the Franks still stood apart, jealously watching over their respective interests. There was no longer any talk of appointing a new Greek Emperor. It was agreed to elect from the crusading host a Latin Emperor and Patriarch, and it was further determined that the party that furnished the Emperor should yield to the other the choice of the Patriarch. A college of six French prelates and six Venetian nobles was set up to elect the Emperor. There was keen rivalry for the post. Boniface of Montferrat, as general, seemed to have an

obvious claim, but the Venetians were unwilling to support
the candidature of an Italian prince, an ally of the Hohenstaufen. Refusing the dangerous honour for their own duke,
the Venetians declared for Count Baldwin of Flanders, who
was duly elected Emperor in May. The papal legate
crowned him in St. Sophia's, and he was invested with
the purple buskins and all the other trappings of the
Basileus of the Romans. Thomas Morosini, a Venetian,
was chosen Patriarch. But the election of the heads of the
Church and State was an easier business than the division of
the spoils amidst a whole swarm of greedy claimants.

Like the conquerors of Jerusalem after the First Crusade,
the conquerors of Constantinople set up a feudal state on the
ruins of the Oriental system that they had destroyed. The
Emperor Baldwin was to be overlord of all the Crusading
chieftains, and was moreover to have as his domains the
capital, saving the Venetian quarter, the greater part of Thrace
with Adrianople, and the eastern islands of the Ægean,
Samothrace, Cos, Lesbos, Samos and Chios. Boniface of
Montferrat was consoled for his disappointment with the title
of King of Thessalonica. He was still strong enough to reject
the offer of a patrimony in Asia which the Latins had still to
conquer, and to profess that he held Thessalonica in his own
right, independently of the Emperor of Romania. He established himself in Macedonia and Thessaly. The Venetians
had the lion's share of the plunder. They had henceforth a
large slice of Constantinople with the practical monopoly of
the trade of the Empire. They also were recognised as
lords of most of the islands and coast lands, including
the Ionian islands, Eubœa, most of the Cyclades and some
of the Sporades, numerous settlements on the coasts of
the Peloponnesus, and a large domain north of the Corinthian
Gulf, along Acarnania, Ætolia, Epirus and Albania, where,
however, they were not strong enough to penetrate far into
the interior. Crete they purchased from Boniface of Montferrat. Dandolo, who assumed the title of *Despotes*, now

styled himself 'lord of a quarter and half-a-quarter' of the Empire. The minor Frankish chiefs also received great fiefs. Louis of Blois became Duke of Nicæa and of Nicomedia: Villehardouin became Prince of Achaia: Odo of La Roche Lord of Athens, and there were counts of Thebes, dukes of Philippopolis, and marquises of Corinth. Each feudatory had still his fief to conquer as best he could, and the lords, to whom lands in Asia were assigned, never obtained effective possession of their territories. The more fortunate European barons could only enjoy their grants by calling in the help of vassal chieftains, whose immunities left them little more than a show of power outside their own domains. No feudal state was ever strong, but no feudal state was ever so weak as the Latin Empire in the East. It had to contend against all the characteristic evils of feudalism, the infinite multiplication of the sovereign power, the constant feuds of rival chieftains, the permanent jealousy of every vassal of the power of his overlord. But it had special difficulties of its own of a kind impossible to be got over. The magnates of the expedition had cleverly manipulated the division of the spoils to their own advantage, and the poorer Crusaders were bitterly discontented. A comparison of the famous history of Villehardouin with the less well known account of the Crusade by the simple Picard knight, Robert of Clari, shows how bitterly the 'poor knights' resented the overbearing conduct of the 'great men,' whose standpoint is represented by the Marshal of Champagne. Moreover, Germans fought with Champenois and Burgundians, North Italians with Flemings, and all with the Venetians. Even if the Crusaders had been united, they were a mere handful of adventurers. The Venetians, who had got for themselves the richest and most accessible parts of the Empire, thought little of colonisation and much of trade. Yet even the Venetians drew wealth from the richly cultivated islands which now became the appanage, and were soon a chief source of wealth, to the noblest houses of the island city. The Ionian islands and

Crete remained Venetian for many centuries; the interior uplands were hardly Latin for two generations. It speaks well for the prowess of the Frankish lords that they held their position so long as this.

There was no attempt at mixing between Latins and Greeks. The quick sympathy that had made the Normans Italians in Sicily, English in England, and Irish in Ireland, no longer remained with the Frankish hosts. Their civilisation was too stereotyped, their ideas too stiff, their contempt for their conquered subjects too profound. It was even less possible for the Greeks to assimilate themselves with their conquerors. The old-world civilisation of the Byzantine realm was infinitely more hide-bound than the feudal system of the Franks. It was impossible to combine French feudalism with Byzantine officialism. The Greek despised the rude and uncultivated 'barbarians' who now ruled the heritage of Rome. The Latin scorned the cunning and effeminate Eastern who had succumbed so readily to his sword. It had been hard enough for the Comneni to keep together the decaying fortunes of the Eastern Empire. It was quite impossible for the French and Flemings to succeed where they had failed.

The barrier of religion would have kept the Latins and Greeks asunder, even if differences of nationality and civilisation had not proved effective causes of separation. The Greek revival. Despite the rejoicings of Innocent III., Orthodox and Catholic were more divided than ever, when the Filioque was chanted by azymites in the choir of St. Sophia, and beardless Latins, who regarded the Pope as the source of all ecclesiastical power, took into their hands every Church dignity and possession, and branded their rightful owners as schismatics. Orthodoxy and the pressure of the Latin invaders united Greek national feeling as it had never been united before. In the mountains of Albania and Epirus, the bolder Greeks fled from the yoke of the conqueror, and maintained their independence against any force that the Latins could bring to bear against them. A bastard of the house of Angelus became Despot of Epirus. Even in Thrace and in the Peloponnesus there were independent Greek States. Into Asia the Crusaders hardly penetrated at all. Two brothers of the house of Comnenus established the independence of distant Trebizond, and dignified themselves, like Isaac in Cyprus, with the title of Emperor. Theodore Lascaris, á brave soldier who escaped from the sack of Constantinople, proclaimed himself Emperor at Nicæa, and ruled over the western parts of Asia Minor. It was well for Greeks and Latins alike that the dissension and decay of the Seljukians of Roum, and the pressure of Tartar invasion, deprived Islam of its power of aggression. In Europe the Wallachio-Bulgarian kingdom easily maintained its independence and enlarged its boundaries at the expense of the crusading state. Nothing but the secure possession of the great military position of Constantinople, and the command of the sea, which the Venetian galleys still kept open for them, allowed the Latin Empire to keep up a feeble existence for nearly sixty years.

Theodore I. Lascaris, 1204-1222.

From the very beginning the Latin settlers had to contend against dissension within and invasion from without. Boniface of Thessalonica married the widow of Isaac Angelus, Margaret of Hungary (called by the Greeks Irene), and posed as an independent prince and the protector of the Greek population. He refused homage to the Emperor, and war broke out between the Flemings of Constantinople and the Lombards of Thessalonica. No sooner were his pretensions rudely shattered than the Emperor was called away to meet the danger of Bulgarian invasion. Johanitsa, the tsar of the Bulgarians, turned his arms against the Crusaders, and invaded Thrace. In April 1205, a decisive battle was fought at Adrianople, when the simulated flight of the wild Bulgar nordes drew the chivalry of the West to break up their solid ranks. Thereupon the Bulgarians rallied, and took advantage of the enemy's disorder to inflict

Rivalry of Constantinople and Thessalonica.

Baldwin I., 1204-1205.

on them a complete defeat. Louis of Blois was among the slain. Baldwin was taken prisoner and murdered. The Marshal of Champagne, and Henry of Flanders, Baldwin's brother, almost alone survived of the Latin chieftains.

Henry of Flanders had already made some progress in the conquest of Greek Asia, when the news of the Bulgarian in-

Henry,
1205-1216.

vasion called him to defend his brother's throne. He was now recognised as Emperor. He was politic as well as brave, and the Greeks themselves admitted that he 'treated the Romans as if they were his own people.' But he could neither conquer Asia, defeat the Bulgarians, nor even permanently conciliate his Greek subjects; though his zeal for shielding them from Catholic persecution drew upon him the thunders of the Vatican. He made a treaty with Theodore Lascaris, which gave him at least a little corner of Asia. He was the strongest of the Latin Emperors. But he profited by the even greater weakness of the kingdom of Thessalonica. In 1207, Boniface of Montferrat perished, like Baldwin, at the hands of the Bulgarians. The Despot of Epirus took advantage of the minority of his infant son, Demetrius, to extend his conquests. The Frankish lords of the kingdom called in the Emperor Henry, who found some consolation for his disappointments in the North, when he gave the law to the Peloponnesus and the islands in a great Diet held in 1210, compelled the regent of the young king to do him homage, and received the submission even of the Venetian lords of the Archipelago, conferring on the great house of Sanudo the Duchy of the Archipelago or the Cyclades. Even the Despot of Epirus formally acknowledged his sovereignty. Henry died in 1216, and with him perished the best hopes of the Latins in Greece.

Peter of Courtenay, Count of Auxerre, a grandson of Louis VI. of France, and the husband of Iolande, sister of

Peter of
Courtenay,
1216-1219.

Baldwin and Henry, was now chosen Emperor. He was in Europe at the time of his election, and hastened to Constantinople to take possession of the Empire. He rashly chose to disembark at Durazzo, and follow the ancient Via Egnatia over the hills to Macedonia and Thrace. When amongst the mountains, his little army was overwhelmed by the Despot of Epirus, and he himself was captured, and died in captivity. His wife, who had more prudently proceeded to Constantinople by sea, now acted as regent for her young son Robert, the next Emperor.

The reign of Robert of Courtenay marked the rapid decline of the Eastern Empire. It witnessed the complete destruction of the Kingdom of Thessalonica. In 1223, Robert, when King Demetrius was abroad, seeking in 1219-1228. vain Western help, Theodore Angelus took possession of his capital, and henceforth ruled without a rival from the Adriatic to the Ægean; and, like the lords of Fall of Nicæa and Trebizond, assumed the pompous Thessalonica, style of Emperor of the Romans. John 1223. Vatatzes, the successor of Theodore Lascaris at Nicæa, renewed the war with the Latins of Constantinople. It seemed almost a race between the two Theodores, as to which should first drive out the Latins. The domain of Robert was reduced to Constantinople and its suburbs. He went to implore help from the West, and died during his journey in 1228.

Baldwin II. (1228-1261), the youngest of Peter of Courtenay's sons, a boy of eleven, was now proclaimed Emperor. John de Brienne, the ex-king of Jerusalem Baldwin II., [see chapter xix.], was soon called in to hold the 1228-1261. regency. He married his daughter to Baldwin, was crowned joint-Emperor, and saved his ward's throne from the Greeks and Bulgarians. On John's death in 1237, new perils beset the young Baldwin. The Latin state had had a few years of breathing time through the rivalry of the Angeli of Thessalonica and the house of Ducas, to which, after the death of Theodore Lascaris, had passed the Empire Union of of Nicæa. John III. Ducas ended the strife Thessalonica in his own favour by the conquest of Thessalonica and Nicæa. in 1241. Henceforth, the Angeli had to be contented with

the title of Despot of Epirus, and were confined to the uplands
of the west.   A single strong Greek power now threatened

John III.
Ducas,
1222-1254.

Constantinople, both from the side of Asia and
the side of Europe.   Moreover, John III. was a
competent administrator, a good warrior, and an
able financier.   Nothing but the mighty walls of Constantinople, which the Greeks had vainly attempted to assault,
and the Venetian command of the sea, now saved the Latin
Empire from immediate extinction.   Baldwin II. spent most
of his long reign in the vain quest of Frankish assistance.
He left his son as a pledge to Western bankers, and sold
the most precious relics of Constantinople to St. Louis.
He had to sell the lead of his palace-roof to buy food, and
warm himself by burning the wood of his outhouses.   But
the death of John III. in 1254 prolonged the long agony of
the Latin Empire.   Michael Palæologus, an ambitious and
unscrupulous soldier, became regent for the infant grandson
of John III., and soon associated himself with his ward as

Michael VIII.
Palæologus,
1259-1282.

joint ruler.   In 1259 Michael was crowned
Emperor at Nicæa, and the rights of his little
colleague were soon forgotten.   But Michael VIII.
showed vigour and military capacity which went some way to
justify his usurpation.   In 1261, he profited by the absence

Conquest of
Constantin-
ople, 1261.

of the Venetian fleet to make a sudden attack on
Constantinople.   The unlucky Baldwin could
offer no effective resistance.   On 15th August,
Michael entered in triumph the ancient capital, and the
Latin Empire perished, unwept and unhonoured.

The Venetians, alarmed to find that Michael had transferred
their privileges to their Genoese rivals, joined with the Franks

The revived
Greek
Empire,
1261-1453.

of the Peloponnesus in raising a cry for a Crusade
against the victorious Greeks, which was further
preached by Pope Urban IV.   Charles of Anjou,
who became King of Naples and Sicily in 1265,
was willing, and seemed eminently fitted, to carry out the old
aggressive policy of the Guiscards.   But, though the proposal

that he should lead a new Crusade against the Orthodox frightened Michael into insincere proposals to buy off Western opposition by ending the Greek schism, his submission had no permanent result when the fear of a Crusade was removed. Michael never ruled with the authority of the Macedonians or the Comneni, but his careful measures of reforms, and his warlike capacity, started the Greek Empire on the last stage of its career, which gave it nearly two centuries more of existence before it succumbed to the Ottoman Turks.

The Latin power still partly continued in the islands and in the Peloponnesus. Not only did the Venetians retain their grip on the Archipelago and the coast, The Latins in but the proximity of the sea enabled some Peloponnesus. of the Franks of Southern Greece to continue to rule their principalities, after Baldwin II. had been driven from his throne. They had as their code of law the Assizes of Romania, a free adaptation of the famous Assizes of Jerusalem. They even effected some sort of partial amalgamation with their native subjects. Their churches and fortresses long remained, as in Cyprus and Syria, the strongest witnesses of their power. It was not till 1310 that the Dukes of Athens, of the house of Brienne, succumbed, not to the Greeks, but to their own Catalan mercenaries. The Princes of Achaia reigned even longer. The Venetians saved both the Ionian islands and Crete alike from the Greeks and from the Turks. To the end of the Middle Ages, titular dukes, princes, and emperors of the Eastern world kept up the memory of one of the strangest and most daring of Western conquests, but one which was useless to the West, and only weakened the Christian East, at a time when the rise of the Ottoman Turks required every effort to be made to stem the tide of that barbarian conquest which was soon to prove fatal to Latin and Greek alike.

GENEALOGY OF THE COMNENI AND ANGELI.

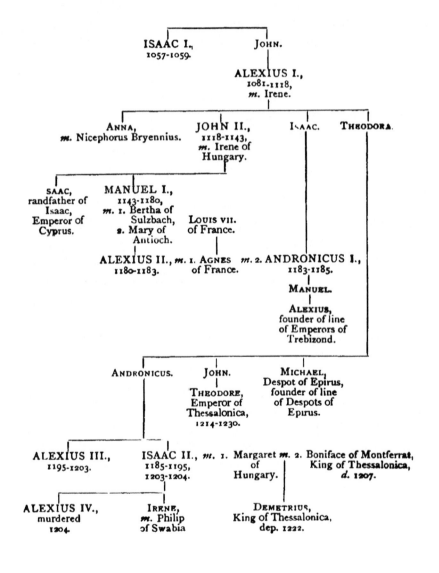

GENEALOGY OF THE LATIN EMPERORS
OF CONSTANTINOPLE.

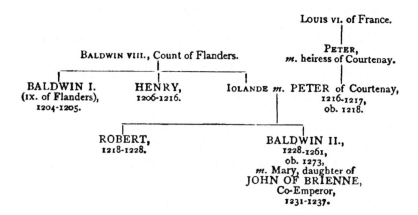

LOUIS VI. of France.

PETER,
m. heiress of Courtenay.

BALDWIN VIII., Count of Flanders.

BALDWIN I.
(IX. of Flanders),
1204-1205.

HENRY,
1206-1216.

IOLANDE *m.* PETER of Courtenay,
1216-1217,
ob. 1218.

ROBERT,
1218-1228.

BALDWIN II.,
1228-1261,
ob. 1273,
m. Mary, daughter of
JOHN OF BRIENNE,
Co-Emperor,
1231-1237.

CHAPTER XVI

FREDERICK II. AND THE PAPACY [1] (1216-1250)

Character and Policy of Frederick II.—His Work in Naples and Sicily—
Frederick and Honorius III.—The Early Struggles of Frederick and
Gregory IX.—Frederick's Crusade and its Consequences—Peace of San
Germano—Germany under Frederick—St. Engelbert and Henry VII.—
German Civilisation under the Later Hohenstaufen—The Eastward Ex-
pansion of Germany—Livonia and Prussia—Frederick and the Lombard
League—Battle of Cortenuova—Renewed Struggle with Gregory IX.—
The Tartars—Innocent IV. and the Council of Lyons—Henry Raspe and
William of Holland—The Italian Struggle—Frederick's Plans for
Ecclesiastical Revolution—Frederick's Death.

FREDERICK II. was just twenty years old when the death of
Innocent III. allowed him to govern as well as to reign. He was
Character of of middle height, and well proportioned, though
Frederick II. becoming somewhat corpulent as he advanced in
age. He had good features and a pleasant appearance. His
light hair, like that of his father and grandfather, inclined

[1] Huillard-Bréholles' *Historia Diplomatica Friderici Secundi* contains a
magnificent collection of Frederick's acts, and a whole volume of introduction, which is the best general commentary on his reign. The same
writer's *Pierre de la Vigne* should also be studied. T. L. Kington's
History of Frederick II. (2 vols.) is a sound and elaborate English
version of the Emperor's career. For Frederick's religious ideas, see also
Gebhart's *L'Italie Mystique*. There is a good essay on Frederick II. in
Freeman's *Historical Essays*, First Series. Freeman's over-emphasis of
the continuity of imperial tradition may be usefully contrasted with the
view held by Mr. E. Jenks, in his interesting *Law and Politics in the
Middle Ages*, 'that the Frank Empire in both its stages was a sham
Empire.' The magnificent editions of the registers of the thirteenth
century Popes, now being published, mainly by the French school at
Rome, will afford a solid basis for the detailed history of the Papacy.

towards redness, but he ultimately became very bald. Despite his troubled childhood, passed in solitude and gloom at the palace of Palermo, he had been carefully educated. He became familiar with many tongues, and versed in many literatures. The half-Greek, half-Arabic cultivation of Sicily had thoroughly permeated a spirit in which keen rationalism and dreamy mysticism were curiously interwoven. He had a true mediæval love for dialectic. He delighted in geometry and in astronomy. He regulated his public and private life by the predictions of his astrologers, among whom Michael Scot held the first place. He was curious in natural history, collecting a great menagerie of strange animals and studying their habits and structure. The camels and dromedaries, employed in carrying his baggage train, excited the wonder of the Italians, and his elephant, a present from the Sultan of Egypt, was almost as famous as the elephant of Charlemagne. In his concern for his own health he busied himself with surgery and medicine, while his care for his animals turned his interests towards veterinary science. He enjoyed hunting and hawking, not only as a sportsman, but as a naturalist. He wrote a treatise on falconry that attests his zoological and anatomical knowledge. Yet with all his love of fresh air and exercise, he was a valetudinarian who depended upon his physicians almost as much as upon his astrologers, regulating his life and diet very carefully, and indulging so frequently in baths that his enemies reproached him with bathing on Sundays.

With advancing life Frederick's personal habits grew more and more oriental. He secluded his wives from the public gaze, keeping them under the custody of eunuchs after the Eastern fashion, and maintaining at Lucera a regular harem of concubines, the expenses of which were duly entered in the public accounts of the realm. Though a respectable strategist, Frederick was no warrior, taking small delight in feats of physical skill, and having little of the rough vigour and determination of his chivalrous contemporaries. But he was a subtle and almost a great statesman, who sought to gain his ends by craft, duplicity, and dexterity. Courteous, polished, and seductive in manner, he seemed to belong to a different race from that of his rude Swabian and Norman ancestors. His many-sided character, so full of contradictions, has nothing of the homogeneity and simplicity of the warriors and statesmen of the Middle Ages, but at one time reflects the astute and effeminate oriental, and at another anticipates the accomplished and brilliant despots of the Italian Renascence. His want of sympathy for the ideals of his time comes out strongly in his dealings with the Church. He was believed to have imbibed from his Arab and Jewish masters an utter scepticism as to all religion. Moses, Mohammed, and Christ, he is reported to have said, were three impostors who had deluded the world in turn; and he is also alleged to have maintained that the soul perished with the body. But if Frederick upheld these views before a select circle, he was careful to submit himself to all the obligations of the Church, and to prove his orthodoxy not only by the most formal and positive denials of these charges, but also by a most sanguinary persecution of heresy.

Frederick's character and policy can best be studied in his favourite Sicilian and South Italian homes. Despite the pro-

Frederick's policy in Naples and Sicily. tection of Innocent III., he had had, as we have seen, the greatest difficulties in maintaining his position both against the untamed descendants of the old Arab lords of Sicily, and against the fierce and turbulent feudal aristocracy that had come in with the Normans. The first years after Innocent's death were taken up with renewed struggles against the Saracens in Sicily. It was not till after an almost constant fight between 1221-1225 that Frederick succeeded in entirely effecting their subjection. He then strove to divide his Arab subjects by transporting a large number of them to the desolate town of Lucera on the mainland. The ruined city was rebuilt on a magnificent scale for its infidel inhabitants. Workers in steel and weavers of silk made Lucera wealthy and prosperous, and the grateful Arabs showed unwavering fidelity to their sympathetic conqueror. Frederick frequently visited Lucera, where he delighted to live the very life of his oriental subjects. Frederick looked upon the Arabs as most kings looked on the Jews. They were his personal slaves and dependants, whom he protected the more since, besides the commercial gifts, which they shared with the Hebrews, they were doughty warriors, who were ever willing to fight for him in his Italian wars. Moreover, their loyalty was superior to the terrors of the papal ban, and their arms proved an admirable counterpoise to the fierce Norman aristocracy, which, allying itself with the Papacy, sought to break down the fabric of centralisation which the Sicilian kings had established at its expense, and which Frederick now strove to elaborate into a strong despotism. The constant feudal revolts were suppressed with firm deliberation and cold-blooded cruelty. Hardly less formidable to Frederick than the feudalists were the great cities such as Messina, Syracuse, and Catania, whose liberties were also menaced by a policy that concentrated all power in the monarch, and whose frequent rebellions were another continued source of trouble. The same firm hand that checked the nobles ultimately managed to triumph over the disaffection of the citizens.

Victorious over Saracens, nobles, and townsmen alike, Frederick skilfully played off one class or race against the others, and banished from his court the turbulent leaders of the lay and spiritual aristocracy. With the help of a handful of faithful prelates and barons, and of a wider circle of lawyers, notaries, and royal dependants, Frederick issued a series of laws for the government of Sicily and Naples that frankly strove to abolish the feudal state in the interests of autocracy. He resumed possession of the estates that had been carved from the royal domain in the days of confusion. Like another Henry of Anjou, he either destroyed the unauthorised castles, erected by the feudal lords, or at least garrisoned them with royal troops under trusty commanders. Private wars were forbidden under pain of death, and even the judicial duel was only allowed in specified cases and under careful precautions. Criminal jurisdiction was withdrawn from the nobles' courts and put in the hands of royal judges. Frederick even made it a merit that he suffered the feudal tribunals to continue to exercise civil justice. The towns were deprived of the right of choosing their magistrates, and put under the rule of royal officials, while councils of notables, chosen by the inhabitants, gave the magistrates some insight into public opinion, or at least proved a convenient channel for receiving the royal commands. The feudal prelates shared in the ruin of their lay colleagues, and every churchman was forced to pay taxes, and to abandon civil office. The Church courts saw their jurisdiction limited and their privileges curtailed. The further growth of ecclesiastical property **was** prevented by a severe law of mortmain.

A great administrative system grew up on the ruins of seignorial, ecclesiastical, and municipal independence. All laws emanated directly from the monarch. The *Magna Curia*, sitting at Capua, took supreme cognisance of all judicial business, while the *Magna Curia Rationum* occupied the position of the Angevin Exchequer. *Chamberlains* looked after the finance and the administration of the provinces, while *Justices*, strangers to the districts in which they bore rule, tried criminals and upheld peace and good order. Local *bailiffs* cared for the royal interests in the villages, and acted as judges in the first instance, while the *Grand Justiciar*, the head of the Court of Capua, made yearly perambulations of the provinces to control the local machinery. Representative *General Courts* anticipated by a generation or more the system of estates of Northern Europe, and brought the autocrat in touch with the needs of the chief orders of the community.

The arts and sciences flourished at the court of the brilliant and enlightened young despot. In 1224 Frederick established the University of Naples, and provided it with every faculty, 'in order that those who have hunger for knowledge may find within the kingdom the food for which they are yearning, and may not be forced to go into exile and beg the bread of learning in strange lands.' It was the first university in Europe established by royal charter, and, all through its history, the rigid dependence of its teachers and students on the State deprived it of that freedom which was necessary to play a real part in the history of thought, though the fostering care of its master, which prohibited his subjects from studying elsewhere, made it an efficient educational instrument, and it had the honour of numbering among its earliest disciples Thomas of Aquino. The more ancient school of medicine at Salerno was revived through Frederick's bounty, and no one was allowed to practise the physician's art within the realm without the licence of the Salerno doctors. At Frederick's accession, we are told, there were few men of letters in Sicily. His largesse soon attracted to his court doctors from every part of the world. The palace itself became a centre of intellectual activity. Michael Scot translated for Frederick many of the works of Aristotle. The famous mathematician, Leonard of Pisa, who introduced Arabic numerals and Arabic algebra into the West, enjoyed the sovereign's patronage. Learned Jews and Arabs were as sure of Frederick's favour as the best of Catholics. Nor were the lighter and more elegant arts forgotten. It is possible that Frederick himself wrote Latin poetry. It is certain that his compositions in the vulgar tongue mark the starting-point of the vernacular literature of Italy, and for the first time gave a currency among the great and learned to the songs of the Sicilian dialect that had hitherto only enjoyed the favour of the poor and humble. Dante regarded Frederick as the father of Italian poetry, and the example of the king and his court gave such vogue to the Sicilian idiom that it was nearly a century before the vernacular poets forsook it for the Tuscan. Frederick also loved the poets of Provence, even if he did not also write verses in

the tongue of the Troubadours. He also favoured the speech
of Northern France, and recognised its general prevalence as
the common language of knights and soldiers. His ministers,
headed by the famous Peter della Vigna, emulated his activity,
and his children, especially the bastard Manfred, strove,
amidst great difficulties, to continue his work. Frederick
loved art so well that he rifled Ravenna to adorn his palace
at Palermo, and collected jewels, plate, and costly furniture
as well as manuscripts. He was a great builder, and his
summer palace at Foggia, where he loved to dwell by reason
of its proximity to the great forest of the Incoronata, which
was reserved for the royal hunting, was, with the still existing
castle of Castel del Monte, a striking example of the severe
yet elegant style which he had adopted.

The successor of Innocent III. was Honorius III., a member
of the noble Roman house of Savelli. He was a gentle,
earnest, mild-mannered man, who had grown grey
while discharging a monotonous round of financial
business in the papal Curia. He was neither a
statesman nor a zealot, yet he was a high-minded
and religious prelate, and intent above all things upon renewing the Crusades. He had been tutor of Frederick, and
wished him well. But though Honorius' conciliatory temper
gave the young king ample opportunities for working out
his Sicilian policy, there were grave matters outstanding that
could not but give rise to difficulties between the Papacy and
its former ward. Frederick had promised Innocent III. to
prevent the permanent union of the Empire and Sicily by
investing his young son Henry with his Italian kingdom, to
be held as a fief of the Papacy. He had also pledged himself
to embark personally upon a Crusade. As success strengthened his love of power and impatience of external control,
Frederick became unwilling to fulfil either of these obligations.
Honorius urged him repeatedly to depart for the East to uphold
the declining cause of the Cross. Frederick exhausted his
ingenuity in piling up excuses for delay, and the meek Pope was

Frederick and Honorius III., 1216-1227.

content to accept them. At last, in April 1220, Frederick allowed his son Henry to be elected King of the Romans, and therefore his successor in the Empire as well as in Sicily. This was an impudent violation of his plighted word and an open defiance of the Pope. He had the effrontery to pretend to Honorius that the election had been made without his knowledge, and in September he returned from Germany to Italy, professing the utmost deference to the papal authority, and offering a settlement of the long-outstanding dispute about the inheritance of the Countess Matilda. He was now profuse in promises to the Pope and clergy. In November 1220 the long-suffering Honorius crowned him Emperor at Rome. The Pope, moreover, allowed him to keep Sicily for his lifetime, on condition that he maintained therein a separate administration from that of the Empire. In return for all this, Frederick again solemnly took the Cross, and lavished concessions on the Church. He annulled all laws hostile to the privileges of the clergy. He declared the Church exempt from all taxes, and conferred on all ecclesiastical persons absolute immunity from lay jurisdiction. He sacrificed the rights of the municipalities in favour of the prelates, and he promised to lend the whole force of the secular power to supplement the Church's efforts for the extirpation of heresy. If he hoped to shift on the towns and the heretics some of the worst disabilities that he had imposed upon himself, he had nevertheless seriously limited his authority and hampered his Sicilian policy. It was not sound statecraft that promised freely in the hope of being able to repudiate the concession when he had obtained the end for which he affected to pay the price.

Frederick seemed at first in earnest about the Crusade, but he again piled up delay upon delay. In 1221 Damietta was lost to the Christians (see chapter xix.), and the Pope, who felt that Frederick was responsible for this severe blow, mildly threatened him with excommunication ; but Frederick soon talked him over, and it was agreed to postpone his Crusade until 1225. Though that term soon passed away, Frederick now contracted his second marriage, with Iolande or Isabella, daughter of John de Brienne, and the heiress of the kingdom of Jerusalem. This match gave him a new and a more personal motive to undertake the promised adventure. Meanwhile papal legates had stirred up Germany with some purpose, and Hermann of Salza, Grand Master of the Teutonic Order, won over many of the princes. The eager Pope at last thought that Europe was again on the verge of making a real effort to redeem the recent failures. But the organisation of Sicily lay nearer the Emperor's heart than the delivery of the Holy Sepulchre from the infidel. The establishment of the Saracens at Lucera was a curious comment on his crusading zeal, and directly threatened the neighbouring papal territories with infidel invasion at the very moment when Frederick was calling on the inhabitants of Spoleto, a fief of the Holy See, to render him military service. The new laws promulgated for his Southern dominions afflicted the clergy with severe disabilities, and gave the lie direct to the promises made after Frederick's coronation. Moreover, in 1226 Frederick held a great diet at Cremona, where he renewed the ancient imperial claims over Lombardy. In their alarm the Lombard cities renewed their league, and blocked the roads by which the imperial troops could cross over the Alps from Germany. Frederick put the guilty cities under the imperial ban, and a German prelate declared an interdict over their lands. Honorius at last lost all patience. He pronounced the interdict invalid, and prepared to renew the ancient league between the Papacy and the Lombard cities. Despite the incredible forbearance of the Pope, the lying and chicanery of the Emperor had wantonly provoked a rupture. The death of Honorius in March 1227 precipitated the inevitable renewal of the old contest of Papacy and Empire.

The next Pope was Ugolino, cardinal bishop of Ostia, a kinsman of Innocent III., a man of the highest character, and

an ardent upholder of the great Pope's ideas. He had long
been known as the special patron of St. Francis and St. Dominic (see chapter xviii.), and the most strenuous The first
foe of all sorts of heretics. Gregory IX. (this was struggle
between
the name he assumed) was already a very old man. Frederick
But the fire of youthful enthusiasm still glowed and
Gregory IX.,
within him, and his strong will and restless energy 1227-1230.
at once brushed aside the specious excuses that had so long
deceived his predecessor. For the moment it seemed as if
Frederick was at last in earnest for the Crusade. Bands
of German, Italian, and French warriors gathered together in
Apulia during the summer, and on 8th September Frederick
himself took ship at Brindisi for the Holy Land. But pestilence had already decimated the crusading army, and after a
few days Frederick put back at Otranto, alleging that a sharp
attack of fever had necessitated his return. The Emperor
soon recovered, but the Landgrave of Thuringia, the com-
mander of his army, now died, and many of the survivors
of the expedition went back to their homes. Frederick's
excuses availed him little with Gregory IX. On 29th September the Pope pronounced him excommunicate, and laid
under interdict every spot wherein he might chance to tarry.
This was the signal for a violent renewal of the ancient strife
between Papacy and Empire. Gregory denounced the
Emperor in threatening manifestos, and swarms of Mendicant
Friars wandered throughout Italy, seeking to turn Frederick's
subjects from their allegiance to the forsworn, grasping, and
profligate Emperor. Frederick did not shrink from the conflict. 'No Roman Emperor,' he declared, 'has ever been so
badly treated by a Pope. The Roman Church is so swollen
with avarice that the goods of the Church will not suffice to
satisfy it, and it is not ashamed to disinherit and make tributary emperors, kings and princes.' For the moment Frederick
was in the stronger position. The Pope's emissaries failed
to turn either Italy or Germany from its allegiance. The
partisans of the Emperor stirred up a tumult in Rome,

and at Easter 1228 Gregory was forced to take flight to Viterbo.

In June Frederick again took ship at Brindisi, and landed in September in Acre. His wife, Isabella of Brienne, died before his embarkation, on the birth of their son Conrad, but Frederick still claimed the crown of Jerusalem. Gregory now forbade the excommunicate Emperor from presumptuously undertaking the holy work, and commanded the faithful to withdraw from his armies. As Frederick still persisted, the sentence of excommunication passed because of his refusal to become a Crusader was renewed because he went to the Holy Land without reconciling himself to the Church. The Patriarch of Jerusalem and the Orders of the Temple and the Hospital obeyed the papal command. But the rash violence of the Pope overreached itself, and many Crusaders, conspicuous among whom was the young Teutonic Order and its famous master, Hermann of Salza, did not scruple to follow Frederick to battle. Public opinion blamed the Pope for his rigour, and a contemporary said that Frederick was the victim of Gregory, as Christ was the victim of Caiaphas. Though not unprepared for battle, Frederick trusted more to negotiation than to his arms. Long before his departure for Palestine, he had been conducting friendly negotiations with El-Kamil, the Sultan of Egypt. In February 1229 he concluded a ten years' truce with the Sultan, by which Bethlehem, Nazareth, and Jerusalem were restored to the Christians, on condition only that the Mosque of Omar remained in Saracen hands. On Mid-Lent Sunday Frederick took the crown of Jerusalem from the high altar of the Church of the Holy Sepulchre, and placed it on his own head. But the Patriarch cast an interdict over the Holy Places, and no priest could be found to hallow the coronation by celebrating the offices of the Church. Frederick gave fresh cause for scandal by visiting the Mosque of Omar. He soon returned to Acre, and in June was back in Italy. Despite the thunders of the Church, the excommunicate

(marginal note) Frederick's Crusade, 1228-1229.

Emperor had done more for the Christian cause than a generation of orthodox pilgrims. Hermann of Salza declared with good reason that Frederick could have obtained still better terms for the Christians had it not been for the hostility of Pope and clergy.

During Frederick's absence, Gregory had devastated Apulia with fire and sword. His dead wife's father, John de Brienne, the ex-king of Jerusalem, acted as captain of the papal mercenaries against him. On Frederick's sudden reappearance, the papal troops were driven over the frontier and the Patrimony of St. Peter itself threatened by the victorious Emperor. Gregory found that his rashness had brought him into an impossible position, and was glad to accept the mediation which Hermann of Salza and Duke Leopold of Austria now proffered. On July 23, 1230, peace was made *The Peace* between Pope and Emperor at San Germano. *of San Germano, 1230.* In return for a promise to protect the Pope's dominions and a confirmation of the papal rights over Sicily, Frederick was released from his excommunication. Soon after, Pope and Emperor met at Anagni with Hermann of Salza as the only witness of their conference. 'The Pope,' wrote Frederick, 'has opened to me his heart, and has calmed my spirit. I will remember the past no longer.' 'The Emperor,' wrote Gregory, 'has come to seek me with the zeal of a devoted son, and has shown to me that he is ready to accomplish all my desires.' Yet, despite these mutual protestations, the Treaty of San Germano so little went to the root of the matter that it was little more than a hollow truce. Both sides still watched each other with jealous suspicion. However, the truce was kept for several years, since neither Pope nor Emperor was ready to strike the decisive blow for power.

Frederick devoted the period succeeding the Treaty of San Germano to the building up of his Southern despotism. His policy now became more exclusively Italian. With the hope of getting help from the German princes in carrying out his Southern schemes, he recklessly played into their hands, and

wantonly destroyed the well-ordered authority over his Northern
kingdom that he had inherited from his father and grandfather.   His German and Sicilian policies stand in
the strongest contrast.   While he trampled down
all feudal communities in the Norman kingdom
in favour of a centralised bureaucracy dependent
upon himself, he threw to the winds every monarchical and national tradition in Germany.   There was something of the wilfulness that is so characteristic of him in this
strangely twofold and contradictory action.   It strikes at the
very root of Frederick's claims to the higher statesmanship.
Their only reconciliation is the fact that the Emperor's policy
was but the policy of the moment.   So long as he could crush
his papal enemy, he was utterly careless of the general tendency
of his work.   The ruin of the Hohenstaufen was already prepared for when Frederick bartered his German kingship for an
immediate triumph over his hated foe.   It was all the more
certain, since the elaborate edifice that he imagined he was
building up in Italy was but a house erected on the sand.

The long civil war between Frederick and Otto of Saxony
had done much to shake the authority of the German king
and stimulate the development of the feudal principle.   A partial recovery was effected during the
years succeeding the collapse of the Guelf, when
the wise rule of Engelbert, archbishop of Cologne,
contributed powerfully towards restoring the prestige of the
absentee sovereign.   Like Barbarossa, Frederick sought to
rule by means of the German episcopate, but the bishops of
his time were no longer in the commanding position which
the warlike prelates of the twelfth century had held.   The
episcopal towns which they had once ruled through their
officials had become great centres of commerce and wealth,
and were rapidly advancing on the road to autonomy.   The
lay princes were more independent, and even the *ministeriales*,
who had played so decisive a part in earlier struggles, were
attaining an independent and permanent position of their own

Marginal notes:

Contrast between Frederick's Italian and German policy.

Government of St. Engel-bert, 1220-1225.

as a lower aristocracy whose imperial offices were becoming hereditary fiefs. There was not time enough for Engelbert's attempts at reformation to succeed. It was not until 1219 that the last partisans of the Guelfs tendered their submission. But even before that, in 1216, Frederick had conferred on his four-year-old son Henry the duchy of Swabia, and in 1220 he had procured, as we have seen, his election as King of the Romans. He smoothed the way to this by a formal alliance with the ecclesiastical princes, conferring upon them a series of privileges that extended to them complete jurisdiction over their fiefs.[1] In 1222 Henry was crowned king at Aachen by Engelbert, who 'cherished him as a son and honoured him as a master.' Henceforth the administration was carried on in the name of the young king.

Engelbert watched with a jealous eye the power of Valdemar II. of Denmark, who had been allowed by Frederick to retain possession of Nordalbingia and the extensive German districts which he had occupied, when fighting as a partisan of Otto IV. But the German lords of the conquered districts were averse to foreign domination, and, headed by Count Henry of Schwerin, sought to restore their estates to their fatherland. In 1223 Henry of Schwerin had the good luck to take the King of Denmark prisoner, and in 1225 Valdemar only obtained his release at the price of renouncing Schwerin, Holstein, and his other German acquisitions. Afterwards Valdemar sought to regain his losses, but in 1227 he was defeated at the bloody battle of Bernhöved in Holstein, and was glad to renew the conditions which he had accepted two years before. Henceforth the Danes were confined to their own territories, and the chief hindrance was removed to the expansion of the German power in the Baltic lands.

Engelbert's war against Denmark was the greatest evidence of his energy and success. Before the struggle was over he

Defeat of Valdemar of Denmark, 1223-1227

[1] It is printed in Altmann and Bernheim, *Ausgewählte Urkunden*, pp. 18-20.

was assassinated in 1225 by a band of robber knights, who resented his strenuous maintenance of public order. The Church honoured him as a martyr, and he was soon added to the catalogue of saints. He left no competent successor,

Henry VII., King of the Romans, 1222-1235.

and the land fell into such anarchy that a chronicler complained that Germany had become as bad as Israel under the Judges, when there was no king, and every man did what was right in

his own eyes. The young Henry VII.—so Frederick's son was generally called—attained man's estate in the midst of these disturbances. He was a dissolute, capricious, featherheaded youth, quite unable to uphold order or frame a clear and consistent policy. Complaints of the disorders arising from his neglect soon crossed the Alps to his father, but Frederick's exhortations and remonstrances only irritated his son against him without turning him from his evil ways. Before long the growing differences between Frederick and Henry added a new element of difficulty to the Emperor's position. The King of the Romans sought, so far as he could, to maintain a diametrically different policy from that approved of by the Emperor. The last generation of the 'ministeriales,' utterly alienated from his father, abetted his designs and gave them some coherence.

In 1231 Frederick forced Henry to promulgate at Worms a *Statutum in favorem principum*, which in 1232 he personally

Frederick's Privileges to the Princes, 1231-1232.

confirmed at a diet at Civitate in Friuli.[1] It was the elaboration and the generalisation of his alliance twelve years earlier with the prelates. 'Let

every prince,' declared the Emperor, 'enjoy in peace, according to the approved custom of his land, his immunities, jurisdictions, counties and hundreds, both those which belong to him in full right, and those which have been granted out to him in fief.' It was a complete recognition of the territorial supremacy of the great nobles, whether churchmen or laymen. No new castle or city was to be set up

Altmann and Bernheim, *Ausgewählte Urkunden*, pp. 20-22.

within their dominions, even by the Emperor. The hundreds-men [*centumgravii*] were to act in their name, and no new money was to be struck in any prince's land that could reduce the currency of his local mintage. The towns and the lesser estates were to be depressed in their favour. The cities were not to exercise jurisdiction outside the circuit of their walls, were not to entertain *Pfahlbürger*, or harbour fugitives or the vassals of any prince. It was a complete renunciation of the earlier policy of the Hohenstaufen. But though powerful in securing the territorial supremacy of the princes, Frederick's law had little effect in checking the growth of municipal autonomy. The greater cities were already getting rid of their episcopal or baronial lords, and Frederick was quite unable to check the flowing tide.

In his shiftless way Henry tried to pose as the champion of the towns and the lesser nobility, that was gradually evolving out of the ancient official class, against the great feudalists whom his father so obstinately favoured. Since Frederick wished to remain for the moment on good terms with the Church, Henry ostentatiously took up an anti-clerical attitude. He had favoured the savage persecntions of heresy which Frederick had allowed Franciscan and Dominican inquisitors to carry out in Germany as well as in Italy (see also chapter xviii.). Conspicuous among them was the Franciscan, Conrad of Marburg, who wandered ' preaching and teaching' all over Germany until 1233, when he was assassinated. Henry now sought to end the persecution which he had once favoured. But in 1234 a regular crusade was fought against the Stedinger of the mouths of the Weser, who had refused to pay their tithes. They were easily defeated, and those who escaped massacre abandoned their homes and took shelter in Friesland.

Henry's relations with Frederick had long been strained. In 1232 he visited his father in Friuli, and was forced to renew his oaths of obedience. But his blunders and follies crowned all his enterprises with failure, and, after his father had been forced to disavow all responsibility for his rash deeds, the young king strove to unite the towns and the lesser

Revolt and Ruin of Henry, 1235. nobles in revolt against the Emperor (1234). In 1235 Frederick was compelled to appear in Germany, where he easily put down his son's rebellion. The cities adhered for the most part to the Emperor, and the 'ministeriales' and lesser nobles were not strong enough to stand alone. On the advice of the peace-loving Hermann of Salza, the young king made his submission to his father. His punishment was perpetual imprisonment in Apulia. In 1242, wearied with the restraint, he rode his horse over a precipice, and perished.

Never was Frederick's power so strongly manifested as during his visit to Germany in 1235. In the summer he celebrated

The Diet of Mainz and the English marriage, 1235. at Worms his third marriage, with Isabella of England, the sister of Henry III., and soon afterwards held a numerously attended Diet at Mainz, where he published a series of famous constitutions, in some of which he sought to extend to Germany some of the principles that had for so long inspired his Sicilian policy. He established a court justiciar [*justiciarius curiæ*], who was to hold sessions of his court on all lawful days, hearing all causes save the high matters which the Emperor reserved for himself. This class included all the questions of dispute that might arise between the great vassals. Frederick strove to limit private war to cases where justice should be denied, and to raise up beside the courts of the princes the imperial court which he had thus reorganised. But at the same time he renewed the former privileges granted to the princes, and thus made his reforms of no effect. The feudal magnates were still to exercise every regalian right, the bishops were still to keep a tight hold over their see towns, and the free municipalities were still to renounce the protection of their 'Pfahlbürger,' and see their independence circumscribed by the local grandees. The lesser nobility soon succumbed before these blows, and the future of Germany was thus intrusted to the great feudatories. A good illustration of this is the circumstance that the ancient power of electing the kings passed away from the general assembly of the barons to the limited circle of magnates, who were later known as the seven electors. In the same conciliatory spirit, those who had a hand in the revolt of King Henry were fully pardoned, and special concessions to the more powerful princes bound them individually to the imperial cause. Among these may be specially mentioned the re cognition of Otto of Lüneburg, the heir of the Guelfs, as Duke of the new duchy of Brunswick (see also page 331). Frederick's friendship with the Guelfs, following closely upon his alliance with England, clearly marks his departure from his ancestors' policy. Even the towns were conciliated by the renewal of their privileges. Only the Duke of Austria, the brother-in-law of Henry VII., still remained unappeased. He was proscribed in the diet of 1236 and his territories invaded. But the Duke resisted so vigorously that Frederick, who had before this returned to Italy, was forced once more to cross the Alps. Early in 1237 the Emperor entered Vienna in triumph, though even after this the stubborn duke held his own, and when peace was at last made in 1239, he secured the full restitution of his estates.

Frederick took with him to Vienna Conrad, his son by Isabella of Brienne, then a boy of nine. The assembled princes declared that the little Conrad was to be preferred to Henry, as David had been put in the place of Saul. He was elected King of the Romans, and on Frederick's speedy return to Italy, the government of Germany was, for a second time, carried on in the name of a boy-king. The troubles that had disturbed the reign of Henry were now quickly renewed.

Conrad, King of the Romans, 1237.

Notwithstanding the rapid diminution of the royal power, the age of Frederick II. is one of no small moment in the development of German civilisation, though little of the credit

for it can be set down to the absentee and incurious Emperor.
But in truth the removal of the imperial authority was not
all loss. It had never been sufficient of a reality

**German
Civilisation
under
Frederick II.**

to secure for all Germany permanent peace, and
even in the days of the strongest of German
kings much of the merit of upholding order and
civilisation had belonged to the local potentates. Their complete recognition and the full legalisation of their power now
substituted a large number of small local centres of authority
for the one unifying power of the old German king. German
unity suffered, but national unity was a far-off ideal in Northern
Europe in the thirteenth century. The great development of
trade, wealth, law, literature, and civilisation showed that
Germany was far from being an absolute loser by the change
of system. Unluckily the power of these lesser rulers did not,
as in France, prepare the way for a strong monarchy when
the time grew ripe for a single government. Germany paid
the penalty for her premature unity under her early kings by
her inability to set up a national authority when national states
became possible.

Despite the hostility of emperor and princes, the towns
more than held their own. Great changes were coming over
the commercial relations of Europe. The volume

**Commerce
and the
Towns.**

of trade was much greater, and now flowed in
channels which gave Germany a larger share
of the world's traffic. The rich products of the East now
came from Venice over the Brenner, and either went down
the Lech to Augsburg and Nürnberg or descended the Rhine
to marts like Cologne, where the traders of the north and
south met together, and the cloth of Flanders or the wool of
England, and the wood, iron, and coarse products of the
Baltic were bartered for the more costly articles of luxury
that had come over the Alps. Safe behind their strong walls,
the citizens could hold their own against prince or emperor,
while their interest in the maintenance of the public peace
and the safety of the roads and waterways attracted them to

the side of any powerful and peace-loving ruler. A few strong princes could keep better order than a mass of robber-nobles levying endless tolls and exactions on all goods passing through their territories. Even before the fall of the Hohenstaufen the towns had not only escaped the direct rule of the Emperor, but had gradually withdrawn themselves from the authority of the neighbouring lords. The extension of the German race and power to the East opened up for them new avenues for trade.

The development of local authorities was marked by the growth of local codes of laws. The earliest code of German customary law, the *Sachsenspiegel*, was drawn up before the fall of Henry VII., and prepared the Law. way for a series of similar collections of customs in the second half of the thirteenth century. The towns followed the same process, and it became the ideal of each community to attain the laws which a more ancient and better established community already enjoyed. For the East the customs of Magdeburg, for the North the laws of Lübeck, which themselves were derived from those of Soest in Westphalia, became the model on which the newer towns based their constitutions.

Literature followed the direction of politics and law. The use of the vernacular tongue spread as, side by side with the Latinised culture of the clergy and the popular epics that had flourished at least since Barbarossa's Literature. days, the lay nobles and knights developed a literary medium of their own. The early part of the thirteenth century was the great period of the Minnesinger, the knightly The Minnepoets of love, whose polished and spontaneous singer lyrics, inspired by the Troubadours of the Langue and the d'oc, celebrated chivalrous devotion to beauty and Romancers. romantic affection in terms that showed how far society had outgrown the rudeness of the Dark Ages. Side by side with them was the great school of romancers, influenced by North-French models, who told to German ears the romances of

Charlemagne and Arthur. Lyrists like the Tyroler Walter von der Vogelweide, and epic poets like Wolfram of Eschenbach and Gottfried of Strassburg, found their best welcome at the courts of the more cultured princes, such as Frederick of Austria and, above all, Hermann of Thuringia, whose castle of the Wartburg, dominating his town of Eisenach, has an almost legendary celebrity in their history. Little as he was in their land, Frederick himself did not neglect to show his favour to the German poets. But the fact that the impulse that inspired so much of their work came from France showed that the Germany of the later Hohenstaufen was not only losing its primacy in politics, but failed even to gain the headship in thought and art. The German builders of Frederick's age continued to construct their churches on Romanesque lines, and the 'French style' of Gothic only came in very slowly and partially. The fact that Germany possessed no university indicated her subordinate position in the world of thought. Though one of the strongest of the thirteenth century scholastics, Albert the Great, was a German, more of his work was accomplished at Paris than at Cologne.

The extension of German influence over the North and East showed that the spirit of the great Saxon and Frankish Emperors continued to inspire the Germans of the thirteenth century. The triumph of St. Engelbert over Valdemar of Denmark had restored German hegemony over the Baltic lands. From it followed the commercial supremacy of Lübeck, the domination of the Margraves of Brandenburg over the Slavonic Dukes of Pomerania, and the extension of German influence beyond the Oder. The ancient strength of the Polish monarchy declined, and the Russian monarchy, which had been so powerful under Saint Vladimir and Iaroslav the Great, split up even more hopelessly than the more western Slavonic state. The only strong Slavonic power was Bohemia, which all through the thirteenth century increased greatly in importance under

Ottocar I. (1197-1230), Wenceslas III. (1230-1253), and Ottocar II. (1253-1278). But the Czech monarchs became so powerfully attracted by German civilisation that they welcomed German merchants, minstrels, priests, and knights, and were soon to profit by the growing weakness of the German power to put themselves among the mightiest of Teutonic states.

The decline of the Slavonic world left to itself the heathenism of the East Baltic lands. From the Gulf of Finland to the borders of Germany the savage and pagan Livonians, Esthonians, Lithuanians, and Prussians still lived their old fierce lives, and it was not till early in the thirteenth century that a pious missionary, named Christian, took up in earnest the long-interrupted work of St. Adalbert, and became the first bishop of the Prussians. A little before this Albert of Buxhöwden, a canon of Bremen, set up the bishopric of Riga, which became the centre of missionary effort among the heathen of Livonia. The result was that Germany had the credit of bringing religion and civilisation to the race that had escaped the nearer influence of Poles and Russians. In 1200 Bishop Albert of Riga established the order of Knights of the Sword, a military brotherhood of the crusading type, specially destined to subdue the heathens of the Livonian lands. More than twenty years later the Prussians pressed Poland so severely that the latter country had to call in German help. The Teutonic Order, engaged for nearly a hundred years in the Holy Land, had never obtained in that region the importance or the wealth of the Temple or the Hospital. Hermann of Salza, the friend of Frederick II., had convinced himself that the affairs of the Christians in Syria were desperate, and even before Frederick's crusade had shown his willingness to transfer his main activity against the Prussians. Frederick II. himself confirmed and enlarged the offers of the Polish duke, and from 1230 onwards the

The Livonian and Prussian Crusades.

The Knights of the Sword and the Teutonic Knights.

Teutonic Knights were busily engaged waging war in Prussia. Bit by bit the military monks overcame the obstinate resistance of the heathen. Even more arduous was the struggle of the Knights of the Sword in Livonia. But in both lands the discipline of the few finally prevailed over the disorderly heroism of the undisciplined barbarians. The two orders formed a close alliance, and before the end of the century Livonia, Curland, and Prussia were altogether in their power, leaving Lithuania alone as the last resting-place of heathenism in Central Europe. Thus was effected the last great expansion of Germany to the east. While the Knights of the Sword remained a limited conquering class, powerless to prevent the continuance of the native idiom and manners of their newly Christianised subjects, Prussia gradually became almost as much Germanised as Pomerania or Silesia. German traders followed the Teutonic warriors, and in both lands a German burgher class supplemented the work of the ruling aristocracy. Even in Poland German towns grew up everywhere. The Baltic bade fair to become a German lake, and the Scandinavian powers shrank back into insignificance and isolation.

While the German race was working its way to fresh destinies with little guidance from its nominal king, Frederick himself was again becoming embroiled in the troubles of Italian and ecclesiastical politics. Even in the quiet times that followed the Treaty of San Germano, the Lombard cities had watched with alarm the despotic and anti-municipal policy of the Emperor. So early as 1232 delegates from Lombardy renewed their league, which was soon to be extended by the inclusion of the chief towns of Romagna and the March. Other leagues grew up in Tuscany and Umbria. Soon Frederick's suspicions were excited, and his anger passed all bounds when the North-Italian cities formed a close alliance with the revolted King Henry, who found south of the Alps the civic support that he had sought in

Marginal note: Breach between Frederick and the Lombard Cities, 1235.

vain to procure in Germany. Frederick at once strove to set up some power antagonistic to the League. Faithful in North Italy to his German policy, he saw in the feudal aristocracy his best immediate support. Even under the shadows of the Alps the Italian barons had not the strength and commanding position of the Teutonic feudalists. But some of the more capable barons were able to extend their authority by exercising influence over the cities, and chief among these was the ancient house of Romano, German in its origin, and now represented by the two brothers Eccelin and Alberic, who had established themselves in Verona and Vicenza respectively. It was upon this bastard feudalism of Italy, that owed half its importance to its capacity for establishing civic tyranny, that Frederick henceforth chiefly relied. It was a policy even more fatal to him than his alliance with the princes in Germany. But for the moment it attained an equal success. After all, feudal ruffians like Eccelin were better fighters than the ill-trained militia of the Lombard cities.

In 1236 Frederick was back in Italy, and found a ready welcome from Eccelin da Romano, who now aspired to appropriate the whole region between the Alps and the Adige, and soon made himself lord of Padua and Treviso. Recalled over the mountains by the Austrian troubles, Frederick again appeared in Italy in 1237. But a small portion of his army came from Germany. He relied for the most part on the Ghibelline barons of Italy, on Eccelin and his following, and on his trusty Saracens from Lucera. The Lombard League sought in vain to withstand his progress. Frederick's clever strategy soon outgeneralled the civic host, and on 27th November 1237 the whole army of the League was signally defeated at Cortenuova, half-way between Brescia and Milan. Taken at a disadvantage, the valour of the citizens was powerless to withstand the skill and discipline of the imperial army. The Milanese abandoned their *carroccio* in their flight, and their Podestâ, the Venetian

Battle of Cortenuova, 27th Nov. 1237.

Tiepolo, fell into the victor's hand?. Frederick celebrated his success by a sort of Roman triumph through the streets of Cremona, where his famous elephant, with its Saracen drivers on its back, dragged the captured *carroccio* of Milan through the town, with the Podestâ Tiepolo tightly bound to its standard-pole. Soon after, Frederick married his daughter to Eccelin, and granted the dominion of Sardinia to his bastard son Enzio, who had wedded the heiress of the island. The majority of the cities desisted from the hopeless struggle and made peace with the victor. Only a few irreconcilable Guelfic strongholds, including Milan, Alessandria, Brescia, Piacenza, and Bologna, persisted in withstanding the Emperor. They could again hope for the support of the Pope, who now thought the time was ripe for breaking with the Emperor.

During the years of peace Gregory IX. had busied himself with the suppression of heresy, the organisation of the Inquisition, the encouragement of the new orders of Mendicant Friars [see Chapter XVIII.], the rekindling of the religious zeal of Europe, and his great work of ecclesiastical legislation. In his war against the heretics he had, as we have seen, the Emperor no less than the Mendicants as his allies. He firmly identified the Papacy with the new religious movement when he canonised Francis and Dominic and the Emperor's kinswoman, St. Elizabeth of Thuringia, the devoted disciple of Conrad of Marburg. With the help of his penitentiary, Raymond of Pennaforte, he collected the constitutions and decretals of earlier Popes in an official code of five books, which was invested with exclusive authority in the courts and the law-schools. Henceforth the Decretals of Gregory IX. stood side by side with the Decretum of Gratian itself among the authoritative texts of the Canon Law. It was, in a measure, an answer to the antagonistic legislation of Frederick in Sicily. But all Gregory's efforts could do little to stop the progress of the Emperor, and he was further hampered by the constant turbulence of the Romans, who

Gregory IX. as legislator and religious leader.

more than once drove him from their city. After the triumph at Cremona, Frederick significantly sent the Milanese *carroccio* to the Roman enemies of the Pope. Gregory's turn would come when the last of the Lombard cities had been reduced. Frederick was already boasting of his intention to restore Middle Italy to its obedience to the Empire. Accordingly Gregory openly declared himself on the side of the Lombard League. Hermann of Salza made his last efforts on behalf of peace, but his death soon removed the one man whom both Pope and Emperor implicitly trusted. In March 1239 Gregory for a second time launched a bull of excommunication against Frederick, and absolved his subjects from their allegiance.

Renewed breach between Gregory and Frederick, 1239.

The new contest between Pope and Emperor was waged with extraordinary and almost unprecedented bitterness and violence. The Emperor reproached the Pope for standing in the way of the repression of heresy in Lombardy, and called upon all kings and princes to unite against the greedy and self-seeking priest who sought to make the humiliation of the Roman Cæsar the first step towards the abasement of all temporal authority. The Pope answered by accusing Frederick of the most outspoken blasphemy, of utter incredulity, and the most shameless profligacy. It was significant that both Frederick and Gregory strove hard to get public opinion on their side, and that neither failed to win over a body of ardent supporters.

Gregory did his best to stir up a revolt in Germany. His legate proposed the election of the King of Denmark, as King of the Romans in place of Conrad; but, despite the adherence of the Duke of Austria and of other discontented magnates, the scheme was shattered through the steady devotion of the German episcopate to the young king. It was equally in vain when Gregory offered the crown to Robert of Artois, St. Louis' brother. The French nobles roundly told the Pope that even if the Emperor deserved deposition, his

Collapse of the German opposition.

deprivation could only be effected by a General Council. Headed by the regent, Siegfried, Archbishop of Mainz, the German clergy rejected the alliance of the Papacy, so that Frederick was able to carry on his war against Gregory in Italy without the distraction of a German revolt. Even the Mendicant preachers of the papal sentence did little to turn German opinion away from the Emperor.

Frederick answered Gregory's attacks by declaring the incorporation of the March of Ancona and the Duchy of Spoleto with the imperial dominions, and by absolving the inhabitants of those regions from their fealty to the Pope. He turned from his Lombard enemies to invade the papal territory, and made himself master of Ravenna and Faenza, and before long of towns so near Rome as Foligno and Viterbo. Nothing but a strange freak of fidelity on the part of the Romans to Gregory saved the holy city from the Emperor's advance. Secure for the moment in his capital, Gregory strove to emphasise the solemnity of his ecclesiastical censures by summoning a Council to Rome, to join with him in the condemnation of the Emperor. But the Pope's violence had alienated even clerical opinion, and a mere handful of prelates answered his summons. Frederick derided the packed Council, and refused safe-conducts to those wishful to take part in it. Nevertheless a certain number of North-Italian, French, and Spanish bishops and abbots collected together in the spring of 1241 at Genoa, and the Pope, by lavish payments, prevailed on the Genoese to provide a fleet to take them to Rome. However, the seafaring towns, with Pisa at their head, were all on the Emperor's side, and an imperial fleet, superior in numbers and fighting capacity, bore down upon the densely packed Genoese galleys near the island of Giglio. After a show of resistance, the mass of the Genoese fleet was captured. Most of the Spanish prelates escaped, but a crowd of French and North-Italian ecclesiastics, including three archbishops and the abbots of Cluny,

Frederick's successes in Italy.

Citeaux, and Clairvaux fell, with the delegates of the Lombard towns, into the hands of the imperialists. The prisoners were taken by Enzio to Naples, 'crowded together in oppression and bonds, and tormented by hunger and thirst,' until the prison wherein they were cast, 'heaped together like pigs,' seemed a 'welcome place of rest.'[1] Flushed with this signal triumph, Frederick once more advanced upon Rome. This time Gregory could not resist his progress. The enemy were at the gates when, on 21st August, the aged Pontiff suddenly ended his long and stormy career.

The capture of a General Council, 1241.

When the rival heads of Christendom were thus fiercely contending for supremacy, Europe was, for the first time since the tenth century, menaced with the horrors of barbarian invasion. The great Tartar Empire, which had already conquered China and threatened the whole Eastern world, now found an easy victim in the divided principalities of Russia, and poured its hordes of fierce warriors over the plains of Poland and Hungary. Germany itself was now threatened by their advance, but Pope and Emperor, though they reproached each other with indifference to the danger, were unable to make even a truce to resist the common enemy. In 1240 the sack of Kiev by the Mongol chieftain Baty, grandson of Genghiz Khan, led directly to the invasion of the West. The young King Conrad armed Germany to meet the savage hosts of Baty. Luckily for Europe the death of the Khan of All the Tartars called Baty back to Asia, and the alarm of the Mongol fury passed away as quickly as it arose.

The Danger from the Tartars.

The triumph of Frederick was further assured by Gregory's death. With affected moderation Frederick withdrew for the moment to Naples, but a mere handful of cardinals ventured to assemble in conclave. Their choice fell upon Celestine IV.,

---

[1] A good account of this 'Capture of a General Council' is given by Mr. G. C. Macaulay in the *English Historical Review*, vol. vi. (1891), pp. 1-17.

who died in a few weeks, before there was time to consecrate him. For more than eighteen months the Holy See now remained vacant, but finally, in June 1243, the cardinals agreed to elect Sinobaldo Fiesco, a Genoese cardinal, who had been professor of law at Bologna, and was reputed to be Ghibelline in his sympathies. But as Pope Innocent IV., the imperialist lawyer showed from the first a stern determination to continue the policy of Gregory IX. The saying attributed to Frederick, 'I have lost a good friend, for no Pope can be a Ghibelline,' though probably never uttered, expressed the facts of the case. Some hollow negotiations for a pacification were entered upon, but soon broke down. Within a year of Innocent's election, Frederick's Saracen hordes were again ravaging the Campagna. In June 1244 Innocent fled from Rome to Genoa, whence he crossed the Alps and took up his abode in the free imperial city of Lyons. It shows the weakness of Frederick in the Arelate that Innocent was able to live in a town nominally subject to the Emperor as long as he chose. So safe did the Pope feel himself that he summoned to Lyons the General Council which, as Gregory IX. had already designed, should strengthen the papal condemnation of the Emperor by the ratification of the prelates of Christendom.

In June 1245 the Council assembled at Lyons. It was reckoned the thirteenth General Council, according to the Roman computation, but even the French refused to acknowledge it as such, and very few German prelates ventured to attend its sessions. However, a fair attendance of prelates was ensured, though the presence of a bishop like Grosseteste, who, five years later, remonstrated before the Pope's face against the exactions of his agents and his abuse of his patronage, showed that there was some spirit left among the fathers of the Council. Five troubles, declared Innocent, grieved his spirit, and the calling of the assembly was destined

[margin note: Innocent IV. and the continuation of the struggle, 1243-1250.]

[margin note: The Council of Lyons and the deposition of Frederick, 1245.]

to relieve Christendom from them. Its business was the protection of Christianity from the Tartars, the ending of the schism between the Eastern and Western Churches, the extirpation of heresy, the revival of the Crusades, and the condemnation of the Emperor. In practice the last item absorbed all the energy of the Council, though the presence of the fugitive Latin Emperor, Baldwin ii., did something to make the fathers realise the sorry plight of Eastern Catholicism and the need of uniting all sorts of Oriental Christians against the Tartars and Turks. Frederick condescended to send as his representative to the Council his chief justiciary, Thaddæus of Suessa, but his condemnation was a foregone conclusion, and Thaddæus had difficulty in obtaining a brief adjournment while he returned to Italy to acquaint his master with the state of affairs at Lyons. Without waiting for the arrival of Peter della Vigna, whom Frederick now despatched to represent him, Innocent on 17th July pronounced in the name of the Council the deposition of his enemy, both as regards the Empire and his two kingdoms. 'We order,' added he, 'those who have the right of election within the Empire to proceed at once to a fresh election. As regards Sicily, we ourselves will do all that is fitting, after taking the advice of our brethren the cardinals.'

The last hope of Christendom lay in the mediation of Louis ix., who saw that the continued contest of Pope and Emperor was fatal to the prospects of a great Crusade. The French king met Innocent at Cluny, and Frederick offered to allow the archbishop of Palermo to thoroughly investigate his orthodoxy. *Henry Raspe and William of Holland, anti-kings.* But nothing came of these projects, and the blame of rejecting all compromise lay mainly at the door of the Pope. The spiritual benefits first awarded to those who had assumed the Cross to free the Holy Sepulchre were now offered to all who would take up arms to carry out the Lyons sentence against the Emperor. In 1246 the papal intrigues so far prevailed in Germany that four archbishops, a considerable number of bishops, and a few temporal princes met together and elected as King of the Romans Henry Raspe, Landgrave of Thur- ingia, the brother-in-law and persecutor of St. Elizabeth. The majority of the Germans remained true to Frederick, though enough Crusaders flocked to Henry's standard to enable him to win a victory over his rival King Conrad, near Frankfurt. 'He shows us his back and not his face,' boasted Henry over his defeated enemy. 'He fled as men are wont to fly who fight with the Holy Empire.' But next year Conrad turned the tables on Henry, who fled home and died soon afterwards in the Wartburg. The imperial crown now went begging for a time. 'I will willingly fight the enemies of the Church,' declared King Haco of Norway, to whom it was offered, 'but I will not fight against the foes of the Pope.' At last the young William, Count of Holland, was persuaded to accept election by the papalists. But only one lay prince, the Duke of Brabant, William's uncle, associated himself with the bishops who assembled for the choosing of the new monarch. For the rest of Frederick's life a fierce fight was fought between William and Conrad. Neither of the two could succeed in crushing the other, and Germany gradually drifted into all the worst horrors of feudal anarchy.

Frederick remained in Italy, struggling with all his might against the papal partisans, and holding his own so far that

Frederick's visions of a lay Papacy and of an Ecclesiasti- cal Revolu- tion.

Innocent found it wise to remain at Lyons. Now that all possibility of reconciliation with the Church was cut off, Frederick threw prudence to the winds. He no longer scrupled against solicit- ing the help of the heretical Cathari that still swarmed all over Lombardy. Visions of power such as he had never imagined in the days of his success now began to flit before his mind. The apocalyptic visions of the Neapolitan seer, the abbot Joachim, began to weigh upon his mystical temperament. Despite the canonisation of Francis of Assisi and the enrolment of his followers under the banners of the Papacy, there was still an undercurrent of revolutionary religious feeling in Italy of the sort that afterwards found expression in the risings of the Fraticelli. Of this opinion Frederick now began to make himself the mouthpiece, hoping thus to be revenged upon his enemies, and to win for himself that first position in the world to which he conceived he was divinely called. He had long used the Franciscan doctrine of Poverty as a weapon against the greedy political Popes. 'It is upon poverty and simplicity,' he wrote in 1227, 'that the Primitive Church was built, in those days when she was the fruitful mother of saints. No one may presume to lay other foundations for her than those appointed by the Lord Jesus.' He now worked out the same idea in a manifesto addressed to all Christian princes. 'God is our witness,' he declared, 'that our intention has always been to force churchmen to follow in the footsteps of the Primitive Church, to live an apostolic life, and to be humble like Jesus Christ. In our days the Church has become worldly. We therefore propose to do a work of charity in taking away from such men the treasures with which they are filled for their eternal damnation.' 'Help us,' he wrote later, 'to put down these proud prelates, that we may give mother Church more worthy guides to direct her.' But his only conception of ecclesiastical reform was the absorption of the Church in the State. Even in their affliction the Orthodox princes of the East seemed to him fortunate, since they had no Pope or independent patriarchs to contend against. He now strove to exclude all papal authority from Naples by condemning to the flames the introducers of papal bulls and all who, under pretext of religion, spoke or acted against his authority. He anticipated Henry VIII. in his effort to abolish the papal power, and, like the great Tudor, condemned as traitors or heretics all who denied his absolute supremacy over the Church. More than that, Frederick proclaimed himself as worthy of the adoration of his subjects, like the pagan Emperors of old. He claimed to be a vicar of Christ, a lay pope, a Christian caliph—nay,

an emanation of the Divinity.   Jesi, his birth-place, was the
blessed Bethlehem where Cæsar first saw the light, and Peter
della Vigna was the apostle of the imperial Messiah, the Peter
who would never betray his master.

The contest was fought out fiercely with sword and fire.
The Guelf and Ghibelline towns were pillaging, burning and

The Italian struggle, 1245-1250. destroying each other. Enzio, the son, and Eccelin,
the son-in-law of Cæsar, strove to stamp out in
blood all Guelfic resistance in Northern Italy.
Frederick of Antioch, another bastard of Frederick's, worked a
similar reign of terror in Tuscany.   So well did Frederick's fortunes go, that he dreamt of crossing the Alps and marching to
Lyons.   In 1247 he was turned from his bold purpose by the
unexpected revolt of Parma.   He hurried back from Turin
eager for revenge.   Before long the dispersed partisans of

The Revolt of Parma. Pope and Emperor flocked to Parma, eager to
defend or attack the city.   With all his energy,
Frederick could only blockade it on one side, and neither
dearth of provisions nor the hideous cruelty of the Emperor
moved the Parmesans to think of surrender.   At last in
despair Frederick built over against Parma a new city called
Vittoria, devastating the whole Parmesan territory to supply
it with building materials and fortifications.   But in 1248 the
Parmesans made a great sally, won an unexpected victory,
slaying the faithful Thaddæus of Suessa, destroying utterly
Frederick's new city, and leading home spoil the *carroccio* of
imperialist Cremona and the whole harem of the Emperor,
that had been unable to keep up with his rapid flight.

Everything now went against Frederick.   Despite the reign
of terror exercised in the South, plots and conspiracies multiplied, and the Apulian barons rose in revolt.

Fall of Peter della Vigna and captivity of Enzio, 1247. The blind rage of the suspicious despot now fell
on Peter della Vigna, his trusted confidant, who
had long kept, as Dante says, the two keys of
Frederick's heart.   He was arrested on charges of
conspiring with the Pope to murder his master.   His eyes

were cruelly torn out, and he sought his own death to avoid further torture. In 1249 Frederick's favourite son Enzio was defeated and taken prisoner by the Bolognese at Fossalta, and spent the rest of his life in hopeless captivity. But Frederick was not yet at the end of his resources. In 1250 fortune smiled once more on his cause. The Ghibellines of Lombardy at last won the upper hand. Good news came from beyond the Alps of Conrad's triumphs over William of Holland. Frederick himself spent most of the year at Foggia, surrounded by his faithful Saracens, in whom he still placed his chief trust. Towards the end of the year he started once more for the north, but he was seized with a mortal illness before he had traversed many stages. He took to his bed at Fiorentino, a hunting lodge a few miles short of Lucera. An ancient prediction of his astrologers that he would die near iron gates at a town called Flora further troubled his spirit. 'This is the spot,' he said, 'long ago foretold to me where I must die. The will of God be done.' He calmly drew up a will, bequeathing to Conrad both the Empire and the kingdom, while his favourite bastard, Manfred, who carefully ministered to his last hours, was to act as his regent in his brother's absence. On 19th December he died, either, as his friends believed, calmly and religiously, clad in the white robe of the Cistercians and reconciled to the Church by the Archbishop of Palermo, or a prey to hideous despair and misery, as the Friars his enemies loved to imagine. He was buried beside his Norman ancestors at Palermo, where his tomb may still be seen. With him expired the Roman Empire as a real claimant to any share of the rule of the world, though for another generation faction raged more fiercely than ever as to the disposal of its heritage. The Papacy had at last triumphed over the Empire. The *sacerdotium* had laid low the *regnum*, and all that remains of the history of the world-strife of Pope and Emperor is to write its epilogue. But the mystic followers of the abbot Joachim could not believe that their hero, the all-powerful Emperor,

Death of Frederick, 1250.

him travelled slowly to the realisation of a brighter future, we shall not think Dante wrong when he puts the golden age of Italy in the time ere Frederick had been hounded to death by his remorseless enemies.

CHAPTER XVII

FRANCE UNDER PHILIP AUGUSTUS AND ST. LOUIS
(1180-1270)[1]

Home Policy of Philip Augustus—The Fall of the Angevins and the Conquest of Normandy and Anjou – The Albigensian Crusade—The establishment of Simon of Montfort in Toulouse, and the Reaction under Raymond VII.—The Relations of Philip and his People—Paris—Administrative Reforms—Death and Character of Philip—Reign of Louis VIII.—The Conquest of Poitou and the Renewal of the Albigensian Crusade—The Regency of Blanche of Castille and the Feudal Reaction—The Treaty of Meaux—Character of St. Louis—His Personal Government—The Settlement of the South and West—Battle of Saintes and Treaty of Lorris—Alfonse in Poitou and Toulouse—Charles in Anjou and Provence—Foreign Policy of St. Louis—His Relations to Pope and Emperor—France the Chief Power of Europe—Home Policy of St. Louis—The Administrative System—Baillages and Sénéchaussées—Enquesteurs—The Parliament of Paris—Finance, Coinage, Trade, Towns—Last Years and Death of St. Louis—The Position of France.

WE have already dealt with the external history of France up to the time of the battle of Bouvines. We have witnessed Philip Augustus' early struggles with Henry of Anjou, his participation in the Third Crusade, his matrimonial difficulties, the struggle they involved him in with Innocent III., and

[1] Delisle's *Catalogue des Actes de Philippe Auguste* and Hutton's *Philip Augustus* cover the early part of this period. For the fall of John, see Bémont's *Condamnation de Jean Sans Terre*, in *Revue Historique*, xxxii., 33-74, 290-311. For the Albigensian Crusade, see Peyrat's *Histoire des Albigeois*, and Douai's *Les Albigeois*, and Lea's *History of the Inquisition in the Middle Ages*. For the reign of Louis VIII., the best work is Petit-Dutaillis' *Règne de Louis VIII.*, in the Bibliothèque de l'école des hautes Études. For St. Louis, Wallon's *Histoire de Saint Louis* is a useful but not an original summary. Joinville's contemporary *Vie de*

the subsequent league between himself and the great Pope which contributed so powerfully towards the abasement of the Guelfs. It remains now to speak of Philip Augustus' reign as affecting France itself, and to show how, by the defeat and disruption of the Angevin monarchy, the royal domain was enormously extended, how by the identification of the monarchical cause with the orthodox Crusade against the Albigensian heretics the way was paved for the subjection of the Langue d'oc to the Langue d'oil, and how the beginnings of the centralised administration of the monarchy, and the establishment of the first modern capital, increased the power of the French state, even more than Philip's conquests increased the extent of its dominions. Under Philip's son, Louis VIII., and his grandson, Louis IX., the same principles of external growth and internal organisation were still further worked out, so that when the collapse of Frederick II. left vacant the hegemony of Europe, the France of St. Louis was more than ready to step into the place left empty by the fall of the Hohenstaufen.

Home policy of Philip Augustus, 1180-1223.

With the return of Philip II. from the Crusade, the interrupted struggle between France and the Angevin monarchy was at once resumed. Despite the advantages which the blundering knight-errantry of Richard I. offered to his more politic antagonist, Philip was not yet in a sufficiently strong position to reap much fruit from his enemy's mistakes. Richard's new castle of Chateau Gaillard blocked the way to the invasion of Normandy, and the South was still a strange region to the King of Paris. In

The Fall of the Angevins.

Saint Louis should above all be studied. Boutaric's *Saint Louis et Alfonse de Poitiers*, the essay in vol. vii. of the *Nouvelle histoire de Languedoc*, and Sternfeld's *Karl von Anjou als Graf von Provence* show well the process of the Southward expansion of France. For Louis' relations to the Papacy consult Berger's *Saint-Louis et Innocent IV*. See also Lecoy de la Marche's *Saint Louis sa famille et sa cour* in *Revue des questions historiques*, t. xxiv., and Beugnot's *Essai sur les constitutions de Saint Louis*. Ch. V. Langlois' *Règne de Philippe le Hardi* gives an admirable summary of the state of France as it was left at St. Louis' death.

1199 Richard perished in an obscure contest with a petty lord of the Limousin, and Philip at once swooped down on Evreux and conquered it with little difficulty. But very soon Philip's quarrel with Innocent III. made him glad to accept the proposals of John's mother, the aged Eleanor of Aquitaine, to revert to his ancient alliance with John. A treaty was signed by which Philip's son Louis was married to Blanche of Castile, the daughter of King Alfonso VIII. and John's sister Eleanor. Evreux, with Philip's other Norman conquests, were made over to the bridegroom as the lady's marriage portion. Before long, however, the wilful and capricious tyranny of John created a widespread discontent in his French dominions, of which Philip was skilful enough to avail himself to the full. No sooner had the French monarch made a partial peace with the Pope than he listened to the complaints of the barons of Poitou, headed by the indignant Hugh of Lusignan, Count of La Marche, whose betrothed, Isabella, the heiress of Angoulême, had been carried off from him and wedded to the English King. In 1202 Philip summoned John to answer before his suzerain's court at Paris the complaints of the Poitevin lords. The English King refused to appear, and was sentenced in default to lose all his French fiefs. The murder of Arthur of Brittany still further increased the ill-will felt against John, and the death of Eleanor of Aquitaine soon afterwards deprived him of his wisest counsellor. In the course of 1203-4 Philip gradually conquered all Normandy, and the Norman barons, disgusted at John's inactivity in defending them, were gradually alienated from his side. Anjou, Touraine, and Maine were won with even less difficulty. After Arthur's death, Brittany passed over from the Angevin to the Capetian obedience, and, after a brief period of French occupation, a new line of Breton began in 1213 with Peter Mauclerc, which, if not very faithful to France, at least acknowledged no other overlord. After Eleanor's death the personal loyalty of Aquitaine to the house of the

The conquest of Normandy, Anjou, and Poitou.

Guilhems was greatly relaxed, and before 1213 most of Poitou had passed over to Philip Augustus. It was John's wish to win back Poitou that led him to interfere actively in the general European struggle that centred round the contest between his nephew Otto and Frederick of Sicily. The victory of Bouvines assured for Philip the permanent domination over Normandy, Maine, Anjou, Touraine, and Poitou. Only the south of Aquitaine remained in the hands of John and his successors. These enormous additions to the monarchy were, for the most part, kept within the royal domain. Their acquisition was the more significant because of the rapidity with which the barons and people of the Angevin dominions accepted the rule of the King of France. Even in England Philip's triumph produced so little irritation that the opposition to John cheerfully called in his son Louis to be their king in the place of the hated tyrant.[1] Though, after John's death, Louis was forced in 1217 to return to France and renounce his English

Louis in England. 1215-1217. throne in favour of the little Henry III., his presence in England, and the long war that preceded and attended it, made impossible any real efforts to win back the Angevin inheritance. The fall of the English power in France first made possible a real French nation united in common obedience to the Capetian monarchs. It was no less vital in fostering a similar national life beyond the Channel. Henceforth England and France were separate and antagonistic though closely inter-related nationalities. Their common destiny, which had begun with the Norman Conquest, was now rudely shattered. The fragments of the Aquitanian heritage that still remained faithful to its English dukes belonged to the feudal and anti-monarchical South. All that England's kings had once ruled in the Langue d'oil was now transferred to Philip, who became henceforward not only the supreme monarch, but the direct feudal lord of the most vigorous and most patriotic regions that constituted his kingdom.

---

1 Petit-Dutaillis' *Louis VIII.*, pp. 30-183, gives by far the best account of this expedition.

While Philip was thus conquering the Angevin North, a North-French Crusade was indirectly preparing the way for the direct rule of the Capetian kings over the South. Philip II. There had long been three chief political and intel- and the lectual centres of South-French nationality. Two South. of these, the duchy of Aquitaine and the county of Toulouse [see pp. 90-91], were within the limits of the French kingdom. The third, the county of Provence, was beyond the Rhone, and, as a part of the ancient Arelate, subject to none save the Emperor. It was, however, a sufficiently representative stronghold of Southern ideas for the term Provençal to be used as an equivalent to the tongue and literature of Oc. At these three courts chiefly flourished the subtle and exquisite literature of the Troubadours, whose delicate lyrics first showed the literary capacity of the vernacular Romance tongues, despite the limitations of their subjects, and the rigid fetters of their metric forms. The end of the twelfth century, the age of Richard the Lion Heart, of Bertrand of The Albi- Born, and of Bernard of Ventadour, was the gensian and Heresy palmiest time in the history of the Troubadours, the Trouba- and the most flourishing period of the brilliant, dours. corrupt, stormy, attractive civilisation of the Languedoc. The heresy, at once social and religious, of the Albigenses [see pp. 216-217], took a deep hold in these wild regions, where the fiercest acts of feudal violence and the hot-house growth of a premature culture stood over-against each other in the strangest contrast. While elsewhere the wild misbelief of the twelfth century easily melted away before the steady influence of the Church, in Languedoc and Provence alone it bade fair to become the faith of a whole people. Toulouse and its neighbourhood were full of open foes of Church and clergy; the barons of the land were either heretics themselves, or favourers of heresy. The clergy were so unpopular that when they went abroad they carefully concealed their tonsure. 'I had rather be a chaplain,' became a popular form of speech in cases where a good Christian had been wont to say, 'I had rather be a Jew.' 'If Black Monks,' wrote the poet Peire Cardinal, 'may win salvation of God by much eating and by the keeping of women, White Monks by fraud, Templars and Hospitallers by pride, Canons by lending money on usury, then for fools I hold St. Peter and St. Andrew, who suffered for God such grievous torments. Kings, emperors, counts, and knights were wont to rule the world, but now I see clerks holding dominion over it by robbery, deceit, hypocrisy, force, and exhortation.'[1] The freebooting barons took this state of feeling as an excuse for laying violent hands on the property of the Church. Moral excesses, wilder than the ordinary immorality of a brutal age, became widespread. The whole land was filled with the tumult and licence of a premature revolution.

Since the absorption of Aquitaine within the Angevin dominions, the court of Toulouse had become more important Raymond VI. than ever as a centre of Languedocian life. of Toulouse. Raymond VI., the great-grandson of Raymond IV., of Saint Gilles, the hero of the First Crusade, was then Count of Toulouse. He was a prince of wide connections, extensive dominions, and considerable personal capacity. Through his mother, Constance, daughter of Louis VI., he was the first cousin of Philip Augustus. His marriage with Joan of Anjou, the sister of Richard I. and John, had secured him peace with his hereditary foe. He ruled not only over Toulouse and its dependencies; as Duke of Narbonne he was lord of the Rouergue and the great coast region that extended from the frontiers of Roussillon to the right bank of the Rhone; as Marquis of Provence, he ruled over a fertile portion of the Arelate on the left bank of the Rhone, extending farther north than Valence, and including the important town of Avignon. He was a notorious enemy of the clergy, and abettor of heretics, and only less conspicuous in the same policy was

[1] Miss Ida Farnell's _Lives of the Troubadours, Translated from the Provençal, with Specimens of their Poetry_, give this (p. 222) and many other interesting illustrations of thirteenth-century Provençal feeling.

his vassal Raymond Roger, Viscount of Béziers. Feeble efforts had long been made by the Church to grapple with the growing heresy, but the only response in Languedoc was fresh murders of priests, and expulsions of bishops from their dioceses, and of abbots from their monasteries. So far back as 1184 Lucius III. had ordered all bishops to make inquiries as to the presence of heretics within their jurisdictions, a step from which the earlier or Episcopal Inquisition first arose. But little was actually effected until the accession of Innocent III. marked the beginning of a more vigorous line of action. In 1198 two Cistercian monks were sent with the position of apostolic legates to win back the Toulousan heretics to the Church. For years they laboured incessantly, wandering and preaching throughout the land, and their unwearied zeal soon led a small band of enthusiasts to join them in their work. Innocent gave further powers to Peter of Castelnau, and Amaury, abbot of Citeaux. In 1206 accident further associated with them the Spanish canon Dominic (see chapter xviii.), who for ten long years preached with infinite perseverance, but little success, and carefully kept himself free from share in the violent measures that ere long supplemented the legitimate propaganda of orthodoxy.

Peaceful means had availed little to win over the Albigenses. Accident rather than design led Innocent III. to fall back on force as well as persuasion. In 1207 Peter of Castelnau excommunicated Raymond VI. for refusing to restore certain churches on which he had laid violent hands. Like his father-in-law *Murder of Peter of Castelnau, 1207.* against Becket, Raymond spoke sharp words against the meddlesome priest, and one of his knights, taking him at his word, went to Saint-Gilles and murdered the legate in January 1208. This deed of blood was soon amply avenged. Innocent III. deposed Raymond and preached a Crusade against him and his heretic subjects, whom he pronounced worse than Saracens. A twenty years' struggle then began in the South, which did not end until

Languedoc lay ruined and helpless at the mercy of the North.

A swarm of North French warriors took the cross in obedience to the papal appeal, though Philip Augustus prudently with-
The Albi-
gensian Cru-
sade and
Simon de
Montfort. held from the whole movement. Some of the greatest of his feudatories, including the Duke of Burgundy, were there, while among the lesser lords, the unbending will and fierce religious zeal of Simon, Count of Montfort, soon gave him the claim for the first position among the leaders of the holy war, though Abbot Amaury of Cîteaux, the Pope's legate, directed the policy of the whole expedition. Raymond quailed before the storm. He submitted himself absolutely to the legate, paid a severe penance for his crime before the abbey church of Saint-Gilles, surrendered his castles, and promised to chastise the heretics that he had favoured. In June 1209 he was absolved, and suffered to take the cross against his own subjects.

Raymond Roger of Béziers scorned to share in his over-lord's submission. The full fury of the Crusaders was turned against him, and after fearful bloodshed his dominions were overrun. After two refusals from greater lords, the legate prevailed upon Simon of Montfort to accept the territory of the heretic viscount, which the Pope had pronounced forfeited. The Crusaders now went home, and the second act of the long struggle began when Montfort began to govern the dominions which his good sword and papal favour had won for him.

After the return of the Northern armies, the cowed South-erners again plucked up courage, and Montfort soon found that he had to hold Béziers and Carcassonne against the hostility of a whole people. The war now assumed a political as well as a religious character, for Simon was resisted not only by reason of his orthodoxy, but as a Northern interloper who had made religious zeal a pretext for personal aggrandise-ment. Before long Raymond VI. forgot his humiliation, and

again took arms.   As the result, a second Crusade was proclaimed in 1211, and once more the South was deluged in
blood.   Peter II. of Aragon, a famous Crusader
beyond the Pyrenees, at last proposed his media-   *Peter of Aragon and*
tion, but so strongly did the lust for Southern   *the battle of Muret, 1213.*
estates sharpen the religious zeal of the army of
the Church that, though Innocent III. was willing to accept
his offers, the French themselves insisted on continuing the
Crusade.   Irritated at the rejection of his offer, Peter himself intervened on behalf of the Count of Toulouse, but in
1213 he lost his army and his life at the battle of Muret,
where Montfort's clever tactics won a decided victory.   This
settled the fate of the South.   Raymond VI. abandoned
Toulouse, and was glad to save his life by another abject
submission.   Simon de Montfort became Count
of Toulouse and Duke of Narbonne.   He divided   *Simon de Montfort, Count of Toulouse.*
his new territories amongst Northern lords who
stipulated to follow the ' customs of France,' that
is, of their own homes.   It was even a favour that some of
the less guilty vassals, such as the Counts of Foix and Com-
minges, were allowed, at the price of a complete humiliation,
to receive back their lands as his subjects.   As a still greater
favour a mere fragment of Toulouse and the imperial marquisate of Provence were conferred on Raymond VII., the son
of the deposed Count, who was glad to abdicate in his favour.
In the midst of the storms of war, the heresy of the Albigenses
was slowly stamped out, and with it perished all that was
most distinctive of Languedocian civilisation.   The stern,
brutal, effective rule of the Northern Count prepared the way
for direct royal government.   The dependence of the South
on the North had begun.

As the struggle proceeded, Philip Augustus gradually departed from his careful policy of non-intervention.   In 1213
he allowed his son Louis to take the cross, and helped
Montfort to destroy the feudal castles of the South.   Philip
himself willingly invested Simon with the fief which his sword

had won. But in a very few years Raymond VII. strove to win back for the house of Saint-Gilles its ancient position, and the Languedoc rose enthusiastically in his favour. The younger Raymond was as orthodox as Montfort, and under his influence the struggle became a mere political contest. As

The Languedocian reaction, Amaury de Montfort, and Raymond VII.

such it waged with varying fortunes for more than thirteen years. Simon was slain in 1218 as he strove to storm revolted Toulouse, and his eldest son, Amaury, who had few of his great gifts, was soon hard pressed by the triumphant Raymond. In 1219 Louis of France again led a Crusade in his favour. The death of the suspected Raymond VI. in 1222 was a further advantage to the Southern cause. Amaury soon saw that his chances were hopeless. When the French king died in 1223, Amaury had already offered to resign his claims in favour of his suzerain.

Thus Philip Augustus by force and cunning made France a great State. There was no longer any vassal of the crown whose power overshadowed that of his sovereign, and the strongest feudatories of the monarchy now found it prudent to be on good terms with their mighty overlord. To them Philip was courteous and friendly. He had so much work to do in absorbing his conquests that he might well leave

Philip II.'s dealings with barons, clergy, and towns.

his vassals a good deal to themselves. Yet he never neglected an opportunity for extending his power, and systematically strove to establish direct relations with all the tenants of his vassals whom he could draw within his reach. Over his own tenants he exercised a constant and watchful superintendence. By the perfection of the administration of his domains, and by the gradual extension of the sphere of the royal courts, he was able to pose as the protector of peace, the friend of the poor, and the champion of the independence and integrity of the nation. The humiliated feudalists took his pay and fought his battles. The conciliated clergy glorified his liberality and piety. Yet all his friendship with Pope and prelates did not prevent Philip from keeping a tight hand over the great dignitaries of the Church. He forced the prelates to pay their full share of suit and service. He strove to minimise the constant interference of the papal authority, even when his interests and his principles forbade him to openly set himself against it. He was a good friend to the townsmen. He felt himself so strong that he could abandon the feeble and tentative policy of his predecessors, and boldly strike an alliance with the communes, though still discouraging the more revolutionary aspects of the communal movement. He was thus able to put even cities outside his domain under the royal protection. Nor did he content himself with giving towns charters of liberties. He loved to strengthen their fortifications, rebuild their walls, encourage their industries, and protect their commerce. He encouraged foreign merchants to attend French markets and purchase French goods. Under his fostering care Paris, already a great Growth of city, became the first modern capital of a cen- Paris. tralised national state. He built a strong wall, taking in the schools of the south bank of the Seine, the royal residence and the cathedral in the island city, and the busy town of merchants and manufactures that was soon to make the north bank of the Seine the largest district of the capital. He ordered that the whole city should be paved with hard and firm stones. In his days the University of Paris received its first royal charters of privilege. Under him a crowd of fair buildings, conspicuous among them the cathedral of the capital, grew up in that new Gothic style that was soon to spread from the Isle of France all over the Western world. As the seat of the most famous schools north of the Alps, as the centre of the only centralised continental monarchy, and as the special haunt of the traders of Northern Gaul, Paris now took a unique place, not only among French towns, but among the cities of Western Europe.

Philip was a soldier and diplomatist rather than an administrator or a legislator. His mission was to endow the
Philip's monarchy with adequate force rather than to
administrative organise it or to govern it after new fashions.
reforms. Yet the circumstances of his position compelled
him to make new departures in the administrative history of
France, and thus to lay the foundation of the system which
was perfected by his famous grandson. The burdens thrown
upon the royal court were now such that they could no
longer be adequately discharged by casual assemblies of
ignorant feudalists. The delicate functions of the chief
officers of state could no longer be put into the hands of
the baron in whose hands happened to lie the hereditary
sergeanty. Hence, under Philip, we observe a further
specialisation of an official class of knights and clerks whose
skill and training could supplement the haphazard and uncertain services of the great barons. The system of administration that was enough for the scanty domains of his
predecessors would have broken down under the responsibilities involved by the conquest of Normandy and Anjou,
had not Philip, before his departure for the Crusade, constituted a new class of royal officials called *baillis*, who were
to act as supervisors and directors of the feudal provosts who
had hitherto administered the royal domain. Each bailli
took charge of a large area of territory, within which he
held monthly assizes to render justice in the king's name to
all his subjects. From time to time he appeared at
Paris, where he handed in an account of their administration, and paid into the exchequer the sums levied by him in
his provinces. But the growth of the royal revenue was
hardly commensurate with the increased strain on it, and
Character of Philip found that success rather added to than
Philip diminished his difficulties. He was a hot-tem-
Augustus. pered, strong, and active man, 'easy to anger
and easy to appease,' whose boisterous joviality, free living,
and robust, vigorous temperament did something to make

him popular, but whose complete personal impression it is hard to grasp, even in the scanty measure in which it is safe to individualise the shadowy statesmen of the Middle Ages.   In his sudden gusts of passion he could be pitilessly cruel, but he was more commonly to be condemned for his violence, his cunning, and his unscrupulous way of overreaching his enemies.   Yet his panegyrist could say of him that he 'loved justice as his own mother, strove to exact mercy above judgment; was ever a follower of the truth, and surpassed all kings in conjugal chastity.'   Such statements show that the contemporary standard was not very high.   But even after time had soured Philip's temper and brutalised his passions, he still laboured manfully to the last.   He was the first French king whose power was so firmly established that there was no need for him to crown his son king in his own lifetime.   He was almost the only king of his age whose son worked faithfully and ungrudgingly in his service, and was content to bide the time when nature should call him to his father's kingdom.

Philip II.'s successor was already six-and-thirty years of age, a tried soldier, a successful statesman, and a man whose private virtues far outshone those of his father, Louis VIII., though he was much less able.   Louis VIII.'s weak 1223-1226. health and cold disposition made him the very opposite of Philip.   His piety, his chastity, his love of truth and justice, were certain.   Despite his poor physique, his personal prowess gave him the surname of the Lion.   He had been long schooled in the execution of his father's policy, and as king he had no wish but to carry it out still further.   Louis' short reign of three years is therefore but a continuation of the reign of Philip Augustus.   His simple mission was to gather the fruits of his predecessor's labours.   His whole reign was occupied in turning to the profit of the crown the results of the collapse of the Angevin power and of the triumph of the Albigensian Crusade.

Despite the earlier conquests of Philip and Louis, the

authority of the crown was still but partially established over
Poitou.   Hugh of Lusignan, though now step-father of the
little Henry III., still played a treacherous and ambiguous
game, and for the moment again declared himself on the

The Con-
quest of
Poitou.

French side. Louis assembled a great army at
Tours and led in on a triumphant progress from
the Loire to the Dordogne.   The regents of the
English king did little but enter into ineffective negotiations.
Louis meanwhile took Niort, Saint Jean d'Angely, and La
Rochelle, after which the barons of the Limousin, Saintonge,
and Périgord made their submission to him.   'Save the
Gascons, who dwell beyond the Garonne,' boasted a French
chronicler, 'all the princes of Aquitaine now promised fealty
to King Louis, and then he went back to France.'

The renewal of the Albigensian Crusade now called Louis
to the South.   Amaury de Montfort had already fled from his
heritage, and had vainly implored the help of Philip Augustus.
Louis VIII. now showed the fugitive greater consideration
than his father had done.   He had already fought as a
Crusader against the Southern heretics.   His piety was kindled
by the renewed appeals of the legate of Honorius III., while
the helplessness of Amaury indicated that the results of
success were bound to fall to the crown.   Early in 1226
Louis again took the cross, and Raymond VII. was again
excommunicated and deposed.   Amaury abdicated his rights
in favour of the king.   The clergy provided funds, and the
Catholic chivalry of the North soon flocked to the crusading
banners.

In the early summer of 1226, Louis with his Crusaders
marched southwards down the Rhone valley, overrunning the

The revival
of the
Albigensian
Crusade.

marquisate of Provence.   He met no opposition
until he approached Avignon, a city long known
to be a hotbed of heresy.   The townsmen refused
him a passage over the Rhone, and it was therefore
necessary to conquer the city before Languedoc could be entered.
After an obstinate struggle Avignon was captured, and Louis

continued his triumphal march up to the gates of Toulouse. But the crusading army broke up before the capital of Raymond had surrendered. The barons were tired of the long and weary marches, and sickness had devastated the host. Louis himself was prostrated by sickness, and after providing for the administration of his conquests hurried back to the North. He had only reached Auvergne when he was carried off by a deadly fever. He had done enough for the monarchy by the great march which had first brought home to the Languedoc the majesty of the Capetian king.

A severe feudal reaction followed the unexpected death of Louis VIII. He had left a numerous family by Blanche of Castile, but the eldest child, who was crowned Louis IX. within three weeks of his father's death, was only twelve years of age, and it required all the skill and courage of his mother to preserve for him even the semblance of authority. The dispositions of her husband's will did not make matters any better. Breaking with the tradition of the early Capetians, Louis VIII. assigned by his testament a large territorial appanage to each of his younger children. Great slices were to be cut out of the royal domain that Robert the second son might be Count of Artois, Alfonse the third Count of Poitou, and Charles the youngest Count of Anjou and Maine. A new race of feudal potentates was thus supplied from the bosom of the royal house itself. The error involved in such a policy is one of the commonplaces of history, and for the next two centuries the hostility to the crown of younger branches of the Capetian family was often to prove almost as formidable as that of the ancient separatist seigneurs. But the fault of Louis has perhaps been unduly censured. Neither the resources of a mediæval monarch, nor the conditions of the time, made it possible for the king to permanently appropriate to himself an indefinite extent of domain, nor to deprive his kinsmen of the state due to their exalted birth. If the policy of Louis lost Artois to France for many centuries, it made it

The Regency of Blanche of Castile and the feudal reaction, 1226-1235.

possible for Alfonse and Charles to act as the most efficient pioneers of the Capetian monarchy in the South. The rule of a royal prince over his appanage was often the best transition from pure independence towards complete incorporation with the monarchy.

A great feudal coalition soon formed against Blanche of Castile. She was a foreigner, haughty and unsympathetic, and strong enough to excite fierce personal antipathy. ' A woman in sex she was,' says Matthew Paris, ' a man in counsel, worthy to be compared with Semiramis.' The younger members of the royal house, headed by Philip Hurepel, Count of Boulogne, the legitimised son of Philip II. and Agnes of Meran, joined with his kinsman Peter Mauclerc of Brittany, whose skill and courage soon made him the head of the league. The persecuted Raymond of Toulouse plucked up courage to unite himself with the coalition. Hugh of La Marche deserted the falling cause of royalty, and again became friendly with his son-in-law, Henry of England, who saw in the distress of the young king a chance of winning back his lost territories in France. Theobald IV. of Champagne, alone of the great feudatories, remained faithful to the royal cause.

The barons demanded the reversal of the policy of the last two reigns, and the restitution of their ancient rights. What power they were willing to leave the crown was to be placed in the hands of Philip of Boulogne, and the Spanish queen was to be sent back to her native country. Blanche did not quail before the storm. She appealed from the barons to the clergy and people. She secured the neutrality of Frederick II., and the open support of Honorius III. By the rapidity and unity of her movements she sought to break up the unwieldy and disorganised levies of her opponents. When she could no longer hold her own in the Isle of France, she went with her young son to Troyes, and threw herself on the protection of the Count of Champagne. Having failed in the first great blow, the feudal coalition slowly dissolved. It kept France in a state of anarchy for several years, but it was not strong enough to do more. Peter of Brittany strove hard to get English support, but it was not until 1230 that the young Henry III. came to France, and then, after an abortive march through Poitou, the English went home again, and the feudalists were as far from success as ever. Next year Peter failed in an intrigue to win over Theobald of Champagne to his side. He finally strove to stir up a revolt against Theobald in favour of Alice, queen of Cyprus, the daughter of Theobald's uncle, Henry, king of Jerusalem. But this also failed, and the queen of Cyprus renounced her claims. In 1234 Theobald attained the climax of his power by succeeding to the kingdom of Navarre as the heir of his uncle Sancho. Philip of Boulogne was dead. Peter of Brittany sullenly made his peace with the triumphant Castilian. The monarchy of Philip Augustus had proved strong enough to survive a minority and the rule of a foreign woman.

A notable result of the triumph of the crown was the settlement of the question of Toulouse by a compromise that was all in favour of the monarchy. The Albigensian Crusade had died away amid the storms of civil war, and against so orthodox a prince as Raymond VII. it had never been more than a sorry pretext for aggression. In 1229 Raymond concluded the Treaty of Meaux with the regent, by which he retained, though on humiliating conditions, a portion of his sovereignty. He yielded up to the crown the duchy of Narbonne, the eastern part of his dominions, from the Rhone to beyond Carcassonne, and was confirmed in his possession of the county of Toulouse. He was, however, to rase the walls of his capital and thirty other towns, to admit a royal garrison into the castle of Toulouse, to wage war against the heretics, to provide orthodox doctors to teach the true faith at Toulouse, and go on pilgrimage to Palestine. He was to

The Treaty of Meaux and the extension of the royal domain to the Mediterranean, 1229.

marry his daughter and heiress to Blanche's younger son
Alfonse, and so secure to the Capetians the ultimate succession to all his dominions.   Another result of the treaty
was the organisation of a systematic effort to stamp out the
last remnants of the Albigensian heresy.   Immediately after

The   the treaty a systematic Episcopal Inquisition,
Inquisition. such   as   Lucius   III.   had   contemplated   in
1184, was set up in every diocese of Languedoc.   In
1233 it was supplemented by a Papal Inquisition, established by Gregory IX.   This latter gave unity to persecution
by overstepping the rigid diocesan limits.   Its direction was
given to the followers of the same Dominic who had preached
so long in vain in Toulouse.   But Gregory did not put his
whole trust in the fires of the inquisitors.   At the same time
that he created their grim tribunal, he established the University of Toulouse, the first *studium generale* set up by papal
bull, and thus gave wider currency to the orthodox teaching
which the care of Honorius had already established there.
The faculty of theology passed at once into Dominican hands,
and the orthodox dialectic of the schoolmen soon replaced the
lay and lax culture of the troubadours.   Only in the county
of Provence did the troubadours still continue their songs.
The independence of the South was at an end, and the royal
domain for the first time touched the Mediterranean.   But the
greater sympathy now shown for the Southern people came
out in the reversal of Montfort's rude efforts to introduce the
customs of the North.

Louis IX.'s personal government began in 1235, when his
mother laid down the regency in his favour.   Though nur-
Character of   tured amidst the storms of rebellion, and exposed
St. Louis.   to all the temptations of one who was a king from
early boyhood, Blanche had so carefully provided for his
education that his simple, just, and straightforward disposition was allowed full scope for its development.   He early
became an example of piety to all his realm.   He regularly
frequented the canonical hours of the Church, rising from

his bed, like a monk, to attend matins at midnight, and again in the early morning for prime. His fasts, his discipline, his rigid self-denial, were beyond all ordinary measure. The length of his private devotions exhausted the patience of his nobles, and even wearied his confessor; but he told the barons that they wasted more time every day in gambling and hunting, and shame compelled them to be silent. His devotion was not merely one of outward forms. His fervent and exalted piety shone through every action of his simple and well-ordered life. He was the soul of honour and chastity. He ate and drank very sparingly, always mixing his wine with water, and consuming whatever meats happened to be set before him. Though on solemn occasions he was clad in gold and rich stuffs, his ordinary garments were of simple cut and sober colour. He detested oaths, violent and impure speech, idle gossip, lies, and tale-bearing. His patience was unending, and his good temper unruffled. His humility was extreme and quite without ostentation. His charity was immense and unbounded. He was not only a great giver of alms and founder of churches, monasteries, and hospitals. He daily fed the poor at his table, and visited the sick and wretched at their own abodes. He washed the feet of repulsive beggars and cripples. He did not shrink from contact with the lepers. His simple enthusiasm for good works powerfully affected the rough barons with whom he was brought into contact. 'To see or hear him,' we are told, 'brought comfort and calm to the most troubled spirit.'

With all his piety and simplicity, there was nothing weak or puerile in Louis' character. His extreme asceticism had no touch of the gloomy moroseness or inhumanity of the baser type of mediæval devotees. His habits were as robust, as manly, as they were simple. He enjoyed vigorous health. His tall, well-knit frame, bright, keen eye, fair flowing hair, and good-humoured blonde face, made him the model of a high-born knight. Not, perhaps, endowed with any high measure of intellectual capacity, he had a firm will, a sane judgment, a shrewd sense of his own limitations, and the strong common-sense that makes a good man of affairs.   He was pleasant and easy of access, delighting in unrestrained intercourse with his friends, and reckless of the etiquette and ceremony that were beginning to hedge even a feudal court.   With all his ambition to live a 'regular' life, he did not scorn the married state nor neglect the softer domestic virtues, and his love for his children caused him early to abandon a hope he at one time entertained of entering a monastery.   As a young man he delighted in the chase, in well-trained hawks and high-mettled horses, and could entertain his barons with sumptuous and regal hospitality.   He was one of the bravest of soldiers, preserving a rare coolness in the fierce hand-to-hand struggle of a mediæval battle, and never losing hope or cheerfulness.   He was as good a king as he was a man, tenacious of all royal rights that had been handed down from his forefathers, and constantly striving to uphold his authority as the best guarantee of the peace and prosperity of his people.   He made his own the policy of his grandfather, though in his hands it lost its original taint of fraud and violence.   He was the friend of the clerk, the friar, the monk, the simple knight, and the burgess.   He depressed the great feudalists the more completely since he was scrupulous to allow them every power that law or custom recognised to be theirs.   He enlarged his dominions the more securely since his scrupulous conscience forbade him taking unfair advantage even of his enemy.   He could withstand the aggressions of a greedy pope or a self-seeking bishop the more effectively since his devotion to the Church and his zeal for her just rights were patent to all men.   He could build up a new administrative system adequate for the government of his vast realm since it was common fame that his motive was not self-aggrandisement, but the well-being of his whole people.   As a Christian and as a man, as a statesman and as a warrior, he was the exemplar of all that was best in his age.

After his death he was raised to the honours of sanctity, and subsequent ages have revered in St. Louis the very ideal of a loyal knight and Christian king.

The first care for the young king was the completion of the conquest of the South-west. His way had already been made smooth for him. Raymond of Toulouse, curbed by the Dominicans and the French garrison, was no longer dangerous, and the greater part of his old dominions were ruled by the royal seneschals of Beaucaire and Carcassonne. In 1237 his heiress Joan was married to Louis's brother, Alphonse, who, on his father-in-law's death, was thus destined to become Count of Toulouse. *The settlement of the South-west.*

Though Alfonse was thus nobly provided for, Louis' strict fidelity to his father's will conferred upon him and his brothers the rich appanages which the previous king had bequeathed to them in their cradles. In 1241 he held a great court at Saumur, where, clad in blue satin and red mantle lined with ermine, he royally feasted with the chief barons of France in the noble hall built by Henry of Anjou. There he made Alfonse a knight, and afterwards, taking him to Poitiers, invested him with the counties of Poitiers and Auvergne. For the moment all was well. Hugh of Lusignan had banqueted at Saumur, and had sworn fealty to Alfonse at Poitiers. But before long his wife, the former queen of England, stirred him up to resist his liege lord and fall back upon his ancient alliance with his step-son. The Poitevin barons met at Parthenay, eager to oppose the crown. 'The French,' they declared, 'have always hated the Poitevins, and will always continue to do so. They would fain trample us under their feet, and use us more contemptuously than the Normans or the Albigeois. In Champagne and Burgundy the king's servants carry all before them, and the nobles dare do nothing without their leave. We had better die than live such a slavish life.' A league was soon formed; the English seneschal of Bordeaux sent immediate help. Even Raymond of Toulouse ventured to revolt, and *Alfonse, Count of Poitou and Auvergne, 1241.*

his subjects murdered inquisitors and chased away the Dominican theologians of the University. All the old spirits of disorder were aroused, and in 1242 Henry of England landed in Saintonge with a considerable army, joyfully profiting by the opportunity to vindicate his ancient claims to Poitou.

Louis IX. was now forced to appear at the head of an army in the South. In a short, one-sided campaign he carried

Battle of Saintes, and final defeat of the English and Poitevins, 1242. all before him. He secured the passage of the Charente by driving the Anglo-Poitevin host from the bridge of Taillebourg, and on 22nd July won a decisive victory outside the walls of Saintes. He pressed on to Blaye on the Gironde, where a sudden sickness alone prevented him from crossing over to the siege of Bordeaux. But he had gained all that he sought. Hugh of La Marche made a humiliating submission, and his sons sought a freer and more adventurous career with their half-brother in England. The Count of

The Treaty of Lorris, and the final humiliation of Raymond VII., 1243. Toulouse yielded before the seneschal of Carcassonne in time to avert a new Crusade. In 1243 the Peace of Lorris renewed the humiliating conditions of the Treaty of Meaux. 'Henceforth,' says William of Nangis, 'the barons no longer attempt to do anything against their king, the Lord's anointed, seeing clearly that the hand of the Lord was with him.'

Nothing now remained but to gather up the spoils. The careful administration of Alfonse at Poitiers prepared the way

Alfonse of Poitiers, Count of Toulouse, 1249. for the direct absorption of the lands between Loire and Garonne within the royal domain. In 1249 the beaten Raymond VII. died, and his son-in-law quietly succeeded to his heritage. Northern laws and manners gradually permeated the South. The improvements of administration which St. Louis had established in his domain were adopted by his intelligent brother. A single parliament or high law court was created for all Alfonse's fiefs, and the South for the first time felt the advantages of law and order. The Langue d'oc receded before the new court tongue of the Langue d'oil. 'Bastides' and 'Villeneuves' were set up as new centres of trade and to diminish the importance and prosperity of the older separatist towns.[1] Vast castles of the northern type kept down the disobedient. Gothic minsters, like the cathedral of Limoges and the choir of Toulouse, were reared by North French workmen side by side with the indigenous Romanesque that had lingered as long in the South as in the Rhineland. When Alfonse died without heirs in 1271, his counties of Toulouse and Poitiers and his land of Auvergne quietly devolved on his nephew Philip III.

There still remained the danger of the English dukes of Gascony, but Henry III. was now Louis' good friend and brother-in-law, and too occupied in quarrels with his subjects to concern himself overmuch with the affairs of Aquitaine. Henry remained, however, tenacious of his rights, and the vigorous rule of his brother-in-law, Simon of Montfort, the younger,[2] showed what a source of strength Aquitaine might become in competent hands. Here St. Louis' moderation and sense of justice stood him in good stead, and led him to make one of the greatest sacrifices ever made by a strong king in the interests of peace. He persuaded the English king to yield up his vain claims on Normandy and Anjou in return for the cession of considerable districts in the South, long conquered and quietly ruled by Louis' seneschals. He yielded at the moment 'all the rights which he had in the three bishoprics of Limoges, Cahors, and Périgueux, in fiefs and in domains,' that is to say, the homages of the barons of those regions, for Louis' domains

The Treaty of Paris and the settlement with Henry III., 1259.

[1] See Curie Seimbres' *Essai sur les villes fondées dans le sud-ouest de la France aux xiii⁴ et xiv⁴ siècles sous le nom de bastides* [Toulouse, 1880].

[2] See on this subject M. Bémont's *Simon de Montfort*. On the general position of the English Dukes of Guienne, see the *Rôles Gascons*, now being published in the *Documents inédits sur l'histoire de France*, with M. Bémont's invaluable introductory sketch.

there were insignificant. He also promised on the death of Alfonse, to yield to Henry Saintonge south of the Charente, the Agenais, and lower Quercy. The treaty was drawn up at Abbeville in 1258 and finally sealed at Paris in the following year. It was the last act in the long struggle for Normandy and Poitou, the legal limitation of the English king's land in France to a small fragment of their Aquitanian heritage. The good faith of St. Louis was not strictly followed by his successor, and Edward I. found some difficulty in obtaining the cessions promised on Alfonse's death. At last, in the treaty of Amiens, 1279, matters were compromised by the cession of the Agenais.[1] Future disputes between the French kings and the Aquitainian dukes were in due course to arise, but they turned on fresh questions. The loyalty of St. Louis had entirely ended the ancient grounds of dispute between overlord and vassal.

No overwhelming growth of the royal domain in Northern France marked the reign of Louis, but the vast acquisitions of Philip II. were quietly absorbed, and their inhabitants became good Frenchmen. Four fiefs of the first order now alone remained in the north, and only two of these—Flanders and Brittany — retained a separatist character.

The King and the northern feudalists.

Appanages of the royal house.

Despite their extension of power over the Pyrenees, the house of Blois-Champagne was ever friendly to Louis, and his purchase of Macon had kept Burgundy in check. No great harm to the central power followed, when in 1237 Louis made his brother Robert Count of Artois, and in 1245 his youngest brother Charles became Count of Anjou and Maine, especially as, in the latter case, Touraine, the ancient dependency of Anjou, was retained within the royal domain. At the later date Louis also granted appanages to his younger sons, Peter becoming Count of Alençon, and Robert Count of Clermont-en-Beauvaisis. But the subsequent marriage of Robert to the heir of

[1] See Tout's *Edward I.* (Twelve English Statesmen), pp. 86-92.

Bourbon brought another great fief under the control of the royal house. Charles's early government of Anjou was vigorous and successful, and did something to reconcile the ancient county to its practical loss of independence. But Charles soon found a better sphere for his energies in the imperial lands adjacent to the French kingdom. He strove for a time to establish himself in the county of Hainault, as the ally of Margaret of Flanders. He finally found a more fruitful field in the Arelate, where he proved a worthy brother to Alfonse of Poitiers, as the precursor of Northern influence over the South.

The fall of Toulouse left the county of Provence the one great centre of the South French national spirit. Though technically no part of the French kingdom, it was one in language, manners, and sympathies with the county of Toulouse, whose princes had indeed acquired possession of the so-called March of Provence, between the Durance and the Isère. So long as the Languedocian civilisation was strong, the hereditary animosities of the Counts of Provence and the Counts of Toulouse did much to weaken the political cohesion of two kindred peoples. In the face of the wave of Northern aggression, signs were not wanting that the ancient feuds of the courts of Aix and Toulouse were abating. Raymond Berengar v. had been Count of Provence since 1209. By his marriage with Beatrix, daughter of Thomas, Count of Savoy, he had established a close union with the active and aggressive house that was beginning to make itself a formidable power in the upper region of the ancient Arelate. But four daughters only were the offspring of the union, and were not some special precautions taken there was the danger lest Raymond Berengar should be the last of his race to rule in Provence. The astute Provençal looked out early for wealthy husbands for his daughters. The eldest, Margaret, became the wife of St. Louis himself in 1234. Two years later Eleanor, the second, was wedded

(marginal note: Provence under Raymond Berengar V.)

(marginal note: Marriages of his daughters.)

to Henry III. of England.   The third, Sanchia, was espoused
in 1244 to Richard earl of Cornwall, the future King of the
Romans.   The youngest, Beatrice, was the destined heiress
of Provence, and everything depended upon her choice of a
husband.   During the crisis of the struggle in the south-west,
Raymond VII. repudiated his Spanish wife and became a
suitor for the hand of Beatrice.   Had such a union been
accomplished, it would have been easy to cheat Alfonse of
Poitiers of the Toulouse succession, and a brilliant prospect
was opened out of a great national state in southern Gaul,
formed by the union of Toulouse and Provence, which
would have surrounded the royal Sénéchaussées of Beaucaire
and Carcassonne, and might well have proved strong
enough to ward off the aggressions of the northerners.
But with the collapse of the English power at Saintes and
the submission of Raymond at Lorris, this glowing vision
vanished for ever.   It was too late in the day to stem the
tide that had already overflowed.   Raymond Berengar died
in 1245, and soon after the marriage of Beatrice to Charles
of Anjou established a Northern court at Aix as well as at
Poitiers.

For the next twenty years (1245-1265) Charles of Anjou
carried on in Provence the same work that Alfonse had long
been doing at Poitiers and was soon to begin at
Toulouse.   The ablest, strongest, fiercest, and
most unscrupulous of the sons of Louis VIII., the
new Count of Provence thoroughly established
Northern methods of government and Northern ideals of
life in the last home of the civilisation of the Troubadours.
Charles's success was brilliant and lasting.   The great churchmen, like the archbishop of Arles, ceased to be temporal
sovereigns.   The feudal nobles lost their independence when
their leader, Barral des Baux, despairing of holding his rock-
built stronghold against his suzerain, gave up his pursuit of
feudal freedom and became one of Charles's most trusted
ministers.   The cities, which had hitherto vied with their

Charles of Anjou, Count of Provence, 1245-1265.

Italian neighbours in their love of absolute autonomy, saw their municipal franchises destroyed when revolted Marseilles was starved into submission, while the care Charles showed for its commercial interests soon did something to reconcile the wealthy citizens to the loss of their liberties. Master of every order of his subjects, Charles welded all Provence together by the skilful execution of good laws. As a result of his careful policy, he was gradually able to dispense with his Northern followers and intrust administration and arms to his Provençal subjects. The last of the Troubadours fled to the more congenial courts of Aragon and northern Italy. The successes of Charles began that long series of French aggressions on the Arelate, which only ceased when Savoy itself became French less than forty years ago. This was the natural and inevitable result of the development of the idea of nationality and the decay of the imperial principle. As the Provençal lands could not form a national state of their own, they ultimately found their salvation in incorporation with the more vigorous nationality of the Langue d'oil.

The foreign policy of St. Louis was inspired by the same spirit of justice and peace that regulated his dealings with his feudatories. We have seen his watchful care Foreign Policy of the just rights of the English king. His of St. Louis. Treaty of Corbeil of 1258, with James I., king of Aragon, was based on the same principles as the Treaty of Paris with Henry III. By it Louis renounced all rights over the county of Barcelona, in return for James's His relations abandonment of his claims over Foix and all to Spain. lands north of Rousillon. By an almost nominal concession, Louis thus broke the close tie between the kindred civilisations north and south of the Pyrenees which, in the days of the Albigensian Wars, had threatened to counterbalance the growing influence of the French crown over the south. By the marriage of Louis's eldest son, Philip, to James's daughter, Isabella of Aragon, the personal tie between the two realms was made the stronger. Two daughters of Louis were wedded to Spanish princes, one to the son of the king of Castile, another to Theobald the Young, king of Navarre and count of Champagne. Even the establishment of the most faithful of the great feudatories in the little kingdom of Navarre helped, rather than hindered, the progress of the French monarchy. The Champenois Joinville became the most attached follower, the most enthusiastic biographer of St. Louis.

The long quarrel of Papacy and Empire gave ample opportunities for an ambitious prince to draw profit to France from their dissensions. The anti-clerical policy of Frederick II. afforded plenty of pretexts to so pious a king as Louis for putting himself on the papal side and making what annexations he could at the expense of Frederick's weakness. But though troubled by the Emperor's ecclesiastical attitude, Louis did not forget Frederick's forbearance in the days when Blanche of Castile was struggling single-handed against the feudal party, and he was by no means satisfied with the rancorous attitude of the Papacy. He therefore strove to take up a strict neutrality between Pope and Emperor. He rejected the offer of the imperial crown which Gregory IX. made to Robert of Artois. He refused to receive Innocent IV. when he fled from Italy, and disregarded the deposition of the Emperor at Lyons. He strove hard at Cluny to reconcile Innocent and Frederick. The only occasion when he prepared to uphold the Pope was when it was believed that Frederick was crossing Mont Cenis with a great army in full march for Lyons. This judicious policy was especially pursued by him since he realised that the essential condition of a new Crusade was the friendship of Cæsar and the Pope. When the last chances of reconciliation were ended, he went, in 1248, to Egypt, to fight single-handed for the cause which he had at heart. On his return in 1254, he found Frederick dead and the Empire as good as destroyed   Yet during the weary years of the Great

Louis and the Empire.

Interregnum, he never, as we shall see, departed from the ancient strictness of his policy. He had no wish that his brother-in-law, Richard of Cornwall, should revive the ancient alliance of England and Germany. He preferred to recognise Alfonso of Castile, but he took no direct action to sustain his preference. The position of Richard in Germany removed his last scruples about the Sicilian inheritance. He allowed Charles of Anjou to accept in 1265 the Sicilian throne, and marred his later policy by his undue deference to his unscrupulous brother. The deviation of the Crusade of 1270 to Tunis was the result of Charles's wish to strengthen his Italian position. Louis's death was thus in a measure due to the influence of the prince who had become the evil spirit of the French royal house.

Towards the end of his reign Louis was incontestably the first prince of Europe. The collapse of the Hohenstaufen, the weakness of his English brother-in- **France the** law, the position of his own brethren in the **chief Power** South and in Italy, the degradation of the feuda- **of Europe.** tories, all contributed to make the power of Louis great, but the unique position which the French monarch now held was due not so much to his authority and resources as to the ascendency won by his personal character and virtues. His reputation for impartiality and his recognised love of peace and justice made him the natural arbiter in every delicate question, the general peace-maker in every European quarrel. Louis's arbitration between Henry III. and his barons, if the least successful of his interventions, was but one example of his activity in this direction, both with regard to foreign princes and his own feudatories. It was too much to expect that even the best of kings would decide otherwise than in favour of a brother monarch against an aristocracy whose avowed object was the transference of the royal authority to a committee of barons. It speaks strongly for Louis that the English barons should ever have consented to submit to his decision

The internal government of Louis IX. must now be considered. His attitude towards the feudal barons has been
Home Policy   already illustrated. The narrowness of his vision
of St Louis.   and the justness of his character combined to
make it impossible for him to adopt an anti-feudal policy like
that of his grandson, Philip the Fair. He was the defender
of all existing lawful authority, but if he intervened to pro-
teet the oppressed barons from the zeal of his too active
officials, he more often used his influence to make the barons
exercise towards their dependants the same rigid justice he was
ever willing to manifest to them. His forbidding of private
war, the judicial duel, and the tournaments which were often
little better than thinly disguised war, were the result of his
love of peace and order; but they cut at the root of feudal
ideas, with which indeed any real measure of peace and order
were almost incompatible.

Louis's relations to the Church bring out strongly the best
sides of his character. No king was ever so anxious to give
Lonis and   the Church its due, and to protect churchmen
the Church.   from grasping barons or greedy crown officials.
He regarded his rights of patronage and his custody of the
temporalities of vacant sees as sacred trusts, and he strove,
so far as he could, to prevail upon his barons to follow in his
footsteps. Guided by the wise counsels of William of Auvergne, bishop of Paris for the first twenty years of his reign,
he safeguarded the interests of the monarchy as well as the
interests of the Church. It was in his reign that the married
clerks engaged in commerce were, at Louis's instance, abandoned to the jurisdiction of the lay tribunals, and yet Louis
more than once associated himself with his barons in protesting against the growing aggressions of the ecclesiastical courts.
It was under Louis that the French clergy first felt the weight
of regular and systematic taxation. The extraordinary favour
which he showed to the Mendicants cost him something of
the good wishes of the secular clergy and of the older
orders. Franciscans and Dominicans were his chaplains and

confessors, his habitual companions, and the instruments even of his secular policy.   Their influence over him contributed towards the establishment of the Mendicants in a strong position in the University of Paris, despite violent secular opposition.   Through the Mendicants Louis was ever inclined to ally himself with the Pope against the secular clergy.   Yet that alliance had, as we have seen, its limits.   The champions of Gallican liberties in the fifteenth century were not altogether at fault in regarding St. Louis as the first upholder of the national freedom of the French Church.   The so-called 'Pragmatic Sanction of St. Louis' is indeed a forgery of the fifteenth century, but the hostility it expresses to simony, to papal taxation, to the temporal claims of Rome and the abuses of ecclesiastical elections, do not go far beyond his practice.   It was, however, quite impossible for a pious churchman of the thirteenth century to formulate the doctrines of national independence that were afterwards upheld by the fathers of Constance and Basel.

The greatest result of St. Louis's home government was the enlargement and definition of the administrative system which first sprang up as the result of the expansion of the monarchy under Philip II.   This arose from the same necessities as the Anglo-Norman system, which had been perfected by Henry of Anjou, and in many details presents remarkable analogies to the polity already established beyond the Channel.   The king was the centre of the whole system.   His advisers were no longer the hereditary functionaries of the primitive monarchy. The royal household (*l'hôtel du roi*) now consisted of a band of clerks and knights, the chaplains, the scribes, the advisers and defenders of the king, and of the subordinate servants, who discharged purely menial and domestic functions.   From the powerful body of clerks and knights of the household sprang the official class which represented the monarchy throughout the kingdom.   Though many of the clerks were doubtless trained lawyers, the ministers of St. Louis were far

Lonis's Administrative System.

from showing that pettifogging and litigious spirit that inspired king and household alike in the days of Philip the
Fair.

All France was divided into great provinces, and at the head
of each was placed a royal official, called a *bailli* in the north

Baillages
and Séné-
chaussées.

and a *sénéchal* in the south, who roughly corre-
sponded to, though they governed a greater extent
of territory than, the sheriffs of the English crown.
They nominated the provosts and inferior officers; they
administered ju·tice; collected the royal revenue; and were
charged with the superintendence of the royal relations to the
neighbouring feudatories as well as with the administration
of their own districts. Their annual visits to the Exchequer
connected them with the central government, and a further
link between the central and local administration was found in

Enquesteurs.

the regular institution by St. Louis of *enquesteurs*,
the *missi dominici*, or the itinerant justices of the
Capetian monarchy, who, though casually employed by
earlier kings, were now made a permanent element in the
administrative system.

Under St. Louis a process of differentiation similar to that
which had evolved the Exchequer, Curia Regis, and other

The Differ-
entiation of
the Royal
Council.

courts from the great councils of the Anglo-
Norman kings, divided into three bodies the
royal court of the Capetian kings. The *Grand
Conseil* became the administrative and political
assembly; the *Parlement* grew into the judicial mouthpiece of
the crown; and *Maîtres des Comptes* received and regulated the
royal revenue. While the political Council still followed
the king in the ceaseless wanderings of a mediæval sovereign, the Parliament gradually settled down permanently at
Paris. With the elaboration of its organisation came an
extension of its competence. Churchmen and lawyers agreed
in believing that the king was the sole source of justice.
Appeals to the king's court became, under St. Louis, the
substitute for the trial by combat, which he abolished. Not

only were the inferior courts of the *baillage* or *prévôté* subordinate to the king's court. It became usual for appeals to be taken to Paris from the highest courts of the greatest feudatories of the realm. The doctrine of the *cas royal*, the plea reserved exclusively for the cognisance of the crown, materially aided the extension of the Parliament of Paris. Alfonse of Poitiers, as we have seen, imitated in his own fief the example of his sovereign and brother. The financial reforms of St. Louis, though important, were not so radical as his judicial changes. The *Gens des Comptes* in session at the Temple in Paris prepared the way for the organisation of the *Chambre des Comptes* under Philip the Fair. But almost alone of mediæval sovereigns, St. Louis was well able ' to live of his own,' and the ordinary revenue of the crown left a surplus for his religious and charitable foundations Only the rare great wars, and the two Crusades of the king, necessitated recourse to exceptional taxation. Yet Louis was able to carry out a thoroughgoing reform of the coinage, and carefully upheld the value and purity of the circulating medium. In 1263 he issued an ordinance by which he gained for the royal mints the monopoly of supplying the monetary needs of the royal domain. Wherever no seignorial money was coined, there the royal money was to circulate exclusively. All that was allowed to the seignorial currency was that it should be accepted concurrently with the king's money in those fiefs where the lord had an established right of mintage. It was, however, to be so struck that every one might see that it plainly differed from the products of the mints of the crown. This reform in itself was a great encouragement to trade. The protection of the communes by the king, the sound peace which enabled merchants to buy and sell without molestation, and the establishment of new towns, especially in the south, all furthered the growth of commerce. The *ville* of Carcassonne, whose plan to this day preserves the right lines

The Parliament of Paris and the Extension of the Royal Jurisdiction.

Finance and the Coinage.

The Towns and Trade.

and measured regularity of an American city, and which, with its Gothic churches and its busy industries stands to this day in such vivid contrast to the desolate *cité* on the height, the witness of departed military glories, is an example of the numerous class

FRANCE
AND ITS
NEIGHBOUR LANDS
IN 1270

Boundary of French kingdom	*Royal domain*
Lands of Alfonse of Poitiers (incorporated with the domain in 1271)	
Lands of Charles of Anjou	*Lands of Robert of Artois*
Lands of English Kings (treaties of 1259 & 1279)	*The other great fiefs*

of *Villeneuves* and *Villefranches* founded by St. Louis in his newly won domains in the Languedoc. Louis's Christian zeal, no

Jews and Cahorsins.

less than his hatred of usury, caused him to deal with excessive rigour with the Jews. He was almost as intolerant of the Lombard and Cahorsin usurers, who had now begun to rival with the Israelites in finance. One of the least pleasing sides of the saint's character was his cruel severity to blasphemers, heretics, and unbelievers. The same zeal led St. Louis twice to abandon France while he went on crusade. [*See* chapter xix.] But neither his long sojourn in Egypt and Syria nor his death at Tunis destroyed the effect of his work for his kingdom. Queen Blanche resumed her vigorous rule of France as regent during Louis's absence from 1248 to her death in 1253, the year before his return. The chief trouble Blanche had was with the strange popular gathering of the *Pastoureaux*, which, assembled The under the pretext that shepherds and workmen Pastoureaux. were to supply the remissness of lords and knights and rescue St. Louis from the Egyptians, soon became a wild carnival of brigandage, which the regent had considerable difficulty in suppressing (1251). In 1270 Philip the Bold, the saint's dull, but pious, docile, hard-fighting, and well-meaning son, succeeded as easily in the camp at Tunis as he could have done in Paris itself. The work of St. Louis was quietly and unostentatiously continued during the first years of Philip III.'s reign. In his later years the baleful influence of Charles of Anjou turned the heir of St. Louis to a more active and greedy policy that prepared the way for the extraordinary success of Philip the Fair, whose triumphant reign marks the end of the process that had begun with the early Capetians.

CHAPTER XVIII

THE UNIVERSITIES AND THE FRIARS [1]

The *Regnum*, the *Sacerdotium*, and the *Studium*—The Beginnings of the
Universities—Their Organisation and their Spirit—Their Relations to the
Church—The Introduction of Aristotle—Intellectual and Popular Heresy
—St. Francis and the Minorites—St Dominic and the Order of Preachers
—Other Mendicant Orders—The Work of the Mendicants—Preaching
and Pastoral Care—The Religious Revival—The Mendicants and the
Universities—The Triumph of the Mendicants—The Great Scholastics
of the Thirteenth Century and the Results of their Influence.

FROM the unorganised schools of the twelfth century proceeded the corporate universities of the thirteenth century.
The same age that witnessed the culmination of
the idea of the 'regnum' under Barbarossa and
Henry VI. and the triumph of the 'sacerdotium'
under Innocent III., saw the establishment of the
'studium' as a new bond of unity and authority, worthy to
be set up side by side with the Empire and the Papacy
themselves. The strong instinct for association that about
the same period led to the organisation of the Lombard

Regnum,
Sacerdotium,
and
Studium.

---

[1] Denifle's *Universitaten des Mittelalters* (vol. i.), and Rashdall's *Universities of Europe in the Middle Ages* supply full information as to the
organisation and studies of the universities. Hauréau's *De la philosophie
scholastique* (2 vols.) summarises clearly the activity and teaching of the
schoolmen. For the Franciscans, Hase's *Franz von Assisi* and Sabatier's
brilliant *Saint François d'Assise*, and Müller's *Anfänge des Minoriten-
ordens und der Bussbruderschaften*. Brewer's *Monumenta Franciscana*
and Little's *Grey Friars at Oxford* illustrate their activity in England.
For the Dominicans, Lacordaire's *Vie de Saint Dominique*, Caro's *Saint
Dominique et les Dominicains*, and Lecoy de la Marche's *La Chaire
française au moyen âge*. For the heretics and their repression, besides
Lea's *History of the Inquisition*, J. Havet's *L'hérésie et le bras séculier
au moyen âge*. The extracts from original authorities in Gieseler, and
Moller's careful summary, remain very useful.

League and the French Communes, that united England under the Angevins and South Italy under Frederick II., that set up merchant guilds in every urban centre and gave fresh life to both the old and the new ecclesiastical societies, brought about the organisation of the masters and scholars into the universities which still remain as the most abiding product of the genius of the Middle Ages. Just as the institution of knighthood had set up a new cosmopolitan principle of union that bound together men of different lands, wealth, and social station, in a common brotherhood of arms, so did the establishment of the corporations of doctors and scholars unite the subtlest brains of diverse countries and ranks in a common professional and social life.

The earliest universities were, like Paris, associations of teachers, or, like Bologna, clubs of foreign students. They had no founders, and based their rights on no The earliest charters of king or pope, but grew up gradually universities. as a natural outcome of the wide spread of intellectual pursuits that had followed upon the twelfth-century Renascence. The accident of the abiding presence of a series of great teachers had made Paris the centre of theological and philosophical study north of the Alps, and had given the schools of Bologna a prestige that attracted to them students Paris and of the civil and canon laws from every country in Bologna. Europe. It was inevitable that sooner or later the accidental and spasmodic character of the earlier schools should give way to systematic organisation. The numerous teachers of arts and theology at Paris gradually became a definite college or guild of doctors and masters, with power to admit and to exclude new members of their profession, and with an increasingly strong corporate spirit and tradition. Before the death of Louis VII. a university, that is to say a corporation, of masters, had replaced the individual schools of the age of Abelard. / Before the century was out Philip Augustus had given the infant university its earliest privileges of exemption from the ordinary municipal organisation. Before the middle of the thirteenth century, the Faculties had been organised, the Four Nations and the Rectorate set up, the authority of the Episcopal Chancellor reduced to a minimum, and the universal acceptation of the teaching rights of the masters secured. Kings and popes vied with each other in showering privileges on a society that controlled with such absolute authority educated public opinion. Moreover, the simple expedient of suspension of lectures or of secession wrung by force the privileges not to be obtained by favour, while a more permanent result of these academic secessions was the creation of other universities, whose rivalry wholesomely stimulated the energies of the teachers of the ancient centre. Bologna did for Italy almost all that Paris did for the North, though the difference of the circumstances of a free municipality and those of a great capital of a national state affected both the organisation of the institution and the character of the studies. Not the teaching masters but the well-to-do and mature students themselves formed the corporations that were the earliest form of the university of Bologna. The

The multiplication of universities. supreme importance of legal studies was the outcome of the social, political, and intellectual condition of Italy. The constant secessions that set up flourishing schools at Padua and Pisa, and covered Italy with smaller universities, were helped by the centrifugal tendency that had already become a marked feature of Italian politics. Yet no mediæval university was in any sense a purely national institution. It was the home of the Latinised, cosmopolitan, clerkly culture that made the wandering scholar as much at home in a distant city of a foreign land as in the schools of his native town. The Studium, like the Regnum and the Sacerdotium, belonged to the old cosmopolitan Roman order that knew nothing of the modern ideas of national life and local states. Yet no local state that aspired to civilised life could dispense with a 'studium generale' or university. The great position of Angevin England made the English school at Oxford the chief northern rival of Paris, from which perhaps it was the most important secession. Thirteenth-century Spain celebrated its deliverance from the Moor and its entrance into the Christian commonwealth by the setting up of new learned corporations. It was a sign of the dethronement of Germany from her ancient predominance that she had no university till long after our period was over. So great were the benefits of an organised general school that kings and popes began to institute, deliberately, imitations of what had earlier grown up spontaneously. Gregory IX. established the first university of papal foundation at Toulouse, and Frederick II. the first university of royal foundation at Naples. Alfonso VIII. of Castile not only conquered at Las Navas de Tolosa, but strove, though to little purpose, to found the first Spanish university at Palencia.

From the remotest parts of Europe eager students of every rank and condition, from highest to lowest, from wealthiest to poorest, flocked to the universities of repute. If many were chiefly eager for a career and professional advancement, there were not wanting a few touched with a higher spirit. The free life, the democratic equality of the teachers, the unrestrained licence of the taught, if leading to constant disorders, brought about a spirit of independence within the academic band such as Europe had not witnessed since the fall of the Roman Empire. This was the more important since the universities of the thirteenth century were no mere abodes of recluse scholars, but exercised a profound influence on every side of human activity. They affected politics and statecraft nearly as much as they affected thought and religion. It is with their influence on the State and the Church that we are mainly concerned now.

The spirit of the universities.

It was an all-important question what would be the relations of the Studium to the Sacerdotium. The universities were in the long-run bound to be either the friends or the foes of the existing order, which was so intimately bound up with the aseendency of the Church. At first there seemed to be little danger

Relation of the universities to the Church.

of rivalry. The reconciliation of orthodoxy and free speculation, which had put the limited but safe activity of a Peter
Lombard in the place of the antagonistic ideas of a Bernard
or an Abelard, still continued during the period that saw the
crystallisation of the European schools into systematic corporations. If the Civilians upheld a Barbarossa, the Canonists
were equally strenuous in upholding the universal bishopric
of the Roman pontiff. North of the Alps every scholar was
a clerk with the privileges of clergy, and the Church alone
provided both the materials of thought and the worldly careers
that were open to scholars. If the Italian scholars were commonly laymen, the spirit of the Italian schools was too averse
to abstract speculation to be likely to lead to formal heresy,
and law was still, even in Italy, the study through which
churchmen rose to greatness. Yet it was by no means clear,
at the beginning of the century, that the intellectual ferment
which the universities had perpetuated would permit the
reconciliation of philosophy with theology, and of law with
the ecclesiastical order. The tradition of Greek thought

The intro-
duction of
Aristotle.
had been revived before the twelfth century was
over, and the full knowledge of the ethical, physical
and metaphysical teachings of Aristotle did not
come in a more Christian shape when it was filtered through
the imperfect translations and free paraphrases through which

Arab and
Jewish
influence.
Arabs and Jews had kept alive a perverted yet
stimulating version of the doctrines of the great
Greek philosopher. The glories of the Arab and
the Jewish schools of Spain had already culminated in
Averroes (*d.* 1198), and Moses Maimonides (*d.* 1204), when
they were made public to the Latin world by scholars like the
translators employed by Archbishop Raymond of Toledo, and
Frederick ii.'s protégé, Michael Scot. The increased intercourse between East and West, which resulted in the Latin
conquest of Constantinople, led before long to a better
acquaintance with Aristotelian texts and to Latin versions
based upon the Greek itself.

The Moorish and Jewish doctors of Spain had endured persecution from the orthodox Mohammedans for the boldness and freedom of their speculations. The materialistic pantheism of Averroes was as famous as his commentaries on Aristotle, and the introduction of the latter was soon followed by the spread of the former. The doctrines of the Averroists stimulated anew the popular heresies of the Cathari, who were now fighting desperately against orthodoxy in Languedoc, and who still filled Lombardy with enemies of the Church. The union of the popular with the scientific heretics might well have led to a violent revolution, especially since the changes involved in the rapid progress of the age threatened social and economic disturbances that imperilled the whole order of society. The ever-increasing wealth and political power of the Church were blighting the best interests of religion. The new orders of the twelfth century had lost their early fervour, and proved almost as susceptible of corruption as their older brethren. The dangers of an earlier age were renewed, and the schools that had long been 'secular' in the mediæval sense bade fair to become secular in a more modern signification of the term. A famous Paris master, Simon of Tournai, boasted to those who had applauded his vindication of the orthodox faith that he could demolish it with equal ease and plausibility. In the early years of the thirteenth century Amalric of Bena taught undisguised pantheism at Paris, and had a following of enthusiastic and outspoken heretics, whose views were as wild and revolutionary as those of any of the Albigenses. The false teaching of Amalric was attributed to the influence of Aristotle and Averroes, and in 1215 the papal legate Courçon drew up a body of statutes for the Paris masters which prohibited the study of the physics and metaphysics of Aristotle—a prohibition renewed later by Gregory IX.—'until they have been examined and purged from all heresy.' In Italy, if there were less speculative theology than in Paris, there was

Intellectual and popular heresy.

more popular heresy, and more political opposition to the church that was also a state. The dangerous mysticism of the abbot Joachim might well become a new source of danger to the hierarchy. Despite all that Innocent III. had done his successors still saw themselves face to face with imminent danger. But the source from which salvation was to arise had already been revealed. From the obscure labours of Francis and Dominic was soon to come not only the reconciliation of the new philosophy with the old orthodoxy, but a revival of spiritual religion, from which asceticism became mighty to do good works, and in which the Church of the Middle Ages attained its loftiest and purest ideals.

In 1182 was born at Assisi John Bernardone, more often known by the nickname Francis, that is the Frenchman, which was given him by his father, a wandering cloth merchant,

St. Francis of Assisi, 1182-1226.

who had travelled much in France and loved its people. The father was well-to-do, and ambitious that his gifted and attractive son should play a great part in the world. But an overmastering religious enthusiasm soon drew Francis from the revels and sports of the wealthy youth of Perugia. He renounced friends, fortune, kinsfolk, and declared that he had wedded the Lady Poverty, the fairest, richest, and purest of brides. His glowing imagination and earnest spiritual longings saw all things through the medium of a divine and ecstatic love. His single-minded devotion to the poor and afflicted, his loving care for the despised and neglected lepers, his holiness, pureness, and goodness soon attracted round him a little band of followers. One day he took them into a church, opened the gospels on the altar and read them the words in which Christ bade His

Beginnings of the Ordo Minorum.

disciples sell all that they have and give to the poor, and take no care of staff nor scrip, nor gold or silver, nor bread nor clothes, but leave all and follow Him. In these words, he told his followers, lay all their life and rule. His one endeavour now became the literal imitation of Christ's life on earth. The doings of Francis and his penitents excited lively opposition as well as unbounded admiration. But in 1210 Francis and eleven companions travelled on foot to Rome, where Innocent III., stranger though he was to their spirit, received them kindly and permitted them to continue to uphold their simple rule of absolute poverty and devotion to good works. The brotherhood grew in numbers, and soon spread beyond the limits of Assisi and central Italy. Francis himself went on missions to the heathen, and pleaded for Christianity before the Sultan of Egypt. Francis called himself and followers the Poor Men of Assisi, or the Order of Lesser Brethren (Ordo Minorum); but the rope-girt grey frock that they wore caused the people to call them the Grey Friars, while the prestige of the founder frequently gave them the name of Franciscans. For years the fraternity in no wise departed from its primitive simplicity. The simple mysticism of Francis, his frank joyousness and cheerfulness, despite his constant perils and rigid asceticism, his strange and forcible preaching, and his utter indifference to all worldly power and influence, won an absolute mastery over men's hearts. He was not a man of learning: he was a simple deacon, who never aspired to the priesthood · he was no organiser, and had an absolute horror of the political forces that kept the Church so absorbed in worldly cares. The grow- The Rule of ing support of great churchmen, the powerful 1223. favour of the zealous Cardinal Ugolino, the future Gregory IX., the establishment of a fixed rule for the order by Honorius III. in 1223, were evidence of the spread of the founder's ideas. Yet they gave Francis as much anxiety as satisfaction. They involved the danger lest the simple gospel of love should be overshadowed by formalism and officialism, lest the doctrine of absolute poverty should be inter- Antagonistic tendencies preted so as to become a snare to the brethren within the as it had been to the older orders of monks. Franciscan Order. The gentle saint retired to his favourite chapels and shrines near Assisi, leaving to the energetic and strenuous

Elias of Cortona the uncongenial but necessary task of organising the new society. Francis died in 1226, full of trouble as to the future, and solemnly warning the brethren to add no glosses or amplifications to the absolute simplicity of the rule which he had prescribed for them. Two years later Gregory IX. made him a saint, and laid the foundation of the great church at Assisi, where the art of Giotto was later to commemorate his glories. But the absorption of the Franciscan spirit to the service of the hierarchy had robbed it of much that was most beautiful and characteristic. Later divisions within the order long bore witness that the literal doctrines of the Testament of St. Francis were still cherished by his more faithful followers. But a great world-wide order could not be controlled by a few pious aspirations and general exhortations to poverty. The work of Gregory and of Elias was as necessary as the life and character of the founder himself, if the Franciscan order were to maintain the place which it had begun to fill in the life of the thirteenth century.

Even before Francis had begun to preach poverty and good works to the scattered towns and villages of central Italy, St. Dominic, Dominic de Guzman had begun his parallel but 1170-1221. yet strangely different career. The son of a mighty Castilian house, a man of learning, zeal, and fiery orthodoxy, Dominic had become a regular canon of the cathedral chapter of Osma, near which town he was born in 1170. The Premonstratensian ideal of living like a monk and working like a clerk was never more fully realised than by this young Spanish canon. Called almost by accident to Languedoc, he resolved to devote his life to the winning over of the Albigensian heretics to orthodoxy. Protected by the bishop of Toulouse, he settled down in a house in that city, where he soon gathered around himself a band of like-minded followers. He remained there during all the storms of the Albigensian wars, and his little society flourished so much that he sought to obtain for himself and his sixteen companions recognition from the Pope as a new religious order specially devoted to the conversion of heretics. But the decision of the Lateran Council of 1215 against the establishment of new orders stood in their way, and Innocent III., though sympathetic, was contented to recommend them to affiliate themselves to one of the recognised regular fraternities. Of these, Dominic's own 'rule of St. Austin' best expressed his ideals, and in 1216 Honorius III. confirmed the adoption by the 'Preaching Brothers *The Preaching Brothers of Toulouse, 1216.* of St. Romanus of Toulouse' of a modification of the Premonstratensian rule. The first four years of the young brotherhood were full of success. Affiliated communities sprang up in Spain, in Italy, and in northern France, where the famous convent of the Jacobins was set up at Paris on the south of the Seine, hard by the Orleans gate. In Rome Dominic found a warm welcome and an establishment within the papal palace, along with the pastoral care of the numerous courtiers and domestics of the pontiff. Cardinal Ugolino was as zealous for Dominic as for the Poor Man of Assisi, and was perhaps the means through which the Spanish canon made the personal acquaintance of St. Francis. The result of this intercourse was that Dominic was strongly impressed with the holiness and beauty of the Franciscan cult of poverty, and resolved that his order also should tread in the footsteps of Christ and the Apostles after the method set forth by the Franciscans. In 1220 the Order of Preachers, as it was now called, took its final form by adopting the doctrine of absolute corporate poverty as well as the life of mendicancy which had become *The Order of Preachers becomes a Mendicant Order, 1220.* usual with the Franciscans. Dominic then went to Bologna, to seek from the doctors there new support against the heretics. In 1221 he died, and was buried at the house of his order in that city. In 1234 Gregory raised him to the list of saints. Long before this his followers were spread all over Europe, rivalling in zeal and energy the Franciscans themselves. The Preaching Friars were called Dominicans from their founder, while their plain but effective garb of a short black cape, over a long white frock, led to their popular name of the Black Friars.

The ideals of Francis and Dominic were widely different, but the methods they adopted to secure them were almost The Mendi- identical. The man of inspiration and love had cant Ideal. won over the man of authority and order to his ideal of absolute poverty; and Franciscans and Dominicans alike agreed so to interpret the monastic vow of poverty that corporate as well as individual possessions were utterly renounced. The early Franciscans had neither houses nor churches. The Dominicans, faithful to their Augustinian traditions, did not push the principles of St. Francis so far as this, but contented themselves with ordaining that the houses of the order should be simple, modest, and of lowly dimensions, and that all ornaments should be reserved for their churches. Gradually, as the spirit of Elias prevailed over the spirit of Francis, the Minorites also had houses and churches of their own, and with the establishment of a systematic conventual life, the isolated brother, working with his hands for his bread, or depending, in his pious wanderings, on passing charity, was replaced by an ordered band of Mendicant Friars, members of a world-wide order, controlled by an almost military discipline that found its expression in the autocracy of the General of the order, and in the annual assembling of a General Chapter, such as the Lateran Council had imposed on all conditions of religious. Thus the Mendicants pushed to further results the great principles of monastic reformation which had already been worked out in the twelfth century. The world-wide organisation and simplicity of life came from the Cistercians, and the vindication of the freedom of the individual as against the excesses of the cœnobitic ideal had belonged to the Carthusians. The combination of the 'religious' life and the work of the ministry characterised the Regular Canons. But the doctrine of absolute Poverty was all their own, and calculated to save them from the dangers before which the new orders had succumbed. The mysticism and love of the poor which had characterised Francis left an enduring impression on his followers. No less strong was the spirit of reasoned orthodoxy and the zeal for popular preaching against heresy which adhered to the Order of Preachers long after its founder had passed away. Francis aimed at the heart, while Dominic appealed to the intellect, but the work of both communities was social and evangelistic, and even when they most differed in spirit they constantly overlapped each other in their labours. Their convents were soon established in every part of Christendom, and exercised the profoundest influence on every section of the community.

So striking was the attraction of the Mendicant ideal that many other attempts were made, besides those of Francis and Dominic, to embody its principles. Even in the lifetime of the Poor Man of Assisi, his influence had gone beyond his own immediate band of followers. So far back as 1212 the spirit of Francis had driven Clara Scifi, a knight's daughter in Assisi, to settle down by the little chapel of St. Damian with a band of followers, pledged to a poverty as absolute and a self-renunciation as complete as that of the Minorites themselves. If Cardinal Ugolino for a time imposed on these 'poor ladies' a rigid form of the rule of Benedictine nuns, the earnest wish of Francis himself procured from Honorius III., in 1224, the approval of a plan of life by which the community was to adopt the principle of absolute poverty (save in respect to cloister and garden), depend for support upon freewill offerings, and promise special obedience to the Pope, brother Francis, and their successors. The 'Claresses' or 'Poor Clares' soon became numerous and did for the religious life of women what St. Francis did for regular communities of men. A more sweeping innovation was the establishment by St. Francis himself of lay brotherhoods of penitents, affiliated to the Mendicant orders, and living

Other Mendicant Orders.

St. Clare and the Claresses.

ordered and religious lives, yet untrammelled by vows and,
The unlike the *conversi* of earlier reforms, continuing in
Tertiaries. the exercise of their worldly professions. In 1230
Gregory IX. formally founded these communities as 'brethren
of the third order of St. Francis.' Similar societies of 'Tertiaries' were also affiliated to the Dominicans. By their means
the Mendicant ideal was still further spread, and the great
framework of affiliated societies established which so closely
connected the new orders with the religious life of the time,
and broke down the ancient breach between 'religion' and
The the 'world.' Moreover, after the triumph of the
Carmelites. Franciscans and Dominicans, other Mendicant
Orders were set up, and some older brotherhoods brought into
the Mendicant fold. Among the latter were the communities
of hermits on Mount Carmel, which in 1219 were constituted
by the Patriarch of Jerusalem as the Hermit Friars of Mount
Carmel, and received from Innocent IV. the stamp of a Mendicant order. The white garb of the Carmelites gave them
the popular name of the White Friars. In 1250 Alexander IV.
The Austin created the Austin Friars out of several societies
Friars. of Italian hermits, to whom he prescribed a
common rule and the Mendicant ideal. Carmelites and
Austin Friars took up a strong position all over Europe,
almost vying with Minorites and Preachers, and constituting
with them the Four Orders of Friars. Other mendicant
societies, such as that of the Friars of the Sack, were also
set up, but in 1274 the second Council of Lyons abolished
The all but the four recognised orders and forbade
Servites. the formation of new ones. Nevertheless, the
Servite Friars, an offshoot of the rule of St. Augustine, received
a separate establishment before the end of the century.

The Mendicants of the thirteenth century worked out to
The Work the fullest result the ideal of St. Augustine of com
of the bining the life of a monk with the work of a clerk,
Mendicants. and thus stand in the strongest contrast to the
older contemplative orders, who sought seclusion from the

world and eschewed even the care of souls as a worldly occupation. If, despite this self-imposed limitation, the earlier orders had been enabled to play so large a part in the religious life of the times of their foundation and early fervour, it is easy to see how much more complete and permanent was the influence of bodies of self-devoted men pledged to redeem their own souls by working out the salvation of others. Through their labours the ascetic and hierarchic ideals of the Church penetrated, as they had never penetrated before, into every rank and every region of the Christian commonwealth. Popular preaching assumed a new importance now that specialists trained to devote their lives to pulpit oratory supplemented the rude and occasional Preaching. efforts of the ill-educated parish priests, and the still more occasional appearances of the dignified clergy as teachers of the people. Preaching was naturally the first care of the followers of Dominic, whose official name was the Order of Preachers, and among whose doctors one at least maintained that preaching was more important for the people than the Mass itself. But, even from the beginning, the Minorites were almost as much devoted to this work as Contrast the Black Friars themselves. While Dominican between preaching tended to be grave, learned, and Franciscan
and argumentative, the Grey Friars rather affected Dominican the simple, straightforward, emotional methods Preaching. of address, through which St. Francis himself had gone straight to the hearts of his hearers. These qualities were strongly illustrated by the career of St. Anthony of Padua (*d.* 1231), a native of Lisbon and an Austin canon, who, like St. Dominic, preached with great effect in Languedoc, and, attaching himself to St. Francis and Poverty, became the most popular of the early Minorite orators, and died in 1231 at Padua, in the enjoyment of a unique reputation for his eloquence and miraculous powers. The best side of the Mendicant gospel was impressed on Germany and the East by the wonderful preaching of another Minorite, Berthold of

Ratisbon (*d.* 1272), whose still surviving German sermons are striking illustrations of the depth and force of the new teaching. Nor did the Order of Preachers neglect the more popular side of its special work. Its greatest intellect, St. Thomas of Aquino, was not only the famous doctor of the schools but a practical preacher to the people in the Italian

Religious vernacular.   Not less effective and more per-
Poetry.   manent than their sermons was the religious poetry inspired by the Mendicants, and especially by the Franciscans, both in the vulgar tongues and in Latin. St. Francis' own famous Song of the Sun struck a chord that was re-echoed in the hearts of his followers. To his biographer, Thomas of Celano, is commonly ascribed the most majestic of mediæval Latin hymns, the *Dies Iræ*. The pathetic *Stabat Mater Dolorosa* is, with less certainty, attributed to Jacopone da Todi, a Grey Friar of the latter part of the century, whose vernacular poems express not only the mystic piety of St. Francis but the fierce glow of indignation of the Fraticelli against the worldliness of the hierarchy.

The pastoral work of the Mendicants among the people was the chief means by which they established that profound

Pastoral hold over the mind of Europe that, despite many
care.   corruptions, they retained until the Reformation. The parish clergy were ignorant and lax, and tended in too many cases to limit themselves to the perfunctory discharge of the routine duties of their office. A new state of things began when the zeal of Gregory ix. assured for both Franciscans and Dominicans the right to preach and hear confessions over all Christendom. Despite the natural but violent opposition which both· the seculars and the older orders offered to their pushing rivals, the Friars soon won by their devotion, their skill, and their sympathy a unique place among the religious teachers of Europe. They chose as their favourite abodes the noisome suburbs where the poorest were huddled together outside the bounds of municipal authority or care. They lived among the sick, the suffering, and the

lepers. Poorer than the poorest, they inspired no envy, but shared the lot of those among whom they lived and worked. They set no rigid limits to their activity. Their care for the sick led them to the study of medicine, while their sympathy with the oppressed made them the natural spokesmen of the cause of popular rights. A nameless Franciscan formulated the English baronial policy in the Song of Lewes. Yet kings like St. Louis or Edward I. chose Friars as their confessors, and their power was as great among the highest as the lowest. Great churches grew up in every city of Europe for each of the four orders of Friars, and were thronged by earnest and zealous congregations. It became a cherished privilege to be allowed burial within their precincts. The extraordinary popularity of the Mendicants soon brought dangers in its train. Their churches became more splendid and adorned with the fairest works of art. Wealth flowed towards them, and this, though at first they held it in trust for the poor, they soon began to regard as virtually their own, with the result that, particularly among the Franciscans, there was a continued feud as to whether the rule of absolute poverty was to be rigidly or laxly interpreted. Long before the danger of wealth had begun, the more subtle temptations of power had exercised their sway. In direct contradiction to the teachings of St. Francis, Mendicants accepted high places in the Church, and became bishops, archbishops, cardinals, and popes. Flushed with the pride of their devotion, they laid their hands on all that they could reach. They called the Benedictines proud epicureans, the Canons little better than laymen, and the Cistercians rude rustics. ‘None of the faithful,’ lamented the Benedictine Matthew Paris, ‘now believe that they can be saved unless they are under the direction of the Preachers or the Minorites.’ Innocent IV. sought to withstand their growing influence by refusing to allow them to exercise the cure of souls in parishes without the permission of the parish priest, and directed that they

The extent of Mendicant influence.

should hand over to the same authority a share of the gifts made to them by the faithful who had bought the right of burial in the friars' churches. But on Innocent's death—hastened, as it was believed, by the prayers of the Mendicants—Alexander IV. reversed his legislation and left the new orders triumphant. With all their feverish grasping after power, they used it with more sense of responsibility than most of their rivals. A real revival of religion followed everywhere upon their work, and was manifested not only in formal acts, in heaping wealth upon ecclesiastics, and in an extension of the power of the Church, but in works of piety and justice, generosity and mercy, that were all too few in the rude Middle Ages.

The Mendicant Orders were everywhere the champions of papal authority, rigid hierarchical pretensions, and uncompromising orthodoxy. Both Franciscans and **The Mendicants and the Inquisition.** Dominicans were intrusted with the administration of the Papal Inquisition which Gregory IX. had established, and did not scruple to hand over to the secular arm the relapsed or unrepentant heretic. But they were not merely persecutors. They were unwearied in their missions to the heretic as well as in those to the heathen and the infidel, and it was now an easier task to deal with popular heresy, since it yielded even more readily to the preaching of the Friars than to the terrors of the Inquisition. The intellectual heresies of the schools, and the vaguer unrestfulness that saw no permanent satisfaction in the traditional teachings, were harder to deal with. Yet even against these the Mendicants waged a long contest, which did not end until they had wrested scholastic philosophy and the new Aristotle to serve as chief buttresses to the authority of the Church.

The special mission of the Order of Preachers made it from the first a great centre of theological study. **The Friars and the Universities.** St. Dominic settled down in Bologna because of its schools, and his death and burial there gave the place an enduring sanctity to his faithful followers.

In 1221, the year of the founder's death, the Dominican Convent of St. James was established at Paris, and very soon made itself a separate and exclusive school of rigidly orthodox theology, without any great care being taken to co-ordinate its teaching and system with those of the public regents of the university. Doctors of great reputation attached themselves to the order, and before long a regular succession of friar-doctors, trained within the convent, set up a definite type of Mendicant theological teaching. The Franciscans were not slow in following the example of the Preachers. Though Francis himself had no learning and few speculative interests, his teaching had never been more effective than among the proud doctors of Bologna, and the spirit of Elias and Ugolino, no less than the necessities of the time and the desire to rival the Preachers, turned even the earlier followers of the saint to theological study. With the establishment of St. Anthony, Francis' close friend, at Padua, where a great university was just being formed by a secession from Bologna, the Minorites enter eagerly on the course marked out by St. Dominic. If Francis inspired Dominic with the worship of poverty, Dominic supplied the followers of Francis with his zeal for theology. Within a year of the foundation of the Jacobin convent, four years before St. Francis' death, the English theologian, Alexander of Hales, who was then teaching with great applause at Paris, entered the Minorite fold, and was celebrated as the 'first Paris doctor of the Franciscan religion.' Before long he resumed his teaching, and henceforth the Parisian convent of the Franciscans was only second to the Dominican cloister in its intellectual activity. Within thirty years the Mendicant schools of theology had taken up so overwhelming a position in Paris, and so ostentatiously kept aloof from all the ordinary regulations and traditions of the university, that a vigorous attack was made upon them by the secular masters. In 1252 the university required the Friars to take an oath of obedience to its statutes,

The struggle between Mendicants and Seculars at Paris.

and, on their refusal, expelled them from its fellowship. A fierce and long struggle followed, in which the chief secular champion, William of Saint-Amour, wrote a book called *The Perils of the Last Times*, which violently attacked the Mendicants and their ideals. The seculars availed themselves of the notorious splits within their enemies' ranks, and regarding the orders as a whole as responsible for the extremer members of one society, signalled out for attack as heretical an 'Introduction to the Eternal Gospel,' in which an Italian Franciscan gave currency to the apocalyptic ideas of the abbot Joachim. The disfavour of Innocent IV. to the Friars increased their difficulties, though they had strong supporters in St. Louis and his brothers. At last Alexander IV. cleared the way for their return, and condemned William's book as scandalous though not heretical. Restored to their chairs in 1255, the Mendicant doctors were contented to abate some of their extreme pretensions. Finally, they decided to accept the oath to the statutes and recognise their responsibilities as members of the corporation of masters. Their doctors were now in so commanding a position that they had no longer reason to desire such exceptional privileges as in the days of their weakness. South of the Alps the Mendicant theologians acquired what there was no chance of their ever getting in the northern universities, a practical monopoly of the teaching of theology. Everywhere the tone of the theological schools was attuned to their teaching. Philosophy was made orthodox, and the most brilliant and fruitful period of scholasticism followed when the ranks of the Friars produced the greatest of the mediæval philosophers and theologians.

The Mendicants' victory.

Alexander of Hales (*d.* 1245), the first Franciscan doctor at Paris, began in his *Summa Theologiæ*, which weighed, said an enemy, as much as a horse, the series of the systematic Mendicant scholastics, and was celebrated as the monarch of theologians and the irrefragable doctor. The first of the great Dominicans was

The Great Mendicant Scholastics.

Albertus Magnus (*d.* 1280), a German, who as doctor at Paris, chief of the Dominican school at Cologne, Albertus Provincial of his order in Germany, and bishop Magnus. of Ratisbon, exercised a profound influence and became known as the universal doctor. Albert's pupil, Thomas of Aquino (1225-1274), represents the culminating Thomas point of scholastic theology. A son of an illustrious Aquinas. Neapolitan house, Thomas renounced the brilliant worldly career promised by his influence and abilities, and entered a Dominican convent. He studied under Albert at Paris, where he acquired a unique reputation. Called back to Italy by Urban IV., he gave a momentary lustre to the struggling university at Naples, which Charles of Anjou had restored. He died in 1274, on his way to the Council of Lyons. Short as was his life, he was not only 'the most authoritative but the most voluminous of the schoolmen. His *Summa Theologiæ* represents the most complete accommodation of Aristotelian doctrine with Catholic orthodoxy, and has profoundly influenced all later ecclesiastical teaching. His political and ethical writings no less faithfully represent the Peripatetic tradition. His friend, the Italian Franciscan Bonaventura (*d.* 1274), a pupil of Alexander of Bonaventura. Hales, gave a scholarly form to the mysticism of the Minorites. Other paths of learning were trodden by writers such as Hugh of Saint-Cher, the chief of the mediæval expositors of Scripture, while the physical speculations and the advocacy of experimental methods by the English Franciscan, Roger Bacon (*d.* 1294), were the most Roger promising results of that contact with nature to Bacon. which the pursuit of medicine had led the Minorite order. Even in their studies the distinct individual impression of the two rival communities was preserved, but they so far worked in common that they had won for the Church the absolute command of the whole field of learning. With the death of Thomas Aquinas and Bonaventura in 1274 the most fruitful period of their activity came to an end.

ï bus the Studium, which might have rivalled the Sacerdotium, became its most strenuous ally, and the little band of The triumph mediæval scholars, who had enough faith and of the character to tear themselves away from bread-Schoolmen. winning studies and all-engrossing professions found their highest satisfaction in justifying the ways of the Church. Before the end of the century the Empire had fallen from its ancient dignity, and within a generation the Papacy itself succumbed to the rough measures of a royal conqueror. But though the Empire might decline and the Papacy itself wane, the command which the Church had acquired of the world of thought and learning remained but little broken until the dawn of the Renascence, and kept alive the papal idea when the popes were captive in a foreign land, and when, through a still more lamentable decline, rival pontiffs at Rome and Avignon disputed the allegiance of Europe and prostituted their dignity by the violence of their brawls. The Studium survived the Regnum, and sustained with its authority the declining might of the Sacerdotium, thus allowing mediæval ideas to remain longer in currency, even when the political and hierarchical system which had engendered them was no longer supreme and triumphant. It is significant that the chief seat of this newly-won power of the mind was at Paris, the one great national capital of the strongest of the national states that had arisen on the ruins of Feudalism and the Empire. But the national principles of the king and his knights and clerks in the Cité were in strange contrast to the fundamental ideas of the cosmopolitan doctors of the univer-Paris and sity. Yet both the physical forces which kings can France. wield and the intellectual influence of teachers and thinkers united to show that France had become the centre of all the chief European movements. In her vernacular literature, more strenuous, copious, robust and varied than that of any other nation, France was showing how in due course a new national culture might supersede the international universal culture of the mediæval schools. No less permanent was her influence on social ideas, on manners, on art, on knightly action and on civic life. It is significant that Brunetto Latini, the master of Dante, wrote his chief work in French, because 'the French tongue is the most delectable and the most common to all peoples.' Even in a land like England, at a time when the national sentiment was becoming strongly anti-French, the French tongue, art, manners and ideals became more profoundly influential than at the time when the island was the province of a French duke. So thorough an Englishman as Matthew Paris called the French monarch the king of earthly kings.[1]

[1] Rex Francorum qui terrestrium rex regum est tum propter ejus cœlestem inunctionem tum propter suam potestatem et militiæ eminentiam. —*Hist. Major*, v. 480

CHAPTER XIX

THE LAST CRUSADES AND THE EAST
IN THE THIRTEENTH CENTURY.[1]

Characteristics of the Thirteenth-Century Crusades—Innocent III. and the Crusades—The Children's Crusade—The State of the Latin Kingdom—The Fifth Crusade—Andrew of Hungary—John of Brienne and the Siege of Damietta—Crusade of Frederick II. and the Recovery of Jerusalem—Crusades of Theobald of Navarre and Richard of Cornwall—The Charismians conquer Jerusalem—The Tartar Crisis—The Sixth Crusade—St. Louis in Egypt—Divisions of the Latin Kingdom—The Mamelukes and Bihars—Fall of Antioch—The Seventh Crusade—Death of St. Louis at Tunis—Crusade of Edward I.—The Fall of Acre and the end of the Crusades.

THE terrible disappointment of the Fourth Crusade showed that the great age of the Holy Wars was over. Yet the century that began with that colossal failure has a place of its own in the history of the Crusades. In no age was the

The place of the Thirteenth Century in the History of the Crusades.

need of new expeditions to the Holy Land more constantly discussed or more commonly recognised. Numerous great Crusades were planned; many leading kings and princes took the Cross; and never was Europe more systematically or regularly taxed to defray the expenses of the projected movements. But very little positive results flowed from all the talk and preparation. The very Crusaders were not in

---

[1] Besides the general authorities referred to in an earlier chapter, special reference may be made to important recent monographs such as Röhricht's *Die Kreuzzugsbewegung im Jahre* 1217 (*Forschungen zur deutschen Geschichte* 1876), *Die Belagerung von Damiette* (Raumer's

earnest with their work, and few of those magnates who signed themselves with the Cross put their whole energy into the redemption of their vows. There were no longer the prospects of rich estates or principalities to attract Crusaders of the baser sort. To most the Crusade was a pious aspiration, or at best an incidental pilgrimage. The great expeditions never came off. St. Louis alone represented the ancient ardour, but the most successful Crusader was the sceptical and self-willed Frederick II. There was no thirteenth-century St. Bernard to direct the enthusiasm of Christendom. It was character-istic that St. Francis went to Egypt not to fight the Sultan but to reason with him, and that his disciple Roger Bacon questioned altogether the utility of the movement. The holy war aga'nst the Moors of Spain brought results that no longer flowed from the struggle in Palestine. Hermann of Salza showed a true instinct when he transferred the operations of his order from Syria to Prussia. Even the Popes began to divert the crusading zeal of Europe to the so-called crusades against heretics, and finally also against the political enemies of the Holy See. Yet to all earnest minds of the century, to fight, pay, or pray for the maintenance of the Latin East remained a Christian duty, while a constant stream of pilgrims and frequent small crusading expeditions kept alive for nearly the whole of the century the poor remnants of the Catholic kingdom of Jerusalem.

Despite the failure of the Fourth Crusade, Innocent III. never lost sight of the need of a more devoted and better-directed expedition that would save the declining fortunes of Latin Syria. Yet he did but a doubt-ful service for the crusading cause when he forced princes so careless as John of England and Frederick of Sicily to pledge themselves to the holy work. The enthusiasm for the Crusades was dying among the mighty, but it still

Innocent III. and the Crusades.

Historisches Taschenbuch 1876), and Riant's article on Edward I.'s Crusade in the *Archives de l'Orient Latin.* Joinville is indispensable for St. Louis's Egyptian Crusade.

lived on in the hearts of the poor, and the strange episodes
known as the Crusade of the Children showed
that the ignorant and disordered zeal that had
preceded the march of Godfrey of Boulogne had
still its representatives in the early thirteenth century. A
shepherd lad from the neighbourhood of Vendôme, named
Stephen, assembled a crowd of boys, peasants, workmen
and women, who made their way to Marseilles, and prevailed
upon two merchants to provide them with a passage to Syria;
but once embarked on the sea, the merchants sold them as
slaves in Egypt. Another swarm of German youths from the
Lower Rhine made their way to Brindisi, where the bishop
wisely prevented them taking ship, though very few ever
managed to make their way back to their distant homes.[1]
The useless devotion of these swarms of children is said to
have provoked from Innocent III. the remark, 'These children
shame us. While we are asleep, they march forth joyously
to conquer the Holy Land.' He had good reason for his
bitterness. Despite all his efforts, no Crusade had been
actually started at the moment of his death. Three kings,
however, had taken the Cross, and the Lateran Council
fixed June 1217 as the moment of their departure for the
East.

The death of John and the calculated delays of Frederick II.
left Andrew of Hungary the only reigning king
who started in 1217 for what is generally called
the Fifth Crusade. Andrew was a hot-headed and chivalrous
prince, who, abandoning the administration of his kingdom to
the great lords who were breaking down the
central power, sought in foreign adventures the
career that was denied him at home. Embarking with a

[1] The authenticity of the story of the Children's Crusade, challenged by
Winkelmann, *Geschichte Friedrichs des Zweiten*, is upheld by the great
authority of Röhricht in his article on *Der Kinderkreuzzug* in the
Historische Zeitschrift, vol. 36.

small army, mainly German and Hungarian, at Spalato, he took ship for Acre, where he found the Latin East in an exceptional state of confusion. The northern principality of Antioch had been wasting its resources in a long and devastating war with the Christian kings of Armenia, while famine, pestilence, and earthquake complicated the difficulties in which a rapid succession of weak rulers had plunged the kingdom of Jerusalem. Luckily the division of the dominions of Saladin among his sons and other kinsmen broke up the unity of Islam and saved the Latins from any real disaster, while the constant flow of small expeditions, the scanty outcome of the great efforts of Henry VI. and Innocent III., still enabled the Latins to carry on the struggle. Henry of Champagne, whom Richard of England had left King of Jerusalem, was accidentally slain in 1197. His widow Isabella, through whom he held his right to rule, chose a new husband in Amalric of Lusignan, the representative of the rival house that Richard had established in Cyprus, who was now crowned as King Amalric II., and reigned vigorously and successfully until his death in 1205. His infant son, who thus became Amalric III., died, as did his mother Isabella, before the year was out. Hugh, Amalric II.'s son by a former wife, now became King of Cyprus, while Isabella's eldest daughter by Conrad of Montferrat succeeded as Queen Mary of Jerusalem. Both princes were children, but a regent and husband was soon found for Mary by Philip Augustus. This was John of Brienne, a warrior of great experience and energy, though of slender resources. He reached Acre in 1210, and was then crowned together with Mary. Too weak to embark on an adventurous policy, John made a truce with the Saracens, and patiently waited until the expected Crusaders came. But the arrival of Andrew did not afford the hoped-for relief. Though a considerable army was collected, and the King of Armenia joined the Western Crusaders at Acre, the Christians

State of the
Latin King-
dom, 1197-
1210.

were not able to force the Saracens to engage in battle, and the kings of Hungary and Armenia soon went home disgusted.

The autumn passage brought many new Crusaders to Acre, and in 1218 John of Brienne prevailed upon his Western allies to take ship for Damietta, hoping thus to attack the Sultan of Egypt near the very centre of his power. At first fortune smiled upon their arms. Damietta was closely besieged, and a strong tower commanding the passage of the Nile was occupied, though the city still held out. The siege was carried on vigorously all through the winter, and many additional Crusaders joined the besieging army, conspicuous among them being the papal legate, Pelagius, who took the supreme command, and a band of English warriors, including Robert Fitzwalter and the Earls of Winchester, Arundel, and Chester. The Christians suffered severely from flood, pestilence, and famine, but at last, on 5th November 1219, Damietta was taken by a sudden assault. The fall of Damietta spread joy throughout Christendom and consternation all over the Mohammedan world. But the Christians quarrelled fiercely over the partition of the spoils, and John de Brienne, indignant at the assumption of Pelagius, withdrew to Syria. Saladin's nephew, El-Kamil, who now became Sultan of Egypt, profited by their slowness to build a new fortress, Mansourah, to block their invasion of the interior of Egypt. Nevertheless, the fear of the Christians was so great that the Sultan offered to yield up Jerusalem itself, if the Crusaders would but restore Damietta. But the Latins expected great things from the projected Crusade of Frederick II., and rejected his proposals. At last, in the summer of 1221, Pelagius advanced against Cairo, having persuaded John de Brienne to come back to his assistance. The expedition was a disastrous failure. The Egyptians flooded the country, and the invaders were soon prevented either from advancing or retreating, and were, moreover, threatened with starvation. John de Brienne prevailed upon the Sultan to allow the

Marginal note: John of Brienne and the Siege of Damietta, 1218-1219.

army to retire unmolested, on condition of Damietta being restored and a long truce granted. Thus the enterprise, from which so much had been hoped, ended in disastrous failure, and the Latin East remained in a worse plight than ever.

John de Brienne wandered through Europe imploring help for his kingdom. By his marriage of his daughter Iolande to Frederick II., he gave the hesitating Emperor a new motive for fulfilling his vow; but a rupture soon broke out between them, and, though Frederick claimed the kingdom on his wife's account, his father-in-law disappeared from the history of Syria, finding fresh fields for adventure in commanding the papal troops in Apulia, and dying in 1237 as regent of the Latin Emperor of Constantinople (see pages 353 and 369). At last Frederick II. went, as we have seen, on his long-deferred Crusade (see page 368). Despite the ban of the Church he obtained a large measure of success, and the treaty of 1229 restored Jerusalem to the Christians, after it had been for more than forty years in the hands of the Infidel. It was the last real triumph of the Crusades.

Crusade of Frederick II., 1227-1229.

Frederick had done a great service to Christendom in recovering Jerusalem, but his attempt to govern the Latin kingdom of Syria as a non-resident sovereign involved the land in fresh disasters. The Syrian lords revolted against the governors of the Emperor, and the continued disfavour of the Church extended with disastrous results the strife of Papacy and Empire into a region where the absolute union of all the Westerns was the essential condition of the maintenance of the Christian cause. Fortunately, the divisions of Islam saved the Syrian monarchy from any immediate danger, especially after El-Kamil's death in 1238, when there was again a general scramble for power among the numerous Ayoubite chieftains. Moreover, a constant stream of Crusaders still flowed to the East, and occasionally regular expeditions were successfully organised.

Decline of the Ayoubite Power.

Conspicuous among these latter was the Crusade of 1239,

Crusades of
Theobald of
Navarre
(1239) and
Richard of
Cornwall
(1240). which Gregory IX. had proclaimed, and then sought to divert, because of his renewed quarrel with the Emperor. Regardless of the Pope's advice, a numerous band of French nobles, headed by Theobald the Great, Count of Champagne and King of Navarre, and including Amalric of Mont-fort, the former Count of Toulouse, set sail for Acre. In 1240 an English Crusade appeared in Palestine, commanded by Richard, Earl of Cornwall, the future King of the Romans, who was joined by his brother-in-law, Amalric's famous brother, Simon, Earl of Leicester. But the King of Navarre had been beaten and had gone home disgusted before the Englishmen had arrived, and Richard, whose name and the fame of his uncle King Richard had excited the liveliest expectations, was able to do little more than make a treaty which secured the freedom of the captives. The fierce feuds of Templars and Hospitallers, and the renewed quarrel of Pope and Emperor, further increased the difficulties of the English prince. The rival attractions of an alliance either with Damascus or Egypt caused violent partisanships among those pledged to general war against the Infidel, while Richard was looked upon with much suspicion by the hier-archical party because he persisted in regarding Frederick II. or his son Conrad as lawful King of Jerusalem.

The great Mongol power was already disturbing all Asia. About 1220 the Charismians, a Turkish race that had estab-

lished itself to the south of the sea of Aral, and had finally reduced all Persia to subjection, were overwhelmed by the hosts of Genghiz Khan. The survivors of the disaster were driven into exile, and forced to earn their bread as the mercenaries of any Eastern prince who could pay for them. Es-Saleh Ayoub, El-Kamil's eldest son, the lord of Damascus, had been so hard pressed by his Christian and Mohammedan enemies that he took some of these fierce hordes into his service. In 1244 they suddenly swooped down on Jerusalem, and captured it, brutally murdering all its inhabitants. Christians and Mohammedans united against the savage Charismians, and provoked them to battle at Gaza. But the Saracens fled early in the fight, leaving the Christians to struggle alone against a superior enemy. The result was the annihilation of the crusading host and the practical end of the Latin Kingdom. Henceforth the Christians were reduced, as after 1187, to a few sea-coast cities. But the fall of Jerusalem now stirred up no such general ferment throughout Christendom as did its first reconquest by the Saracens. The news arrived when Innocent IV. was fulminating his final deposition against Frederick. The Crusade against the Emperor seemed to all followers of the papal teaching a more pressing necessity than the Crusade against Islam. Under such circumstances, the proclamation of a new Crusade at the Council of Lyons could lead to no real result. It was not by talk only that Jerusalem could be restored to the Cross.

The spirit of a former age was not quite extinct, but the only great prince who was still under its influence was the King of France. St. Louis had long desired to go upon Crusade, and would gladly have accompanied the King of Navarre in 1239. The state of his dominions was now so satisfactory that he at last felt able to embark upon the undertaking. After striving in vain to make the Crusade general by uniting Pope and Emperor, he saw that the effort would have to be made by himself alone. In the summer of 1248 he embarked from Aigues Mortes and took ship to Cyprus, where during the winter a large but almost exclusively French army of pilgrims gathered together. Among the adventurers was the lord of Joinville, who has in his *Life of St. Louis* left an imperishable account of the expedition.

Egypt was still the chief seat of Ayoub's power, and, as in 1218, it was thought more profitable to attack Egypt

than Palestine.　Thus the Sixth Crusade became almost a
repetition of the Fifth.　In the spring of 1249,
the Christian host sailed from Cyprus and landed
near Damietta.　They were luckier than John
de Brienne and Pelagius, for their arrival threw the Mussulman
garrison into such alarm that it withdrew in the night, and
Damietta was occupied without any difficulty.　Precious time
was now wasted waiting for Alfonse of Poitiers, who at last
arrived with reinforcements.　The army was also joined by
William Longsword, Earl of Salisbury, and a band of Englishmen.　Hot disputes arose as to the method of carrying on the
campaign.　The prudent were in favour of a gradual conquest
of the sea-coast, and advised a march on Alexandria.　But
Robert of Artois urged a direct march on Cairo, and his
opinion prevailed.　In November 1249 the Crusaders made
their way inwards through the Delta, untaught by the disasters
of thirty years before.　The result was a further repetition of
the blunders and ill-luck of Pelagius.　The vast host marched
from Damietta and invested Mansourah, but their progress was
made excessively slow by the difficult nature of the country,
cut up by broad canals and arms of the Nile.　The fatal rashness of Robert of Artois led a part of the army to a premature
attack, in which Robert was slain.　Before long the besiegers
were themselves almost besieged.　Wasted by heat and lack
of food, the Crusaders lost all heart, and finally a terrible
epidemic devastated the camp and completed their demoralisa-
tion.　Louis at last ordered a retirement on Damietta,
but the Saracens threw themselves on the retreating host.
Louis fought valiantly at the post of danger in the rear.　He
was before long taken prisoner, whereupon the whole army
laid down its arms.　The mass of the captives was put to the
sword, but Louis and the great lords were ransomed, in
consideration of an enormous payment and the surrender of
Damietta.　The King on his release went on pilgrimage to
Palestine.　He sent his brothers Alfonse and Charles back to
France, but himself abode for more than three years in the

Holy Land, labouring strenuously at restoring the Christian fortresses, and atoning for his failure in Egypt by works of piety and self-sacrifice. The Sultan of Damascus offered him a safe-conduct to Jerusalem, but he refused to see the Holy City since he could not rescue it from the hands of the enemies of the faith. At last the death of his mother necessitated his return to France (June 1254). He was the last Western king who led a great army to the East. *St. Louis in Palestine, 1251-1254.*

In the years after the return of Louis the Crusading State managed to hold its own. The Tartars still pressed on Islam on the east, and it was no time for the Saracens to make fresh conquests when their very existence was in danger. Moreover, constant changes in the Mohammedan world further limited its power of aggression. Es-Saleh died while St. Louis was in Egypt, whereupon in 1254 the Mameluke mercenaries finally destroyed the Ayoubite power, and, inspired by their leader Bibars, the soul of the resistance to St. Louis, set up sultans at their discretion and murdered them when they were weary of them. *The Rise of the Mame-lukes.*

It was small praise to the Franks themselves that the Crusading State still continued. The fierce factions of the Latins grew worse than ever. A line of bailiffs of the house of Ibelin ruled in the name of the absentee Hohenstaufen, Henry, Conrad and Conradin. With the execution of the latter, the house of Hohenstaufen became extinct, and the King of Cyprus, Hugh III. of Lusignan, was crowned in 1269 as King of Jerusalem, though his title was contested by his aunt, Mary of Antioch. His rule was not strong enough to keep order, so that Templars and Hospitallers, Pullani and emigrants, Venetians and Genoese, carried out their feuds with little hindrance. Acre, the crusading capital, remained, despite the disorder, a considerable commercial centre, and the trading rivalries of the Italian cities were the most fruitful of all sources of disorder. In 1258 a pitched battle between great fleets of Venetians *Vicissitudes of the Latin Kingdom.*

and Genoese was fought off the coast of Acre, in which the
Genoese were so severely beaten that they were obliged to
abandon their quarter in the capital and establish their factory
at Tyre.

While this was going on, the contest of Saracen and Tartar
reached its height. In 1258 the Tartars took Bagdad and
The Tartar   ended the nominal Caliphate.   Next year they
Crisis, 1258- appeared in Syria and captured Damascus.   The
1260.   Western Christians hoped that the Tartars would
root out Islam and then turn Christians, but the Syrian
Franks knew better.   Though the Prince of Antioch appeared
as a suppliant in the Tartar camp, the barbarians soon turned
their arms against Acre.   All that the Christians could hope
for was from the dissensions of their enemies.   Even this
did not avail them long.   In 1260 the Sultan Kutuz of
Egypt defeated the Tartars at Ain Talut.   It was the Eastern
counterpart of the victories of Conrad, and equally decisive.
The barbarians withdrew to the East, leaving Islam again
triumphant.

Kutuz went back to Egypt, and was murdered by his
Mameluke soldiers.   The time was now ripe for Bihars to
The Sultan   mount his throne, and the former Turkman slave
Bibars, 1260. and Mameluke captain soon proved himself the
most dangerous enemy that the Eastern Christians had seen
since the death of Saladin.   A stern but just ruler of his own
subjects, and a pious and ascetic Mussulman, he was willingly
obeyed by the Mohammedans of the Levant.   A strenuous
warrior against the Christians, he was also statesman enough
to seek allies among the Christian states of Europe, whose
friendship soon proved as useful to him as the valour of his
soldiers.   In 1262 Bibars began his attacks on the Latin
Kingdom.   Though town after town fell into his hands, the
Franks could not end their quarrels even in the face of the
enemy.   In 1267 the Genoese waged war against Acre, now
wholly given over to the commerce of Venice.   At that
very time Bihars, having already conquered the Templars'

stronghold of Safed, was devastating the country about Acre. In the spring of 1268 he conquered Jaffa, and then, turning his arms northwards, overran the princi- Fall of Jaffa pality of Antioch. Before the end of the year and Antioch, 1268. Antioch had surrendered, after a disgracefully short resistance. The northern crusading state was thus brought to an end, and once more Europe was confronted with the imminent danger of the few remaining towns, like Acre and Tripoli, that still resisted Bibars.

St. Louis again took the Cross, but even in France the crusading fever was dying out, and Joinville himself refused to accompany the king on his second adventure Seventh against Islam. Other sovereigns promised to Crusade, follow Louis's example. James of Aragon actually 1270. embarked, but a tempest shattered his ships, and he piously withdrew from an enterprise of which, he argued, God had shown His disapproval. Edward of England did not hesitate to leave his aged father to follow his uncle, the French king, but his following was small, and his departure was delayed. But the worst was that the host of St. Louis was no longer St. Louis an army of pilgrims or enthusiasts, but of highly again takes paid mercenaries or of reluctant barons, whom the Cross. duty to the king alone withdrew from their homes. Even more fatal was the presence of Charles of Anjou, established in Sicily since 1266, with whom Bibars had established friendly rela- tions, and who had striven hard to divert his The Crusade brother's army from Egypt or Syria to a place diverted to where it would more directly play the game of Tunis. the house of Anjou. His craft proved only too successful. He persuaded Louis to direct his forces against Tunis, an ancient dependency of the Norman kings of Sicily, whose sultans had always continued to pay tribute to the Hohen- staufen, though they had refused it to their Angevin sup- planter. Accordingly St. Louis disembarked at Tunis, and took up his quarters amidst the ruins of Carthage. He had hoped that the presence of his army would frighten the enemy

into yielding and accepting Christianity, but he soon found
Its Failure. himself blockaded in his camp. Plague followed
Death of the heats of summer, and on 25th August St.
St. Louis. Louis died. The new king, Philip the Bold,
who was in the camp, was almost forced by his barons to
conclude a truce by which the ancient tribute to the King
of Sicily was promised henceforth in double measure. The
remnants of the host then went sadly home, reverently con-
veying with them the remains of their dead monarch.

Edward of England appeared off Tunis after the truce had
been signed. He indignantly refused to be bound by the
Crusade of disgraceful accommodation, and sailed with his
Edward of little fleet of thirteen ships to Acre, where his
England, energy infused a little life into the resistance of
1270-1272. the Latins. Even there the subtle influence of
Charles of Anjou made itself felt. He offered his mediation
with Bibars, and the dispirited Syrian Franks could not refuse
the chance of enjoying a short period of rest. As at Carthage,
Edward contemptuously held aloof, but the truce was signed,
and the Sultan sought to assassinate the last champion of
resistance. The attempt failed, and as soon as his wounds
were cured, Edward went home to claim his kingdom. A
companion of his pilgrimage to Acre, Theobald of Liége, now
became Pope Gregory X., and strove once more to preach a
The Second great Crusade. At the Council of Lyons of 1274,
Council of which saw the temporary union of the Greek and
Lyons and Latin Churches, the whole Western Church was
the failure
to revive the called upon to contribute a tenth of its revenues
Crusades, for six years to equip the new Crusade. The
1274. Holy War was preached all over Christendom,
but the appeal fell on deaf ears. Gregory soon died, and his
successors allowed the kings of Europe to lay hands on the
sacred treasure, a power which Edward I. himself did not
scruple to exercise. The hopes of a new rising of Christendom became fainter and fainter as years rolled on and nothing
was done. The hollow union of Orthodox and Catholic soon

came to an end. The death of Bihars rather than the arms of the Westerns still kept alive the remnants of the Latin East. At last Islam descended upon its prey. In 1289 Tripoli fell, and in 1291 Acre itself surrendered. Henceforth the Latin East was only represented by the power of the Lusignans in Cyprus, and by the Hospitallers' stronghold of Rhodes. The crusading impulse still survived among a few enthusiasts : but with its decay as a real force over the minds of men the noblest period of the Middle Ages was at an end. Yet the Crusaders had not died in vain. With all their violence and fanaticism, they had afforded Europe the most striking embodiment of the universal monarchy of the Church. They had made a long and valiant effort to stem the tide of Eastern fury, and their long resistance lessened and lightened the shock of its impact. Had they succeeded permanently the Eastern Mediterranean would have been saved from the horrors of Turkish rule, and the Cross might never have yielded to the Crescent on the shores of the Bosporus.

End of the Latin Kingdom, 1291.

THE GROWTH OF CHRISTIAN SPAIN [1]

Characteristics of Spanish History—The Caliphate of Cordova and its decline
—The Christian States—Navarre under Sancho the Great—Beginning of
the Christian advance—Alfonso VI. and the Conquest of Toledo—The
Cid—The Almoravides and the Battle of Zallaca—The Divisions of
Islam—Rivalry of Almoravides and Almohades—Alfonso I. and the Rise
of Aragon—Affonso Henriquez and the Capture of Lisbon—Triumph of
the Almohades—Innocent III. and the Spanish Crusades—Las Navas de
Tolosa—James I. of Aragon and St. Ferdinand of Castile—Completion of
the Reconquest—Organisation of Christian Spain—Peter of Aragon and
Alfonso the Wise of Castile.

THE period covered by this volume is marked by the gradual
re-entry of the Spanish peninsula into the Christian Commonwealth. At the beginning of the tenth century
the Christian states of Spain were still confined to
the extreme north, while nearly all the land worth
having was subject to the sway of the Caliphs

Character-
istics of
Spanish
History.

of Cordova. Before the end of the thirteenth century Islam
had been driven back into the hills of southern Andalusia.
Four strong Christian kingdoms ruled the greater part of the
peninsula, and acquired, as a result of the continued Crusade
that gave them existence, a character intensely warlike, turbulent, religious, and enthusiastic. On the ruins of the civilisation of Islam arose one of the most characteristic types of
mediæval Christianity.

[1] Ulick R. Burke's *History of Spain*, 2 vols. (1895), S. Lane-Poole's
Moors in Spain, Watts' *Spain*, and Professor Morse Stephens' *Portugal*
(these three in 'The Story of the Nations'); Southey's *Chronicle of the
Cid*, H. B. Clarke's *The Cid* ('Heroes of the Nations'). Fuller accounts
in Dozy, *Histoire des Mussulmans d'Espagne*, and Schäfer and Schirrmacher's *Geschichte von Spanien*.

It is impossible to follow in detail either the unending revolutions of the Spanish Mohammedans, or the constant fluctuations of victory and defeat between them and their Christian rivals, or the intricate domestic history and perpetual unions and divisions of the Spanish states themselves. Yet the history of Europe, and of the great contest of Christianity and Islam round which so much of our history turns, would be very incompletely narrated were all reference to the Spanish struggle omitted. In the present chapter this can only be told in the baldest and briefest outline.

Among the first signs of the dissolution of Islam had been the establishment by a branch of the Ommiades of a schismatic Caliphate at Cordova. Yet so long as the divisions of the Mohammedan world were not too inveterate, the followers of the Prophet, if no longer active or aggressive, still upheld great and flourishing states. Nowhere did Mohammedan civilisation attain a greater glory than under the Caliphs of Cordova. The wealth, the luxury, the trade, the science and the arts of the East never shone more brilliantly than in the days when Cordova rivalled in splendour, luxury, and culture both the Fatimite Court at Cairo and the orthodox Abbaside Caliphs of Bagdad. Both the Jews and Christians enjoyed tolerable prosperity under the Ommiad yoke, and the schools of Cordova preserved a tradition of Greek culture which made them famous even in the Christian world. The Caliphs ruled over all Spain south of the lower Douro and the mountains of the Guadarrama, restricting the kings of Leon and Navarre and the counts of Castile within the rugged region of the north, while a series of half-independent Moorish states ran like a wedge from the Ebro to the Pyrenees, and utterly separated the kingdom of Navarre from the county of Barcelona or Catalonia, which in its weakness remained dependent upon the West-Frankish kings, as it had been since Charlemagne first organised the Spanish March between Pyrenees and Ebro. Wars of aggression seemed over; religious wars even

The Caliphate of Cordova.

were almost dead. The Christian warriors of the north held frequent intercourse with their infidel neighbours, and did not scruple to avail themselves of their aid in their ceaseless feuds with one another.

The decline of the Caliphate of Cordova destroyed these fair prospects. The dismemberment of Moorish Spain amongst The Decline a series of rival Ameers increased the opportu- of Cordova. nities of Christian aggression, while it destroyed the peace and prosperity of Islam. In 1002 the death of the great minister Almansor ended the prosperity of the Caliphate. In 1028 the fall of the Ommiades was completed. Yet Moorish culture died very slowly, and it was not until the next century was nearly over that the glory of Arab science attained its culmination in the career of Averroes (1126-1198), the greatest of the Cordovan doctors, and the teacher of the schoolmen of Christendom. But political supremacy had long passed away from the Moors. The disunion of Islam was the opportunity of the Christians, and, despite several Mohammedan revivals, the fortunes of Christian Spain were now assured, though for a long time the advance was fitful and exceedingly slow. The divided Moors fell back upon the support of their brethren in Africa, without whose help their decline would have been much more rapid.

At the time of the fall of the Calipate there were four Christian states in Spain, the kingdoms of Leon and Navarre, The and the counties of Barcelona and Castile. Christian Under the rule of Sancho the Great (970-1035) States. the little upland kingdom of Navarre held for the moment the first place among them. But Sancho turned his main energies towards conquering his Christian neighbours, Supremacy and before his death he dominated, with the title of Navarre of Emperor, all Christian Spain, save the Spanish under Sancho March. On his death his dominions were the Great. divided among his children. Among these was Castile, already erected into a kingdom in favour of his second son Ferdinand. Another son, Ramiro, had received

the little knot of mountain land which subsequently grew
into the kingdom of Aragon, and which under Alfonso I.
extended its territories towards the Ebro valley, Union of
at the expense of the Ameers of Saragossa. Mean- Castile and
while the preponderance formerly enjoyed by Leon and
Sancho the Great was transferred to central Spain beginning of
by the union of the ancient kingdom of Leon with advance.
the great monarchy of Castile, under Ferdinand I. Before
this prince's death in 1065 the conquest of the valley of the
Douro began the period of definitive expansion. In the
lower Douro valley Ferdinand set up the vassal county of
Oporto, and, between that stream and the Mondego, another
tributary county of Coimbra. Under Alfonso VI. the time
of the great conquests began. The Castilians crossed the
high mountains of Guadarrama, and penetrated into the valley
of the Tagus. For a long time Alfonso feared to break
openly with the Ameer of Toledo, the lord of that region,
but he found an ally in the rival Ameer of Seville, whose
daughter he now took as his concubine. While the Alfonso VI.
Moors of Toledo fought against their co-religionists conquers
at Seville, Alfonso conquered the upper valley of Toledo.
the Tagus, and became lord of Madrid, the modern capital
of Spain. In vain the Ameer offered to become the vassal
of the triumphant Castilian for the rest of his dominions.
Alfonso swept steadily down the course of the great river. In
1085 he entered in triumph into Toledo itself.

The history of Alfonso's alliances shows how little of
religious fanaticism entered into the wars of the two races.
Even his crowning conquest of Toledo was due not so much
to his prowess as to a treacherous league with some of its
disloyal defenders. Alfonso's famous subject, The Cid.
Ruy Diaz, the Cid Campeador, the most famous
legendary hero of early Spain, though figuring in romance
as a Christian hero, was in history a brave and self-seeking
condottiere, who sold his sword to the Moors, or took
the pay of the rival King of Aragon almost as cheerfully

as he fought for his native Castile. But the fall of the ancient Gothic capital created a terrible panic in the Mohammedan world, and something like a Crusade was started by Islam to win back the ground that it had lost. The frightened Ameers of Spain met together, and agreed to seek foreign help against the overbearing foe. A sect of

The Almoravides. Mohammedan enthusiasts, called the Almoravides, and mainly composed of the Berbers of the Sahara, had recently overrun all northern Africa, displacing the ancient Arab dynasts, and rekindling the ancient zeal of the followers of the Prophet. The Spanish Moors now turned to Yussuf, the Almoravides' leader, and begged him to come to their assistance. After some hesitation Yussuf accepted the challenge. In 1086 he crossed the Straits of Gibraltar. His army of fierce and barbarous nomads of the desert soon wrought infinitely greater havoc on the Christians than the lax and effeminate Arabs of the Peninsula had been wont to do. Alfonso VI., who was besieging Saragossa when he heard of Yussuf's arrival, turned south to resist the new foe, and the kings of Aragon and Navarre sent reinforcements to the strongest representative of the Christian cause. But on

Battle of Zallaca. 23rd October 1086 the host of Alfonso was utterly destroyed at the battle of Zallaca, near Badajoz, and the victorious African was proclaimed Ameer of Andalous or Moorish Spain.

Spanish Christianity was now saved by the dissensions that broke out between the Spanish Arabs and their African cham

Divisions of Islam. pion. The petty Ameers of Spain were disgusted at Yussuf remaining behind in the Peninsula and striving to be its effective ruler. Hostilities soon broke out between them and Yussuf, who, finding allies in the fanatic party in Andalous itself, diverted his arms from the Christians against the subordinate lords of Islam. Within the next few years he had conquered every Ameer save the ruler of Saragossa, who was suffered to hold his northern marchland against the aggressive Aragonese. During this period Alfonso VI.

resumed his conquests. He devastated the lower valley of the Tagus from Toledo to the sea, and for the time Alfonso VI. made himself master of Lisbon. Meanwhile the takes Lisbon. Cid profited by the dissensions of Islam to pursue a bolder career. He deserted his paymaster, the Ameer of Saragossa, and at the head of his trusty mercenaries sought to carve a state for himself out of the ruins of the power of Islam in eastern Spain. In 1094 he made himself Conquest of master of Valencia, after performing prodigies Valencia by of valour. But a disastrous failure cost him the the Cid. lives of the best of his troops, and in 1099 the Cid died of grief at the loss of his faithful followers. His widow strove in vain to hold Valencia against the Moors, but her only possible helper was the king of Castile, and he was too far off to give effective assistance. Three years later she abandoned the smoking ruins of Valencia to the Moorish hosts, and retired with the bones of her husband to a safe refuge in Castile. Before this Yussuf had become master of Mohammedan Spain. He again turned his arms against Alfonso, and easily drove the Castilians from Lisbon and their other recent conquests. It was all that Alfonso could do to maintain himself in Toledo. His death in 1108 saved him from further disasters.

Yussuf had already died in 1106, but the dissensions of Castile and Leon that followed the death of Alfonso VI. made it easy for his successors to hold their own. The rivalry Before long, however, the short term of activity of Almora- of an Oriental dynasty had ended; and the vides and Almoravides saw their African possessions taken Almohades. away from them by the newer and fiercer power of the Almohades, the Berbers of the Atlas, who had long resented the rule of their brethren of the desert. Meanwhile the Almoravides' hold over Spain was becoming weakened. The Berber soldiers still ruled over the Moslem as conquered subjects, and their fanatic zeal still more disgusted the Mozarabic Christians (*i.e.* the Christians subject to the Arab yoke) who had borne with equanimity the tolerant yoke of the Spanish

Alfonso I. and the Rise of Aragon. Arabs. A new saviour of the Christians now arose in Alfonso I. of Aragon, the true founder of the Aragonese power. In 1118 he had won for Aragon its natural capital in Saragossa. He led destructive forays into the heart of Andalusia, and brought home with him numerous Mozarabic families, to whom he afforded a new home in the north. By the time of his death before the walls of Valencia, Aragon had become second only to Castile among the kingdoms of Christian Spain. Nor were the successes of the Cross only in Aragon. Count Raymond Berengar IV. of Barcelona united for a time his county with Aragon and conquered Tortosa in 1148. In the extreme west the little counties of Oporto and Coimbra had long been united to form the county of Portugal, now ruled by Affonso

Affonso Henriquez and the Capture of Lisbon. Henriquez, the founder of Portuguese greatness. In 1139 Affonso penetrated far into the heart of the Moorish country beyond the Tagus and won the famous battle of Ourique. Next year he assumed the title of King of Portugal. In 1147, with the help of a fleet of English and German warriors on their way to join the Second Crusade, Affonso drove the Moors out of Lisbon, which now became the capital of the infant kingdom. The Crusaders to the East now joined hands with the Crusaders of the West. While the Northern pilgrims helped to conquer Lisbon, French Crusaders fought for Raymond Berengar of Barcelona and Provence, and the Knights of the Temple and the Hospital stationed themselves in the valley of the Ebro as well as in Syria. Spain soon had Military Orders of her own. In 1149 Sancho IX. of Castile captured Calatrava, on the upper Guadiana,

The Spanish Military Orders. from the Moors, and made it over to the Cistercians, who, inspired by St. Bernard, were already establishing themselves in Spain and proclaiming the Crusade against the infidel. In 1158 the knightly order of Calatrava was set up to defend the

Cistercian possession. The order was the 'holy soldiery of Citeaux,' a sort of martial section of the White Monks, and in close dependence upon them. In an equally close relation to the Cistercians stood the order of St. Julian, founded even earlier, in 1152, by the king of Leon, which became, in 1218, the order of Alcantara, when that strong-hold on the lower Tagus was won from the Moors and handed over to the knights to defend it. Both orders took the full monastic vows, but a less ascetic regimen prevailed with the order of Evora in Portugal, set up in 1162 as a sort of 'conversi' or lay brethren of the Cistercians, and allowed marriage and the enjoyment of property. On the same lines was formed, under the patronage of Alexander III. and Inno-cent III., the most famous of the Spanish orders, that of Santiago, which, alone of its class, was quite independent of Citeaux. Under the Cistercian guidance the Spanish struggle took more and more the character of a religious war. Instead of local wars between neighbouring *The Crusades in Spain.* chieftains, the contest now became part of the general struggle between the two civilisations and religions that had so long divided the world.

The deepening feud of the Almoravides and Almohades allowed the Christians, despite their own divisions, to win fresh ground. In 1146 Morocco was captured by the Almohades, who immediately afterwards crossed the Straits to extend their rule from Africa to *Triumph of the Almohades.* Andalous. The fierce sectarian conflict of the rival Moham-medans had for its natural result the almost simultaneous cap-tures of Tortosa, Lisbon, and Calatrava. But the Almohades soon made themselves masters of infidel Spain, and turned fiercely against the Christians. In 1185 they won the battle of Alarcos over Alfonso VIII. of Castile. Their victory stayed for the time the progress of the Cross, and restored Calatrava to the rule of the Crescent. For the rest of the century the constant wars between Leon, Castile, Navarre, and Aragon played the game of the infidel.

Innocent III. revived the Crusading ardour of Spain, and
inspired great bands of Northern warriors to cross the Pyrenees
Innocent III. and join in the struggle against Islam. Alfonso
and the VIII. sought to atone for the disasters of his youth
Spanish by victories in his old age. A vast Crusading host
Crusade. collected at Toledo, and showed its ardour by
mercilessly butchering the Jews of that city. The threats
and entreaties of the great Pope inspired King Peter of
Aragon and the king of Navarre to join the army of Alfonso
of Castile. The local military orders were well to the fore,
and only the king of Leon held aloof from the greatest
Battle of Las combined effort that had as yet ever been made
Navas de against Spanish Islam. The crusading host
Tolosa. crossed the mountains of Toledo and restored the
rule of Castile in the upper valley of the Guadiana, where
Calatrava was now restored to its Cistercian lords. It was
with much difficulty that the Christians could be persuaded to
advance farther south, but a shepherd showed them a path
which enabled them to avoid the Moorish host that was
waiting for them in the defiles of the Sierra Morena, and
they successfully crossed the mountains to Las Navas de
Tolosa, an upland valley watered by a tributary of the Guadalquivir. There, on 16th July 1212, was fought the famous
battle of Las Navas de Tolosa, which secured for ever the
preponderance of Christianity in Spain. Within fifty years
of the victory the Moors had all they could do to hold their
own in the little kingdom of Granada that alone represented
the ancient Andalous.

James I. (1213-1276) of Aragon and Ferdinand III. (the
Saint) completed the work which Alfonso VIII. had thus suc-
James I. of cessfully begun. The son of that Peter of Aragon
Aragon. who had fought so well at Las Navas de Tolosa,
James was called to his kingdom as a child by his father's
death on the fatal field of Muret. He was a true hero of
chivalry, one of the greatest warriors of the Middle Ages,
ardent, pious, merciful, and ignorant of the very name of fear.

Though a soldier of the Cross, his matrimonial irregularities did not escape papal censure. While first of all a warrior, he did not shun the arts of peace, writing in his native Catalan tongue an autobiographical chronicle which is one of the most precious records of the thirteenth century.[1] His first exploit was the conquest of the Balearic Islands between 1229 and 1232. He then turned against Valencia, anxious to do over again the work of the Cid. In 1238 Valencia opened her gates to him, and Aragon thus established her limits such as they remained so long as she remained an independent kingdom.

Saint Ferdinand (Ferdinand III.) of Castile reigned from 1214-1252, and was enabled in 1230 to effect the definitive union of Leon with his original inheritance. He fought with great brilliancy and courage with the Moors in the valley of the Guadalquivir, and before his death succeeded in utterly expelling them from the most famous of their haunts. In 1236 he conquered the ancient seat of the Caliphs at Cordova, and turned the famous mosque of many columns into a Christian cathedral, while in 1246 his triumphs in this region were completed by his capture of Jaen. Before that, in 1244, he had entered Seville, and in 1250 the capture of Xeres and Cadiz gave him access to the Atlantic. His successor, Alfonso X., completed the conquest of Murcia in conjunction with James of Aragon. Meanwhile Portugal had acquired her modern limits by 1262, by the conquest of Algarve, Spanish Algarve being also won by Alfonso X. When Islam was thus nearly overthrown the tide of conquest was stayed, and for more than two hundred years longer Granada, but Granada alone, remained in Moorish hands.

After the land had been won back from the Moors, the Spanish kings had to deal with the organisation and

St. Ferdinand of Castile.

[1] *The Chronicle of James I. of Aragon*, translated by John Foster, with an introduction by Pascual de Gayangos.

government of their conquests. The withdrawal of the
Mohammedans left great tracts of territory open to
the settlement of the hardy northerners, among
whom the land was divided out, like a new country
for the first time opened up to civilisation.
Foreign countries, especially the south of France, contributed
to these emigrations. The Mozarabs soon amalgamated with
the settlers, and even after constant expulsions a strong
Moorish and a considerable Jewish element remained, especially in the south, for the central provinces of Old and New
Castile were cleared of the Moors. The whole of Spanish
institutions bore a deep impress of the character of the
conquest. The military orders, who had fought so well, had
enormous territories in the reconquered lands. The clergy
were invested with higher authority than in any other
Christian country. The kings were proud to obtain from the
Papacy a confirmation of their right to govern their realms.
But the nobility was also very powerful, and the division
of interests between the greater and the lesser barons was so
marked that in Aragon they formed separate Estates of the
realm. In Castile the monarchical authority was the strongest,
but the grants of privileges to the king's partners in the
conquest had even here given the institutions a markedly
aristocratic character, and no country was fuller of hereditary feuds and local dissensions. Aragon was a thoroughly
feudalised country, where the maintenance of public rights
was intrusted to a supreme magistrate called the *Justicia*, before
whose tribunal all disputes between the king and his subjects
might be carried, and whose influence overshadowed that of
the monarch. The *Justicia* was always chosen from the lesser
nobility, a class that the Aragonese kings favoured as their
best supporters against the feudal magnates. Even the towns
of Spain bore the military and ecclesiastical impress that the
Moorish wars had given to the whole nation. They were an
important element of the *Cortes*, or Estates-General, that
grew up very early in the Peninsula. Their associations or

hermandads were almost as formidable to the crown as the leagues of the nobility.

After the reconquest from the Moors was over, Spanish history takes a new character. Under Alfonso X. of Castile (1252-1284), Peter III. of Aragon (1276-1285), and Affonso III. of Portugal (1245-1279) the internal development of the three chief Spanish kingdoms falls into line with that of the rest of Europe.

The New Spain.

Alfonso X., surnamed the Wise, of Castile, was one of the most remarkable sovereigns of the thirteenth century, and is well worthy to be classed with St. Louis, with Frederick II., or with his brother-in-law, Edward I. of England. His rare gifts gave him fame as a man of learning, a poet, a historian, and a legislator, but his violent and unmeasured ambition paid but too little regard to the narrowness of his resources, and he had not the iron will and strong, resolute character without which no mediæval king could be a successful ruler. Thus it was that Alfonso failed in his early struggles with his neighbour Affonso III. of Portugal, whose more limited ambitions better enabled him to carry out his ideas. While the Castilian strove to play a great part in Europe, the Portuguese built cities, encouraged trade and agriculture, and struggled successfully even with the Papacy. While Portugal secured its rights over the Algarves, Alfonso plunged into a long contest with his Castilian nobles, in which he was by no means triumphant. The marriage of Alfonso's sister with his Portuguese rival at last secured peace between the two realms. Alfonso X. was a theorist even in his famous legislation, called the *Siete Partidas*, in which he laid down a high theory of monarchy, though he could not live up to his pretensions. His contest with Richard of Cornwall for the Holy Roman Empire was the extreme example of his desire to cut a great figure in the world, but his subjects would not allow him to take any real steps to assert his claims. His quarrel with his son Sancho led to bloody

Alfonso X. of Castile.

Affonso III. of Portugal.

civil wars that were continued after his death, and made it
impossible for Castile to play a great part in Europe; but
with all his errors Alfonso the Wise had first made her a
European power. Even greater difficulties beset Alfonso's
Peter III. contemporary Peter III. in Aragon. Like James I.,
of Aragon. Peter III. had to yield before the nobles and the
confederate cities, while his intervention in the affairs of Italy
involved him in a fierce contest with the Papacy, and
seemed for long to be utterly futile. But, like Alfonso X.,
Peter prepared for others the way that he was unable to
traverse himself. More than two hundred years were still
to elapse before the rulers of the Peninsula were able to
realise the monarchical theories of Alfonso, and push to a
successful result the Italian policy of Peter.

SPAIN

AT THE END OF THE 12TH CENTURY.

The dates are those of Christian Conquest, except those of battles which are marked thus _____
The limits of the Christian states at the beginning of the 10th century shaded thus _____
The limits of Moorish Spain at the end of the 12th century shaded thus _____

SPAIN

AT THE END OF THE 13TH CENTURY

The dates are those of Christian Conquest, except those of battles which are marked thus ⚔

The limits of Moorish Spain at the end of the 13th century shaded thus

CHAPTER XXI

THE FALL OF THE HOHENSTAUFEN
AND THE GREAT INTERREGNUM [1250-1273].[1]

The Reign of Conrad IV.—Innocent IV. and Manfred—Alexander IV. and
Edmund of England—Manfred King of Sicily—Fall of Eccelin da
Romano—Ghibelline triumph in Tuscany—Urban IV.—Clement IV.—
Coronation of Charles of Anjou—Battle of Grandella and Death of Man-
fred—Charles conquers Sicily—Guelfic Revolution in Tuscany—Conradin's
Expedition to Italy—Battle of Tagliacozzo—The Papal Vacancy and the
Restoration of Peace by Gregory IX.—the Great Interregnum in Germany
—Rivalry of Richard of Cornwall and Alfonso of Castile—Destruction of
the German Kingdom—The Triumph of the Princes and the Town
Leagues—The Election of Rudolf of Hapsburg.

ACCORDING to his father's testament, King Conrad succeeded
on Frederick II.'s death-bed to the Empire and the kingdom of
The Reign of Sicily.   Conrad remained in Germany.   Manfred,
Conrad IV.,   Frederick's bastard son, acted as lieutenant for
1250-1254.   his brother in Sicily, and received as his share
in the inheritance the principality of Taranto.   To Henry,
Frederick's son by Isabella of England, was assigned either
Jerusalem or Burgundy, at Conrad's discretion, while to
Frederick, son of the dead Henry VII., Austria and Styria,

---

[1] To the authorities earlier given may be added Schirrmacher's *Die
letzten Hohenstaufen* and Kempf's *Geschichte des deutschen Reichs während
des grossen Interregnum*. A considerable literature of monographs and
dissertations has been written in Germany as to the Interregnum. Refer-
ences to it will be found in the present writer's article on Richard Io
Cornwall in the *Dictionary of National Biography*, vol. xlviii. pp.
165-175.

his mother's heritage, were allotted. But the hostility of the Church was not abated by the death of the chief offender. 'Root out the name of the Babylonian, and what remains of him, his succession and his seed,' was now the cry of Innocent IV. The careful precautions taken by the dead Emperor to maintain the union of the Empire and Sicily showed that the long struggle was still far from its end.

Conrad IV., finding that he made no way against his rival, William of Holland, left his wife with her father, Duke Otto of Bavaria, his chief supporter, and abandoned Germany. Early in 1252 he appeared in Italy. After rally- Conrad in ing his partisans in Upper Italy, he took ship at Italy, 1252- Venice for Siponto, where Manfred and the Apu- 1254. lian barons gave him a hearty welcome. His appearance within his kingdom was followed by a strong reaction in his favour. The magnates generally recognised him, and Naples and Capua were forced to open their gates. But misfortunes still dogged the house of Hohenstaufen. Conrad's position in southern Germany was now shattered by the death of his father-in-law, the Duke of Bavaria, which was rapidly followed by that of Conrad's nephew, the young Duke Frederick of Austria and Styria. Early in 1254 Henry, Conrad's half-brother, also died, and his removal destroyed the last ties which bound the Hohenstaufen to England. Worse than all, Conrad and Manfred began to disagree, and their dispute gave the Papacy an oppor- Innocent tunity to intervene with effect in Apulia. So IV.'s hosti- early as 1250 Innocent had sought to set up lity to him. candidates of his own for the Sicilian throne. He had sounded Richard, Earl of Cornwall, brother of Henry III., as to his willingness to accept it, and in 1252 he had renewed his offer. But neither Richard nor his brother, the King of England, were willing to break from the Hohenstaufen, though, after the death of Isabella's son, in 1253, their scruples were removed, and in the same year Henry III. accepted another offer of the Sicilian throne on behalf of his younger son Edmund. Meanwhile Innocent had returned m 1251 from Lyons to Italy, and had, after a progress through the north-Italian cities, taken up his residence at Perugia. Before the end of 1253 he was strong enough to return to Rome. Active hostilities were now threatened. Mendicant Friars vigorously proclaimed the Crusade against Conrad, and in the spring of 1254 Innocent renewed his

Death of excommunication. But in May 1254 Conrad
Conrad, 1254 died suddenly, when only twenty-six years old, leaving Conradin, a child of two, as his heir, and, in his distrust of Manfred, intrusting the regency to the Margrave Berthold of Hohenburg. The body of the deceased king had hardly been laid in its tomb at Messina when the ancient hatred of the Germans and South Italians burst out as violently as of old. Berthold found himself so powerless that he cheerfully

Innocent IV. gave up the regency, and Manfred was put in his
and Manfred. place. Meanwhile Innocent's troops had invaded
1254. the kingdom, and took possession of the important border stronghold of San Germano. The barons of the neighbourhood sent in their submission, and the Margrave Berthold made overtures to the Pope. Manfred was forced to negotiate with Innocent, and in September 1254 a peace was signed, in which Innocent recognised Manfred as Prince of Taranto and reconciled him to the Church. Nothing was said as to the rights of Conradin, and in October Innocent himself went on progress through the cities of the kingdom, and took up his quarters at Naples, where he posed as feudal lord of the realm, the disposal of which rested entirely in his hands. Manfred had hoped that his submission would be followed by the recognition, if not of his nephew, at least of himself as King of Sicily. He now saw that he had been tricked by the Pope, and that the king whom the Pope would acknowledge

Death of was not himself but the young Edmund of Eng-
Innocent, land. He rode hastily to the trusty Saracens of
1254. Lucera, and with their help gathered together an army to withstand the aggressions of the Pope. Before any

decisive action could take place, Innocent died on 7th December at Naples.

The Conclave assembled at Naples and elected a nephew of Gregory IX., who took the name of Alexander IV. The new Pope was described by Matthew Paris as 'kindly Alcxauder and pious, assiduous in prayer and strenuously IV., 1254-1261. ascetic, but easily moved by flatterers and inclined to avarice.' He had not the inflexible will of his predecessor and (though he continued Innocent's policy) he was not very successful in his efforts, despite the fact that it was easier to carry on the war against the Hohenstaufen now that the legitimate stock was almost extinct and Germany entirely isolated from Sicily. He soon found it prudent to withdraw from Naples to his own territories, but he excommunicated Manfred and renewed Innocent's offer of the Sicilian throne Edmund of England to Edmund of England. In April 1255 the King of Sicily. conditions were drawn up on which Edmund was to obtain the proffered kingship. He was to pay a yearly tribute of two thousand ounces of pure gold, and be responsible for all past and future expenses involved in the prosecution of the war against Manfred, besides sending an army and a general to assist in the conquest of his kingdom. Edmund was still a mere child, and remained in England while papal legates waged war against the usurper in his name and sent in the bills to King Henry, who exhansted his last resources in a vain effort to extract from the clergy and laity of England the sums necessary for their payment. Meanwhile Manfred more than held his own against the papalists, and showed in the struggle a Manfred daring courage and force of character that proved conquers Naples and that he was no unworthy son of his father. Before Sicily, 1255- the end of 1255 the bastard of Frederick had 1256. established his position on the mainland. Early in 1256 he crossed over to Sicily, and soon subjected the whole of the island to his obedience. Alexander now found that there was no prospect of the promised English army and subsidies. In

1257 the Pope's difficulties were increased by a popular revolt in Rome, where the Senator Brancaleone drove him to take refuge in Viterbo, while a violent and sanguinary democracy lorded over the capital and entered into friendly relations with Manfred, to whom the Ghibelline towns now turned as their best protector against Pope and Clergy.   By politic commercial treaties Manfred secured the active alliance of both Genoa and Venice.   At last he grew so strong that he scorned any longer to rule merely as the regent of his nephew. An untrue report of Conradin's death gave him a pretext for

Manfred's accepting the offer of the throne from the Sicilian
Coronation, magnates, and in August 1258 he was crowned
1258.   at Palermo.   He soon learnt that Conradin was still alive, but he did not lay down his crown.   For a brief space Naples and Sicily enjoyed peace and prosperity under his rule.   The early years of Frederick II. seemed revived, and the strong national traditions of the South Italian kingdom were never more capably expressed than in the brilliant court of Manfred at Palermo.

The cause of the Hohenstaufen seemed once more in the ascendant.   Even in Germany, where the little Conradin had hitherto found but scanty acknowledgment outside his hereditary estates in Swabia, things took a turn for the better. William of Holland died in 1256, and nearly a year elapsed before a new election was made.   Even then the papalists disagreed, and, instead of a single strong partisan with an undoubted title, two weak foreign claimants, neither of whom were very zealous for Rome, disputed, as we shall see, the title

Guelfs and of King of the Romans.   In Italy the success
Ghibellines of Manfred had led to a strong Ghibelline revival,
in Northern
and Central and the one apparent reverse which their cause
Italy.   now suffered in the fall of Eccelin da Romano did good by relieving the party from complicity in the odious deeds of the 'most cruel and redoubtable tyrant that ever was among Christians.'   The cities of north-eastern Italy began to revolt against the horrors of his rule, and the

papal Crusade preached against him now found a welcome even among his own subjects. But Eccelin lacked **Fall of Eccelin da Romano, 1259.** neither energy nor ability, and in September 1258 he signally defeated the Guelfic Crusaders at Torricella. But his comrade in victory, the Marquis Pallavicino, soon deserted his blood-stained cause, and was joined by Cremona, Mantua, Ferrara, and revolted Padua. Manfred himself expressed his goodwill to the confederates. Eccelin's days were now numbered. He made a last desperate effort to regain power by allying himself with the Milanese nobles who had been recently exiled from their city by the popular leader, Martin della Torre. But the attack on Milan failed, and Eccelin himself was wounded and taken prisoner at Casciano by Pallavicino and the Cremonese. Conscious that the game was up, he tore off his bandages and perished (7th October 1259). The allies now wreaked their revenge on his brother Alberic, murdering his wife and eight children before his eyes, and then tearing him to pieces with wild horses. The house of Romano had fought for its own hand rather than for the Emperor, and their fall did little towards helping forward the papal cause. Yet Eccelin was the prototype of the swarm of Ghibelline tyrants who in subsequent generations were the most characteristic upholders of a once great cause in Italy.

The fall of Eccelin made Manfred the uncontested head of the Italian Ghibellines. In 1258 the Guelfic city of Florence had driven out the local Ghibellines, who took refuge in Siena and appealed to Manfred for help. In 1260 the Florentines marched out against Siena with their *carroccio*. They were utterly defeated on 4th September at Montaperto, a battle which secured the triumph of the Ghibel- **Battle of Montaperto and Ghibelline triumph in Tuscany, 1260.** lines over all Tuscany save Lucca. The victors proposed to reduce Florence to open villages, but the patriotism and courage of the exiled Farinata degli Uberti dissuaded his fellow-countrymen from this act of sacrilege. Manfred had sent a troop of German horsemen to help the allies at Montaperto. He now, says Villani, 'rose to great lordship and state, and all the imperial party in Tuscany and in Lombardy greatly increased in power, and the Church and its devout and faithful followers were much abased.' The baffled Guelfs were now reduced to the sorry shift of sending to Conradin's mother in Germany, hoping to stir up her and her son to resent the power of Manfred.

Alexander IV. was now so hopeless that he vainly sought to make peace with Manfred. He died in May 1261, and a three

Urban IV. months' vacancy showed even more clearly the im-
1261-1264. potence of the cardinals and the abasement of the
Church. At last the choice of the conclave fell upon the nominal Patriarch of Jerusalem, James of Court Palais, the son of a cobbler of Troyes, who took the title of Urban IV. During the three years of his pontificate, the French Pope lived mostly at Viterbo and Orvieto, while at Rome the Ghibellines again won the upper hand, and talked of making Manfred their Senator. But Urban was a hot-tempered, strong and active partisan, who brought back the Papacy to the policy of Innocent IV., and struggled with all his might to lay low the power of Manfred, and strove, though in vain, to end the schism of rival kings in Germany. He was clear-sighted enough to see that it was no use fighting Manfred in the name of a nominal king like Edmund of England, especially since, after 1258, the Provisions of Oxford had effectually deprived

Charles his father of money and power. Urban therefore
of Anjou prudently threw over the creature of Innocent
offered and Alexander, and offered the Sicilian throne to
Sicily. Charles of Anjou, the brother of St. Louis, whose
successful rule of Provence had shown his fitness for the difficult task of withstanding the son of Frederick. St. Louis shrank from countenancing the aggression of his brother, but Charles was ambitious, and brushing aside all objections, gladly accepted the offer. Manfred meanwhile grew more powerful than ever, and was steadily extending his authority

over the States of the Church. Before the Angevin could come to his assistance, Urban IV. died on 2nd October 1264.

There was no delay in electing the next Pope. Guy Foulquois, a native of Saint Gilles, and a born subject of the King of France, who had attained the cardinal bishopric of Sabina, and was at the moment striving as papal legate to uphold Henry III. against his barons, was chosen in his absence by the cardinals, and assumed the name Clement IV., of Clement IV. A capable man and a strong parti- 1264-1268. san, Clement at once entered into the enjoyment of the results of the labours of his predecessors. He proclaimed a Crusade against Manfred, and in May 1265 Charles of Anjou himself appeared in Rome, where the fickle Romans, among whom the Pope never ventured to risk himself, received him with enthusiasm and named him their Senator. Next month a commission of cardinals conferred upon him the investiture of Sicily, and received his acceptance of the onerous condi- Charles of tions on which he was permitted to occupy the Anjou papal fief. He was to pay 8000 ounces of gold as King of tribute, to surrender Benevento to the Apostolic Sicily, 1266. See, and to renounce the office of Roman Senator as soon as he had conquered Manfred's dominions. Charles returned to Provence to raise an adequate army. Before the end of the year he was back in Rome, where on 6th January 1266 he and his wife Beatrice were crowned King and Queen of Sicily.

Within a few weeks of his hallowing, Charles invaded Manfred's dominions with an army of Provençals, North-French adventurers, and Italian Guelfs. The Neapolitans were unprepared to fight a winter campaign, and many towns and castles opened their gates to the French. Manfred retreated from Capua to Benevento, where he resolved to strike his great blow. On 26th February the Battle of decisive battle was fought in the plain of Gran- Grandella della, north-westward of Benevento. Manfred's of Manfred, Saracens easily scattered the Provençal foot, but 1267. were in their turn overwhelmed by the mail-clad mounted knights. The German cavalry, that were still faithful to the Hohenstaufen, sought to redress the fortunes of the day. Charles hastily directed the flower of his army against the Germans, who after a short sharp fight were outnumbered and defeated. The chivalry of Apulia took fright at the discomfiture of the Germans, and rode off the field with-

Charles conquers Sicily. out striking a blow. Manfred saw the hopelessness of the situation, spurred his horse into the thick of the fight, and valiantly met his fate. His wife and children fell into the victor's hands, and on that one day Charles gained his new kingdom, which he now sought to tame by stern and systematic cruelty. He was soon able to give material help to the struggling Guelfs of Tuscany. On the news of Charles's victory reaching Florence, the Ghibellines were expelled, and the Guelfs availed themselves of their triumph to reorganise the constitution. It was the

Guelfic Revolution in Tuscany, 1266-1267. first faint beginning of Florentine democracy, and the turning-point in the whole history of the city. Fearing for the permanence of their power, the Florentines called upon Charles to aid them. On Easter Day 1267, Count Guy of Montfort, the fiercest and wildest of the banished sons of Leicester, marched into the city at the head of a band of French horse. Charles was made lord of Florence for ten years. The Guelfs were almost as triumphant in Tuscany as in Naples.

Conradin was in his fifteenth year when the death of his uncle made him the sole surviving representative of the house

Conradin's Italian Expedition, 1267-1268. of Hohenstaufen. He was a precocious and gallant youth, conscious that there was no prospect of his playing a great part in Germany, and greedily listening to the stories which Ghibelline exiles told of the wrongs of Italy and the violence of the Angevin usurper. The triumph of Charles had been too rapid to be permanent, and a strong reaction set in both in Apulia and Tuscany against the brutal violence of his partisans. A revolt broke out in Calabria. The Pope himself trembled at the completeness of his ally's success, and Rome chose Henry of Castile, brother of Alfonso x. and an old enemy of Charles, as her Senator. Pisa raised the Ghibelline standard in Tuscany, and the northern feudalists vied with the Ghibelline cities in stemming the Guelfic tide. Conradin judged the moment opportune to try his fortunes in Italy. At the head of a small army, and accompanied by his uncle, Duke Louis of Bavaria, and by his closest friend, Frederick, the nominal Duke of Austria, the young prince crossed the Brenner, and in October 1267 entered Verona. But he was not strong enough to act at once, and Charles profited by the delay to prepare thoroughly for the struggle. At the approach of danger the jealousies of the Guelfs vanished, and Clement was as eager as Charles to destroy the 'basilisk sprung from the seed of the dragon.'

Early in 1268 Conradin began to move. Welcomed in January in Ghibelline Pavia, in April he was nobly received in Pisa, where he long tarried, hoping to make head against the Guelfic reaction which, thanks to Charles's energy, was already apparent in Tuscany. In July he entered Rome, where the Senator Henry of Castile joined his forces with the Ghibelline host. He pressed on into Apulia, hoping to join hands with the revolted Saracens of Lucera. But Charles hurried to meet him, and on 23rd August annihilated his army at the battle of Tagliacozzo. Conradin fled from the ruin of his hopes, but was betrayed to Charles, and was beheaded at Naples along with his comrade Frederick of Austria. He was the last of his race, and his death ensured the Guelfic triumph in Italy, which was henceforth to be utterly separate from Germany, and was to go through long generations of anguish before she could work out her destinies for herself. Clement iv. only just outlived the success of his policy. After his death, in November 1268, a three years' vacancy in the Papacy completed the victory of Charles of Anjou by depriving him of the only control that could be set over his actions. It was

Battle of Tagliacozzo and Death of Conradin, 1268.

during this period that he attained that fatal ascendency over Louis IX. that led to the expedition to Tunis, where even the sacred crusading cause was made subservient to the ambition of the lord of Naples. Yet, fierce and violent as he was, Charles's power alone kept Italy from absolute anarchy.

While Italy was distracted by the contest between Guelfs and Ghibellines, Germany was equally divided by the troubles of the Great Interregnum which followed the death of William of Holland in 1256. After Conrad IV.'s departure to Italy, William had begun to make way in Germany, and his marriage with the daughter of Duke Otto of Brunswick connected him closely with the traditional leaders of the German Guelfs. After Conrad's death many of the partisans of the Hohenstaufen, including the Rhenish cities, recognised his claim, and no attempt was made to set up the infant Conradin as his rival. But if he thus gained formal recognition, William never aspired to be more than a king in name. The chief event of his reign was the union in 1254 of the Rhenish cities in a league which extended beyond its original limits as far as Ratisbon, and gave a precedent for other and even more memorable unions of German towns. The local alliance between Lübeck and Hamburg, established as far back as 1241, proved the nucleus of the famous Hanseatic League. William's death was only important because of the troubles that a contested election evoked. The friends of the Hohenstaufen found it useless to pursue the candidature of Conradin, and were anxious to effect a compromise. They sought to find some prince who, while friendly to the Swabian traditions, was acceptable to the Pope and his partisans. Even the Rhenish archbishops, who had procured the elections of Henry and William, felt the need for peace. Thus both the Bavarian kinsfolk of Conradin, and Conrad of Hochstaden, the Guelfic archbishop of Cologne, agreed in the sort of candidate that they would welcome. They soon found no one in Germany

Margin notes:

Germany, 1254-1273.

King William of Holland, 1254-1256.

who answered their requirements. Ottocar, King of Bohemia, possessed a power that far outshadowed that of any native prince, and his recent acquisition of Austria and Styria gave him a sort of claim to be considered a German. But all parties viewed with alarm the aggrandisement of so powerful and dangerous a neighbour, and looked further afield, hoping to find a candidate who, though not strong enough to overwhelm their independence, was rich and energetic enough to save them from the ambitious Czech. Conrad of Hochstaden, already well acquainted with England, declared himself in favour of Richard, Earl of Cornwall, whose wealth and reputation were great, and whose rejection of the Sicilian throne, afterwards bestowed by the Pope on his nephew Edmund, showed that he would keep clear from the complications of Italian politics. Henry III., delighted that his brother and son should divide the Hohenstaufen inheritance between them, backed up his candidature. Richard was a good friend of the Pope, and yet had been the brother-in-law and ally of Frederick II. He scattered his money freely, and the Jews, his faithful dependants in England, actively furthered his candidature. But France took the alarm at the extension of the power of her English enemies, and the inveterate Ghibelline partisans of the Italian cities would hear of no Emperor indifferent to their ancient feuds. The citizens of Pisa suggested that Alfonso X. of Castile would be a better candidate than the Earl of Cornwall, and the French party eagerly took up his claims. The ancient rights of all the German nobles to choose their king had fallen into disuse during the recent troubles, and the right of election had gradually passed to seven of their leaders, who on this occasion first definitely exercised the power that belonged to the Seven Electors of later times.

In January 1257 the Archbishop of Cologne appeared with the Count Palatine Otto of Bavaria and the proxy of the captive Archbishop of Mainz before the walls of Frankfurt. On being refused admission to the city, they formally elected

Richard as King of the Romans before the gates. The Archbishop of Trier, who had held the town against them, was soon joined by the Duke of Saxony and the Margrave of Brandenburg, and on 1st April these three elected Alfonso of Castile. Ottocar of Bohemia, the remaining elector, for some time hesitated between the two, but his declaration in favour of Richard gave the English earl a majority of the votes of the electoral college. In May Richard crossed over the North Sea, and was crowned at Aachen by Archbishop Conrad. He remained nearly two years in Germany, and succeeded in getting himself generally recognised by the estates of the Rhineland. But the rest of Germany took little interest in his movements, and as soon as his money was exhausted, even his Rhenish friends grew lukewarm in his cause. More hopeful was the support of Alexander IV. and the alliance of Milan and other Italian cities. The Castilians refused to allow Alfonso to prosecute his candidature in person, and an absentee competitor might safely be neglected. Richard now hoped to be able to seek the Imperial crown at Rome. But his absorption in English politics required his return to his native land, and the death of Alexander IV. deprived him of his best chance of formal recognition.

The Great Interregnum, 1257-1293.

Richard paid three subsequent visits to Germany, but never obtained any greater power. Neither his character nor his resources were adequate to the difficult task that he had undertaken, and his divided allegiance to his old and new country made real success quite impossible. His simple policy was to obtain formal recognition from the princes by making them lavish grants of privileges. A striking example of this was when in 1262 he secured the permanent friendship of Ottocar by confirming his acquisitions of Austria and Styria. For all practical purposes Germany had no king at all. The abeyance of the central power forced the princes to exercise all sovereign rights, and their feuds and factions reduced the realm to a deplorable state of anarchy. Richard's gold had broken up the league of the Rhenish cities, and for the time the feudal party seemed to have it all their own way. Richard, despairing of general recognition, at last agreed to submit his claims to the judgment of Clement IV., though he had refused similar proffers from Urban IV. Clement died in 1268 before anything could be decided, and three years' vacancy of the Papacy between 1268 and 1271 left the world without either a spiritual or a temporal head. The great days of Papacy and Empire were plainly over.

Henceforth the Empire was little more than an unrealised theory, but the Papacy was still a practical necessity for the age, however much the furious Guelfic partisanship of recent pontiffs had deprived the Apostolic See of its former position as spiritual director of Europe. Only a good and a strong Pope could restore peace to Italy and Germany, and in September 1271 the election of the holy Theobald of Piacenza, Archdeacon of Liége, then actually on pilgrimage in the Holy Land, secured for Europe a high-minded spiritual leader. The short pontificate of Theobald, who took the name of Gregory x. *Gregory x. and the restoration of peace 1271-1276.* (1271-1276), stands in noble contrast to the reigns of a Gregory IX., an Innocent IV., or a Clement IV. With the wise and peace-loving pontiff, who sought to win back Europe to better ways, the highest spirit of the Roman Church was restored. We have seen how Gregory laboured in the second Council of Lyons for the organisation of the Mendicant Orders, for the union of East and West, and for the renewal of the Crusades. He devoted himself with equal energy to ending the long anarchy in Germany. Richard of Cornwall submitted to his decision, but died in 1272 before it could be pronounced. In 1273 the Electors chose Rudolf, Count of Hapsburg, in his stead. Gregory smoothed over the difficulties which might have attended his candidature, and established friendly relations with him. But the peace that the Pope loved was but of short duration. The Papacy again succumbed to the spirit of intrigue and violence, and before long fell at the hands of the grandson of St. Louis, the great-nephew of Charles of Anjou. The glory of the Papacy only outlasted the glory of the Empire for two generations: but while the Empire had become little more than a mere name, the Papacy, even in the days of the Captivity, continued, though with diminished lustre, to command the spiritual allegiance of Europe. Germany and Italy, the chief names of the Imperial idea, had hopelessly lost any prospect of national unity, while losing the wider unity of the Roman State. The real future thus remained with the localised national states, which were best represented by France, England, and the Spanish kingdoms. With their establishment on the ruins of the older system, the age of the Papacy and Empire came to an end.

APPENDIX

TABLES OF SOVEREIGNS

(1) POPES.

John X., 914-928.
Leo VI., 928-929.
Stephen VII., 929-931.
John XI., 931-936.
Leo VII., 936-939.
Stephen VIII., 939-942.
Martin III. or Marinus II., 942-946.
Agapet II., 946-955.
John XII., 955-963.
Leo VIII., 963-964.
Benedict V., 964-965.
John XIII., 965-972.
Benedict VI., 972-974
Benedict VII., 974-983.
John XIV., 983-984.
Boniface VII., Antipope, 974-984 ; recognised, 984-985.
John XV., 985-996.
Gregory V., 996-999.
John XVI., 997-998 (partisan of Crescentius).
Sylvester II., 999-1003.
John XVII., 1003.
John XVIII., 1003-1009.
Sergius IV., 1009-1012.
Benedict VIII., 1012-1024.
John XIX., 1024-1033.

Benedict IX., 1033-1046. ⎫
[Antipope, Sylvester III., 1044-1046.] ⎬ deposed in 1046.
Gregory VI., 1044-1046. ⎭
Clement II., 1046-1047.
Damasus II., 1048.
Leo IX., 1048-1054.
Victor II., 1055-1057.
Stephen IX., 1057-1058.
[Antipope, Benedict X., 1058-1059.]
Nicholas II., 1058-1061.
Alexander II., 1061-1073.
[Antipope, Honorius, 1061-1062.]
Gregory VII., 1073-1085.
[Antipope, Clement III., 1080-1100.]
Victor III., 1086-1087.
Urban II., 1088-1099.
Paschal II., 1099-1118.
[Antipopes, Albert, Theodoric, and Sylvester IV.]
Gelasius II., 1118-1119.
[Antipope, Gregory VIII., 1118-1121.]

Calixtus II., 1119-1124.
Honorius II., 1124-1130.
Innocent II., 1130-1143.
  [Antipopes, Anacletus, 1130-
      1138.
      Victor, 1138 (ab-
      dicated).]
Celestine II., 1143-1144.
Lucius II., 1144-1145.
Eugenius III., 1145-1153.
Anastasius IV., 1153-1154.
Adrian IV., 1154-1159.
Alexander III., 1159-1181.
  [Antipopes, Victor,   1159-
      1164.
      Paschal III., 1164-
      1168.

[Antipopes, Calixtus III.,
      1168-1178.
      Lando, 1178-1180.]
Lucius III., 1181-1185.
Urban III., 1185-1187.
Gregory VIII., 1187.
Clement III., 1187-1191.
Celestine III., 1191-1198.
Innocent III., 1198-1216.
Honorius III., 1216-1227.
Gregory IX., 1227-1241.
Celestine IV., 1241.
Innocent IV., 1243-1254.
Alexander IV., 1254-1261.
Urban IV., 1261-1264.
Clement IV., 1265-1268.
Gregory X., 1271-1276.

(2) Emperors and Kings of the Romans.

Henry I. (the Fowler), 918-936.
*Otto I. (the Great), 936-973.
*Otto II., 973-983.
*Otto III., 983-1002.
*Henry II. (the Saint), 1002-1024.
*Conrad II. (the Salic), 1024-
    1039.
*Henry III. (the Black), 1039-
    1056.
*Henry IV., 1056-1106.
  [Rivals, Rudolf of Swabia,
      1077-1080.
      Hermann of Luxem-
      burg, 1082-1093.
      Conrad of Franconia,
      1093-1101.]
*Henry V., 1106-1125.
*Lothair II., 1125-1138.

Conrad III., 1138-1152.
*Frederick I. (Barbarossa), 1152-
    1190.
*Henry VI., 1190-1197.
*Otto IV., 1197-1212, } Rivals.
Philip II., 1197-1208, }
*Frederick II., 1212-1250.
[Rivals — Henry Raspe, 1246-
    1247 ; William of Holland,
    1247-1256.]
Conrad IV., 1250-1254.
The Great Interregnum, 1254-
    1273.
Richard, Earl of⎫
  Cornwall,   ⎬ Rivals,
Alfonso X., King of⎪ 1257-1272.
  Castile, ⎭

---

* An asterisk is affixed to these Kings who were crowned Emperors by the Pope.

(3) Eastern Emperors.

Constantine VII. (Porphyrogenitus), 912-959.
[Joint-rulers—Alexander, 912-913.
    Romanus I. (Lecapenus), 919-945.]
Romanus II., 959-963.
Basil II. (Bulgaroctonus), 963-1025.
[Joint-rulers—Nicephorus II. (Phocas), 963-969.
    John I. (Zimisces), 969-976.]
Constantine VIII., 1025-1028.
Romanus III. (Argyrus), 1028-1034.
Michael IV. (the Paphlagonian), 1034-1041.
Michael V., 1041-1042.
Constantine IX. (Monomachus), 1042-1054.
Theodora, 1054-1057.
Michael VI. (Stratioticus), 1057.

Isaac I. (Comnenus), 1057-1059.
Constantine X. (Ducas), 1059-1067.
Michael VII. (Ducas), 1067-1078.
[Joint-ruler — Romanus IV. (Diogenes), 1068-1071.]
Nicephorus III. (Botaniates), 1078-1081.
Alexius I. (Comnenus), 1081-1118.
John II. (Comnenus), 1118-1143.
Manuel I. (Comnenus), 1143-1180.
Alexius II. (Comnenus), 1180-1183.
Andronicus I.(Comnenus), 1183-1185.
Isaac II. (Angelus), 1185-1195.
Alexius III. (Angelus), 1195-1203.
Isaac II. (restored) ⎱ Joint-rulers
Alexius IV. ⎰ 1203-1204.
    (Angelus)
Alexius V. (Ducas), 1204.

(4) Latin Emperors of the East.

Baldwin I , 1204-1205.
Henry of Flanders, 1205-1216.
Peter of Courtenay, 1216-1219.

Robert, 1219-1228.
Baldwin II., 1228-1261.

(5) Kings of Jerusalem.

Godfrey of Boulogne, 1099-.100 [refused the title].
Baldwin I. of Edessa, 1100-1118.
Baldwin II. of Edessa, 1118-1130.
Fulk of Anjou, 1130-1143.
Baldwin III., 1143-1163.
Amalric I., 1163-1174.
Baldwin IV. (the Leper), 1173-1185.
Baldwin V. (the Child), 1185-1186.

Guy of Lusignan, 1186-1194.
[Conrad of Montferrat, 1191-1192.]
[Henry of Champagne, 1192-1197.]
Amalric II. of Lusignan, 1197-1205.
Amalric III., 1205-1206.
John of Brienne, 1210-1225.
Iolande of Brienne, 1225-1228.
Frederick II., 1228-1250.
Hugh of Lusignan (King of Cyprus), 1268-1284.

(6) Kings of France.

Charles the Simple, 896-929.
[Rivals—Robert of Paris, 922-
923; Rudolf of Burgundy,
923-936.]
Rudolf of Burgundy, 929-936.
Louis IV., 936-954.
Lothaire, 954-986.
Louis V., 986-987.
Hugh Capet, 987-996.

Robert II., 996-1031.
Henry I., 1031-1060.
Philip I., 1060-1108.
Louis VI., 1108-1137.
Louis VII., 1137-1180.
Philip II., Augustus, 1180-1223.
Louis VIII., 1223-1226.
Louis IX. (Saint Louis), 1226-
1270.

INDEX

AACHEN, 18, 46, 51, 139, 141, 258, 331, 371.
—— palace at, 46, 80.
Aarhuus, 22.
Aba, king of Hungary, 61.
Abbassides, the, 158.
Abbeville, 416.
Abelard, 7, 208, 211-214, 239, 240, 241, 429, 432.
Abotrites, the, 21, 226, 227, 264.
Abul Cassim, 39.
Acarnania, 348.
Acerra, Diepold of. *See* Diepold.
Achaia, Villehardouin, Prince of, 349.
—— Princes of, 355.
Acre, 186, 192, 300, 302-303, 304, 312, 337, 368, 453, 461, 462, 463.
—— battle of, 459-460.
—— St. Thomas of. *See* Thomas, St.
Adalbero, Archbishop of Reims, 44, 70, 71, 74, 77.
—— Archbishop of Trier, 231.
Adalbert, St., 43, 45, 379.
—— Archbishop of Bremen, 121, 122, 123, 223, 236.
—— —— of Mainz, 144, 146, 231.
Adela, daughter of William the Conqueror, 87.
—— of Champagne, third wife of Louis VII., 290, 291.
Adelaide of Burgundy, wife of Otto I., 28, 29, 31, 41.
—— of Maurienne, queen of Louis VI., 282.
—— of Poitou, 69.
Adenulfus, Duke of Benevento, 106.
Adhemar, bishop of Le Puy, 182, 183.
Adige, the, 29, 258.
Adolf of Holstein, 265.
—— Archbishop of Cologne, 311.
Adrian IV., Pope, 249-250, 252-254, 256.
Adrianople, 155, 162, 299, 348; battle at, 351.
Ægean, islands of, 158, 348; crusaders in, 345.
Ætolia, 348.

Affonso Henriquez, king of Portugal, 325, 470-471, 475.
Afghanistan, 168.
Africa, 158, 170, 236-237, 468, 469, 471.
—— Christianity in, 103.
Agenais, the, 416.
Agnes of Poitou, wife of Henry III., 62, 121, 122, 128.
—— daughter of Henry IV., 221.
—— wife of Henry of Brunswick, and daughter of Conrad, Count Palatine, 308, 319.
—— of France, daughter of Louis VII., and wife of Alexius II., 340.
—— of Meran, wife of Philip Augustus, 323-324, 408.
Agriculture under Frederick I., 272.
Aigues Mortes, 457.
Ain Talut, battle of, 460.
Aix (in Provence), 417, 418.
Alan 'of the Twisted Beard,' first Count of Brittany, 85.
Alarcos, battle of, 471.
Albania, 164, 348; Greeks in, 350.
Alberic I., Marquis of Camerino, 30.
—— II., 30, 38.
—— 381.
—— da Romano, 483.
Albert the Bear, the Margrave, 226, 232, 233, 251, 264, 265, 268.
—— of Brabant, claimant to Liège, 307.
—— of Buxhöwden, 379.
—— the Great, 378, 447.
Albi, 216.
Albigenses, the, 216-217, 334, 394, 397, 398, 401, 419, 433, 436.
Albigensian Crusade, the, 332. *See also* Albigenses.
Albigeois, 287.
Albina, daughter of Tancred, 317.
Alcantara, Order of, 207, 471.
Alençon, Peter, Count of. *See* Peter.
Aleppo, 158, 195; Ameer of, 159-160.

PERIOD II.

In Eight Volumes. Crown 8vo. 6s. net, each.

The Complete Set £2, 8s. net.

PERIODS OF EUROPEAN HISTOR

General Editor—ARTHUR HASSALL, M.A.,
Student of Christ Church, Oxford.

THE object of this Series is to present in separate Volumes comprehensive and trustworthy account of the general develop ment of European History, and to deal fully and carefully wit the more prominent events in each century.

No such attempt to place the History of Europe in a compre hensive, detailed, and readable form before the English Publi has previously been made, and the Series forms a valuabl continuous History of Mediæval and Modern Europe.

Period I.—The Dark Ages. 476-918.
By C. W. C. OMAN, M.A., Deputy Chichele Professor of Moder History in the University of Oxford. 6s. *net.*

Period II.—The Empire and the Papacy. 918-1273.
By T. F. TOUT, M.A., Professor of Mediæval and Modern History a Owens College, Victoria University, Manchester. 6s. *net.*

Period III.—The Close of the Middle Ages. 1273-1494.
By R. LODGE, M.A., Professor of History at the University c Edinburgh. 6s. *net.*

Period IV.—Europe in the 16th Century. 1494-1598.
By A. H. JOHNSON, M.A., Historical Lecturer to Merton, Trinity and University Colleges, Oxford. 6s. *net.*

Period V.—The Ascendancy of France. 1598-1715.
By H. O. WAKEMAN, M.A., late Fellow of All Souls' College Oxford. 6s. *net.*

Period VI.—The Balance of Power. 1715-1789.
By A. HASSALL, M.A., Student of Christ Church, Oxford. 6s. *net.*

Period VII.—Revolutionary Europe. 1789-1815.
By H. MORSE STEPHENS, M.A., Professor of History at Cornel University, Ithaca, U.S.A. 6s. *net.*

Period VIII.—Modern Europe. 1815-1899.
By W. ALISON PHILLIPS, M.A., formerly Senior Scholar of St. John' College, Oxford. 6s. *net.*

LONDON: RIVINGTONS

RIVINGTONS' COMPLETE COURSE OF ENGLISH HISTORY TEACHING FOR SCHOOLS, ETC.

1. A FIRST HISTORY OF ENGLAND. *By* Mrs. CYRIL RANSOME. *Small Fcap. 8vo. With numerous Illustrations.* 2s. 6d.

'In its comprehensiveness, accuracy, and sequence of events, we have seen no elementary compilation to equal it.'—*Aberdeen Daily Journal.*

'Mrs Ransome writes at young children's level, but at the same time shows the *why* as well as the *how* of the events she chronicles.'—*University Correspondent.*

'Youths would not be ill off who never saw any other history of England than Mrs. Ransome's during their whole school course.'—*Glasgow Herald.*

2. AN ELEMENTARY HISTORY OF ENGLAND. For the use of the Lower Forms in Schools. *By* CYRIL RANSOME, M.A., *late Professor of Modern History, Yorkshire College, Victoria University. Small Fcap. 8vo. With Maps and Plans.* 1s. 9d.

'Has discharged his task in a practically faultless manner.'—*Aberdeen Journal.*
'Is carefully and well compiled to the very last page.'—*Manchester Examiner.*

3. A CLASS BOOK OF ENGLISH HISTORY. For the use of Middle Forms of Schools, Training Colleges, Army, Intermediate, and Oxford and Cambridge Local Examinations, the Central Welsh Board, Irish Intermediate, Scottish Leaving Certificates, etc. With Maps, Plans, Lists of Important Dates, Subjects for Class, Blackboard Illustrations, Chief Names, Notes and Index. *By* ARTHUR HASSALL, M.A., *Student of Christ Church, Oxford. Crown 8vo.* 3s. 6d.

'It is, I think, the most completely equipped History of its size in the market. It is singularly full of matter carefully arranged and clearly expressed ; its maps, genealogies, and elucidatory notes are all very much to the point. I have recommended it to my class, and shall hope to find that it is widely used.'
D. J. MEDLEY, *Professor of History in the University of Glasgow.*

'The best text-book of English History . . . Mr. Hassall has provided.'
R. LODGE, *Professor of History in the University of Edinburgh.*

'I have decided to introduce it into my upper forms, comprising about 100 boys.'
ALBERT J. MEAD, *Head Master of Wallasey Grammar School, Cheshire.*

'By far the best book of its kind I have seen. I shall certainly adopt it.'—W. H. PEARSALL, *Head Master of the Senior Mixed Board School, Dalton-in-Furness.*

We advise all managers who are wanting a history text-book for the senior classes n their schools to buy and test the one before us '—*School Guardian.*

4. AN ADVANCED HISTORY OF ENGLAND. For use in Upper Forms of Schools and in Colleges. *By* CYRIL RANSOME, M.A. *Crown 8vo. One Volume. With Maps and Plans.* 7s. 6d.

MAY ALSO BE HAD IN TWO PERIODS:--

Period I.—To Elizabeth, 1603. 4s.
Period II.—To Victoria, 1895. 4s.

'Sure to be widely used for educational purposes. . . . An excellent, well-arranged clear, temperate, just, and patriotic book, deserving wide and] hearty welcome.'-*Spectator.*

Printed in Great Britain
by Amazon

17909856R10312